T0192548

Securing Systems

Applied Security Architecture and Threat Models

Securing Systems

Applied Security Architecture and Threat Models

Brook S.E. Schoenfield

Forewords by John N. Stewart and James F. Ransome

CRC Press
Taylor & Francis Group
Boca Raton London New York

CRC Press is an imprint of the
Taylor & Francis Group, an **informa** business

CRC Press
Taylor & Francis Group
6000 Broken Sound Parkway NW, Suite 300
Boca Raton, FL 33487-2742

First issued in paperback 2021

© 2015 by Taylor & Francis Group, LLC
CRC Press is an imprint of Taylor & Francis Group, an Informa business

No claim to original U.S. Government works

Version Date: 20150427

ISBN 13: 978-1-03-202740-1 (pbk)
ISBN 13: 978-1-4822-3397-1 (hbk)

Visit the Taylor & Francis Web site at
http://www.taylorandfrancis.com

and the CRC Press Web site at
http://www.crcpress.com

Publisher's Note
The publisher has gone to great lengths to ensure the quality of this reprint but points out that some imperfections in the original copies may be apparent.

Dedication

To the many teachers who've pointed me down the path; the managers who have supported my explorations; the many architects and delivery teams who've helped to refine the work; to my first design mentors—John Caron, Roddy Erickson, and Dr. Andrew Kerne—without whom I would still have no clue; and, lastly, to Hans Kolbe, who once upon a time was our human fuzzer.

Each of you deserves credit for whatever value may lie herein.

The errors are all mine.

Contents

Foreword

As you read this, it is important to note that despite hundreds to thousands of people-years spent to date, we are still struggling mightily to take the complex, de-compose into the simple, and create the elegant when it comes to information systems. Our world is hurtling towards an always on, pervasive, interconnected mode in which software and life quality are co-dependent, productivity enhancements each year require systems, devices and systems grow to 50 billion connected, and the quantifiable and definable risks all of this creates are difficult to gauge, yet intuitively unsettling, and are slowly emerging before our eyes.

"Arkhitekton"—a Greek word preceding what we speak to as architecture today, is an underserved idea for information systems, and not unsurprisingly, security architecture is even further underserved. The very notion that through process and product, systems filling entire data centers, information by the pedabyte, transaction volumes at sub-millisecond speed, and compute systems doubling capability every few years, is likely seen as impossible—even if needed. I imagine the Golden Gate bridge seemed impossible at one point, a space station also, and buildings such as the Burj Khalifa, and yet here we are admiring each as a wonder unto themselves. None of this would be possible without formal learning, training architects in methods that work, updating our training as we learn, and continuing to require a demonstration for proficiency. Each element plays that key role.

The same is true for the current, and future, safety in information systems. Architecture may well be the savior that normalizes our current inconsistencies, engenders a provable model that demonstrates efficacy that is quantifiably improved, and tames the temperamental beast known as risk. It is a sobering thought that when systems are connected for the first time, they are better understood than at any other time. From that moment on, changes made—documented and undocumented—alter our understanding, and without understanding comes risk. Information systems must be understood for both operational and risk-based reasons, which means tight definitions must be at the core—and that is what architecture is all about.

For security teams, both design and protect, it is our time to build the tallest, and safest, "building." Effective standards, structural definition, deep understanding with validation, a job classification that has formal methods training, and every improving and learning system that takes knowledge from today to strengthen systems installed yesterday, assessments and inspection that look for weaknesses (which happen over time), all surrounded by a well-built security program that encourages if not demands security architecture, is the only path to success. If breaches, so oftentimes seen as avoidable ex post facto, don't convince you of this, then the risks should.

We are struggling as a security industry now, and the need to be successful is higher than it has ever been in my twenty-five years in it. It is not good enough just to build something and try and secure it, it must be architected from the bottom up with security in it, by professionally trained and skilled security architects, checked and validated by regular assessments for weakness, and through a learning system that learns from today to inform tomorrow. We must succeed.

– John N. Stewart
SVP, Chief Security & Trust Officer
Cisco Systems, Inc.

About John N. Stewart:

John N. Stewart formed and leads Cisco's Security and Trust Organization, underscoring Cisco's commitment to address two key issues in boardrooms and on the minds of top leaders around the globe. Under John's leadership, the team's core missions are to protect Cisco's public and private customers, enable and ensure the Cisco Secure Development Lifecycle and Trustworthy Systems efforts across Cisco's entire mature and emerging solution portfolio, and to protect Cisco itself from the never-ending, and always evolving, cyber threats.

Throughout his 25-year career, Stewart has led or participated in security initiatives ranging from elementary school IT design to national security programs. In addition to his role at Cisco, he sits on technical advisory boards for Area 1 Security, BlackStratus, Inc., RedSeal Networks, and Nok Nok Labs. He is a member of the Board of Directors for Shape Security, Shadow Networks, Inc., and the National Cyber-Forensics Training Alliance (NCFTA). Additionally, Stewart serves on the Cybersecurity Think Tank at University of Maryland University College, and on the Cyber Security Review to Prime Minister & Cabinet for Australia. Prior, Stewart served on the CSIS Commission on Cybersecurity for the 44th Presidency of the United States, the Council of Experts for the Global Cyber Security Center, and on advisory boards for successful companies such as Akonix, Cloudshield, Finjan, Fixmo, Ingrian Networks, Koolspan, Riverhead, and TripWire. John is a highly sought public and closed-door speaker and most recently was awarded the global Golden Bridge Award and CSO 40 Silver Award for the 2014 Chief Security Officer of the Year.

Stewart holds a Master of Science degree in computer and information science from Syracuse University, Syracuse, New York.

Foreword

Cyberspace has become the 21st century's greatest engine of change. And it's everywhere. Virtually every aspect of global civilization now depends on interconnected cyber systems to operate. A good portion of the money that was spent on offensive and defensive capabilities during the Cold War is now being spent on cyber offense and defense. Unlike the Cold War, where only governments were involved, this cyber challenge requires defensive measures for commercial enterprises, small businesses, NGOs, and individuals. As we move into the Internet of Things, cybersecurity and the issues associated with it will affect everyone on the planet in some way, whether it is cyber-war, cyber-crime, or cyber-fraud.

Although there is much publicity regarding network security, the real cyber Achilles' heel is insecure software and the architecture that structures it. Millions of software vulnerabilities create a cyber house of cards in which we conduct our digital lives. In response, security people build ever more elaborate cyber fortresses to protect this vulnerable software. Despite their efforts, cyber fortifications consistently fail to protect our digital treasures. Why? The security industry has failed to engage fully with the creative, innovative people who write software and secure the systems these solutions are connected to. The challenges to keep an eye on all potential weaknesses are skyrocketing. Many companies and vendors are trying to stay ahead of the game by developing methods and products to detect threats and vulnerabilities, as well as highly efficient approaches to analysis, mitigation, and remediation. A comprehensive approach has become necessary to counter a growing number of attacks against networks, servers, and endpoints in every organization.

Threats would not be harmful if there were no vulnerabilities that could be exploited. The security industry continues to approach this issue in a backwards fashion by trying to fix the symptoms rather than to address the source of the problem itself. As discussed in our book *Core Software Security: Security at the Source*,[*] the stark reality is that the

---

[*] Ransome, J. and Misra, A. (2014). *Core Software Security: Security at the Source.* Boca Raton (FL): CRC Press.

vulnerabilities that we were seeing 15 years or so ago in the OWASP and SANS Top Ten and CVE Top 20 are almost the same today as they were then; only the pole positions have changed. We cannot afford to ignore the threat of insecure software any longer because software has become the infrastructure and lifeblood of the modern world.

Increasingly, the liabilities of ignoring or failing to secure software and provide the proper privacy controls are coming back to the companies that develop it. This is and will be in the form of lawsuits, regulatory fines, loss of business, or all of the above. First and foremost, you must build security into the software development process. It is clear from the statistics used in industry that there are substantial cost savings to fixing security flaws early in the development process rather than fixing them after software is fielded. The cost associated with addressing software problems increases as the lifecycle of a project matures. For vendors, the cost is magnified by the expense of developing and patching vulnerable software after release, which is a costly way of securing applications. The bottom line is that it costs little to avoid potential security defects early in development, especially compared to costing 10, 20, 50, or even 100 times that amount much later in development. Of course, this doesn't include the potential costs of regulatory fines, lawsuits, and or loss of business due to security and privacy protection flaws discovered in your software after release.

Having filled seven Chief Security Officer (CSO) and Chief Information Security Officer (CISO) roles, and having had both software security and security architecture reporting to me in many of these positions, it is clear to me that the approach for both areas needs to be rethought. In my last book, Brook helped delineate our approach to solving the software security problem while also addressing how to build in security within new agile development methodologies such as Scrum. In the same book, Brook noted that the software security problem is bigger than just addressing the code but also the systems it is connected to.

As long as software and architecture is developed by humans, it requires the human element to fix it. There have been a lot of bright people coming up with various technical solutions and models to fix this, but we are still failing to do so as an industry. We have consistently focused on the wrong things: vulnerability and command and control. But producing software and designing architecture is a creative and innovative process. In permaculture, it is said that "the problem is the solution." Indeed, it is that very creativity that must be enhanced and empowered in order to generate security as an attribute of a creative process. A solution to this problem requires the application of a holistic, cost-effective, and collaborative approach to securing systems. This book is a perfect follow-on to the message developed in *Core Software Security: Security at the Source*[*] in that it addresses a second critical challenge in developing software: security architecture methods and the mindset that form a frame for evaluating the security of digital systems that can be used to prescribe security treatments for those systems. Specifically, it addresses an applied approach to security architecture and threat models.

---

[*] Ibid.

It should be noted that systems security, for the most part, is still an art not a science. A skilled security architect must bring a wealth of knowledge and understanding—global and local, technical, human, organizational, and even geopolitical—to an assessment. In this sense, Brook is a master of his craft, and that is why I am very excited about the opportunity to provide a Foreword to this book. He and I have worked together on a daily basis for over five years and I know of no one better with regard to his experience, technical aptitude, industry knowledge, ability to think out of the box, organizational collaboration skills, thoroughness, and holistic approach to systems architecture—specifically, security as it relates to both software and systems design and architecture. I highly recommend this book to security architects and all architects who interact with security or to those that manage them. If you have a reasonable feel for what the security architect is doing, you will be able to accommodate the results from the process within your architectures, something that he and I have been able to do successfully for a number of years now. Brook's approach to securing systems addresses the entire enterprise, not only its digital systems, as well as the processes and people who will interact, design, and build the systems. This book fills a significant gap in the literature and is appropriate for use as a resource for both aspiring and seasoned security architects alike.

– Dr. James F. Ransome, CISSP, CISM

About Dr. James F. Ransome:

Dr. James Ransome, CISSP, CISM, is the Senior Director of Product Security at McAfee—part of Intel Security—and is responsible for all aspects of McAfee's Product Security Program, a corporate-wide initiative that supports the delivery of secure software products to customers. His career is marked by leadership positions in private and public industries, having served in three chief information officer (CISO) and four chief security officer (CSO) roles. Prior to the corporate world, Ransome had 23 years of government service in various roles supporting the United States intelligence community, federal law enforcement, and the Department of Defense. He holds a Ph.D. specializing in Information Security from a NSA/DHS Center of Academic Excellence in Information Assurance Education program. Ransome is a member of Upsilon Pi Epsilon, the International Honor Society for Computing and Information Disciplines and a Ponemon Institute Distinguished Fellow. He recently completed his 10th information security book *Core Software Security: Security at the Source.*[*]

---

[*] Ibid.

Preface

This book replies to a question that I once posed to myself. I know from my conversations with many of my brother and sister practitioners that, early in your security careers, you have also posed that very same question. When handed a diagram containing three rectangles and two double-headed arrows connecting each box to one of the others, each of us has wondered, "How do I respond to this?"

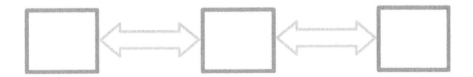

This is a book about security architecture. The focus of the book is upon how security architecture methods and mindset form a frame for evaluating the security of digital systems in order to prescribe security treatments for those systems. The treatments are meant to bring the system to a particular and verifiable risk posture.

"System" should be taken to encompass a gamut running from individual computers, to networks of computers, to collections of applications (however that may be defined) and including complex system integrations of all the above, and more. "System" is a generic term meant to encompass rather than exclude. Presumably, a glance through the examples in Part II of this book should indicate the breadth of reach that has been attempted?

I will endeavor along the way, to provide situationally appropriate definitions for "security architecture," "risk," "architecture risk assessment," "threat model," and "applied." These definitions should be taken as working definitions, fit only for the purpose of "applied security architecture" and not as proposals for general models in any of these fields. I have purposely kept a tight rein on scope in the hope that the book retains enough focus to be useful. In my very humble experience, applied security architecture will make use of whatever skills—technical, interpersonal, creative, adaptive, and so forth—that you have or can learn. This one area, applied security architecture, seems big enough.

Who May Benefit from This Book?

Any organization that places into service computer systems that have some chance of being exposed to digital attack will encounter at least some of the problems addressed within *Securing Systems*. Digital systems can be quite complex, involving various and sometimes divergent stakeholders, and they are delivered through the collaboration of multidisciplinary teams. The range of roles performed by those individuals who will benefit from familiarity with applied security architecture, therefore, turns out to be quite broad. The following list comprises nearly everyone who is involved in the specification, implementation, delivery, and decision making for and about computer systems.

- Security architects, assessors, analysts, and engineers
- System, solution, infrastructure, and enterprise architects
- Developers, infrastructure engineers, system integrators, and implementation teams
- Managers, technical leaders, program and project managers, middle management, and executives

Security architecture is and will remain, for some time, an experience-based practice. The security architect encounters far too many situations where the "right" answer will be "it depends." Those dependencies are, in part, what this book is about.

Certainly, engineering practice will be brought to bear on secure systems. Exploit techniques tend to be particular. A firm grasp of the engineering aspects of software, networks, operating systems, and the like is essential. Applied cryptography is not really an art. Cryptographic techniques do a thing, a particular thing, exactly. Cryptography is not magic, though application is subtle and algorithms are often mathematically and algorithmically complex. Security architecture cannot be performed without a firm grounding in many aspects of computer science. And, at a grosser granularity, there are consistent patterns whose solutions tend to be amenable to clear-cut engineering resolution.

Still, in order to recognize the patterns, one must often apply deep and broad experience. This book aims to seed precisely that kind of experience for practitioners. Hopefully, alongside the (fictitious but commonly occurring) examples, I will have explained the reasoning and described the experience behind my analysis and the decisions depicted herein such that even experts may gain new insight from reading these and considering my approaches. My conclusions aren't necessarily "right." (Being a risk-driven practice, there often is no "right" answer.)

Beyond security architects, all architects who interact with security can benefit from this work. If you have a reasonable feel for what the security architect is doing, you will be able to accommodate the results from the process within your architectures. Over the years, many partner architects and I have grown so attuned, that we could finish each other's sentences, speak for each other's perspectives, and even include each other's likely requirements within our analysis of an architecture. When you have achieved this level of understanding and collaboration, security is far more easily incorporated from the very inception of a new idea. Security becomes yet another emerging attribute of the architecture and design, just like performance or usability. That, in my humble opinion, is an ideal to strive for.

Developers and, particularly, development and technical leaders will have to translate the threat model and requirements into things that can be built and coded. That's not an easy transformation. I believe that this translation from requirement through to functional test is significantly eased through a clear understanding of the threat model. In fact, at my current position, I have offered many participatory coaching sessions in the ATASM process described in this book to entire engineering teams. These sessions have had a profound effect, causing everyone involved—from architect to quality engineer—to have a much clearer understanding of why the threat model is key and how to work with security requirements. I hope that reading this book will provide a similar grounding for delivery teams that must include security architecture in their work.

I hope that all of those who must build and then sustain a security architecture practice will find useful tidbits that foster high-functioning technical delivery teams that must include security people and security architecture—namely, project and program managers, line managers, middle management, or senior and executive management. Beyond the chapter specifically devoted to building a program, I've also included a considerable explanation of the business and organizational context in which architecture and risk assessment programs exist. The nontechnical factors must comprise the basis from which security architecture gets applied. Without the required business acumen and understanding, security architecture can easily devolve to ivory tower, isolated, and unrealistic pronouncements. Nobody actually reads those detailed, 250-page architecture documents that are gathering dust on the shelf. My sincere desire is that this body of work remains demonstratively grounded in real-world situations.

All readers of this book may gain some understanding of how the risk of system compromise and its impacts can be generated. Although risk remains a touted cornerstone of computer security, it is poorly understood. Even the term, "risk," is thrown about with little precision, and with multiple and highly overloaded meanings. Readers will be provided with a risk definition and some specificity about its use, as well as given a proven methodology, which itself is based upon an open standard. We can all benefit from just a tad more precision when discussing this emotionally loaded topic, "risk." The approach explained in Chapter 4 underlies the analysis in the six example (though fictitious) architectures. If you need to rank risks in your job, this book will hopefully provide some insight and approaches.

Background and Origins

I was thrown into the practice of securing systems largely because none of the other security architects wanted to attend the Architecture Technical Review (ATR) meetings. During those meetings, every IT project would have 10 minutes to explain what they were intending to accomplish. The goal of the review was to uncover the IT services required for project success. Security was one of those IT services.

Security had no more than 5 minutes of that precious time slot to decide whether the project needed to be reviewed more thoroughly. That was a hard task! Mistakes and misses occurred from time to time, but especially as I began to assess the architectures of the projects.

When I first attended ATR meetings, I felt entirely unqualified to make the engagement decisions; in fact, I felt pretty incompetent to be assessing IT projects, at all. I had been hired to provide long-term vision and research for future intrusion detection systems and what are now called "security incident event management systems." Management then asked me to become "Infosec's" first application security architect. I was the newest hire and was just trying to survive a staff reduction. It seemed a precarious time to refuse job duties.

A result that I didn't expect from attending the ATR meetings was how the wide exposure would dramatically increase my ability to spot architecture patterns. I saw hundreds of different architectures in those couple of years. I absorbed IT standards and learned, importantly, to quickly cull exceptional and unique situations. Later, when new architects took ATR duty, I was forced to figure out how to explain what I was doing to them. And interacting with all those projects fostered relationships with teams across IT development. When inevitable conflicts arose, those relationships helped us to cooperate across our differences.

Because my ATR role was pivotal to the workload for all the security architects performing reviews, I became a connecting point for the team. After all, I saw almost all the projects first. And that connecting role afforded me a view of how each of these smart, highly skilled individuals approached the problems that they encountered as they went through their process of securing IT's systems and infrastructures.

Security architecture was very much a formative practice in those days. Systems architecture was maturing; enterprise architecture was coalescing into a distinct body of knowledge and practice. The people performing system architecture weren't sure that the title "architect" could be applied to security people. We were held somewhat at arm's length, not treated entirely as peers, not really allowed into the architects' "club," if you will? Still, it turns out that it's really difficult to secure a system if the person trying does not have architectural skills and does not examine the system holistically, including having the broader context for which the system is intended. A powerful lesson.

At that time, there were few people with a software design background who also knew anything about computer security. That circumstance made someone like me a bit of a rarity. When I got started, I had very little security knowledge, just enough knowledge to barely get by. But, I had a rich software design background from which to draw. I could "do" architecture. I just didn't know much about security beyond having written simple network access control lists and having responded to network attack logs. (Well, maybe a little more than that?)

Consequently, people like Steve Acheson, who was already a security guru and had, in those early days, a great feel for design, were willing to forgive me for my inexperience. I suspect that Steve tolerated my naiveté because there simply weren't that many people who had enough design background with whom he could kick around the larger issues encountered in building a rigorous practice of security architecture. At any rate, my conversations with Steve and, slightly later, Catherine Blackader Nelson, Laura Lindsey, Gavin Reid, and somewhat later, Michele Guel, comprise the seeds out of which this book was born. Essentially, perhaps literally, we were trying to define the very nature of security architecture and to establish a body of craft for architecture risk assessment and threat models.

A formative enterprise identity research team was instigated by Michele Guel in early 2001. Along with Michele, Steve Acheson and I, (then) IT architect Steve Wright, and (now) enterprise architect, Sergei Roussakov, probed and prodded, from diverse angles, the problems of identity as a security service, as an infrastructure, and as an enterprise necessity. That experience profoundly affects not only the way that I practice security architecture but also my understanding of how security fits into an enterprise architecture. Furthermore, as a team encompassing a fairly wide range of different perspectives and personalities, we proved that diverse individuals can come together to produce seminal work, and relatively easily, at that. Many of the lessons culled from that experience are included in this volume.

For not quite 15 years, I have continued to explore, investigate, and refine these early experiments in security architecture and system assessment in concert with those named above, as well as many other practitioners. The ideas and approaches set out herein are this moment's summation of not only of my experience but also that of many of the architects with whom I've worked and interacted. Still, it's useful to remember that a book is merely a point in time, a reflection of what is understood at that moment. No doubt my ideas will change, as will the practice of security architecture.

My sincere desire is that I'm offering both an approach and a practicum that will make the art of securing systems a little more accessible. Indeed, ultimately, I'd like this book to unpack, at least a little bit, the craft of applied security architecture for the many people who are tasked with providing security oversight and due diligence for their digital systems.

Brook S.E. Schoenfield
Camp Connell, California, USA, December 2014

Acknowledgments

There are so many people who have contributed to the content of this book—from early technical mentors on through my current collaborators and those people who were willing to wade through my tortured drivel as it has come off of the keyboard. I direct the reader to my blog site, brookschoenfield.com, if you're curious about my technical history and the many who've contributed mightily to whatever skills I've gained. Let it suffice to say, "Far too many to be named here." I'll, therefore, try to name those who contributed directly to the development of this body of work.

Special thanks are due to Laura Lindsey, who coached my very first security review and, afterwards, reminded me that, "We're not the cops, Brook." Hopefully, I continue to pass on your wisdom?

Michelle Koblas and John Stewart not only "got" my early ideas but, more importantly, encouraged me, supporting me through the innumerable and inevitable mistakes and missteps. Special thanks are offered to you, John, for always treating me as a respected partner in the work, and to both of you for offering me your ongoing personal friendship. Nasrin Rezai, I continue to carry your charge to "teach junior people," so that security architecture actually has a future.

A debt of gratitude is owed to every past member of Cisco's "WebArch" team during the period when I was involved. Special thanks go to Steve Acheson for his early faith in me (and friendship).

Everyone who was involved with WebArch let me prove that techniques gleaned from consensus, facilitation, mediation, and emotional intelligence really do provide a basis for high-functioning technical teams. We collectively proved it again with the "PAT" security architecture virtual team, under the astute program management of Ferris Jabri, of "We're just going to do it, Brook," fame. Ferris helped to manifest some of the formative ideas that eventually became the chapter I wrote (Chapter 9) in *Core Software Security: Security at the Source,*[*] by James Ransome and Anmol Misra, as well.

---

[*] Schoenfield, B. (2014). "Applying the SDL Framework to the Real World" (Ch. 9). In *Core Software Security: Security at the Source*, pp. 255–324. Boca Raton (FL): CRC Press.

A special note is reserved for Ove Hansen who, as an architect on the WebArch team, challenged my opinions on a regular basis and in the best way. Without that countervail, Ove, that first collaborative team experiment would never have fully succeeded. The industry continues to need your depth and breadth.

Aaron Sierra, we proved the whole concept yet again at WebEx under the direction and support of Dr. James Ransome. Then, we got it to work with most of Cisco's burgeoning SaaS products. A hearty thanks for your willingness to take that journey with me and, of course, for your friendship.

Vinay Bansal and Michele Guel remain great partners in the shaping of a security architecture practice. I'm indebted to Vinay and to Ferris for helping me to generate a first outline for a book on security architecture. This isn't that book, which remains unwritten.

Thank you to Alan Paller for opportunities to put my ideas in front of wider audiences, which, of course, has provided an invaluable feedback loop.

Many thanks to the readers of the book as it progressed: Dr. James Ransome, Jack Jones, Eoin Carroll, Izar Tarandach, and Per-Olof Perrson. Please know that your comments and suggestions have improved this work immeasurably. You also validated that this has been a worthy pursuit.

Catherine Blackader Nelson and Dr. James Ransome continue to help me refine this work, always challenging me to think deeper and more thoroughly. I treasure not only your professional support but also the friendship that each of you offers to me.

Thanks to Dr. Neal Daswani for pointing out that XSS may also be mitigated through output validation (almost an "oops" on my part).

This book simply would not exist without the tireless logistical support of Theron Shreve and the copyediting and typesetting skills of Marje Pollack at DerryField Publishing Services. Thanks also go to John Wyzalek for his confidence that this body of work could have an audience and a place within the CRC Press catalog. And many thanks to Webb Mealy for help with graphics and for building the Index.

Finally, but certainly not the least, thanks are owed to my daughter, Allison, who unfailingly encourages me in whatever creative efforts I pursue. I hope that I return that spirit of support to you. And to my sweetheart, Cynthia Mealy, you have my heartfelt gratitude. It is you who must put up with me when I'm in one of my creative binges, which tend to render me, I'm sure, absolutely impossible to deal with. Frankly, I have no idea how you manage.

Brook S.E. Schoenfield
Camp Connell, California, USA, October 2014

About the Author

Brook S.E. Schoenfield is a Master Principal Product Security Architect at a global technology enterprise. He is the senior technical leader for software security across a division's broad product portfolio. He has held leadership security architecture positions at high-tech enterprises for many years.

Brook has presented at conferences such as RSA, BSIMM, and SANS What Works Summits on subjects within security architecture, including SaaS security, information security risk, architecture risk assessment and threat models, and Agile security. He has been published by CRC Press, SANS, Cisco, and the IEEE.

Brook lives in the Sierra Mountains of California. When he's not thinking about, writing about, and speaking on, as well as practicing, security architecture, he can be found telemark skiing, hiking, and fly fishing in his beloved mountains, or playing various genres of guitar—from jazz to percussive fingerstyle.

Part I

Part I

Introduction

The Lay of Information Security Land

[S]ecurity requirements should be developed at the same time system planners define the requirements of the system. These requirements can be expressed as technical features (e.g., access controls), assurances (e.g., background checks for system developers), or operational practices (e.g., awareness and training).[1]

How have we come to this pass? What series of events have led to the necessity for pervasive security in systems big and small, on corporate networks, on home networks, and in cafes and trains in order for computers to safely and securely provide their benefits? How did we ever come to this? Isn't "security" something that banks implement? Isn't security an attribute of government intelligence agencies? Not anymore.

In a world of pervasive and ubiquitous network interconnection, our very lives are intertwined with the successful completion of millions of transactions initiated on our behalf on a rather constant basis. At the risk of stating the obvious, global commerce has become highly dependent upon the "Internet of Things."[2] Beyond commerce, so has our ability to solve large, complex problems, such as feeding the hungry, understanding the changes occurring to the ecosystems on our planet, and finding and exploiting resources while, at the same time, preserving our natural heritage for future generations. Indeed, war, peace, and regime change are all dependent upon the global commons that we call "The Public Internet." Each of these problems, as well as all of us connected humans, have come to rely upon near-instant connection and seamless data exchange, just as each of us who use small, general-purpose computation devices—that is, your "smart phone,"—expect snappy responses to our queries and interchanges. A significant proportion of the world's 7 billion humans* have become interconnected.

---

* As of this writing, the population of the world is just over 7 billion. About 3 billion of these people are connected to the Internet.

And we expect our data to arrive safely and our systems and software to provide a modicum of safety. We'd like whatever wealth we may have to be held securely. That's not too much to expect, is it?

We require a modicum of security: the same protection that our ancestors expected from the bank and solicitor. Or rather, going further back, these are the protections that feudal villages expected from their Lord. Even further back, the village or clan warriors supposedly provided safety from a dangerous "outside" or "other."

Like other human experiments in sharing a commons,* the Internet seems to suffer from the same forces that have plagued common areas throughout history: bandits, pirates, and other groups taking advantage of the lack of barriers and control.

Early Internet pundits declared that the Internet would prove tremendously democratizing:

> *As we approach the twenty-first century, America is turning into an electronic republic, a democratic system that is vastly increasing the people's day-to-day influence on the decisions of state . . . transforming the nature of the political process . . .*[3]

Somehow, I doubt that these pundits quite envisioned the "democracy" of the modern Internet, where salacious rumors can become worldwide "facts" in hours, where news about companies' mistakes and misdeeds cannot be "spun" by corporate press corps, and where products live or die through open comment and review by consumers.

Governments are not immune to the power of instant interconnectedness. Regimes have been shaken, even toppled it would seem, by the power of the instant message. Nation-state nuclear programs have been stymied through "cyber offensives." Corporate and national secrets have been stolen. Is nothing on the Internet safe?

Indeed, it is a truism in the Age of the Public Internet (if I may title it so?), "You can't believe anything on the Internet." And yet, Wikipedia has widely replaced the traditional, commercial encyclopedia as a reference source. Wikipedia articles, which are written by its millions of participants—"crowd-sourced"—rather than being written by a hand-selected collection of experts, have proven to be quite reliable, if not always perfectly accurate. "Just Good Enough Reference"? Is this the power of Internet democracy?

Realizing the power of unfettered interconnection, some governments have gone to great lengths to control connection and content access. For every censure, clever technicians have devised methods of circumventing those governmental controls. Apparently, people all over the world prefer to experience the content that they desire and to communicate with whom they please, even in the face of arrest, detention, or other sanction.

Alongside the growth of digital interconnection have grown those wishing to take advantage of the open structure of our collective, global commons. Individuals seeking

---

* A commons is an asset held in common by a community—for example, pasture land that every person with livestock might use to pasture personal animals. The Public Internet is a network and a set of protocols held in common for everyone with access to it.

advantage of just about every sort, criminal gangs large and small, pseudo-governmental bodies, cyber armies, nation-states, and activists of every political persuasion have all used and misused the openness built into the Internet.

Internet attack is pervasive. It can take anywhere from less than a minute to as much as eight hours for an unprotected machine connected to the Internet to be completely compromised. The speed of attack entirely depends upon at what point in the address space any of the hundreds of concurrent sweeps happen to be at the moment. Compromise is certain; the risk of compromise is 100%. There is no doubt. An unprotected machine that is directly reachable (i.e., has a routable and visible address) from the Internet will be controlled by an attacker given a sufficient exposure period. The exposure period has been consistently shortening, from weeks, to days, then to hours, down to minutes, and finally, some percentage of systems have been compromised within seconds of connection.

In 1998, I was asked to take over the security of the single Internet router at the small software house for which I worked. Alongside my duties as Senior Designer and Technical Lead, I was asked, "Would you please keep the Access Control Lists (ACL) updated?"* Why was I chosen for these duties? I wrote the TCP/IP stack for our real-time operating system. Since supposedly I knew something about computer networking, we thought I could add few minor maintenance duties. I knew very little about digital security at the time. I learned.

As I began to study the problem, I realized that I didn't have a view into potential attacks, so I set up the experimental, early Intrusion Detection System (IDS), Shadow, and began monitoring traffic. After a few days of monitoring, I had a big shock. We, a small, relatively unknown (outside our industry) software house with a single Internet connection, were being actively attacked! Thus began my journey (some might call it descent?) into cyber security.

Attack and the subsequent "compromise," that is, complete control of a system on the Internet, is utterly pervasive: constant and continual. And this has been true for quite a long time. Many attackers are intelligent and adaptive. If defenses improve, attackers will change their tactics to meet the new challenge. At the same time, once complex and technically challenging attack methods are routinely "weaponized," turned into point-and-click tools that the relatively technically unsophisticated can easily use. This development has exponentially expanded the number of attackers. The result is a broad range of attackers, some highly ingenious alongside the many who can and will exploit well-known vulnerabilities if left unpatched. It is a plain fact that as of this writing, we are engaged in a cyber arms race of extraordinary size, composition, complexity, and velocity.

Who's on the defending side of this cyber arms race? The emerging and burgeoning information security industry.

As the attacks and attackers have matured, so have the defenders. It is information security's job to do our best to prevent successful compromise of data, communications,

---

* Subsequently, the company's Virtual Private Network (VPN) was added to my security duties.

the misuse of the "Internet of Things." "Infosec"* does this with technical tools that aid human analysis. These tools are the popularly familiar firewalls, intrusion detection systems (IDS), network (and other) ACLs, anti-virus and anti-malware protections, Security Information and Event Managers (SIEM), the whole panoply of software tools associated with information security. Alongside these are tools that find issues in software, such as vulnerability scanners and "static" analysis tools. These scanners are used as software is written.†

Parallel to the growth in security software, there has been an emerging trend to codify the techniques and craft used by security professionals. These disciplines have been called "security engineering," "security analysis," "security monitoring," "security response," "security forensics," and most importantly for this work, "security architecture." It is security architecture with which we are primarily concerned. Security architecture is the discipline charged with integrating into computer systems the security features and controls that will provide the protection expected of the system when it is deployed for use. Security architects typically achieve a sufficient breadth of knowledge and depth of understanding to apply a gamut of security technologies and processes to protect systems, system interconnections, and the data in use and storage: Securing Systems.

In fact, nearly twenty years after the publication of NIST-14 (quoted above), organizations large and small—governmental, commercial, and non-profit—prefer that some sort of a "security review" be conducted upon proposed and/or preproduction systems. Indeed, many organizations *require* a security review of systems. Review of systems to assess and improve system security posture has become a mandate.

Standards such as the NIST 800-53 and ISO 27002, as well as measures of existing practice, such as the BSIMM-V, all require or measure the maturity of an organization's "architecture risk assessment" (ARA). When taken together, it seems clear that a security review of one sort or another has become a security "best practice." That is, organizations that maintain a cyber-security defense posture typically require some sort of assessment or analysis of the systems to be used by the organization, whether those systems are homegrown, purchased, or composite. Ergo, these organizations believe it is in their best interest to have a security expert, typically called the "security architect."‡

However "security review" often remains locally defined. Ask one practitioner and she will tell you that her review consists of post-build vulnerability scanning. Another answer might be, "We perform a comprehensive attack and penetration on systems before deployment." But neither of these responses captures the essence and timing of, *"[S]ecurity requirements should be developed at the same time system planners define*

---

* "Infosec" is a common nickname for an information security department.
† Static analyzers are the security equivalent of the compiler and linker that turn software source code written in programming languages into executable programs.
‡ Though these may be called a "security engineer," or a "security analyst," or any number of similar local variations.

the requirements of the system."[4] That is, the "review," the discovery of "requirements" is supposed to take place proactively, *before* a system is completely built! And, in my experience, for many systems, it is best to gather security requirements at various points during system development, and at increasing levels of specificity, as the architecture and design are thought through. The security of a system is best considered just as all the other attributes and qualities of the system are pulled together. It remains an ongoing mistake to leave security to the end of the development cycle.

By the time a large and complex system is ready for deployment, the possibility of structural change becomes exponentially smaller. If a vulnerability (hole) is found in the systems logic or that its security controls are incomplete, there is little likelihood that the issue can or will be repaired before the system begins its useful life. Too much effort and resources have already been expended. The owners of the system are typically stuck with what's been implemented. They owners will most likely bear the residual risk, at least until some subsequent development cycle, perhaps for the life of the system.

Beyond the lack of definition among practitioners, there is a dearth of skilled security architects. The United States Department of Labor estimated in 2013 that there would be zero unemployment of information security professionals for the foreseeable future. Demand is high. But there are few programs devoted to the art and practice of assessing systems. Even calculating the risk of any particular successful attack has proven a difficult problem, as we shall explore. But risk calculation is only one part of an assessment. A skilled security architect must bring a wealth of knowledge and understanding—global and local, technical, human, organizational, and even geopolitical—to an assessment. How does a person get from here to there, from engineer to a security architect who is capable of a skilled security assessment?

Addressing the skill deficit on performing security "reviews," or more properly, security assessment and analysis, is the object of this work. The analysis must occur while there is still time to make any required changes. The analyst must have enough information and skill to provide requirements and guidance sufficient to meet the security goals of the owners of the system. That is the goal of this book and these methods, to deliver the right security at the right time in the implementation lifecycle. In essence, this book is about addressing pervasive attacks through securing systems.

The Structure of the Book

There are three parts to this book: Parts I, II, and III. Part I presents and then attempts to explain the practices, knowledge domains, and methods that must be brought to bear when performing assessments and threat models.

Part II is a series of linked assessments. The assessments are intended to build upon each other; I have avoided repeating the same analysis and solution set over and over again. In the real world, unique circumstances and individual treatments exist within a universe of fairly well known and repeating architecture patterns. Alongside the need for a certain amount of brevity, I also hope that each assessment may be read by itself, especially for experienced security architects who are already familiar with the typical, repeating patterns of their practice. Each assessment adds at least one new architecture and its corresponding security solutions.

Part III is an abbreviated exploration into building the larger practice encompassing multiple security architects and engineers, multiple stakeholders and teams, and the need for standards and repeating practices. This section is short; I've tried to avoid repeating the many great books that already explain in great detail a security program. These usually touch upon an assessment program within the context of a larger computer security practice. Instead, I've tried to stay focused on those facets that apply directly to an applied security architecture practice. There is no doubt that I have left out many important areas in favor of keeping a tight focus.

I assume that many readers will use the book as a reference for their security architecture and system risk-assessment practice. I hope that by clearly separating tools and preparation from analysis, and these from program, it will be easier for readers to find what they need quickly, whether through the index or by browsing a particular part or chapter.

In my (very humble) experience, when performing assessments, nothing is as neat as the organization of any methodology or book. I have to jump from architecture to attack surface, explain my risk reasoning, only to jump to some previously unexplored technical detail. Real-world systems can get pretty messy, which is why we impose the ordering that architecture and, specifically, security architecture provides.

References

1. Swanson, M. and Guttman B. (September 1996). "Generally Accepted Principles and Practices for Securing Information Technology Systems." National Institute of Standards and Technology, Technology Administration, US Department of Commerce (NIST 800-14, p. 17).
2. Ashton, K. (22 June 2009). "That 'Internet of Things' Thing: In the real world things matter more than ideas." *RFID Journal*. Retrieved from http://www.rfidjournal.com/articles/view?4986.
3. Grossman, L. K. (1995). *Electronic Republic: Reshaping American Democracy for the Information Age* (A Twentieth Century Fund Book), p. 3. Viking Adult.
4. Swanson, M. and Guttman B. (September 1996). "Generally Accepted Principles and Practices for Securing Information Technology Systems." National Institute of Standards and Technology, Technology Administration, US Department of Commerce (NIST 800-14, p. 17).

Chapter 1

Introduction

Often when the author is speaking at conferences about the practice of security archi-tecture, participants repeatedly ask, "How do I get started?" At the present time, there are few holistic works devoted to the art and the practice of system security assessment.*

Yet despite the paucity of materials, the practice of security assessment is growing rapidly. The information security industry has gone through a transformation from reactive approaches such as Intrusion Detection to proactive practices that are embed-ded into the Secure Development Lifecycle (SDL). Among the practices that are typi-cally required is a security architecture assessment. Most Fortune 500 companies are performing some sort of an assessment, at least on critical and major systems.

To meet this demand, there are plenty of consultants who will gladly offer their expensive services for assessments. But consultants are not typically teachers; they are not engaged long enough to provide sufficient longitudinal mentorship. Organizations attempting to build an assessment practice may be stymied if they are using a typi-cal security consultant. Consultants are rarely geared to explaining what to do. They usually don't supply the kind of close relationship that supports long-term training. Besides, this would be a conflict of interest—the stronger the internal team, the less they need consultants!

Explaining security architecture assessment has been the province of a few mentors who are scattered across the security landscape, including the author. Now, therefore, seems a like a good time to offer a book describing, in detail, how to actually perform a security assessment, from strategy to threat model, and on through producing security requirements that can and will get implemented.

---

* There are numerous works devoted to organizational "security assessment." But few describe in any detail the practice of analyzing a system to determine what, if any, security must be added to it before it is used.

Training to assess has typically been performed through the time-honored system of mentoring. The prospective security architect follows an experienced practitioner for some period, hoping to understand what is happening. The mentee observes the mentor as he or she examines in depth systems' architectures.

The goal of the analysis is to achieve the desired security posture. How does the architect factor the architecture into components that are relevant for security analysis? And, that "desired" posture? How does the assessor know what that posture is? At the end of the analysis, through some as yet unexplained "magic"—really, the experience and technical depth of the security architect—requirements are generated that, when implemented, will bring the system up to the organization's security requirements. The author has often been asked by mentees, "How do you know what questions to ask?" or, "How can you find the security holes so quickly?"

Securing Systems is meant to step into this breach, to fill the gap in training and mentorship. This book is more than a step-by-step process for performing an analysis. For instance, this book offers a set of prerequisite knowledge domains that is then brought into a skilled analysis. What does an assessor need to understand before she or he can perform an assessment?

Even before assembling the required global and local knowledge set, a security architect will have command of a number of domains, both within security and without. Obviously, it's imperative to have a grasp of typical security technologies and their application to systems to build the defense. These are typically called "security controls," which are usually applied in sets intended to build a "defense-in-depth," that is, a multilayered set of security controls that, when put together, complement each other as well as provide some protection against the failure of each particular control. In addition, skilled security architects usually have at least some grounding in system architecture—the practice of defining the structure of large-scale systems. How can one decompose an architecture sufficiently to provide security wisdom if one cannot understand the architecture itself? Implicit in the practice of security architecture is a grasp of the process by which an architect arrives at an architecture, a firm grasp on how system structures are designed. Typically, security architects have significant experience in designing various types of computer systems.

And then there is the ongoing problem of calculating information security risk. Despite recent advances in understanding, the industry remains largely dependent upon expert opinion. Those opinions can be normalized so that they are comparable. Still, we, the security industry, are a long way from hard, mathematically repeatable calculations. How does the architect come to an understanding whereby her or his risk "calculation" is more or less consistent and, most importantly, trustworthy by decision makers?

This book covers all of these knowledge domains and more. Included will be the author's tips and tricks. Some of these tips will, by the nature of the work, be technical. Still, complex systems are built by teams of highly skilled professionals, usually crossing numerous domain and organizational boundaries. In order to secure those systems, the skilled security architect must not alienate those who have to perform the work or who may have a "no" vote on requirements. Accumulated through the "hard dint" of experience, this book will offer tricks of the trade to cement relationships and to work with inevitable resistance, the conflict that seems to predictably arise among teams with different viewpoints and considerations who must come to definite agreements.

There is no promise that reading this book will turn the reader into a skilled security architect. However, every technique explained here has been practiced by the author and, at least in my hands, has a proven track record. Beyond that endorsement, I have personally trained dozens of architects in these techniques. These architects have then taught the same techniques and approaches down through several generations of architecture practice. And, indeed, these techniques have been used to assess the security of literally thousands of individual projects, to build living threat models, and to provide sets of security requirements that actually get implemented. A few of these systems have resisted ongoing attack through many years of exposure; their architectures have been canonized into industry standards.*

My promise to the reader is that there is enough information presented here to get one started. Those who've been tasked for the first time with the security assessment of systems will find hard answers about what to learn and what to do. For the practitioner, there are specific techniques that you can apply in your practice. These techniques are not solely theoretical, like, "programs should . . ." And they aren't just "ivory tower" pronouncements. Rather, these techniques consist of real approaches that have delivered results on real systems. For assessment program managers, I've provided hints along the way about successful programs in which I've been involved, including a final chapter on building a program. And for the expert, perhaps I can, at the very least, spark constructive discussion about what we do and how we do it? If something that I've presented here can seed improvement to the practice of security architecture in some significant way, such an advance would be a major gift.

1.1 Breach! Fix It!

Advances in information security have been repeatedly driven by spectacular attacks and by the evolutionary advances of the attackers. In fact, many organizations don't really empower and support their security programs until there's been an incident. It is a truism among security practitioners to consider a compromise or breach as an "opportunity." Suddenly, decision makers are paying attention. The wise practitioner makes use of this momentary attention to address the weaker areas in the extant program.

For example, for years, the web application security team on which I worked, though reasonably staffed, endured a climate in which mid-level management "accepted" risks, that is, vulnerabilities in the software, rather than fix them. In fact, a portfolio of

---

* Most notably, the Cisco SAFE eCommerce architecture closely models Cisco's external web architecture, to which descendant architects and I contributed.

thousands of applications had been largely untested for vulnerabilities. A vulnerability scanning pilot revealed that every application tested had issues. The security "debt," that is, an unaddressed set of issues, grew to be much greater than the state of the art could address. The period for detailed assessment grew to be estimated in multiple years. The application portfolio became a tower of vulnerable cards, an incident waiting to happen. The security team understood this full well.

This sad state of affairs came through a habit of accepting risk rather than treating it. The team charged with the security of the portfolio was dispirited and demoralized. They lost many negotiations about security requirements. It was difficult to achieve security success against the juggernaut of management unwilling to address the mounting problem.

Then, a major public hack occurred.

The password file for millions of customers was stolen through the front end of a web site pulling in 90% of a multi-billion dollar revenue stream. The attack was successful through a vector that had been identified years before by the security team. The risk had been accepted by corporate IT due to operational and legacy demands. IT didn't want to upset the management who owned the applications in the environments.

Immediately, that security team received more attention, first negative, then constructive. The improved program that is still running successfully 10 years later was built out on top of all this senior management attention. So far as I know, that company has not endured another issue of that magnitude through its web systems. The loss of the password file turned into a powerful imperative for improvement.

Brad Arkin, CSO for Adobe Systems, has said, "Never waste a crisis."[1] Savvy security folk leverage significant incidents for revolutionary changes. For this reason, it seems that these sea changes are a direct result, even driven out of, successful attacks. Basically, security leaders are told, "There's been a breach. Fix it!" Once into a "fix it" cycle, a program is much more likely to receive the resource expansions, programmatic changes, and tool purchases that may be required.

In parallel, security technology makers are continually responding to new attack methods. Antivirus, anti-malware, next-generation firewall, and similar vendors continually update the "signatures," the identifying attributes, of malicious software, and usually very rapidly, as close to "real-time" as they are able. However, it is my understanding that new variations run in the hundreds every single day; there are hundreds of millions of unique, malicious software samples in existence as of this writing. Volumes of this magnitude are a maintenance nightmare requiring significant investment in automation in order to simply to keep track, much less build new defenses. Any system that handles file movements is going to be handling malicious pieces of software at some point, perhaps constantly exposed to malicious files, depending upon the purpose of the system.

Beyond sheer volume, attackers have become ever more sophisticated. It is not unusual for an Advanced Persistent Attack (APT) to take months or even years to plan, build, disseminate, and then to execute. One well-known attack described to the author involved site visits six months before the actual attack, two diversionary probes in parallel to the actual data theft, the actual theft being carried out over a period of days and perhaps involving an attack team staying in a hotel near the physical attack site. Clever name-resolution schemes such as fast-flux switching allow attackers to efficiently hide their identities without cost. It's a dangerous cyber world out there on the Internet today.

The chance of an attempted attack of one kind or another is certain. The probability of a web attack is 100%; systems are being attacked and will be attacked regularly and continually. Most of those attacks will be "door rattling," reconnaissance probes and well-known, easily defended exploit methods. But out of the fifty million attacks each week that most major web sites must endure, something like one or two within the mountain of attack events will likely be highly sophisticated and tightly targeted at that particular set of systems. And the probability of a targeted attack goes up exponentially when the web systems employ well-known operating systems and execution environments.

Even though calculating an actual risk in dollars lost per year is fairly difficult, we do know that Internet system designers can count on being attacked, period. And these attacks may begin fairly rapidly upon deployment.

There's an information security saying, "the defender must plug all the holes. The attacker only needs to exploit a single vulnerability to be successful." This is an over-simplification, as most successful data thefts employ two or more vulnerabilities strung together, often across multiple systems or components.

Indeed, system complexity leads to increasing the difficulty of defense and, inversely, decreasing the difficulty of successful exploitation. The number of flows between systems can turn into what architects call, "spaghetti," a seeming lack of order and regularity in the design. Every component within the system calls every other component, perhaps through multiple flows, in a disorderly matrix of calls. I have seen complex systems from major vendors that do exactly this. In a system composed of only six components, that gives $6^2=36$ separate flows (or more!). Missing appropriate security on just one of these flows might allow an attacker a significant possibility to gain a foothold within the trust boundaries of the entire system. If each component blindly trusts every other component, let's say, because the system designers assumed that the surrounding network would provide enough protection, then that foothold can easily allow the attacker to own the entire system. And, trusted systems make excellent beach heads from which to launch attacks at other systems on a complex enterprise network. Game over. Defenders 0, attacker everything.

Hence, standard upon standard require organizations to meet the challenge through building security into systems *from the very start of the architecture and then on through design*. It is this practice that we will address.

- When should the architect begin the analysis?
- At what points can a security architect add the most value?
- What are the activities the architect must execute?
- How are these activities delivered?
- What is the set of knowledge domains applied to the analysis?

- What are the outputs?
- What are the tips and tricks that make security architecture risk assessment easier?

If a breach or significant compromise and loss creates an opportunity, then that opportunity quite often is to build a security architecture practice. A major part or focus of that maturing security architecture practice will be the assessment of systems for the purpose of assuring that when deployed, the assessed systems contain appropriate security qualities and controls.

- Sensitive data will be protected in storage, transmission, and processing.
- Sensitive access will be controlled (need-to-know, authentication, and authorization).
- Defenses will be appropriately redundant and layered to account for failure.
- There will be no single point of failure in the controls.
- Systems are maintained in such a way that they remain available for use.
- Activity will be monitored for attack patterns and failures.

1.2 Information Security, as Applied to Systems

One definition of security architecture might be, "applied information security." Or perhaps, more to the point of this work, security architecture applies the principles of security to system architectures. It should be noted that there are (at least) two uses of the term, "security architecture." One of these is, as defined above, to ensure that the correct security features, controls, and properties are included into an organization's digital systems and to help implement these through the practice of system architecture.

The other branch, or common usage, of "security architecture" is the architecture of the security systems of an organization. In the absence of the order provided through architecture, organizations tend to implement various security technologies "helter-skelter," that is, *ad hoc*. Without security architecture, the intrusion system (IDS) might be distinct and independent from the firewalls (perimeter). Firewalls and IDS would then be unconnected and independent from anti-virus and anti-malware on the end-point systems and entirely independent of server protections. The security architect first uncovers the intentions and security needs of the organization: open and trusting or tightly controlled, the data sensitivities, and so forth. Then, the desired security posture (as it's called) is applied through a collection of coordinated security technologies. This can be accomplished very intentionally when the architect has sufficient time to strategize before architecting, then to architect to feed a design, and to have a sound design to support implementation and deployment.[*]

---

[*] Of course, most security architects inherit an existing set of technologies. If these have grown up piecemeal over a significant period of time, there will be considerable legacy that hasn't been architected with which to contend. This is the far more common case.

[I]nformation security solutions are often designed, acquired and installed on a tactical basis. . . . [T]here is no strategy that can be identifiably said to support the goals of the business. An approach that avoids these piecemeal problems is the development of an enterprise security architecture which is business-driven and which describes a structured inter-relationship between the technical and procedural solutions to support the long-term needs of the business.[2]

Going a step further, the security architect who is primarily concerned with deploying security technologies will look for synergies between technologies such that the sum of the controls is greater than any single control or technology. And, there are products whose purpose is to enhance synergies. The purpose of the security information and event management (SIEM) products is precisely this kind of synergy between the event and alert flows of disparate security products. Depending upon needs, this is exactly the sort of synergistic view of security activity that a security architect will try to enhance through a security architecture (this second branch of the practice). The basic question the security architect implementing security systems asks is, "How can I achieve the security posture desired by the organization through a security infrastructure, given time, money, and technology restraints."

Contrast the foregoing with the security architect whose task it is to build security into systems whose function *has nothing to do with information security.* The security architecture of any system *depends upon and consumes* whatever security systems have been put into place by the organization. Oftentimes, the security architecture of non-security systems *assumes* the capabilities of those security systems that have been put into place. The systems that implement security systems are among the tools that the system security architect will employ, the "palette" from which she or he draws, as systems are analyzed and security requirements are uncovered through the analysis. You may think of the security architect concerned with security systems, the designer of security systems, as responsible for the coherence of the security *infrastructure.* The architect concerned with non-security systems will be utilizing the security infrastructure in order to add security into or underneath the other systems that will get deployed by the organization.

In smaller organizations, there may be no actual distinction between these two roles: the security architect will design security systems and will analyze the organization's other systems in light of the security infrastructure. The two, systems and security systems, are intimately linked and, typically, tightly coupled. Indeed, as stated previously, at least a portion of the security infrastructure will usually provide security services such as authentication and event monitoring for the other systems. And, firewalls and the like will provide protections that surround the non-security systems.

Ultimately, the available security infrastructure gives rise to an organization's technical standards. Although an organization might attempt to create standards and then build an infrastructure to those standards, the dictates of resources, technology, skill, and other constraints will limit "ivory tower" standards; very probably, the ensuing infrastructure will diverge significantly from standards that presume a perfect world and unlimited resources.

When standards do not match what can actually be achieved, the standards become empty ideals. In such a case, engineers' confidence will be shaken; system project teams are quite likely to ignore standards, or make up their own. Security personnel will lose considerable influence. Therefore, as we shall see, it's important that standards match capabilities closely, even when the capabilities are limited. In this way, all participants in the system security process will have more confidence in analysis and requirements. Delivering ivory tower, unrealistic requirements is a serious error that must be avoided. Decision makers need to understand precisely what protections can be put into place and have a good understanding of any residual, unprotected risks that remain.

From the foregoing, it should be obvious that the two concentrations within security architecture work closely together when these are not the same person. When the roles are separate disciplines, the architect concerned with the infrastructure must understand what other systems will require, the desired security posture, perimeter protections, and security services. The architect who assesses the non-security systems must have a very deep and thorough understanding of the security infrastructure such that these services can be applied appropriately. I don't want to over specify. If an infrastructure provides strong perimeter controls (firewalls), there is no need to duplicate those controls locally. However, the firewalls may have to be updated for new system boundaries and inter-trust zone communications.

In other words, these two branches of security architecture work very closely together and may even be fulfilled by the same individual.

No matter how the roles are divided or consolidated, the art of security analysis of a system architecture is the art of applying the principles of information security to that system architecture. A set of background knowledge domains is applied to an architecture for the purpose of discovery. The idea is to uncover points of likely attack: "attack surfaces." The attack surfaces are analyzed with respect to active threats that have the capabilities to exercise the attack surfaces. Further, these threats must have access in order to apply their capabilities to the attack surfaces. And the attack surfaces must present a weakness that can be exploited by the attacker, which is known as a "vulnerability." This weakness will have some kind of impact, either to the organization or to the system. The impact may be anywhere from high to low.

We will delve into each of these components later in the book. When all the requisite components of an attack come together, a "credible attack vector" has been discovered. It is possible in the architecture that there are security controls that protect against the exercise of a credible attack vector. The combination of attack vector and mitigation indicates the risk of exploitation of the attack vector. Each attack vector is paired to existing (or proposed) security controls. If the risk is low enough after application of the mitigation, then that credible attack vector will receive a low risk. Those attack vectors with a significant impact are then prioritized.

The enumeration of the credible attack vectors, their impacts, and their mitigations can be said to be a "threat model," which is simply the set of credible attack vectors and their prioritized risk rating.

Since there is no such thing as perfect security, nor are there typically unlimited resources for security, the risk rating of credible attack vectors allows the security architect to focus on meaningful and significant risks.

Securing systems is the art and craft of applying information security principles, design imperatives, and available controls in order to achieve a particular security posture. The analyst must have a firm grasp of basic computer security objectives for confidentiality, integrity, and availability, commonly referred to as "CIA." Computer security has been described in terms of CIA. These are the attributes that will result from appropriate security "controls." "Controls" are those functions that help to provide some assurance that data will only be seen or handled by those allowed access, that data will remain or arrive intact as saved or sent, and that a particular system will continue to deliver its functionality. Some examples of security controls would be authentication, authorization, and network restrictions. A system-monitoring function may provide some security functionality, allowing the monitoring staff to react to apparent attacks. Even validation of user inputs into a program may be one of the key controls in a system, preventing misuse of data handling procedures for the attacker's purposes.

> *The first necessity for secure software is specifications that define secure behavior exhibiting the security properties required. The specifications must define functionality and be free of vulnerabilities that can be exploited by intruders. The second necessity for secure software is correct implementation meeting specifications. Software is correct if it exhibits only the behavior defined by its specification – not, as today is often the case, exploitable behavior not specified, or even known to its developers and testers.*[3]

The process that we are describing is the first "necessity" quoted above, from the work of Redwine and Davis[*] (2004)[3]: "specifications that define secure behavior exhibiting the security properties required." Architecture risk assessment (ARA) and threat modeling is intended to deliver these specifications such that the system architecture and design includes properties that describe the system's security. We will explore the architectural component of this in Chapter 3.

The assurance that the implementation is correct—that the security properties have been built as specified and actually protect the system and that vulnerabilities have not been introduced—is a function of many factors. That is, this is the second "necessity" given above by Redwine and David (2004).[3] These factors must be embedded into processes, into behaviors of the system implementers, and for which the system is tested. Indeed, a fair description of my current thinking on a secure development lifecycle (SDL) can be found in *Core Software Security: Security at the Source*, Chapter 9 (of which I'm the contributing author), and is greatly expanded within the entire book, written by Dr. James Ransome and Anmol Misra.[4] Architecture analysis for security fits within a mature SDL. Security assessment will be far less effective standing alone, with-

---

[*] With whom I've had the privilege to work.

out all the other activities of a mature and holistic SDL or secure project development lifecycle. However, a broad discussion of the practices that lead to assurance of implementation is not within the scope of this work. Together, we will limit our exploration to ARA and threat modeling, solely, rather than attempting cover an entire SDL.

A suite of controls implemented for a system becomes that system's defense. If well designed, these become a "defense-in-depth," a set of overlapping and somewhat redundant controls. Because, of course, things fail. One security "principle" is that no single control can be counted upon to be inviolable. Everything may fail. Single points of failure are potentially vulnerable.

I drafted the following security principles for the enterprise architecture practice of Cisco Systems, Inc. We architected our systems to these guidelines.

1. **Risk Management:** We strive to manage our risk to acceptable business levels.
2. **Defense-in-Depth:** No one solution alone will provide sufficient risk mitigation. Always assume that every security control will fail.
3. **No Safe Environment:** We do not assume that the internal network or that any environment is "secure" or "safe." Wherever risk is too great, security must be addressed.
4. **CIA:** Security controls work to provide some acceptable amount of Confidentiality, Integrity, and/or Availability of data (CIA).
5. **Ease Security Burden:** Security controls should be designed so that doing the secure thing is the path of least resistance. Make it easy to be secure, make it easy to do the right thing.
6. **Industry Standard:** Whenever possible, follow industry standard security practices.
7. **Secure the Infrastructure:** Provide security controls for developers not by them. As much as possible, put security controls into the infrastructure. Developers should develop business logic, not security, wherever possible.

The foregoing principles were used[*] as intentions and directions for architecting and design. As we examined systems falling within Cisco's IT development process, we applied specific security requirements in order to achieve the goals outlined through these principles. Requirements were not only technical; gaps in technology might be filled through processes, and staffing might be required in order to carry out the processes and build the needed technology. We drove toward our security principles through the application of "people, process, and technology." It is difficult to architect without knowing what goals, even ideals, one is attempting to achieve. Principles help

---

[*] These principles are still in use by Enterprise Architecture at Cisco Systems, Inc., though they have gone through several revisions. National Cyber Security Award winner Michele Guel and Security Architect Steve Acheson are coauthors of these principles.

to consider goals as one analyzes a system for its security: The principles are the properties that the security is supposed to deliver.

These principles (or any similar very high level guidance) may seem like they are too general to help? But experience taught me that once we had these principles firmly communicated and agreed upon by most, if not all, of the architecture community, discussions about security requirements were much more fruitful. The other architects had a firmer grasp on precisely why security architects had placed particular requirements on a system. And, the principles helped security architects remember to analyze more holistically, more thoroughly, for all the intentions encapsulated within the principles.

ARAs are a security, "rubber meets the road" activity. The following is a generic statement about what the practice of information security is about, a definition, if you will.

Information assurance is achieved when information and information systems are protected against attacks through the application of security services such as availability, integrity, authentication, confidentiality, and nonrepudiation. The application of these services should be based on the protect, detect, and react paradigm. This means that in addition to incorporating protection mechanisms, organizations need to expect attacks and include attack detection tools and procedures that allow them to react to and recover from these unexpected attacks. [5]

This book is not a primer in information security. It is assumed that the reader has at least a glancing familiarity with CIA and the paradigm, "protect, detect, react," as described in the quote above. If not, then perhaps it might be of some use to take a look at an introduction to computer security before proceeding? It is precisely this paradigm whereby:

- Security controls are in-built to protect a system.
- Monitoring systems are created to detect attacks.
- Teams are empowered to react to attacks.

The Open Web Application Security Project (OWASP) provides a distillation of several of the most well known sets of computer security principles:

- Apply defense-in-depth (complete mediation).
- Use a positive security model (fail-safe defaults, minimize attack surface).
- Fail securely.
- Run with least privilege.
- Avoid security by obscurity (open design).
- Keep security simple (verifiable, economy of mechanism).
- Detect intrusions (compromise recording).
- Don't trust infrastructure.

o Don't trust services.
o Establish secure defaults[6]

Some of these principles imply a set of controls (e.g., access controls and privilege sets). Many of these controls, such as "Avoid security by obscurity" and "Keep security simple," are guides to be applied during design, approaches rather than specific demands to be applied to a system. When assessing a system, the assessor examines for attack surfaces, then applies specific controls (technologies, processes, etc.) to realize these principles.

These principles (and those like the ones quoted) are the tools of computer security architecture. Principles comprise the palette of techniques that will be applied to systems in order to achieve the desired security posture. The prescribed requirements fill in the three steps enumerated above:

- Protect a system through purpose-built security controls.
- Attempt to detect attacks with security-specific monitors.
- React to any attacks that are detected.

In other words, securing systems is the application of the processes, technologies, and people that "protect, detect, and react" to systems. Securing systems is essentially applied information security. Combining computer security with information security risk comprises the core of the work.

The output of this "application of security to a system" is typically security "requirements." There may also be "nice-to-have" guidance statements that may or may not be implemented. However, there is a strong reason to use the word "requirement." Failure to implement appropriate security measures may very well put the survival of the organization at risk.

Typically, security professionals are assigned a "due diligence" responsibility to prevent disastrous events. There's a "buck stops here" part of the practice: Untreated risk must never be ignored. That doesn't mean that security's solution will be adopted. What it does mean is that the security architect must either mitigate information security risks to an acceptable, known level or make the appropriate decision maker aware that there is residual risk that either cannot be mitigated or has not been mitigated sufficiently.

Just as a responsible doctor must follow a protocol that examines the whole health of the patient, rather than only treating the presenting problem, so too must the security architect thoroughly examine the "patient," any system under analysis, for "vital signs"—that is, security health.

The requirements output from the analysis are the collection of additions to the system that will keep the system healthy as it endures whatever level of attack is predicted for its deployment and use. Requirements must be implemented or there is residual risk. Residual risk must be recognized because of due diligence responsibility. Hence, if the analysis uncovers untreated risk, the output of that analysis is the necessity to bring the security posture up and risk down to acceptable levels. Thus, risk practice and architecture analysis must go hand-in-hand.

So, hopefully, it is clear that a system is risk analyzed in order to determine how to apply security to the system appropriately. We then can define Architecture Risk Analysis (ARA) as the process of uncovering system security risks and applying information security techniques to the system to mitigate the risks that have been discovered.

1.3 Applying Security to Any System

This book describes a process whereby a security architect analyzes a system for its security needs, a process that is designed to uncover the security needs for the system.

Some of those security needs will be provided by an existing security infrastructure. Some of the features that have been specified through the analysis will be services consumed from the security infrastructure. And there may be features that need to be built solely for the system at hand. There may be controls that are specific to the system that has been analyzed. These will have to be built into the system itself or added to the security architecture, depending upon whether these features, controls, or services will be used only by this system, or whether future systems will also make use of these.

A typical progression of security maturity is to start by building one-off security features into systems during system implementation. During the early periods, there may be only one critical system that has any security requirements! It will be easier and cheaper to simply build the required security services as a part of the system as it's being implemented. As time goes on, perhaps as business expands into new territories or different products, there will be a need for common architectures, if for no other reason than maintainability and shared cost. It is typically at this point that a security infrastructure comes into being that supports at least some of the common security needs for many systems to consume. It is characteristically a virtue to keep complexity to a minimum and to reap scales of economy.

Besides, it's easier to build and run a single security service than to maintain many different ones whose function is more or less the same. Consider storage of credentials (passwords and similar).

Maintaining multiple disparate stores of credentials requires each of these to be held at stringent levels of security control. Local variations of one of the stores may lower the overall security posture protecting all credentials, perhaps enabling a loss of these sensitive tokens through attack, whereas maintaining a single repository at a very high level, through a select set of highly trained and skilled administrators (with carefully controlled boundaries and flows) will be far easier and cheaper. Security can be held at a consistently high level that can be monitored more easily; the security events will be consistent, allowing automation rules to be implemented for raising any alarms. And so forth.

An additional value from a single authentication and credential storing service is likely to be that users may be much happier in that they have only a single password to remember! Of course, once all the passwords are kept in a single repository, there may be a single point of failure. This will have to be carefully considered. Such considerations are precisely what security architects are supposed to provide to the organization.

It is the application of security principles and capabilities that is the province and domain of security architecture as applied to systems.

The first problem that must be overcome is one of discovery.

- What risks are the organization's decision makers willing to undertake?
- What security capabilities exist?
- Who will attack these types of systems, why, and to attain what goals?

Without the answers to these formative questions, any analysis must either treat every possible attack as equally dangerous, or miss accounting for something important. In a world of unlimited resources, perhaps locking everything down completely may be possible. But I haven't yet worked at that organization; I don't practice in that world. Ultimately, the goal of a security analysis isn't perfection. The goal is to implement just enough security to achieve the surety desired and to allow the organization to take those risks for which the organization is prepared. It must always be remembered that there is no usable perfect security.

A long-time joke among information security practitioners remains that all that's required to secure a system is to disconnect the system, turn the system off, lock it into a closet, and throw away the key. But of course, this approach disallows all purposeful use of the system. A connected, running system in purposeful use is already exposed to a certain amount of risk. One cannot dodge taking risks, especially in the realm of computer security. The point is to take those risks that can be borne and avoid those which cannot. This is why the first task is to find out how much security is "enough." Only with this information in hand can any assessment and prescription take place.

Erring on the side of too much security may seem safer, more reasonable. But, security is expensive. Taken among the many things to which any organization must attend, security is important but typically must compete with a host of other organizational priorities. Of course, some organizations will choose to give their computer security primacy. That is what this investigation is intended to uncover.

Beyond the security posture that will further organizational goals, an inventory of what security has been implemented, what weaknesses and limitations exist, and what security costs must be borne by each system is critical.

Years ago, when I was just learning system assessment, I was told that every application in the application server farm creating a Secure Sockets Layer (SSL)* tunnel was required to implement bidirectional, SSL certificate authentication. Such a connection

---

* This was before the standard became Transport Layer Security (TLS).

presumes that at the point at which the SSL is terminated on the answering (server) end, the SSL "stack," implementing software, will be tightly coupled, usually even controlled by the application that is providing functionality over the SSL tunnel. In the SSL authentication exchange, first, the server (listener) certificate is authenticated by the client (caller). Then, the client must respond with its certificate to be authenticated by the server. Where many different and disparate, logically separated applications coexist on the same servers, each application would then have to be listening for its own SSL connections. You typically shouldn't share a single authenticator across all of the applications. Each application must have its own certificate. In this way, each authentication will be tied to the relevant application. Coupling authenticator to application then provides robust, multi-tenant application authentication.

I dutifully provided a requirement to the first three applications that I analyzed to use bidirectional, SSL authentication. I was told to require this. I simply passed the requirement to project teams when encountering a need for SSL. Case closed? Unfortunately not.

I didn't bother to investigate how SSL was terminated for our application server farms.

SSL was not terminated at the application, at the application server software, or even at the operating system upon which each server was running. SSL was terminated on a huge, specialized SSL adjunct to the bank of network switches that routed network traffic to the server farm. The receiving switch passed all SSL to the adjunct, which terminated the connection and then passed the normal (not encrypted SSL) connection request onwards to the application servers.

The key here is that this architecture separated the network details from the application details. And further and most importantly, SSL termination was quite a distance (in an application sense) from any notion of application. There was no coupling whatsoever between application and SSL termination. That is, SSL termination was entirely independent from the server-side entities (applications), which must offer the connecting client an authentication certificate. The point being that the infrastructure had designed "out" and had not accounted for a need for application entities to have individual SSL certificate authenticators. The three applications couldn't "get there from here"; there was no capability to implement bidirectional SSL authentication. I had given each of these project teams a requirement that couldn't be accomplished without an entire redesign of a multi-million dollar infrastructure. Oops!

Before rushing full steam ahead into the analysis of any system, the security architect must be sure of what can be implemented and what cannot, what has been designed into the security infrastructure, and what has been designed out of it. There are usually at least a few different ways to "skin" a security problem, a few different approaches that can be applied. Some of the approaches will be possible and some difficult or even impossible, just as my directive to implement bidirectional SSL authentication was impossible given the existing infrastructure for those particular server farms and networks. No matter how good a security idea may seem on the face of it, it is illusory if it cannot be made real, given the limits of what exists or accounting for what can be put into place. I prefer never to assume; time spent understanding existing security infra-structure is always time well spent. This will save a lot of time for everyone involved. Some security problems cannot be solved without a thorough understanding of the existing infrastructure.

Almost every type and size of a system will have some security needs. Although it may be argued that a throw-away utility, written to solve a singular problem, might not have any security needs, if that utility finds a useful place beyond its original problem scope, the utility is likely to develop security needs at some point. Think about how many of the UNIX command line programs gather a password from the user. Perhaps many of these utilities were written without the need to prompt for the user's creden-tials and subsequently to perform an authentication on the user's behalf? Still, many of these utilities do so today. And authentication is just one security aspect out of many that UNIX system utilities perform. In other words, over time, many applications will eventually grapple with one or more security issues.

Complex business systems typically have security requirements up front. In addi-tion, either the implementing organization or the users of the system or both will have security expectations of the system. But complexity is not the determiner of security. Consider a small program whose sole purpose is to catch central processing unit (CPU) memory faults. If this software is used for debugging, it will probably have to, at the very least, build in access controls, especially if the software allows more than one user at a time (multiuser). Alternatively, if the software catches the memory faults as a part of a security system preventing misuse of the system through promulgation of memory faults, preventing say, a privilege escalation through an executing program via a mem-ory fault, then this small program will have to be self-protective such that attackers cannot turn it off, remove it, or subvert its function. Such a security program must not, under any circumstances, open a new vector of attack. Such a program will be targeted by sophisticated attackers if the program achieves any kind of broad distribution.

Thus, the answer as to whether a system requires an ARA and threat model is tied to the answers to a number of key questions:

- What is the expected deployment model?
- What will be the distribution?
- What language and execution environment will run the code?
- On what operating system(s) will the executables run?

These questions are placed against probable attackers, attack methods, network exposures, and so on. And, of course, as stated above, the security needs of the organi-zation and users must be factored against these.

The answer to whether a system will benefit from an ARA/Threat model is a func-tion of the dimensions outlined above, and perhaps others, depending upon consider-ation of those domains on which analysis is dependent. The assessment preprocess or triage will be outlined in a subsequent chapter. The simple answer to "which systems?"

is any size, shape, complexity, but certainly not all systems. A part of the art of the security architecture assessment is deciding which systems must be analyzed, which will benefit, and which may pass. That is, unless in your practice you have unlimited time and resources. I've never had this luxury. Most importantly, even the smallest application may open a vulnerability, an attack vector, into a shared environment.

Unless every application and its side effects are safely isolated from every other application, each set of code can have effects upon the security posture of the whole. This is particularly true in shared environments. Even an application destined for an endpoint (a Microsoft Windows™ application, for instance) can contain a buffer overflow that allows an attacker an opportunity, perhaps, to execute code of the attacker's choosing. In other words, an application doesn't have to be destined for a large, shared server farm in order to affect the security of its environment. Hence, a significant step that we will explore is the security triage assessment of the need for analysis.

Size, business criticality, expenses, and complexity, among others, are dimensions that *may* have a bearing, but are not solely deterministic. I have seen many Enterprise IT efforts fail, simply because there was an attempt to reduce this early decision to a two-dimensional space, yes/no questions. These simplifications invariably attempted to achieve efficiencies at scale. Unfortunately, in practice today, the decision to analyze the architecture of a system for security is a complex, multivariate problem. That is why this decision will have its own section in this book. It takes experience (and usually more than a few mistakes) to ask appropriate determining questions that are relevant to the system under discussion.

The answer to "Systems? Which systems?" cannot be overly simplified. Depending upon use cases and intentions, analyzing almost any system may produce significant security return on time invested. And, concomitantly, in a world of limited resources, some systems and, certainly, certain types of system changes may be passed without review. The organization may be willing to accept a certain amount of unknown risk as a result of not conducting a review.

References

1. Arkin, B. (2012). "Never Waste a Crisis - Necessity Drives Software Security." RSA Conference 2012, San Francisco, CA, February 29, 2012. Retrieved from http://www.rsaconference.com/events/us12/agenda/sessions/794/never-waste-a-crisis-necessity-drives-software.

2. Sherwood, J., Clark, A., and Lynas, D. "Enterprise Security Architecture." SABSA White Paper, SABSA Limited, 1995–2009. Retrieved from http://www.sabsa-institute.com/members/sites/default/inline-files/SABSA_White_Paper.pdf.

3. Redwine, S. T., Jr., and Davis, N., eds. (2004). "Processes to Produce Secure Software: Towards more Secure Software." Software Process Subgroup, Task Force on Security across the Software Development Lifecycle, National Cyber Security Summit, March 2004.

4. Ransome, J. and Misra, A. (2014). *Core Software Security: Security at the Source.* Boca Raton (FL): CRC Press.

5. NSA. "Defense in Depth: A practical strategy for achieving Information Assurance in today's highly networked environments." National Security Agency, Information Assurance Solutions Group - STE 6737. Available from: https://www.nsa.gov/ia/_files/support/defenseindepth.pdf.

6. Open Web Application Security Project (OWASP) (2013). *Some Proven Application Security Principles*. Retrieved from https://www.owasp.org/index.php/Category:Principle.

Chapter 2

The Art of Security Assessment

Despite the fact that general computer engineering is taught as a "science," there is a gap between what can be engineered in computer security and what remains, as of this writing, as "art." Certainly, it can be argued that configuring Access Control Lists (ACL) is an engineering activity. Cold hard logic is employed to generate linear steps that must flow precisely and correctly to form a network router's ACL. Each ACL rule must lie in precisely the correct place so as not to disturb the functioning of the other rules. There is a definite and repeatable order in the rule set. What is known as the "default deny" rule must be at the very end of the list of rules. For some of the rules' ordering, there is very little slippage room, and sometimes absolutely no wiggle room as to where the rule must be placed within the set. Certain rules must absolutely follow other rules in order for the entire list to function as designed.

Definition of "engineering":

The branch of science and technology concerned with the design, building, and use of engines, machines, and structures.[1]

Like an ACL list, the configuration of alerts in a security monitoring system, the use of a cryptographic function to protect credentials, and the handling of the cryptographic keying material are all engineering tasks. There are specific demands that must be met in design and implementation. This is engineering. Certainly, a great deal in computer security can be described as engineering.

There is no doubt that the study of engineering requires a significant investment in time and effort. I do not mean to suggest otherwise. In order to construct an effective

ACL, a security engineer must understand network routing, TCP/IP, the assignment and use of network ports for application functions, and perhaps even some aspects and details of the network protocols that will be allowed or blocked. Alongside this general knowledge of networking, a strong understanding of basic network security is essential. And, a thorough knowledge of the configuration language that controls options for the router or firewall on which the rule set will be applied is also essential. This is a considerable and specific knowledge set. In large and/or security-conscious organizations, typically only experts in all of these domains are allowed to set up and maintain the ACL lists on the organization's networking equipment.

Each of these domains follows very specific rules. These rules are deterministic; most if not all of the behaviors can be described with Boolean logic. Commands must be entered precisely; command-line interpreters are notoriously unforgiving. Hence, hopefully, few will disagree that writing ACLs is an engineering function.

2.1 Why Art and Not Engineering?

In contrast, a security architect must use her or his understanding of the currently active threat agents in order to apply these appropriately to a particular system. Whether a particular threat agent will aim at a particular system is as much a matter of understanding, knowledge, and experience as it is cold hard fact.* Applying threat agents and their capabilities to any particular system is an essential activity within the art of threat modeling. Hence, a security assessment of an architecture is an act of craft.

> *Craftsmen know the ways of the substances they use. They watch. Perception and systematic thinking combine to formulate understanding.*[2]

Generally, effective security architects have a strong computer engineering background. Without the knowledge of how systems are configured and deployed, and without a broad understanding of attack methods—maybe even a vast array of attack methods and their application to particular scenarios—the threat model will be incomplete. Or the modeler will not be able to prioritize attacks. All attacks will, therefore, have to be considered as equally probable. In security assessment, art meets science; craft meets engineering; and experience meets standard, policy, and rule. Hence, the methodology presented here is a combination of art and science, craft and engineering.

> *It would be prohibitively expensive and impractical to defend every possible vulnerability.*[3]

---

* Though we do know with absolute certainty that any system directly addressable on the Public Internet will be attacked, and that the attacks will be constant and unremitting.

Perhaps someday, security architecture risk assessment (ARA) and threat modeling will become a rigorous and repeatable engineering activity? As of the writing of this book, however, this is far from the case. Good assessors bring a number of key knowledge domains to each assessment. It is with these domains that we will start. Just as an assessment begins before the system is examined, so in this chapter we will explore the knowledge and understanding that feeds into and underpins an analysis of a system for security purposes.

You may care to think of these pre-assessment knowledge domains as the homework or pre-work of an assessment. When the analyst does not have this information, she or he will normally research appropriately before entering into the system assessment. Of course, if during an assessment you find that you've missed something, you can always stop the analysis and do the necessary research. While I do set this out in a linear fashion, the linearity is a matter of convenience and pedagogy. There have been many times when I have had to stop an assessment in order to research a technology or a threat agent capability about which I was unsure.

It is key to understand that jumping over or missing any of the prerequisite knowledge sets is likely to cause the analysis to be incomplete, important facets to be missed. The idea here is to help you to be holistic and thorough. Some of the biggest mistakes I've made have been because I did not look at the system as a whole but rather focused on a particular problem to the detriment of the resulting analysis. Or I didn't do thorough research. I assumed that what I knew was complete when it wasn't. My assessment mistakes could likely fill an entire volume by themselves. Wherever relevant, I will try to highlight explanations with both my successes and my failures.

Because we are dealing with experience supporting well-educated estimates, the underpinning knowledge sets are part of the assessor's craft. It is in the application of controls for risk mitigation that we will step into areas of hard engineering, once again.

2.2 Introducing "The Process"

It certainly may appear that an experienced security architect can do a system assessment, even the assessment of something fairly complex, without seeming to have any structure to the process at all. Most practitioners whom I've met most certainly do have a system and an approach. Because we security architects have methodologies, or I should say, I have a map in my mind while I assess, I can allow myself to run down threads into details without losing the whole of both the architecture and the methodology. But, unfortunately, that's very hard to teach. Without structure, the whole assessment may appear aimless and unordered? I've had many people follow me around through many, many reviews. Those who are good at following and learning through osmosis "get it." But many people require a bit more structure in order to fit the various elements that must be covered into a whole and a set of steps.

Because most experienced architects actually have a structure that they're following, that structure gives the architect the opportunity to allow discussion to flow where it needs to rather than imposing a strict agenda. This approach is useful, of course, in helping everyone involved feel like they're part of a dialogue rather than an interrogation. Still, anyone who doesn't understand the map may believe that there is no structure at all. In fact, there is a very particular process that proceeds from threat and attack methods, through attack surfaces, and ultimately resulting in requirements. Practitioners will express these steps in different ways, and there are certainly many different means to express the process, all of them valid. The process that will be explained in this book is simply one expression and certainly not absolute in any sense of the word.

Further, there is certain information, such as threat analysis, that most practitioners bring to the investigation. But the architect may not take the time to describe this pre-assessment information to other participants. It was only when I started to teach the process to others that I realized I had to find a way to explain what I was doing and what I knew to be essential to the analysis.

Because this book explains how to perform an assessment, I will try to make plain all that is necessary. Please remember when you're watching an expert that she or he will apply existing knowledge to an analysis but may not explain all the pre-work that she or he has already expended. The security architect will have already thought through the appropriate list of threat agents for the type of system under consideration. If this type of system is analyzed every day, architects live and breathe the appropriate information. Hence, they may not even realize the amount of background that they bring to the analysis.

I'm going to outline with broad strokes a series of steps that can take one from prerequisite knowledge through a system assessment. This series of steps assumes that the analyst has sufficient understanding of system architecture and security architecture going into the analysis. It also assumes that the analyst is comfortable uncovering risk, rating that risk, and expressing it appropriately for different audiences. Since each of these, architecture and risk, are significant bodies of knowledge, before proceeding into the chapters on analysis, we will take time exploring each domain in a separate section. As you read the following list, please remember that there are significant prerequisite understandings and knowledge domains that contribute to a successful ARA.

- Enumerate inputs and connections
- Enumerate threats for this type of system and its intended <u>deployment</u>
  - Consider threats' usual attack methods
  - Consider threats' usual goals
- Intersect threat's attack methods against the inputs and connections. These are the set of attack surfaces
- Collect the set of *credible* attack surfaces
- Factor in each existing security control (mitigations)
- Risk assess each attack surface. Risk rating will help to prioritize attack surfaces and remediations

Each of the foregoing steps hides a number of intermediate steps through which an assessment must iterate. The above list is obviously a simplification. A more complete list follows. However, these intermediate steps are perceived as a consequence of the investigation. At this point, it may be more useful to understand that relevant threats are applied to the attack surfaces of a system to understand how much additional security needs to be added.

The analysis is attempting to enumerate the set of "credible attack surfaces." I use the word "credible" in order to underline the fact that every attack method is not applicable to every input. In fact, not every threat agent is interested in every system. As we consider different threat agents, their typical methods, and most importantly, the goals of their attacks, I hope that you'll see that some attacks are irrelevant against some systems: These attacks are simply not worth consideration. The idea is to filter out the noise such that the truly relevant, the importantly dangerous, get more attention than anything else.

Credible attack vector: A credible threat exercising an exploit on an exposed vulnerability.

I have defined the term "credible attack vector." This is the term that I use to indicate a composite of factors that all must be true before an attack can proceed. I use the term "true" in the Boolean sense: there is an implicit "if" statement (for the programming language minded) in the term "credible": if the threat can exercise one of the threat's exploit techniques (attack method) upon a vulnerability that is sufficiently exposed such that the exploit may proceed successfully.

There are a number of factors that must each be true before a particular attack surface becomes relevant. There has to be a known threat agent who has the capability to attack that attack surface. The threat agent has to have a reason for attacking. And most importantly, the attack surface needs to be exposed in some way such that the threat agent can exploit it. Without each of these factors being true, that is, if any one of them is false, then the attack cannot be promulgated. As such, that particular attack is not worth considering. A lack of exposure might be due to an existing set of controls. Or, there might be architectural reasons why the attack surface is not exposed. Either way, the discussion will be entirely theoretical without exposure.

Consider the following pseudo code:

Credible attack vector = (active threat agent & exploit & exposure & vulnerability)

The term "credible attack vector" may only be true if each of the dependent conditions is true. Hence, an attack vector is only interesting if its component terms all return a "true" value. The operator combining each terms is Boolean And. Understanding the combinatory quality of these terms is key in order to filter out hypothetical attacks in favor of attacks that have some chance of succeeding if these attacks are not well defended.

Also important: If the attacker cannot meet his or her goals by exploiting a particular attack surface, the discussion is also moot. As an example, consider an overflow condition that can only be exploited with elevated, super-user privileges. At the point at which attackers have gained superuser privileges, they can run any code they want on most operating systems. There is no advantage to exploiting an additional overflow. It has no attack value. Therefore, any vulnerability such as the one outlined here is theoretical. In a world of limited resources, concentrating on such an overflow wastes energy that is better spent elsewhere.

In this same vein, a credible attack vector has little value if there's no reward for the attacker. Risk, then, must include a further term: the impact or loss. We'll take a deeper dive into risk, subsequently.

An analysis must first uncover all the credible attack vectors of the system. This simple statement hides significant detail. At this point in this work, it may be sufficient to outline the following mnemonic, "ATASM." Figure 2.1 graphically shows an ATASM flow:

Figure 2.1 Architecture, threats, attack surfaces, and mitigations.

Threats are applied to the attack surfaces that are uncovered through decomposing an architecture. The architecture is "factored" into its logical components—the inputs to the logical components and communication flows between components. Existing mitigations are applied to the credible attack surfaces. New (unimplemented) mitigations become the "security requirements" for the system. These four steps are sketched in the list given above. If we break these down into their constituent parts, we might have a list something like the following, more detailed list:

- Diagram (and understand) the logical architecture of the system.
- List all the possible threat agents for this type of system.
- List the goals of each of these threat agents.
- List the typical attack methods of the threat agents.
- List the technical objectives of threat agents applying their attack methods.
- Decompose (factor) the architecture to a level that exposes every possible attack surface.
- Apply attack methods for expected goals to the attack surfaces.
- Filter out threat agents who have no attack surfaces exposed to their typical methods.

- Deprioritize attack surfaces that do not provide access to threat agent goals.
- List all existing security controls for each attack surface.
- Filter out all attack surfaces for which there is sufficient existing protection.
- Apply new security controls to the set of attack services for which there isn't sufficient mitigation. Remember to build a defense-in-depth.
- The security controls that are not yet implemented become the set of security requirements for the system.

Even this seemingly comprehensive set of steps hides significant detail. The details that are not specified in the list given above comprise the simplistic purpose of this book. Essentially, this work explains a complex process that is usually treated atomically, as though the entire art of security architecture assessment can be reduced to a few easily repeated steps. However, if the process of ARA and threat modeling really were this simple, then there might be no reason for a lengthy explication. There would be no need for the six months to three years of training, coaching, and mentoring that is typically undertaken. In my experience, the process cannot be so reduced. Analyzing the security of complex systems is itself a complex process.

2.3 Necessary Ingredients

Just as a good cook pulls out all the ingredients from the cupboards and arranges them for ready access, so the experienced assessor has at her fingertips information that must feed into the assessment. In Figure 2.2, you will see the set of knowledge domains that

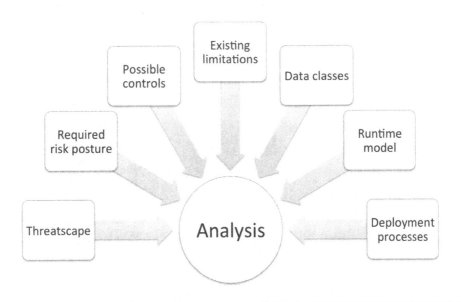

Figure 2.2   Knowledge sets that feed a security analysis.

feed into an architecture analysis. Underlying the analysis set are two other domains that are discussed, separately, in subsequent chapters: system architecture and specifically security architecture, and information security risk. Each of these requires its own explanation and examples. Hence, we take these up below.

The first two domains from the left in Figure 2.2 are strategic: threats and risk posture (or tolerance). These not only feed the analysis, they help to set the direction and high-level requirements very early in the development lifecycle. For a fuller discussion on early engagement, please see my chapter, "The SDL in the Real World," in *Core Software Security*.[4] The next two domains, moving clockwise—possible controls and existing limitations—refer to any existing security infrastructure and its capabilities: what is possible and what is difficult or excluded. The last three domains—data sensitivity, runtime/execution environment, and expected deployment model—refer to the system under discussion. These will be discussed in a later chapter.

Figure 2.3 places each contributing knowledge domain within the area for which it is most useful. If it helps you to remember, these are the "3 S's." Strategy, infrastructure and security structures, and specifications about the system help determine what is important: "Strategy, Structures, Specification." Indeed, very early in the lifecycle, perhaps as early as possible, the strategic understandings are critically important in order to deliver high-level requirements. Once the analysis begins, accuracy, relevance, and deliverability of the security requirements may be hampered if one does not know what security is possible, what exists, and what the limitations are. As I did in my first couple of reviews, it is easy to specify what cannot actually be accomplished. As an architecture begins to coalesce and become more solid, details such as data sensitivity, the runtime and/or execution environment, and under what deployment models the system will run become clearer. Each of these strongly influences what is necessary, which threats and attack methods become relevant, and which can be filtered out from consideration.

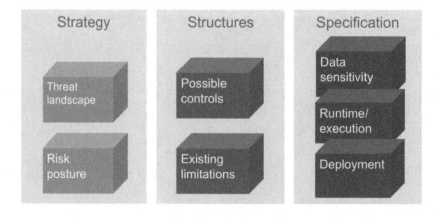

Figure 2.3 Strategy knowledge, structure information, and system specifics.

It should be noted that the process is not nearly as linear as I'm presenting it. The deployment model, for instance, may be known very early, even though it's a fairly specific piece of knowledge. The deployment model can highly influence whether security is inherited or must be placed into the hands of those who will deploy the system. As soon as this is known, the deployment model will engender some design imperatives and perhaps a set of specific controls. Without these specifics, the analyst is more or less shooting in the dark.

2.4 The Threat Landscape

Differing groups target and attack different types of systems in different ways for different reasons. Each unique type of attacker is called a "threat agent." The threat agent is simply an individual, organization, or group that is capable and motivated to promulgate an attack of one sort or another. Threat agents are not created equal. They have different goals. They have different methods. They have different capabilities and access. They have different risk profiles and will go to quite different lengths to be successful. One type of attacker may move quickly from one system to another searching for an easy target, whereas another type of attacker or threat agent may expend considerable time and resources to carefully target a single system and goal. This is why it is important to understand who your attackers are and why they might attack you. Indeed, it helps when calculating the probability of attack to know if there are large numbers or very few of each sort of attackers. How active is each threat agent? How might a successful attack serve a particular threat agent's goals?

You may note that I use the word "threat" to denote a human actor who promulgates attacks against computer systems. There are also inanimate threats. Natural disasters, such as earthquakes and tornadoes, are most certainly threats to computer systems. Preparing for these types of events may fall onto the security architect. On the other hand, in many organizations, responding to natural disasters is the responsibility of the business continuity function rather than the security function. Responding to natural disaster events and noncomputer human events, such as riots, social disruption, or military conflict, do require forethought and planning. But, it is availability that is mostly affected by this class of events. And for this reason generally, the business continuity function takes the lead rather than security. We acknowledge the seriousness of disastrous events, but for the study of architecture analysis for security, we focus on human attackers.

It should be noted that there are research laboratories who specialize in understanding threat agents and attack methods. Some of these, even commercial research, are regularly published for the benefit of all. A security architect can consume these public reports rather than trying to become an expert in threat research. What is important is to stay abreast of current trends and emerging patterns. Part of the art of security assessment is planning for the future. As of this writing, two very useful reports are produced by Verizon and by McAfee Labs.*

Although a complete examination of every known computer attacker is far beyond the scope of this work, we can take a look at a few examples to outline the kind of knowledge about threats that is necessary to bring to an assessment.

There are three key attributes of human attackers, as follows:

- Intelligence
- Adaptivity
- Creativity

This means that whatever security is put into place can and will be probed, tested, and reverse engineered. I always assume that the attacker is as skilled as I am, if not more so. Furthermore, there is a truism in computer security: "The defender must close every hole. The attacker only needs one hole in order to be successful." Thus, the onus is on the defender to understand his adversaries as well as possible. And, as has been noted several times previously, the analysis has to be thorough and holistic. The attackers are clever; they only need one opportunity for success. One weak link will break the chain of defense. A vulnerability that is unprotected and exposed can lead to a successful attack.

2.4.1 Who Are These Attackers? Why Do They Want to Attack My System?

Let's explore a couple of typical threat agents in order to understand what it is we need to know about threats in order to proceed with an analysis.† Much media attention has been given to cyber criminals and organized cyber crime. We will contrast cyber criminals with industrial espionage threats (who may or may not be related to nation-state espionage). Then we'll take a look at how cyber activists work, since their goals and methods differ pretty markedly from cyber crime. These three threat agents might be the only relevant ones to a particular system. But these are certainly not the only threat agents who are active as of this writing. It behooves you, the reader, to take advantage of public research in order to know your attackers, to understand your adversaries.

---

* Full disclosure: At the time of this writing, the author works for McAfee Inc. However, citing these two reports from among several currently being published is not intended as an endorsement of either company or their products. Verizon and McAfee Labs are given as example reports. There are others.
† The threat analysis presented in this work is similar in intention and spirit to Intel's Threat Agent Risk Assessment (TARA). However, my analysis technique was developed independently, without knowledge of TARA. Any resemblance is purely coincidental.

Currently, organized cyber criminals are pulling in billions and sometimes tens of billions of dollars each year. Email spam vastly outweighs in volume the amount of legitimate email being exchanged on any given day. Scams abound; confidence games are ubiquitous. Users identities are stolen every day; credit card numbers are a dime a dozen on the thriving black market. Who are these criminals and what do they want?

The simple answer is money. There is money to be made in cyber crime. There are thriving black markets in compromised computers. People discover (or automate existing) and then sell attack exploits; the exploit methods are then used to attack systems. Fake drugs are sold. New computer viruses get written. Some people still do, apparently, really believe that a Nigerian Prince is going to give them a large sum of money if they only supply a bank account number to which the money will supposedly be wired.

Each of these activities generates revenue for someone. That is why people do these things, for income. In some instances, lots of income. The goal of all of this activity is really pretty simple, as I understand it. The goal of cyber criminals can be summed up with financial reward. It's all about the money.

But, interestingly, cyber criminals are not interested in computer problems, *per se.* These are a means to an end. Little hard exploit research actually occurs in the cyber crime community. Instead, these actors tend to prefer to make use of the work of others, if possible. Since the goal is income, like any business, there's more profit when cost of goods, that is, when the cost of research can be minimized.

This is not to imply that cyber criminals are never sophisticated. One only has to investigate fast flux DNS switching to realize the level of technical skill that can be brought to bear. Still, the goal is not to be clever, but to generate revenue.

Cyber crime can be an organized criminal's "dream come true." Attacks can be largely anonymous. Plenty of attack scenarios are invisible to the target until after success: Bank accounts can be drained in seconds. There's typically no need for heavy handed thuggery, no guns, no physical interaction whatsoever. These activities can be conducted with far less risk than physical violence. "Clean crime?"

Hence, cyber criminals have a rather low risk tolerance, in general. Attacks tend to be poorly targeted. Send out millions of spams; one of them will hit somewhere to someone. If you wonder why you get so many spams, it's because these continue to hit pay dirt; people actually do click those links, they do order those fake drugs, and they do believe that they can make $5000 per week working from home. These email scams are successful or they would stop. The point here is that if I don't order a fake drug, that doesn't matter; the criminal moves on to someone who will.

If a machine can't easily be compromised, no matter. Cyber criminals simply move on to one that can fall to some well-known vulnerability. If one web site doesn't offer any cross-site scripting (XSS) opportunities from which to attack users, a hundred thousand other web sites do offer this vulnerability. Cyber criminals are after the gullible, the poorly defended, the poorly coded. They don't exhibit a lot of patience. "There's a sucker born every day," as T.E. Barnum famously noted.

From the foregoing, you may also notice that cyber criminals prefer to put in as little work as possible. I call this a low "work factor." The pattern then is low risk, low work factor. The cyber criminal preference is for existing exploits against existing vulnerabilities. Cyber criminals aren't likely to carefully target a system or a particular individual, as a generalization. (Of course, there may be exceptions to any broad characterization.)

There are documented cases of criminals carefully targeting a particular organization. But even in this case, the attacks have gone after the weak links of the system, such as poorly constructed user passwords and unpatched systems with well-known vulnerabilities, rather than highly sophisticated attack scenarios making use of unknown vulnerabilities.

Further, there's little incentive to carefully map out a particular person's digital life. That's too much trouble when there are so many (unfortunately) who don't patch their systems and who use the same, easily guessed password for many systems. It's a simple matter of time and effort. When not successful, move on to the next mark.

> *This Report [2012 Attorney General Breach Report*], and other studies, have repeatedly shown that cybercrime is largely opportunistic.† In other words, the organizations and individuals who engage in hacking, malware, and data breach crimes are mostly looking for "low-hanging fruit" — today's equivalent of someone who forgets to lock her car door.*[5]

If you've been following along, I hope that you have a fair grasp of the methods, goals, and profile of the cyber criminal? Low work factor, easy targets, as little risk as possible.

Let's contrast cyber crime to some of the well-known industrial espionage cases. Advanced persistent threats (APTs) are well named because these attack efforts can be multi-year, multidimensional, and are often highly targeted. The goals are information and disruption. The actors may be professionals (inter-company espionage), quasi-state sponsored (or, at least, state tolerated), and nation-states themselves. Many of the threat agents have significant numbers of people with which to work as well as being well funded. Hence, unlike organized cyber criminals, no challenge is too difficult. Attackers will spend the time and resources necessary to accomplish the job.

> *I am convinced that every company in every conceivable industry with significant size and valuable intellectual property and trade secrets has been compromised (or will be shortly) . . . In fact, I divide the entire set of Fortune Global 2,000 firms into two categories: those that know they've been compromised and those that don't yet know.*[6]

---

* Harris, K. D. (2013). 2012 Attorney General Breach Report. Retrieved from http://oag. ca.gov/news/press-releases/attorney-general-kamala-d-harris-releases-report-data-breaches-25-million> (as of Jan. 8, 2014).

† VERIZON 2014 DATA BREACH INVESTIGATIONS REPORT, 2014. Retrieved from http://www.verizonenterprise.com/DBIR/2014/reports/rp_Verizon-DBIR-2014_en_xg.pdf.

We have collected logs that reveal the full extent of the victim population since mid-2006 when the log collection began.[7]

That is, Operation "Shady RAT" likely began in 2006, whereas the McAfee research was published in 2011. That is an operation of at least five years. There were at least 70 organizations that were targeted. In fact, as the author suggests, all of the Fortune 2000 companies were likely successfully breached. These are astounding numbers.

More astounding then the sheer breadth of Shady RAT is the length, sophistication, and persistence of this single set of attacks, perhaps promulgated by a single group or under a single command structure (even if multiple groups). APT attacks are multi-month, often multi-year efforts. Sometimes a single set of data is targeted, and sometimes the attacks seem to be after whatever may be available. Multiple diversionary attacks may be exercised to hide the data theft. Note the level of sophistication here:

- Carefully planned and coordinated
- Highly secretive
- Combination of techniques (sometimes highly sophisticated)

The direct goal is rarely money (though commercial success or a nation-state advantage may ultimately be the goal). The direct goal of the attack is usually data, information, or disruption. Like cyber criminals, APT is a risk averse strategy, attempting to hide the intrusion and any compromise. Persistence is an attribute. This is very unlike the pattern of cyber criminals, who prefer to find an easier or more exposed target. For industrial spies, breaking through a defense-in-depth is an important part of the approach. Spies will take the time necessary to study and then to target individuals. New software attacks are built. Nation-states may even use "zero day" (previously unknown) vulnerabilities and exploits. The United States' STUXNET attack utilized an exploit never before seen.

Although both cyber criminals and industrial spies are fairly risk averse, their methods differ somewhat—that is, both threats make use of anonymizing services, but spies will attempt to cover their tracks completely. They don't want the breach to be discovered, ever, if possible. In contrast, criminals tend to focus on hiding only their identity. Once the theft has occurred, they don't want to be caught and punished; their goal is to hang on to their illegitimate gains. The fact that a crime has occurred will eventually be obvious to the victim.

These two approaches cause different technical details to emerge through the attacks. And, defenses need to be different.

Since the cyber criminal will move on in the event of resistance, an industry standard defense is generally sufficient. As long as the attack work-factor is kept fairly high, the attackers will go somewhere else that offers easier pickings. The house with the dog and burglar alarm remains safe. Next door, the house with poor locks that is regularly unoccupied is burglarized repeatedly.

The industrial spy spends weeks, months, years researching the target organization's technology and defenses. The interests and social relations of potentially targetable users are carefully studied. In one famous attack, the attacker knew that on a particular day, a certain file was distributed to a given set of individuals with an expected file name. By spoofing the document and the sender, several of the recipients were fooled into opening the document, which contained the attack.

It is difficult to resist a targeted "spear phishing" attack: An email or URL that appears to be sent such that the email masquerades as something expected, of particular interest, from someone trusted. To resist an APT effort, defenses must be thorough and in depth. No single defense can be a single point of failure. Each defense is assumed to fail. As the principles previously outlined state, each defense must "fail securely." The entire defense cannot count on any single security control surviving; controls are layered, with spheres of control overlapping significantly. The concept being that one has built sufficient barriers for the attackers to surmount such that an attack will be identified before it can fully succeed.* It is assumed that some protections will fail to the technical excellence of the attackers. But the attacks will be slower than the reaction to them.

Figure 2.4 attempts to provide a visual mapping of the relationships between various attributes that we might associate with threat agents. This figure includes inanimate threats, with which we are not concerned here. Attributes include capabilities, activity level, risk tolerance, strength of the motivation, and reward goals.

If we superimpose attributes from Table 2.1's cyber-crime attributes onto Figure 2.4, we can render Figure 2.5. Figure 2.5 gives us a visual representation of cyber criminal threat agent attributes and their relationships in a mind map format.

> [I]f malicious actors are interested in a company in the aerospace sector, they may try to compromise the website of one of the company's vendors or the website of an aerospace industry-related conference. That website can become a vector to exploit and infect employees who visit it in order to gain a foothold in the intended target company.[8]

We will not cover every active threat here. Table 2.1 summarizes the attributes that characterize each of the threat agents that we're examining. In order to illustrate the differences in methods, goals, effort, and risk tolerance of differing threat agents, let's now briefly examine the well-known "hacktivist" group, Anonymous.

Unlike either cyber criminals or spies, activists typically want the world to know about a breach. In the case of the HP Gary Federal hack (2011), the email, user credentials, and other compromised data were posted publicly after the successful breach. Before the advent of severe penalties for computer breaches, computer activists sometimes did

---

* Astute readers may note that I did not say, "attack prevented." The level of focus, effort, and sophistication that nation-state cyber spies can muster implies that most protections can be breached, if the attackers are sufficiently motivated.

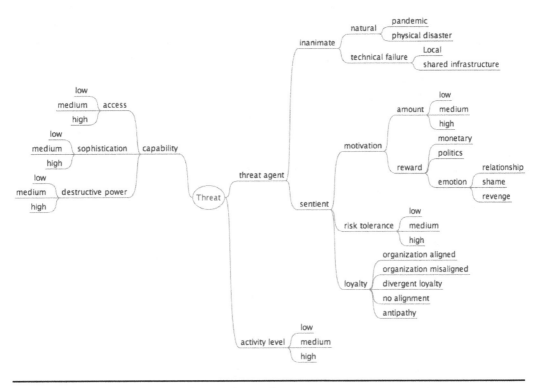

Figure 2.4   Threat agent attribute relationships.

not hide their attack at all.* As of this writing, activists do try to hide their identities because current US law provides serious penalties for any breach, whether politically motivated or not: All breaches are treated as criminal acts. Still, hacktivists go to no great pains to hide the compromise. Quite the opposite. The goal is to uncover wrong-doing, perhaps even illegal actions. The goal is an open flow of information and more transparency. So there is no point in hiding an attack. This is completely opposite to how spies operate.

---

* Under the current US laws, an activist (Aaron Schwartz) who merely used a publicly available system (MIT library) faced terrorism charges for downloading readily available scientific papers without explicit permission from the library and each author. This shift in US law has proven incredibly chilling to transparent cyber activism.

Table 2.1 Summarized Threat Attributes

Threat Agent	Goals	Risk Tolerance	Work Factor	Methods
Cyber criminals	Financial	Low	Low to medium	Known proven
Industrial spies	Information and disruption	Low	High to extreme	Sophisticated and unique
Hacktivists	Information, disruption, and media attention	Medium to high	Low to medium	System administration errors and social engineering

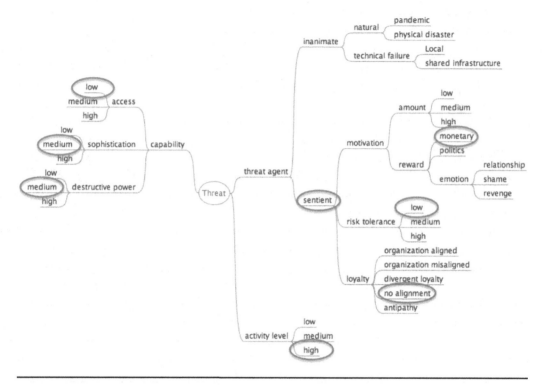

Figure 2.5 Cyber criminal attributes.

The technical methods that were used by Anonymous were not particularly sophisticated.* At HP Gary Federal, a very poorly constructed and obvious password was used for high-privilege capabilities on a key system. The password was easily guessed or otherwise forced. From then on, the attackers employed social engineering, not technical acumen. Certainly, the attackers were familiar with the use of email systems and the manipulation of servers and their operating systems. Any typical system administrator would have the skills necessary. This attack did not require sophisticated reverse engineering skills, understanding of operating system kernels, system drivers, or wire-level network communications. Anonymous didn't have to break any industrial-strength cryptography in order to breach HB Gary Federal.

Computer activists are volunteers. They do not get paid (despite any propaganda you may have read). If they do have paying jobs, their hacktivism has to be performed during

---

* I drew these conclusions after reading a technically detailed account of the HB Gary attack in *Unmasked*, by Peter Bright, Nate Anderson, and Jacqui Cheng (Amazon Kindle, 2011).[9] The conclusions that I've drawn about Anonymous were further bolstered by an in-depth analysis appearing in *Rolling Stone Magazine*, "The Rise and Fall of Jeremy Hammond: Enemy of the State," by Janet Reitman, appearing in the December 7, 2012, issue.[10] It can be retrieved from: http://www.rollingstone.com/culture/news/the-rise-and-fall-of-jeremy-hammond-enemy-of-the-state-20121207.

their non-job hours. Although there is some evidence that Anonymous did coordinate between the various actors, group affiliation is loose. There are no leaders who give the orders and coordinate the work of the many to a single goal. This is quite unlike the organization of cyber criminals or cyber spies.

In our short and incomplete survey, I hope you now have a feel for the differences between at least some of the currently active threat agents.

- **Cyber crimes:** The goal is financial. Risk tolerance is low. Effort tends to be low to medium; cyber criminals are after the low hanging fruit. Their methods tend to be proven.
- **Industrial espionage:** The goal is information and disruption. Risk tolerance is low. Effort can be quite high, perhaps even extreme. Difficult targets are not a barrier. Methods are very sophisticated.
- **Computer activists:** The goal is information, disruption, and media attention. Risk tolerance is medium to high (they are willing to go to jail for their beliefs). Their methods are computer savvy but not necessarily sophisticated. They are willing to put in the time necessary to achieve their goal.

These differences are summarized in Table 2.1, above.

Each of these threat agents operates in a different way, for different motivations, and with different methods. Although many of the controls that would be put into place to protect against any of them are the same, a defense-in-depth has to be far more rigorous and deep against industrial espionage or nation-state spying versus cyber criminals or activists.

If a system does not need to resist industrial espionage, it may rely on a less rigorous defense. Instead, shoring up significant barriers to attack at the entrances to systems should be the focus. On the other hand, preparing to resist a nation-state attack will likely also discourage cyber criminals. Attending to basics appropriately should deter many external activists.*

Hopefully, at this point you can see that knowing who your attackers are and something about them influences the way you build your defenses. An organization will need to decide which of the various threat agents pose the most likely attack scenarios and which, if any, can be ignored. Depending upon the use of the system, its exposure, the data it handles, and the organizations that will deploy and use the system, certain threat agents are likely to be far more important and dangerous to the mission of the organization than others. An organization without much controversy may very well not have to worry about computer activism. An organization that offers little financial reward may not have to worry about cyber crime (other than the pervasive cyber crime

---

* Edward Snowden, the NSA whistleblower, was given almost free rein to access systems as a trusted insider. In his case, he required no technical acumen in order to retrieve much of the information that he has made public. He was given access rights.

that's aimed at every individual who uses a computer). And likewise, an organization that handles a lot of liquid funds may choose to focus on cyber crime.

I do not mean to suggest that there's only one threat that any particular system must resist. Rather, the intersection of organization, organizational mission, and systems can help focus on those threats that are of concern while, at the same time, allowing some threat agents and their attack methods to be de-prioritized.

2.5 How Much Risk to Tolerate?

As we have seen, different threat agents have different risk tolerances. Some attempt near perfect secrecy, some need anonymity, and some require immediate attention for success. In the same way, different organizations have different organizational risk postures. Some businesses are inherently risky; the rewards need to be commensurate with the risk. Some organizations need to minimize risk as much as possible. And, some organizations have sophisticated risk management processes. One only needs to consider an insurance business or any loan-making enterprise. Each of these makes a profit through the sophisticated calculation of risk. An insurance company's management of its risk will, necessarily, be a key activity for a successful business. On the other hand, an entrepreneurial start-up run by previously successful businesspeople may be able to tolerate a great deal of risk. That, in fact, may be a joy for the entrepreneur.

Since there is no perfect security, and there are no guarantees that a successful attack will always be prevented, especially in computer security, risk is always inherent in the application of security to a system. And, since there are no guarantees, how much security is enough? This is ultimately the question that must be answered before the appropriate set of security controls can be applied to any system.

I remind the reader of a definition from the Introduction:

> *Securing systems is the art and craft of applying information security principles, design imperatives, and available controls in order to achieve* <u>*a particular security posture*</u>.

I have emphasized "a particular security posture." Some security postures will be too little to resist the attacks that are most likely to come. On the other hand, deep, rigorous, pervasive information security is expensive and time consuming. The classic example is the situation where the security controls cost more than the expected return on investment for the system. It should be obvious that such an expensive security posture would then be too much? Security is typically only one of many attributes that contribute to the success of a particular system, which then contributes to the success of the organization. When resources are limited (and aren't they always?), difficult choices need to be made.

In my experience, it's a great deal easier to make these difficult choices when one has a firm grasp on what is needed. A system that I had to assess was subject to a number of the organization's standards. The system was to be run by a third party, which brought it under the "Application Service Provider Policy." That policy and standard was very clear: All third parties handling the organization's data were required to go through an extensive assessment of their security practices. Since the proposed system was to be exposed to the Internet, it also fell under standards and policies related to protection of applications and equipment exposed to the Public Internet. Typically, application service provider reviews took two or three months to complete, sometimes considerably longer. If the third party didn't see the value in participating or was resistive for any other reason, the review would languish waiting for their responses. And, oftentimes the responses would be incomplete or indicate a misunderstanding of one or more of the review questions. Though unusual, a review could take as long as a year to complete.

The Web standards called for the use of network restrictions and firewalls between the various components, as they change function from Web to application to data (multi-tier protections). This is common in web architectures. Further, since the organization putting forth the standards deployed huge, revenue-producing server farms, its standards were geared to large implementations, extensive staff, and very mature processes. These standards would be overwhelming for a small, nimble, poorly capitalized company to implement.

When the project manager driving the project was told about all the requirements that would be necessary and the likely time delays that meeting the requirements would entail, she was shocked. She worked in a division that had little contact with the web security team and, thus, had not encountered these policies and standards previously. She then explained that the company was willing to lose all the money to be expended on this project: The effort was an experiment in a new business model. That's why they were using a third party. They wanted to be able to cut loose from the effort and the application on a moment's notice. The company's brand name was not going to be associated with this effort. So there was little danger of a brand impact should the system be successfully breached. Further, there was no sensitive data: All the data was eminently discardable. This application was to be a tentative experiment. The goal was simply to see if there was interest for this type of application. In today's lexicon, the company for which I worked was searching for the "right product," rather than trying to build the product "right."

Any system connected to the Internet, of course, must have some self-protection against the omnipresent level of attack it must face. But the kind of protections that we would normally have put on a web system were simply too much for this particular project. The required risk posture was quite low. In this case, we granted exceptions to the policies so that the project could go forward quickly and easily. The controls that we actually implemented were just sufficient to stave off typical, omnipresent web attack. It was a business decision to forgo a more protective security posture.

The primary business requirements for information security are business-specific. They will usually be expressed in terms of protecting the availability, integrity, authenticity and confidentiality of business information, and providing accountability and auditability in information systems.[11]

There are two risk tolerances that need to be understood before going into a system security assessment.

- What is the general risk tolerance of the owners of the system?
- What is the risk tolerance for this particular system?

Systems critical to the functioning of an organization will necessarily have far less risk tolerance and a far higher security posture than systems that are peripheral. If a business can continue despite the loss of a system or its data, then that system is not nearly as important as a system whose functioning is key. It should be noted that in a shared environment, even the least critical application within the shared environment may open a hole that degrades the posture of the entire environment. If the environment is critical, then the security of each component, no matter how peripheral, must meet the standards of the entire environment. In the example above, the system under assessment was both peripheral and entirely separate. Therefore, that system's loss could not have significant impact on the whole. On the other hand, an application on that organization's shared web infrastructure with a vulnerability that breached the tiered protections could open a disastrous hole, even if completely insignificant. (I did prevent an application from doing exactly that in another, unrelated, review.)

It should be apparent that organizations willing to take a great deal of risk as a general part of their approach will necessarily be willing to lose systems. A security architect providing security controls for systems being deployed by such an organization needs to understand what risks the organization is willing to take. I offer as an example a business model that typically interacts with its customers exactly one single time. In such a model, the business may not care if customers are harmed through their business systems. Cross-site scripting (XSS) is typically an attack through a web system against the users of the system. In this business model, the owners of the system may not care that some percentage of their customers get attacked, since the organization won't interact with these customers again; they have no need for customer loyalty.*

On the other hand, if the business model requires the retention, loyalty, and goodwill of as many customers as possible, then having one's customers get attacked because of flaws in one's commerce systems is probably not a risk worth taking. I use these two polar examples to illustrate how the organization's operational model influences its risk stance. And, the risk tolerance of the organization significantly influences how much security is required to protect its systems.

How does one uncover the risk tolerance of an organization? The obvious answer is to simply ask. In organizations that have sophisticated and/or mature risk management

---

* I do not mean to suggest that ignoring your customers' safety is a particularly moral stance. My own code entreats me to "do no harm." However, I can readily imagine types of businesses that don't require the continuing goodwill of their customers.

practices, it may be a matter of simply asking the right team or group. However, for any organization that doesn't have this information readily available, some investigation is required. As in the case with the project manager whose project was purely experimental and easily lost, simply asking, "What is the net effect of losing the data in the system?" may be sufficient. But in situations where the development team hasn't thought about this issue, the most likely people to understand the question in the broader organizational sense will be those who are responsible and accountable. In a commercial organization, this may be senior management, for instance, a general manager for a division, and others in similar positions. In organizations with less hierarchy, this may be a discussion among all the leaders—technical, management, whoever's responsible, or whoever takes responsibility for the success of the organization.

Although organizational risk assessment is beyond the scope of this book, one can get a good feel simply by asking pointed questions:

- How much are we willing to lose?
- What loss would mean the end of the organization?
- What losses can this organization sustain? And for how long?
- What data and systems are key to delivering the organizational mission?
- Could we make up for the loss of key systems through alternate means? For how long can we exist using alternate means?

These and similar questions are likely to seed informative conversations that will give the analyst a better sense of just how much risk and of what sort the organization is willing to tolerate.

As an example, for a long time, an organization at which I worked was willing to tolerate accumulating risk through its thousands of web applications. For most of these applications, loss of any particular one of them would not degrade the overall enterprise significantly. While the aggregate risk continued to increase, each risk owner, usually a director or vice president, was willing to tolerate this isolated risk for their particular function. No one in senior management was willing to think about the aggregate risk that was being accumulated. Then, a nasty compromise and breach occurred. This highlighted the pile of unmitigated risk that had accumulated. At this point, executive management decided that the accumulated risk pile needed to be addressed; we were carrying too much technology debt above and beyond the risk tolerance of the organization. Sometimes, it takes a crisis in order to fully understand the implications for the organization. As quoted earlier, in Chapter 1, "Never waste a crisis."[12] The short of it is, it's hard to build the right security if you don't know what "secure enough" is. Time spent fact finding can be very enlightening.

With security posture and risk tolerance of the overall organization in hand, specific questions about specific systems can be placed within that overall tolerance. The questions are more or less the same as listed above. One can simply change the word "organization" to "system under discussion."

There is one additional question that should be added to our list: "What is the highest sensitivity of the data handled by the system?" Most organizations with any security maturity at all will have developed a data-sensitivity classification policy and scale. These usually run from public (available to the world) to secret (need-to-know basis only). There are many variations on these policies and systems, from only two classifications to as many as six or seven. An important element for protecting the organization's data is to understand how restricted the access to particular data within a particular system needs to be. It is useful to ask for the highest sensitivity of data since controls will have to be fit for that, irrespective of other, lower classification data that is processed or stored.

Different systems require different levels of security. A "one-size-fits-all" approach is likely to lead to over specifying some systems. Or it may lead to under specifying most systems, especially key, critical systems. Understanding the system risk tolerance and the sensitivity of the data being held are key to building the correct security.

For large information technology (IT) organizations, economies of scale are typically achieved by treating as many systems as possible in the same way, with the same processes, with the same infrastructure, with as few barriers between information flow as possible. In the "good old days" of information security, when network restrictions ruled all, this approach may have made some sense. Many of the attacks of the time were at the network and the endpoint. Sophisticated application attacks, combination attacks, persistent attacks, and the like were extremely rare. The castle walls and the perimeter controls were strong enough. Security could be served by enclosing and isolating the entire network. Information within the "castle" could flow freely. There were only a few tightly controlled ingress and egress points.

Those days are long gone. Most organizations are so highly cross-connected that we live in an age of information ecosystems rather than isolated castles and digital city-states. I don't mean to suggest that perimeter controls are useless or passé. They are one part of a defense-in-depth. But in large organizations, certainly, there are likely to be several, if not many, connections to third parties, some of whom maintain radically different security postures. And, on any particular day, there are quite likely to be any number of people whose interests are not the same as the organization's but who've been given internal access of one kind or another.

Added to highly cross-connected organizations, many people own many connecting devices. The "consumerization" of IT has opened the trusted network to devices that are owned and not at all controlled by the IT security department. Hence, we don't know what applications are running on what devices that may be connecting (through open exchanges like HTTP/HTML) to what applications. We can authenticate and authorize the user. But from how safe a device is the user connecting? Generally, today, it is safer to assume that some number of the devices accessing the organization's network and resources are already compromised. That is a very different picture from the highly restricted networks of the past.

National Cyber Security Award winner Michelle Guel has been touting "islands of security" for years now. Place the security around that which needs it rather than trusting the entire castle. As I wrote above, it's pretty simple: Different systems require different security postures. Remember, always, that one system's security posture affects all the other systems' security posture in any shared environment.

What is a security posture?

Security posture is the overall capability of the security organization to assess its unique risk areas and to implement security measures that would protect against exploitation.[13]

If we replace "organization" with "system," we are close to a definition of a system's security posture. According to Michael Fey's definition, quoted above, an architecture analysis for security is a part of the security posture of the system (replacing "organization" with "system"). But is the analysis to determine system posture a part of that posture? I would argue, "No." At least within the context of this book, the analysis is outside the posture. If the analysis is to be taken as a part of the posture, then simply performing the analysis will change the posture of the system. And our working approach is that the point of the analysis is to determine the current posture of the system and then to bring the system's posture to a desired, intended state. If we then rework the definition, we have something like the following:

System security posture: The unique risk areas of a system against which to implement security measures that will protect against exploitation of the system.

Notice that our working definition includes both risk areas and security measures. It is the sum total of these that constitute a "security posture." A posture includes both risk and protection. Once again, "no risk" doesn't exist. Neither does "no protection," as most modern operating environments have some protections in-built. Thus, posture must include the risks, the risk mitigations, and any residual risk that remains unprotected. The point of an ARA—the point of securing systems—is to bring a system to an *intended* security posture, the security posture that matches the risk tolerance of the organization and protects against those threats that are relevant to that system and its data.

Hence, one must ascertain what's needed for the system that's under analysis. The answers that you will collect to the risk questions posed above point in the right direction. An analysis aims to discover the existing security posture of a system and to calculate through some risk-based method, the likely threats and attack scenarios. It then requires those controls that will bring the system to the intended security posture.

The business model (or similar mission of system owners) is deeply tied into the desired risk posture. Let's explore some more real-life examples. We've already examined a system that was meant to be temporary and experimental. Let's find a polar opposite, a system that handles financial data for a business that must retain customer loyalty.

In the world of banking, there are many offerings, and competition for customers is fierce. With the growth of online banking services, customers need significant reasons to bank with the local institution, even if there is only a single bank in town. A friend of mine is a bank manager in a small town of four thousand people, in central California. Even in that town, there are several brick and mortar banks. She vies for the loyalty of her customers with personal services and through paying close attention to individual needs and the town's overall economic concerns.

Obviously, a front-end banking system available to the Internet may not be able to offer the human touch that my friend can tender to her customers. Hopefully, you still agree that loyalty is won, not guaranteed? Part of that loyalty will be the demonstration, over time, that deposits are safely held, that each customer's information is secure.

Beyond the customer-retention imperative, in most countries, banks are subject to a host of regulations, some of which require and specify security. The regulatory picture will influence the business' risk posture, alongside its business imperatives. Any system deployed by the bank for its customers will have to have a security posture sufficient for customer confidence and that meets jurisdictional regulations, as well.[*]

As we have noted, any system connected to the Public Internet is guaranteed to be attacked, to be severely tested continuously. Financial institutions, as we have already examined, will be targeted by cyber criminals. This gives us our first posture clue: The system will have to have sufficient defense to resist this constant level of attack, some of which will be targeted and perhaps sophisticated.

But we also know that our customers are targets and their deposits are targeted. These are two separate goals: to gain, through our system, the customers' equipment and data (on their endpoint). And, at the same time, some attackers will be targeting the funds held in trust. Hence, this system must do all that it can to prevent its use to attack our customers. And, we must protect the customers' funds and data; an ideal would be to protect "like a safety deposit box."

Security requirements for an online bank might include demilitarized zone (DMZ) hardening, administration restrictions, protective firewall tiers between HTTP terminations, application code and the databases to support the application, robust authentication and authorization systems (which mustn't be exposed to the Internet, but only to the systems that need to authenticate), input validation (to prevent input validation errors), stored procedures (to prevent SQL injection errors), and so forth. As you can see, the list is quite extensive. And I have not listed everything that I would expect for this system, only the most obvious.

If the bank chose to outsource the system and its operations, then the chosen vendor would have to demonstrate all of the above and more, not just once, but repeatedly through time.

Given these different types of systems, perhaps you are beginning to comprehend why the analysis can only move forward successfully with both the organization posture

---

[*] I don't mean to reduce banking to two imperatives. I'm not a banking security expert. And, online banking is beyond our scope. I've reduced the complexity, as an example.

and the system posture understood? The bank's internal company portal through which employees get the current company news and access various employee services, would, however, have a different security posture. The human resources (HR) system may have significant security needs, but the press release feed may have significantly less. Certainly, the company will prefer not to have fake news posted. Fake company news postings may have a much less significant impact on the bank than losing the account holdings of 30% of the banks customers?

Before analysis, one needs to have a good understanding of the shared services that are available, and how a security posture may be shared across systems in any particular environment. With the required system risk posture and risk tolerance in hand, one may proceed with the next steps of the system analysis.

2.6 Getting Started

Before I can begin to effectively analyze systems for an organization, I read the security policy and standards. This gives me a reasonable feel for how the organization approaches security. Then, I speak with leaders about the risks they are willing to take, and those that they cannot—business risks that seem to have nothing to do with computers may still be quite enlightening. I further query technical leaders about the security that they think systems have and that systems require.

I then spend time learning the infrastructure—how it's implemented, who administers it, the processes in place to grant access, the organization's approach to security layers, monitoring, and event analysis. Who performs these tasks, with what technology help, and under what response timing ("SLA"). In other words, what security is already in place and how does a system inherit that security?

My investigations help me understand the difference between past organization expectations and current ones. These help me to separate my sense of appropriate security from that of the organization. Although I may be paid to be an expert, I'm also paid to execute the organization's mission, not my own. As we shall see, a big part of risk is separating my risk tolerance from the desired risk tolerance.

Once I have a feel for the background knowledge sets listed in this introduction, then I'm ready to start looking at systems. I try to remember that I'll learn more as I analyze. Many assessments are like peeling an onion: I test my understandings with the stakeholders. If I'm off base or I've missed something substantive, the stakeholders will correct me. I may check each "fact" as I believe that I've come to understand something about the system. There are a lot of questions. I need to be absolutely certain of every relevant thing that can be known at the time of the assessment. I reach for absolute technical certainty. Through the process, my understanding will mature about each system under consideration and about the surrounding and supporting environment. As always, I will make mistakes; for these, I prepare myself and I prepare the organization.

References

1. *Oxford Dictionary of English*. (2010). 3rd ed. UK: Oxford University Press.
2. Buschmann, F., Henney, K., and Schmidt, D. C. (2007). "Foreword." In *Pattern-Oriented Software Architecture: On Patterns and Pattern Languages*. Vol. 5. John Wiley & Sons.
3. Rosenquist, M. (2009). "Prioritizing Information Security Risks with Threat Agent Risk Assessment." IT@Intel White Paper, Intel Information Technology. Retrieved from http://media10.connectedsocialmedia.com/intel/10/5725/Intel_IT_Business_Value_Prioritizing_Info_Security_Risks_with_TARA.pdf.
4. Schoenfield, B. (2014). "Applying the SDL Framework to the Real World" (Ch. 9). In *Core Software Security: Security at the Source*, pp. 255–324. Boca Raton (FL): CRC Press.
5. Harris, K. D. (2014). "Cybersecurity in the Golden State." California Department of Justice.
6. Alperovitch, D. (2011-08-02). "Revealed: Operation Shady RAT." McAfee, Inc. White Paper.
7. Ibid.
8. Global Threat Report 2013 YEAR IN REVIEW, Crowdstrike, 2013. Available at: http://www.crowdstrike.com/blog/2013-year-review-actors-attacks-and-trends/index.html.
9. Bright, P., Anderson, N., and Cheng, J. (2011). *Unmasked*. Amazon Kindle. Retrieved from http://www.amazon.com/Unmasked-Peter-Bright.
10. Reitman, J. (Dec. 7, 2012). "The Rise and Fall of Jeremy Hammond: Enemy of the State." *Rolling Stone Magazine*. Retrieved from http://www.rollingstone.com/culture/news/the-rise-and-fall-of-jeremy-hammond-enemy-of-the-state-20121207.
11. Sherwood, J., Clark, A., and Lynas, D. "Enterprise Security Architecture." SABSA White Paper, SABSA Limited, 1995–2009. Retrieved from http://www.sabsa-institute.com/members/sites/default/inline-files/SABSA_White_Paper.pdf.
12. Arkin, B. (2012). "Never Waste a Crisis-Necessity Drives Software Security." RSA Conference 2012, San Francisco, CA, February 29, 2012. Retrieved from http://www.rsaconference.com/events/us12/agenda/sessions/794/never-waste-a-crisis-necessity-drives-software.
13. Fey, M., Kenyon, B., Reardon, K. T., Rogers, B., and Ross, C. (2012). "Assessing Mission Readiness" (Ch. 2). In *Security Battleground: An Executive Field Manual*. Intel Press.

Chapter 3

Security Architecture of Systems

A survey of 7,000 years of history of human kind would conclude that the only known strategy for accommodating extreme complexity and high rates of change is architecture. If you can't describe something, you can't create it, whether it is an airplane, a hundred storey building, a computer, an automobile . . . or an enterprise. Once you get a complex product created and you want to change it, the basis for change is its descriptive representations.[1]

If the only viable strategy for handling complex things is the art of architecture, then surely the practice of architecture is key to the practice of security for computers. This is John Zachman's position in the quote introducing this chapter. The implication found in this quote is that the art of representing a complex system via an abstraction helps us cope with the complexity because it allows us to understand the structure of a thing— for our purposes, computer systems.

Along with a coping strategy for complexity, the practice of architecture gives us a tool for experimenting with change *before* we actually build the system. This is a profound concept that bears some thinking. By creating an abstraction that represents a structure, we can then play with that structure, abstractly. In this way, when encountering change, we can try before we build, in a representative sense.

For a fairly common but perhaps trivial example, what happens when we place the authentication system in our demilitarized zone (DMZ)—that is, in the layer closest to the Internet? What do we have to do to protect the authentication system? Does this placement facilitate authentication in some way? How about if we move the authentication system to a tier behind the DMZ, thus, a more trusted zone? What are the implications of doing so for authentication performance? For security? I've had precisely these discussions, more than once, when architecting a web platform. These are discussions about structures; these are architecture discussions.

Computer security is a multivariate, multidimensional field. Hence, by its very nature, computer security meets a test for complexity. Architecture then becomes a tool to apply to that complexity.

Computer security is dynamic; the attackers are adaptive and unpredictable. This dynamism guarantees change alongside the inherent complexity. The complexity of the problem space is mirrored within the complexity of the systems under discussion and the security mechanisms that must be built in order to protect the systems. And as John Zachman suggests in the quote introducing this chapter, complex systems that are going to change require some kind of descriptive map so as to manage the change in an orderly fashion: "the basis for change is its descriptive representations."[2]

3.1 Why Is Enterprise Architecture Important?

The field of enterprise architecture supplies a mapping to generate order for a modern, cross-connected digital organization.* I think Pallab Saha sums up the discipline of Enterprise architecture in the following quote. Let this be our working definition for enterprise—that is, an enterprise of "systems"—architecture.

> *Enterprise architecture (EA) is the discipline of designing enterprises guided with principles, frameworks, methodologies, requirements, tools, reference models, and standards.*[3]

Enterprise architecture is focused on the entire enterprise, not only its digital systems, including the processes and people who will interact, design, and build the systems. An often-quoted adage, "people, process, and technology," is used to include human, non-digital technology, and digital domains in the enterprise architecture. Enterprise architects are not just concerned with technology. Any process, manual or digital, that contributes to the overall goals of the enterprise, of the entire system taken as a whole, is then, necessarily, a part of the "enterprise architecture." Thus, a manually executed process will, by definition, include the people who execute that process: "People, process, and technology."

I've thrown around the term "enterprise" since the very beginning of this book. But, I haven't yet defined it. I've found most definitions of "enterprise," in the sense that it is used here and in enterprise architecture, rather lacking. There's often some demarcation below which an organization doesn't meet the test. Yet, the organizations who fail to meet the criteria would still benefit from architecture, perhaps enterprise architecture, certainly enterprise security architecture. Consider the following criteria:

---

* Large business organizations are often called "enterprises."

- Greater than 5000 employees (10,000? 50,000? 100,000?)
- Greater than $1 billion in sales ($2 billion? $5 billion? $10 billion?)
- Fortune 1000 company (Fortune 500? Fortune 100? Fortune 50?)

Each of these measures presumes a for-profit goal. That leaves out non-governmental organizations (NGOs) and perhaps governments.

A dictionary definition also doesn't seem sufficient to our purpose:

[A] unit of economic organization or activity; especially : a business organization[4]

For the purposes of this book, I will offer a working definition not meant for any purposes but my own:

Enterprise: An organization whose breadth and depth of activities cannot easily be held simultaneously in one's conscious mind.

That is, for our purposes only, if a person (you? I?) can't keep the relationships and processes of an organization in mind, it's probably complex enough to meet our, not very stringent, requirement and, thus, can be called an "enterprise."

The emphasis here is on complexity. At the risk of forming a tautology, if the organization needs an architecture practice in order to transcend ad hoc and disparate solutions to create some semblance of order, then it's big enough to benefit from enterprise architecture. Our sole concern in this discussion concerns whether or not an organization may benefit from enterprise architecture as a methodology to provide order and to reap synergies between the organization's activities. If benefit may be derived from an architectural approach, then we can apply enterprise architecture to the organization, and specifically, a security architecture.

If enterprise architecture is concerned with the structure of the enterprise as a functioning system, then enterprise security architecture will be concerned with the security of the enterprise architecture as a functioning system. We emphasize the subset of enterprise security architecture that focuses on the security of digital systems that are to be used within the enterprise architecture. Often, this more granular architecture practice is known as "solutions" architecture although, as of this writing, I have not seen the following term applied to security: "solutions security architecture." The general term, "security architecture," will need to suffice (though, as has been previously noted, the term "security architecture" is overloaded).

Generally, if there is an enterprise architecture practice in an organization, the enterprise architecture is a good place from which to start. Systems intended to function within an enterprise architecture should be placed within that overall enterprise structure and will contribute to the working and the goals of the organization. The enterprise architecture then is an abstract, and hopefully ordered, representation of those systems and their interactions. Because the security architecture of the organization is one part of the overarching architecture (or should be!), it is useful for the security architect to understand and become conversant in architectures at this gross, organizational level of granularity. Hence, I introduce some enterprise architecture concepts in order to place system security assessments within the larger framework in which they may exist.

Still, it's important to note that most system assessments—that is, architecture risk assessment (ARA) and threat modeling—will take place at the systems or solutions level, not at the enterprise view. Although understanding the enterprise architecture helps to find the correct security posture for systems, the system-oriented pieces of the enterprise security architecture emerge from the individual systems that make up the total enterprise architecture. The caveat to this statement is the security infrastructure into which systems are placed and which those systems consume for security services. The security infrastructure must be one key component of an enterprise architecture. This is why enterprise security architects normally work closely with, and are peers of, the enterprise architects in an organization. Nevertheless, security people charged with the architectural assessment of systems will typically be working at the system or solution level, placing those systems within the enterprise architecture and, thus, within an enterprise security architecture.

> *Being a successful security architect means thinking in business terms at all times, even when you get down to the real detail and the nuts and bolts of the construction. You always need to have in mind the questions: Why are you doing this? What are you trying to achieve in business terms here?*[5]

In this book, we will take a cursory tour through some enterprise architecture concepts as a grounding and path into the practice of security architecture. In our security architecture journey, we can borrow the ordering and semantics of enterprise architecture concepts for our security purposes. Enterprise architecture as a practice has been developing somewhat longer than security architecture.* Its framework is reasonably mature.

An added benefit of adopting enterprise security architecture terminology will then be that the security architect can gently and easily insert him or herself in an organization's architecture practice without perturbing already in-flight projects and processes. A security architect who is comfortable interacting within existing and accepted architecture practices will likely be more successful in adding security requirements to an architecture. By using typical enterprise architecture language, it is much easier for non-security architects to accept what may seem like strange concepts—attack vectors and misuse cases, threat analysis and information security risk rating, and so forth. Security concepts can run counter to the goals of the other architects. The bridge

---

* The Open Group offers a certification for Enterprise Architects. In 2008, I asked several principals of the Open Group about security architecture as a practice. They replied that they weren't sure such an architecture practice actually existed. Since then, the Open Group has initiated an enterprise security architect certification. So, apparently we've now been recognized.

between security and solution is to understand enterprise and solutions architecture first, and then to build the security picture from those practices.

> *I would suggest that architecture is the total set of descriptive representations relevant for describing something, anything complex you want to create, which serves as the baseline for change if you ever want to change the thing you have created.*[6]

I think that Zachman's architecture definition at the beginning of the chapter applies very well to the needs of securing systems. In order to apply information security principles to a system, that system needs to be describable through a representation—that is, it needs to have an architecture. As Izar Taarandach told me, "if you *can't* describe it—it is not time to do security architecture yet." A security assessment doesn't have to wait for a completely finished system architecture. Assessment can't wait for perfection because high-level security requirements need to be discovered early enough to get into the architecture. But Izar is right in that without a system architecture, how does the security architect know what to do? Not to mention that introducing even more change by attempting to build security before sufficient system architecture exists is only going to add more complexity before the structure of the system is understood well enough. Furthermore, given one or more descriptive representations of the system, the person who assesses the system for security will have to understand the representation as intended by the creators of the representation (i.e., the "architects" of the system).

3.2 The "Security" in "Architecture"

The assessor cannot stop at an architectural understanding of the system. This is where security architecture and enterprise, solutions, or systems architects part company. In order to assess for security, the representation must be viewed both as its functioning is intended and, just as importantly, as it may be misused. The system designers are interested in "use cases." Use cases must be understood by the security architect in the context of the intentions of the system. And, the security architect must generate the "misuse cases" for the system, how the system may be abused for purposes that were not intended and may even run counter to the goals of the organization sponsoring the system.

An assessor (usually a security architect) must then be proficient in architecture in order to understand and manipulate system architectures. In addition, the security architect also brings substantial specialized knowledge to the practice of security assessment. Hence, we start with solutions or systems architectures and their representations and then apply security to them.

This set of descriptive representations thereby becomes the basis for describing the security needs of the system. If the security needs are not yet built, they will cause a "change" to the system, as explained in Zachman's definition describing architecture as providing a "baseline for change" (see above).[7]

Let me suggest a working definition for our purposes that might be something similar to the following:

System architecture is the descriptive representation of the system's component functions and the communication* flows between those components.

My definition immediately raises some important questions.

- What are "components"?
- Which functions are relevant?
- What is a communication flow?

It is precisely these questions that the security architect must answer in order to understand a system architecture well enough to enumerate the system's attack surfaces. Ultimately, we are interested in attack surfaces and the risk treatments that will protect them. However, the discovery of attack surfaces is not quite as straightforward a problem as we might like. Deployment models, runtime environments, user expectations, and the like greatly influence the level of detail at which a system architecture will need to be examined. Like computer security itself, the architectural representation is the product of a multivariate, complex problem. We will examine this problem in some detail.

Mario Godinez et al. (2010)[8] categorize architectures into several different layers, as follows:

- **Conceptual Level**—This level is closest to business definitions, business processes, and enterprise standards.
- **Logical Level**—This level of the Reference Architecture translates conceptual design into logical design.
- **Physical Level**—This level of the Reference Architecture translates the logical design into physical structures and often products.

The **Logical Level** is broken down by Godinez et al. (2010) into two interlocking and contributing sub-models:

o **Logical Architecture**—The Logical Architecture shows the relationships of the different data domains and functionalities required to manage each type of information.

---

* I use "communication flow" because, sometimes, people forget those communications between systems that aren't considered "data" connections. In order to communicate, digital entities need to exchange data. So, essentially, all communication flows are data flows. In this context we don't want to constrain ourselves to common conceptions of data flows, but rather, all exchange of bits between one function and another.

o **Component Model**—Technical capabilities and the architecture building blocks that execute them are used to delineate the Component Model.[9]

For complex systems, and particularly at the enterprise architecture level, a single representation will never be sufficient. Any attempt at a complete representation is likely to be far too "noisy" to be useful to any particular audience: There are too many possible representations, too many details, and too many audiences. Each "audience"—that is, each stakeholder group—has unique needs that must be reflected in a representation of the system. Organizational leaders (senior management, typically) need to understand how the organization's goals will be carried out through the system. This view is very different from what is required by network architects building a network infrastructure to support the system. As we shall see, what the security architect needs is also different, though hopefully not entirely unique. Due to these factors, the practice of enterprise architecture creates different views representing the same architecture.

For the purposes of security evaluation, we are concerned primarily with the Logical Level—both the logical architecture and component model. Often, the logical architecture, the different domains and functionalities, as well as the component model, are superimposed upon the same system architecture diagram. For simplicity, we will call this the "logical system architecture." The most useful system architecture diagram will contain sufficient logical separation to represent the workings of the system and the differing domains. And the diagram should explain the component model sufficiently such that the logical functions can be tied to technical components.

Security controls tend to be "point"—that is, they implement a single function that will then be paired to one or more attack vectors. The mapping is not one-to-one, vector to control or control to attack method. The associations are much looser (we will examine this in greater detail later). Due to the lack of absolute coherence between the controls that can be implemented and the attack vectors, the technical components are essential for understanding just precisely which controls can be implemented and which will contribute towards the intended defense-in-depth.

Eventually, any security services that a system consumes or implements will, of course, have to be designed at the physical level. Physical servers, routers, firewalls, and monitoring systems will have to be built. But these are usually dealt with logically, first, leaving the physical implementation until the logical and component architectures are thoroughly worked out. The details of firewall physical implementation often aren't important during the logical security analysis of a system, so long as the logical controls produce the tiers and restrictions, as required. Eventually, the details will have to be decided upon, as well, of course.

3.3 Diagramming For Security Analysis

Circles and arrows leave one free to describe the interrelationships between things in a way that tables, for example, do not.[10]

Figure 3.1 A simplistic Web architecture diagram.

It may be of help to step back from our problem (assessing systems for security) to examine different ways in which computer systems are described visually. The architecture diagram is a critical prerequisite for most architects to conduct an assessment. What does an architecture diagram look like?

In Figure 3.1, I have presented a diagram of an "architecture" that strongly resembles a diagram that I once received from a team.* The diagram does show something of the system: There is some sort of interaction between a user's computer and a server. The server interacts with another set of servers in some manner. So there are obviously at least three different components involved. The brick wall is a standard representation of a firewall. Apparently, there's some kind of security control between the user and the middle server. Because the arrows are double headed, we don't know which component calls the others. It is just as likely that the servers on the far right call the middle server as the other way around. The diagram doesn't show us enough specificity to begin to think about trust boundaries. And, are the two servers on the right in the same trust area? The same network? Or are they separated in some manner? We don't know from this diagram. How are these servers managed? Are they managed by a professional, security-conscious team? Or are they under someone's desk, a pilot project that has gone live without any sort of administrative security practice? We don't know if these are web and database protocols or something else. We also do not know anything about the firewall. Is it stateful? Deep packet inspection? A web application firewall (WAF)? Or merely a router with an Access Control List (ACL) applied?

An astute architect might simply make queries about each of these facets (and more). Or the architect might request more details in order to help the team create a diagram with just a little bit more specificity.

I include Figure 3.2 because although this diagram may enhance the sales of a product, it doesn't tell us very much about those things with which we must deal. This diagram is loosely based upon the "architecture" diagram that I received from a business data processing product† that I was reviewing. What is being communicated by the diagram, and what is needed for an assessment?

---

* Figure 3.1 includes no references that might endanger or otherwise identify a running system at any of my former or current employers.

† Although based upon similar concepts, this diagram is entirely original. Any resemblance to an existing product is purely coincidental.

From Figure 3.2, we know that, somehow, a "warehouse" (whatever that is) communicates with data sources. And presumably, the application foundation supports various higher-level functions? This may be very interesting for someone buying the product. However, this diagram does not give us sufficient information about any of the components for us to begin to identify attack surfaces, which is the point of a security analysis. The diagram is too high level, and the components displayed are not tied to things that we can protect, such as applications, platforms, databases, applications, and so forth.

Even though we understand, by studying Figure 3.2, that there's some sort of "application platform"—an operating environment that might call various modules that are being considered as "applications"—we do not know what that execution entails, whether "application" in this diagram should be considered as atomic, with attack surfaces exposed, or whether this is simply a functional nomenclature to express functionality about which customers will have some interest. Operating systems provide application execution. But so do "application servers." Each of these presents rather different attack possibilities. An analysis of this "architecture" could not proceed without more specificity about program execution.

In this case, the real product's platform was actually a Java web application server (a well-known version), with proprietary code running within the application server's usual web application runtime. The actual applications were packaged as J2EE servelets. That means that custom code was running within a well-defined and publicly available specification. The diagram that the vendor had given to me did not give me much useful information; one could not even tell how "sources" were accessed, for what

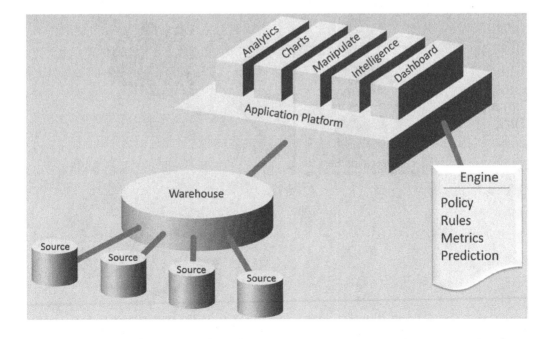

Figure 3.2   Marketing architecture for a business intelligence product.

operations (Read only? Write? Execute?). And which side, warehouse or source, initiated the connection? From the diagram, it was impossible to know. Do the source communications require credentials? How might credentials be stored and protected? We don't have a clue from the diagram that authentication by each source is even supported.

> *[T]he System Context Diagram . . . is a methodological approach to assist in the detailing of the conceptual architecture all the way down to the Operational Model step by step and phase by phase.*[11]

As may be seen from the foregoing explanation, the diagram in Figure 3.2 was quite insufficient for the purposes of a security assessment. In fact, neither of these diagrams (Figures 3.1 or 3.2) meets Zachman's definition, "the total set of descriptive representations relevant for describing something."[12] Nor would either of these diagrams suitably describe "all the way down to the Operational Model step by step."[13] Each of these diagrams describes some of the system in an incomplete way, not only for the purposes of security assessment, but incomplete in a more general architectural sense, as well. Figures 3.1 and 3.2 may very well be sufficient for other purposes beyond general system architecture or security architecture. My point is that these representations were

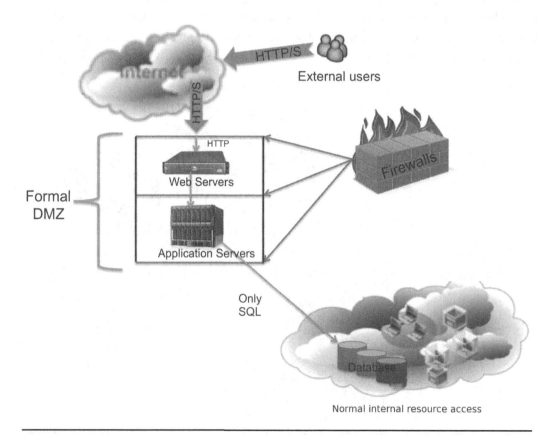

Figure 3.3   Sample external web architecture.[14] (Courtesy of the SANS Institute.)

insufficient for the kind of analysis about which this book is written. Since systems vary so tremendously, it is difficult to provide a template for a system architecture that is relevant across the extant variety and complexity. Still, a couple of examples may help?

Figure 3.3 is reproduced from an ISA Smart Guide that I wrote to explain how to securely allow HTTP traffic to be processed by internal resources that were not originally designed to be exposed to the constant attack levels of the Internet. The diagram was not intended for architecture analysis. However, unlike Figure 3.1, several trust-level boundaries are clearly delineated. Internet traffic must pass a firewall before HTTP/S traffic is terminated at a web server. The web server is separated by a second firewall from the application server. Finally, there is a third firewall between the entire DMZ network and the internal networks (the cloud in the lower right-hand corner of the diagram).

Further, in Figure 3.3, it is clear that only Structured Query Language (SQL) traffic will be allowed from the application server to internal databases. The SQL traffic originates at the application server and terminates at the internal databases. No other traffic from the DMZ is allowed onto internal networks. The other resources within the internal cloud do not receive traffic from the DMZ.

Figure 3.3 is still too high level for analyzing the infrastructure and runtime of the components. We don't know what kind of web server, application server, or database may be implemented. Still, we have a far better idea about the general layout of the architecture than from, say, Figure 3.1. We certainly know that HTTP and some variant of SQL protocols are being used. The system supports HTTPS (encrypted HTTP) up to the first firewall. But communications are not encrypted from that firewall to the web server. From Figure 3.3, we can tell that the SSL/TLS tunnel is terminated at the first firewall. The diagram clearly demonstrates that it is HTTP past the firewall into the DMZ.

We know where the protocols originate and terminate. We can surmise boundaries of trust[*] from highly exposed to internally protected. We know that there are functional tiers. We also know that external users will be involved. Since it's HTTP, we know that those users will employ some sort of browser or browser-like functionality. Finally, we know that the infrastructure demarks a formal DMZ, which is generally restricted from the internal network.

The security architect needs to understand bits of functionality that can be treated relatively independently. Unity of any particular piece of the architecture we'll call "atomic." The term "atomic" has a fairly specific meaning in some computer contexts. It is the third Oxford Dictionary definition of atomic that applies to the art of securing systems:

---

[*] "Boundaries" in this context is about levels of exposure of networks and systems to hostile networks, from exposed to protected. These are usually called "trust boundaries." It is generally assumed that as a segment moves closer to the Internet the less it is trusted. Well protected from external traffic has higher trust. We will examine boundaries in greater detail, later.

[O]f or forming a single irreducible unit or component in a larger system[15]

"Irreducible" in our context is almost never true, until one gets down to the individual line of code. Even then, is the irreducible unit a single binary computer instruction? Probably. But we don't have to answer this question,* as we work toward the "right" level of "single unit." In the context of security assessments of systems, "atomic" may be taken as *treat as* irreducible or *regard as* a "unit or component in a larger system."[16]

In this way, the security architect has a requirement for abstraction that is different from most of the other architects working on a system. As we shall see further along, we reduce to a unit that presents the relevant attack surfaces. The reduction is dependent on other factors in an assessment, which were enumerated earlier:

- Active threat agents that attack similar systems
- Infrastructure security capabilities
- Expected deployment model
- Distribution of executables or other deployable units
- The computer programming languages that have been used
- Relevant operating system(s) and runtime or execution environment(s)

This list is essentially synonymous with the assessment "background" knowledge, or pre-assessment "homework" that has already been detailed. Unfortunately, there is no single architecture view that can be applied to every component of every system. "Logical" and "Component" are the most typical.

Depending upon on the security architect role that is described, one of two likely situations prevail:

1. The security architect must integrate into existing architecture practices, making use of whatever architecture views other architects are creating.
2. The security architect is expected to produce a "security view" of each architecture that is assessed.†

In the first case, where the organization expects integration, essentially, the assessor is going to "get what's on offer" and make do. One can attempt to drive artifacts to some useful level of detail, as necessary. When in this situation, I take a lot of notes about the architecture because the diagrams offered are often incomplete for my purposes.

The second case is perhaps the luxury case? Given sufficient time, producing both an adequate logical and component architecture, and then overlaying a threat model onto them, delivers a working document that the entire team may consider as they

---

* I cannot remember a single instance of needing to go down to the assembly or binary code level during a review.

† The author has personally worked under each of these assumptions.

architect, design, code, and test. Such an artifact (diagram, or better, layered diagram) can "seed" creative security involvement of the entire team.

Eoin Carroll, when he worked as a Senior Quality Engineer at McAfee, Inc., innovated exactly this practice. Security became embedded into Agile team consideration to the benefit of everyone involved with these teams and to the benefit of "building security in from the start." As new features were designed,* teams were able to consider the security implications of the feature and the intended design *before* coding, or while iterating through possible algorithmic solutions.

If the security architect is highly shared across many teams, he or she will likely not have sufficient time to spend on any extensive diagramming. In this situation, because diagramming takes considerable time to do well, diagramming a security architecture view may be precluded.

And, there is the danger that the effort expended to render a security architecture may be wasted, if a heavyweight document is only used by the security architect during the assessment. Although it may be useful to archive a record of what has been considered during the assessment, those building programs will want to consider cost versus benefit carefully before mandating that there be a diagrammatic record of every assessment. I have seen drawings on a white board, and thus, entirely ephemeral, suffice for highly complex system analysis. Ultimately, the basic need is to uncover the security needs of the system—the "security requirements."

The decision about exactly which artifacts are required and for whose consumption is necessarily an organizational choice. Suffice it to note that, in some manner, the security architect who is performing a system analysis will require enough detail to uncover all the attack surfaces, but no more detail than that. We will explore "decomposing" and "factoring" architectures at some length, below. After our exploration, I will offer a few guidelines to the art of decomposing an architecture for security analysis.

Let's turn our attention for a moment to the "mental" game involved in understanding an architecture in order to assess the architecture for security.

It has also been said that architecture is a practice of applying patterns. Security patterns are unique problems that can be described as arising within disparate systems and whose solutions can be described architecturally (as a representation).

Patterns provide us with a vocabulary to express architectural visions, as well as examples of representative designs and detailed implementations that are clear and to the point. Presenting pieces of software in terms of their constituent patterns also allows us to communicate more effectively, with fewer words and less ambiguity.[17]

For instance, the need for authentication occurs not just between users, but wherever in a software architecture a trust boundary occurs. This can be between eCommerce

---

* In SCRUM Agile, that point in the process when user stories are pulled from the backlog for implementation during a Sprint.

tiers (say, web to application server) or between privilege boundaries among executables running on top of an operating system on a computer. The pattern named here is the requirement of proof that the calling entity is not a rogue system, perhaps under control of an attacker (say, authentication before allowing automated interactions). At a very gross level, ensuring some level of trust on either side of a boundary is an authentication pattern. However, we can move downwards in specificity by one level and say that all tiers within a web stack are trust boundaries that should be authenticated. The usual authentication is either bidirectional or the less trusted system authenticates to those of higher trust. Similarly, any code that might allow attacker access to code running at a higher privilege level, especially across executable boundaries, presents this same authentication pattern.

That is, entities at higher trust levels should authenticate communication flows from entities of lower trust. Doing so prevents an attacker from pretending to be, that is, "spoofing," the lower trust entity. "Entity" in this discussion is both a web tier and an executable process. The same pattern expresses itself in two seemingly disparate architectures.

Figure 3.4 represents the logical Web architecture for the Java application development environment called "AppMaker."* AppMaker produces dynamic web applications without custom coding by a web developer. The AppMaker application provides a plat-

---

* AppMaker is not an existing product. There are many offerings for producing web applications with little or no coding. This example demonstrates a typical application server and database architecture.

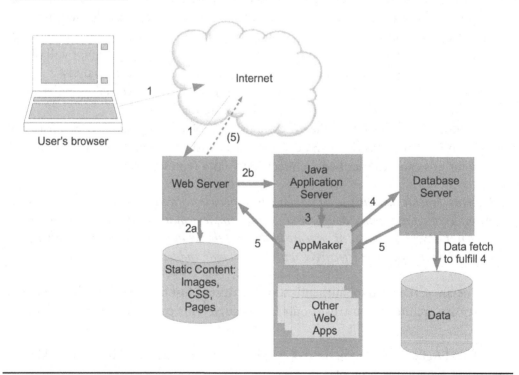

Figure 3.4 AppMaker Web architecture.

form for creating dynamic web applications drawing data from a database, as needed, to respond to HTTP requests from a user's browser. For our purposes, this architecture represents a classic pattern for a static content plus dynamic content web application. Through this example, we can explore the various logical components and tiers of a typical web application that also includes a database.

The AppMaker architecture shows a series of arrows representing how a typical HTTP request will be handled by the system. Because there are two different flows, one to return static content, and an alternate path for dynamic content built up out of the database, the return HTTP response flow is shown ("5" from database server to AppMaker, and then from AppMaker through the webserver). Because there are two possible flows in this logical architecture, there is an arrow for each of the two response flows.

Quite often, an HTTP response will be assumed; an architecture diagram would only show the incoming request. If the system is functioning normally, it will generate a response; an HTTP response can be assumed. HTTP is a request/response protocol.

But in this case, the program designers want potential implementers to understand that there are two possible avenues for delivering a response: a static path and a dynamic path. Hence, you can see "2a" being retrieved from the disk available to the Web server (marked "Static Content"). That's the static repository.

Dynamic requests (or portions of requests) are delivered to the AppMaker web application, which is incoming arrow "2b" going from the Web server to the application server in the diagram. After generating the dynamic response through interactions with custom code, forms, and a database server (arrows 3 and 4), the response is sent back in the outgoing arrows, "5."

Digging a little further into Figure 3.4, you may note that there are four logical tiers. Obviously, the browser is the user space in the system. You will often hear security architects exclude the browser when naming application tiers, whereas the browser application designers will consider the browser to be an additional web application tier, for their purposes. Inclusion of the browser as a tier of the web application is especially common when there is scripting or other application-specific code that is downloaded to the browser, and, thus, a portion of the system is running in the context of the user's browser. In any case, whether considering the browser as a tier in the architecture or not, the user's browser initiates a request to the web application, regardless of whether there is server-supplied code running in the browser.

This opposing viewpoint is a function of what can be trusted and what can be protected in a typical Web application. The browser must always be considered "untrusted." There is no way for a web application to know whether the browser has been compromised or not. There is no way for a web application to confirm that the data sent as HTTP requests is not under the control of an attacker.[*] By the way, authentication of the user only reduces the attack surface. There is still no way to guarantee that an

---

[*] Likewise, a server may be compromised, thus sending attacks to the user's browser. From the user's perspective, the web application might be considered untrusted.

attacker hasn't previously taken over the user's session or is otherwise misusing a user's login credentials.

> *Manipulating the variables in the URL is simple. But attackers can also manipulate almost all information going from the client to the server like form fields, hidden fields, content-length, session-id and http methods.*[18]

Due to the essential distrust of everything coming into any Web application, security architects are likely to discount the browser as a valid tier of the application. Basically, there is very little that a web application designer can do to enhance the protection of the web browsers. That is not to say that there aren't applications and security controls that can't be applied to web browser; there most certainly are. Numerous security vendors offer just such protections. However, for a web application that must serve content to a broad population, there can be no guarantees of browser protection; there are no guarantees that the browser hasn't already been compromised or controlled by an attacker. Therefore, from a security perspective, the browser is often considered outside the defensible perimeter of a web application or web system. While in this explanation we will follow that customary usage, it must be noted that there certainly are applications where the browser would be considered to lie within the perimeter of the web application. In this case, the browser would then be considered as the user tier of the system.

Returning then to Figure 3.4, from a defensible perimeter standpoint, and from the standpoint of a typical security architect, we have a three-tier application:

1. Web server
2. Application server
3. Database

For this architecture, the Web server tier includes disk storage. Static content to be served by the system resides in this forward most layer. Next, further back in the system, where it is not directly exposed to HTTP-based attacks (which presumably will be aimed at the Web server?), there is an application server that runs dynamic code. We don't know from this diagram what protocol is used between the Web server and the application server. We do know that messages bound for the application server originate at the Web server. The arrow pointing from the Web server to the application server clearly demonstrates this. Finally, as requests are processed, the application server interacts with the database server to construct responses. Figure 3.4 does not specify what protocol is used to interact with the database. However, database storage is shown as a separate component from the database server. This probably means that storage can be separated from the actual database application code, which could indicate an additional tier, if so desired.

What security information can be harvested from Figure 3.4? Where are the obvious attack surfaces? Which is the least-trusted tier? Where would you surmise that the greatest trust resides? Where would you put security controls? You will note that no security boundaries are depicted in the AppMaker logical architecture.

In Chapter 6, we will apply our architecture assessment and threat modeling methodology to this architecture in an attempt to answer these questions.

Figure 3.5 represents a completely different type of architecture compared to a web application. In this case, there are only two components (I've purposely simplified the architecture): a user interface (UI) and a kernel driver. The entire application resides on some sort of independent computing device (often called an "endpoint"). Although a standard desktop computer is shown, this type of architecture shows up on laptops, mobile devices, and all sorts of different endpoint types that can be generalized to most operating systems. The separation of the UI from a higher privileged system function is a classic architecture pattern that crops up again and again.

Under most operating systems where there is some user-accessible component that then opens and perhaps controls a system level piece of code, such as a kernel driver, the kernel portion of the application will run at a higher privilege level than the user interface. The user interface will run at whatever privilege level the logged-in user's account runs. Generally, pieces of code that run as part of the kernel have to have access to all system resources and must run at a much higher privilege level, usually the highest privilege level available under the operating system. The bus, kernel drivers, and the like are valuable targets for attackers. Once an attacker can insert him or herself into the kernel: "game over." The attacker has the run of the system to perform whatever actions and achieve whatever goals are intended by the attack. For system takeover, the kernel is the target.

For system takeover, the component presents a valuable and interesting attack surface. If the attacker can get at the kernel driver through the user interface (UI) in some

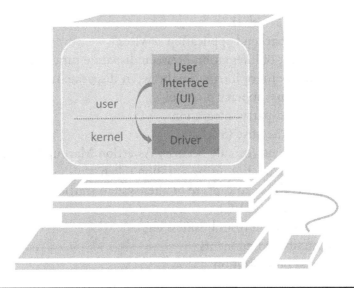

Figure 3.5 Two-component endpoint application and driver.

fashion, then his or her goals will have been achieved. Whatever inputs the UI portion of our architecture presents (represented in Figure 3.5) become critical attack surfaces and must be defended. If Figure 3.5 is a complete architecture, it may describe enough of a logical architecture to begin a threat model. Certainly, the key trust boundary is obvious as the interface between user and system code (kernel driver). We will explore this type of application in somewhat more depth in a subsequent chapter.

3.4 Seeing and Applying Patterns

A **pattern** *is a common and repeating idiom of solution design and architecture. A pattern is defined as a solution to a problem in the context of an application.*[19]

Through patterns, unique solutions convert to common patterns that make the task of applying information security to systems much easier. There are common patterns at a gross level (trust/distrust), and there are recurring patterns with more specificity. Learning and then recognizing these patterns as they occur in systems under assessment is a large part of assessing systems for security.

Identifying patterns is a key to understanding system architectures. Understanding an architecture is a prerequisite to assessing that architecture. Remediating the security of an architecture is a practice of applying security architecture patterns to the system patterns found within an architecture. Unique problems generating unique solutions do crop up; one is constantly learning, growing, and maturing one's security architecture practice. But after a security architect has assessed a few systems, she or he will start to apply security patterns as solutions to architectural patterns.

There are architectural patterns that may be abstracted from specific architectures:

- Standard e-commerce Web tiers
- Creating a portal to backend application services
- Database as the point of integration between disparate functions
- Message bus as the point of integration between disparate functions
- Integration through proprietary protocol
- Web services for third-party integration
- Service-oriented architecture (SOA)
- Federated authentication [usually Security Assertion Markup Language (SAML)]
- Web authentication validation using a session token
- Employing a kernel driver to capture or alter system traffic
- Model–view–controller (MVC)
- Separation of presentation from business logic
- JavaBeans for reusable components
- Automated process orchestration
- And more

There are literally hundreds of patterns that repeat, architecture to architecture. The above list should be considered as only a small sample.

As one becomes familiar with various patterns, they begin to "pop out," become obvious. An experienced architect builds solutions from these well-known patterns. Exactly which patterns will become usable is dependent upon available technologies and infrastructure. Typically, if a task may be accomplished through a known or even implemented pattern, it will be more cost-effective than having to build an entirely new technology. Generally, there has to be a strong business and technological motivation to ignore existing capabilities in favor of building new ones.

Like architectural patterns, security solution patterns also repeat at some level of abstraction. The repeatable security solutions are the security architecture "patterns." For each of the architectural patterns listed above, there are a series of security controls that are often applied to build a defense-in-depth. A security architect may fairly rapidly recognize a typical architecture pattern for which the security solution is understood. To the uninitiated, this may seem mysterious. In actuality, there's nothing mysterious about it at all. Typical architectural patterns can be generalized such that the security solution set also becomes typical.

As an example, let's examine a couple of patterns from the list above.

- Web services for third-party integration:
  o Bidirectional, mutual authentication of each party
  o Encryption of the authentication exchange
  o Encryption of message traffic
  o Mutual distrust: Each party should carefully inspect data that are received for anomalous and out-of-range values (input validation)
  o Network restrictions disallowing all but intended parties
- Message bus as a point of integration:
  o Authentication of each automated process to the message bus before allowing further message traffic
  o Constraint on message destination such that messages may only flow to intended destinations (ACL)
  o Encryption of message traffic over untrusted networks
  o In situations where the message bus crosses the network trust boundaries, access to the message bus from less-trusted networks should require some form of access grant process

Hopefully, as may be seen, each of the foregoing patterns (listed) has a fairly well-defined security solution set.* When a system architecture is entirely new, of course, the

---

* The security solutions don't include specific technology; the implementation is undefined—lack of specificity is purposive at this level of abstraction. In order to be implemented, these requirements will have to be designed with specific technologies and particular semantics.

security assessor will need to understand the architecture in a fairly detailed manner (as we will explain in a later chapter). However, architectural patterns repeat over and over again. The assessment process is more efficient and can be done rapidly when repeating architectural patterns are readily recognized. As you assess systems, hopefully, you will begin to notice the patterns that keep recurring?

As you build your catalog of architectural patterns, so you will build your catalog of security solution patterns. In many organizations, the typical security solution sets become the organization's standards.

I have seen organizations that have sufficient standards (and sufficient infrastructure to support those standards in an organized and efficient manner) to allow designs that strictly follow the standards to bypass security architecture assessment entirely. Even when those standard systems were highly complex, if projects employed the standard architectural patterns to which the appropriate security patterns were applied, then the organization had fairly strong assurance that there was little residual risk inherent in the new or updated system. Hence, the ARA could be skipped. Such behavior is typically a sign of architectural and security maturity. Often (but not always), organizations begin with few or no patterns and little security infrastructure. As time and complexity increase, there is an incentive to be more efficient; every system can't be deployed as a single, one-off case. Treating every system as unique is inefficient. As complexity increases, so does the need to recognize patterns, to apply known solutions, and to make those known solutions standards that can then be followed.

I caution organizations to avoid attempting to build too many standards before the actual system and security patterns have emerged. As has been noted above, there are classic patterns that certainly can be applied right from the start of any program. However, there is a danger of specifying capabilities that will never be in place and may not even be needed to protect the organization. Any hints of "ivory tower," or other idealized but unrealistic pronouncements, are likely to be seen as incompetence or, at the very least, misunderstandings. Since the practice of architecture is still craft and relatively relationship based, trust and respect are integral to getting anything accomplished.

When standards reflect reality, they will be observed. But just as importantly, when the standards make architectural and security sense, participants will implicitly understand that a need for an exception to standards will need to be proved, not assumed. Hence, blindly applying industry "standards" or practices without first understanding the complexities of the situation at hand is generally a mistake and will have costly repercussions.

Even in the face of reduced capabilities or constrained resources, if one understands the normal solution to an architectural pattern, a standard solution, or an industry-recognized solution, one can creatively work from that standard. It's much easier to start with something well understood and work towards an implementable solution, given the capabilities at hand. This is where a sensible risk practice is employed. The architect must do as much as possible and then assess any remaining residual risk.

As we shall see, residual risk must be brought to decision makers so that it can either be accepted or treated. Sometimes, a security architect has to do what he or she can within the limits and constraints given, while making plain the impact that those limits are likely to generate. Even with many standard patterns at hand, in the real world, applying patterns must work hand-in-hand with a risk practice. It has been said that information security is "all about risk."

In order to recognize patterns—whether architectural or security—one has to have a representation of the architecture. There are many forms of architectural representation. Certainly, an architecture can be described in a specification document through descriptive paragraphs. Even with a well-drawn set of diagrams, the components and flows will typically need to be documented in prose as well as diagramed. That is, details will be described in words, as well. It is possible, with sufficient diagrams and a written explanation, that a security assessment can be performed with little or no interaction. In the author's experience, however, this is quite rare. Inevitably, the diagram is missing something or the descriptions are misleading or incomplete. As you begin assessing systems, prepare yourself for a fair amount of communication and dialogue. For most of the architects with whom I've worked and who I've had the privilege to train and mentor, the architectural diagram becomes the representation of choice. Hence, we will spend some time looking at a series of diagrams that are more or less typical. Like Figure 3.3, let's try to understand what the diagram tells us, as well as from a security perspective, what may be missing.

3.5 System Architecture Diagrams and Protocol Interchange Flows (Data Flow Diagrams)

Let's begin by defining what we mean by a representation. In its simplest form, the representation of a system is a graphical representation, a diagram. Unfortunately, there are "logical" diagrams that contain almost no useful information. Or, a diagram can contain so much information that the relevant and important areas are obscured.

A classic example of an overly simplified view would be a diagram containing a laptop, a double-headed arrow from the laptop to the server icon with, perhaps, a brick wall in between representing a firewall (actual, real-world "diagrams"). Figure 3.1 is more less this simple (with the addition of some sort of backend server component). Although it is quite possible that the system architecture is really this simple (there are systems that only contain the user's browser and the Web server), we still don't know a key piece of information without asking, namely, which side, laptop or server, opens the connection and begins the interaction. Merely for the sake of understanding authentication, we have to understand that one key piece of the communication flow.* And for most modestly complex systems, it's quite likely that there are many more components

---

* Given the ubiquity of HTTP interactions, if the protocol is HTTP and the content is some form of browser interaction (HTML+dynamic content), then origination can safely be assumed from the user, from the user's browser, or from an automated process, for example, a "web service client."

involved than just a laptop and a server (unless the protocol is telnet and the laptop is logging directly into the server).

Figure 3.6 represents a conceptual sample enterprise architecture. Working from the abovementioned definition given by Godinez et al. (2010)[20] of a conceptual architecture, Figure 3.6 then represents the enterprise architect's view of the business relationships of the architecture. What the conceptual architecture intends to represent are the business functions and their interrelationships; technologies are typically unimportant,

We start with an enterprise view for two reasons:

1. Enterprise architecture practice is better described than system architecture.
2. Each system under review must fit into its enterprise architecture.

Hence, because the systems you will review have a place within and deliver some part of the intent of the enterprise architecture, we begin at this very gross level. When one possesses some understanding of enterprise architectures, this understanding provides a basis for the practice of architecture and, specifically, security architecture. Enterprise architecture, being a fairly well-described and mature area, may help unlock that which is key to describing and then analyzing all architectures. We, therefore, begin at the enterprise level.

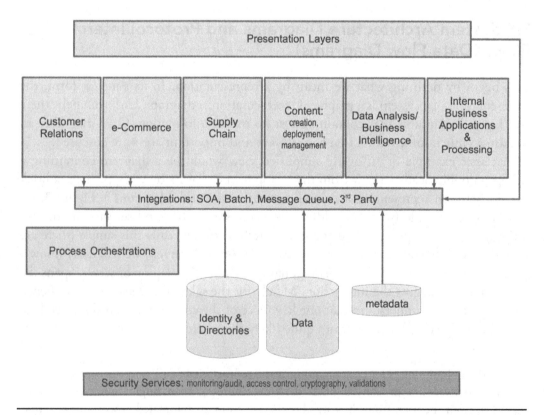

Figure 3.6 Conceptual enterprise architecture.

In a conceptual enterprise architecture, a very gross level of granularity is displayed so that viewers can understand what business functions are at play. For instance, in Figure 3.6, we can understand that there are integrating services that connect functions. These have been collapsed into a single conceptual function: "Integrations." Anyone who has worked with SOA knows that, at the very least, there will be clients and servers, perhaps SOA managing software, and so on. These are all collapsed, along with an enterprise message bus, into a single block. "Functions get connected through integrations" becomes the architecture message portrayed in Figure 3.6.

Likewise, all data has been collapsed into a single disk. In an enterprise, it is highly unlikely that terrabytes of data could be delivered on a single disk icon. Hence, we know that this representation is conceptual: There is data that must be delivered to applications and presentations. The architecture will make use of "integrations" in order to access the data. Business functions all are integrated with identity, data, and metadata, whereas the presentations of the data for human consumption have been separated out from the business functions for a "Model, View, Controller" or MVC separation. It is highly unlikely that an enterprise would use a single presentation layer for each of the business functions. For one thing, external customers' presentations probably shouldn't be allowed to mix with internal business presentations.

In Figure 3.6, we get some sense that there are technological infrastructures that are key to the business flows and processes. For instance, "Integrations" implies some sort of messaging bus technology. Details like a message bus and other infrastructures might be shown in the conceptual architecture only if the technologies were "standards" within the organization. Details like a message bus might also be depicted if these details will in some manner enhance the understanding of what the architecture is trying to accomplish at a business level. Mostly, technologies will be represented at a very gross level; details are unimportant within the conceptual architecture. There are some important details, however, that the security architect can glean from a conceptual architecture.

Why might the security architect want to see the conceptual architecture? As I wrote in Chapter 9 of *Core Software Security*,[21] early engagement of security into the Secure Development Lifecycle (SDL) allows for security strategy to become embedded in the architecture. "Strategy" in this context means a consideration of the underlying security back story that has already been outlined, namely, the organization's risk tolerance and how that will be implemented in the enterprise architecture or any specific portion of that architecture. Security strategy will also consider the evolving threat landscape and its relation to systems of the sort being contemplated. Such early engagement will enhance the conceptual architecture's ability to account for security. And just as importantly, it will make analysis and inclusion of security components within the logical architecture much easier, as architectures move to greater specificity.

From Figure 3.6 we can surmise that there are "clients," "line of business systems," "presentations," and so on who must connect through some sort of messaging or other exchange semantic [perhaps file transfer protocol (FTP)] with core business services. In this diagram, two end-to-end, matrix domains are conceptualized as unitary:

- Process Orchestrations
- Security and privacy services

This is a classic enterprise architect concept of security; security is a box of services rather than some distinct services (the security infrastructure) and some security

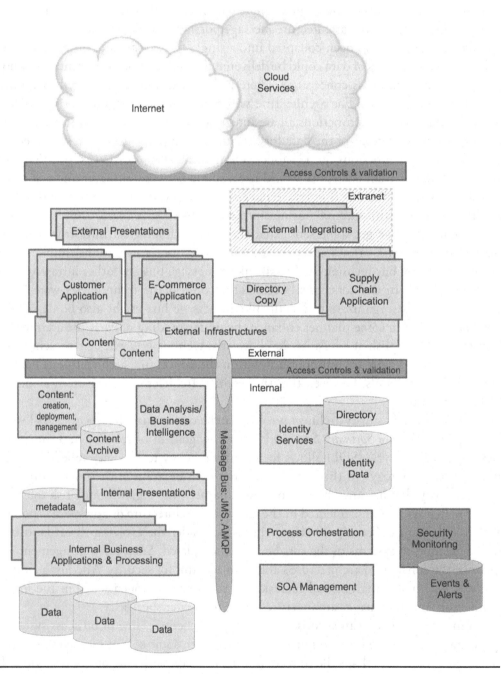

Figure 3.7   Component enterprise architecture.

capabilities built within each component. It's quite convenient for an enterprise architect to imagine security (or orchestrations, for that matter) as unitary. Enterprise architects are generally not domain experts. It's handy to unify into a "black box," opaque, singular function that one needn't understand, so one can focus on the other services. (I won't argue that some security controls are, indeed, services. But just as many are not.)

Figure 3.6 also tells us something about the integration of the systems: "service-oriented." This generally means service-oriented architecture (SOA). At an enterprise level, these are typically implemented through the use of Simple Object Access protocol (SOAP) services or Web services. The use of Web services implies loose coupling to any particular technology stack. SOAP implementation libraries are nearly ubiquitous across operating systems. And, the SOAP clients and servers don't require programming knowledge of each other's implementation in order to work: loosely coupled. If mature, SOA may contain management components, and even orchestration of services to achieve appropriate process stepping and process control.

You might take a moment at this point to see what questions come up about this diagram (see Figure 3.6). What do you think is missing? What do you want to know more of? Is it clear from the diagram what is external to the organization and what lies within possible network or other trust boundaries?

Figure 3.7 represents the same enterprise architecture that was depicted in Figure 3.6. Figure 3.6 represents a conceptual view, whereas Figure 3.7 represents the component view.

3.5.1 Security Touches All Domains

For a moment, ignore the box second from the left titled "Infrastructure Security Component" found in the conceptual diagram (Figure 3.6). For enterprise architects, it's quite normal to try and treat security as a black box through which communications and data flow. Somehow the data are "magically" made secure. If you work with enough systems, you will see these "security" boxes placed into diagrams over and over again.

Like any practice, the enterprise architect can only understand so many factors and so many technologies. Usually, anyone operating at the enterprise level will be an expert in many domains. The reason they depend upon security architects is because the enterprise architects are typically not security experts. Security is a matrix function across every other domain. Some security controls are reasonably separate and distinct, and thus, can be placed in their own component space, whereas other controls must be embedded within the functionality of each component. It is our task as security architects to help our sister and brother architects understand the nature of security as a matrix domain.[*]

---

[*] Annoying as the treatment of security as a kind of unitary, magical transformation might be, I don't expect the architects with whom I work to be security experts. That's my job.

In Figure 3.7, the security functions have been broken down into four distinct components:

1. Internet facing access controls and validation
2. External to internal access controls and validation
3. Security monitoring
4. A data store of security alerts and events that is tightly coupled to the security monitoring function

This component breakout still hides much technological detail. Still, we can see where entrance and exit points are, where the major trust boundaries exist. Across the obvious trust boundary between exposed networks (at the top of the diagram) and the internal networks, there is some sort of security infrastructure component. This component is still largely undefined. Still, placing "access controls and validation" between the two trust zones allows us to get some feel for where there are security-related components and how these might be separated from the other components represented in Figure 3.7. The security controls that must be integrated into other components would create too much visual noise in an already crowded representation. Another security-specific view might be necessary for this enterprise architecture.

3.5.2 Component Views

Moving beyond the security functions, how is the component view different from the conceptual view?

Most obviously, there's a lot more "stuff" depicted. In Figure 3.7, there are now two very distinct areas—"external" and "internal." Functions have been placed such that we can now understand where within these two areas the function will be placed. That single change engenders the necessity to split up data so that co-located data will be represented separately. In fact, the entire internal data layer has been sited (and thus associated to) the business applications and processing. Regarding those components for which there are multiple instances, we can see these represented.

"Presentations" have been split from "external integrations" as the integrations are sited in a special area: "Extranet." That is typical at an enterprise, where organizations are cross-connected with special, leased lines and other point-to-point solutions, such as virtual private networks (VPN). Access is granted based upon business contracts and relationships. Allowing data exchange after contracts are confirmed is a different relationship than encouraging interested parties to be customers through a "presentation" of customer services and online shopping ("eCommerce"). Because these two modes of interaction are fundamentally different, they are often segmented into different zones: web site zone (for the public and customers) and Extranet (for business partners). Typically, both of these will be implemented through multiple applications, which are usually deployed on a unitary set of shared infrastructure services that are sited in the externally accessible environment (a formal "DMZ").

In Figure 3.7 you see a single box labeled, "External Infrastructures," which cuts across both segments, eCommerce and Extranet. This is to indicate that for economies of scale, there is only one set of external infrastructures, not two. That doesn't mean that the segments are not isolated from each other! And enterprise architects know full well that infrastructures are complex, which is why the label is plural. Still, at this granularity, there is no need to be more specific than noting that "infrastructures" are separated from applications.

Take a few moments to study Figures 3.6 and 3.7, their similarities and their differences. What functions have been broken into several components and which can be considered unitary, even in the component enterprise architecture view?

3.6 What's Important?

The amount of granularity within any particular architecture diagram is akin to the story of *Goldilocks and the Three Bears*. "This bed is too soft! This bed is too hard! This bed is just right." Like Goldilocks, we may be presented with a diagram that's "too soft." The diagram, like Figure 3.1, doesn't describe enough, isn't enough of a detailed representation to uncover the attack surfaces.

On the other hand, a diagram that breaks down the components that, for the purposes of analysis, could have been considered as atomic (can be treated as a unit) into too many subcomponents will obscure the attack surfaces with too much detail: "This diagram is too hard!"

As we shall see in the following section, what's "architecturally interesting" is dependent upon a number of factors. Unfortunately, there is no simple answer to this problem. When assessing, if you're left with a lot of questions, or the diagram only answers one or two, it's probably "too soft." On the other hand, if your eyes glaze over from all the detail, you probably need to come up one or two levels of granularity, at least to get started. That detailed diagram is "too hard." There are a couple of patterns that can help.

3.6.1 What Is "Architecturally Interesting"?

This is why I wrote "component functions." If the interesting function is the operating system of a server, then one may think of the operating system in an atomic manner. However, even a command-line remote access method such as telnet or secure Shell (SSH) gives access to any number of secondary logical functions. In the same way, unless a Web server is only sharing static HTML pages, there is likely to be an application, some sort of processing, and some sort of data involved beyond an atomic web server. In this case, our logical system architecture will probably need a few more components and the methods of communication between those components: Web server, application, data store. There has to be a way for the Web server to instantiate the application processing and then return the HTTP response from that processing. And the application will need to fetch data from the data store and perhaps update the data based on whatever processing is taking place. We have now gone from two components to five. We've gone from one communication flow to three. Typical web systems are considerably more complex than this, by the way.

On the other hand, let's consider the web tier of a large, commercial server. If we know with some certainty that web servers are only administered by security savvy, highly trained and highly trusted web masters, then we can assume a certain amount of restriction to any attacker-attractive functionality. Perhaps we already know and have approved a rigorous web server and operating environment hardening standard. Storage areas are highly restricted to only allow updates from trusted sources and to only allow read operations from the web servers. The network on which these web servers exist is highly restricted such that only HTTP/S is allowed into the network from untrusted sources, only responses from the web servers can flow back to untrusted sources, and administrative traffic comes only from a trusted source that has considerable access restrictions and robust authorization before grant of access. That administrative network is run by security savvy, highly trusted individuals handpicked for the role through a formal approval process, and so forth.*

In the website case outlined above, we may choose to treat web servers as atomic without digging into their subcomponents and their details. The web servers inherit a great deal of security control from the underlying infrastructure and the established formal processes. Having answered our security questions once to satisfaction, we don't need to ask each web project going into the environment, so long as the project uses the environment in the intended and accepted manner, that is, the project adheres to the existing standards. In a security assessment, we would be freed to consider other factors, given reasonably certain knowledge and understanding of the security controls already in place. Each individual server can be considered "atomic." In fact, we may even be able to consider an entire large block of servers hosting precisely the same function as atomic, for the purposes of analysis.

Besides, quite often in these types of highly controlled environments, the application programmer is not given any control over the supporting factors. Asking the application team about the network or server administration will likely engender a good deal of frustration. Also, since the team members actually don't have the answers, they may be encouraged to guess. In matters relating to security due diligence, guessing is not good enough. An assessor must have near absolute certainty about everything about which certainty can be attained. All unknowns must be treated as potential risks.

Linked libraries and all the different objects or other modular interfaces inside an executable program usually don't present any trust boundaries that are interesting. A

---

* We will revisit web sites more thoroughly in later chapters.

single process (in whatever manner the execution environment defines "process") can usually be considered atomic. There is generally no advantage to digging through the internal software architecture, the internal call graph of an executable process space.

The obvious exception to the guideline to treat executable packages as atomic are dynamically linked executable forms,* such as DLLs under the Microsoft operating systems or dynamic link libraries under UNIX. Depending upon the rest of the architecture and the deployment model, these communications might prove interesting, since certain attack methods substitute a DLL of the attacker's choosing.

The architecture diagram needs to represent the appropriate logical components. But, unfortunately, what constitutes "logical components" is dependent upon three factors:

1. Deployment model
2. Infrastructure (and execution environment)
3. Attack methods

In the previous chapter, infrastructure was mentioned with respect to security capabilities and limitations. Alongside the security capabilities that are inherited from the infrastructure and runtime stack, the very *type* of infrastructure upon which the system will run influences the level at which components may be considered atomic. This aspect is worth exploring at some length.

3.7 Understanding the Architecture of a System

The question that needs answering in order to factor the architecture properly for attack surfaces is at what level of specificity can components be treated as atomic? In other words, how deep should the analysis decompose an architecture? What constitutes meaningless detail that confuses the picture?

3.7.1 Size Really Does Matter

As mentioned above, any executable package that is joined to a running process after it's been launched is a point of attack to the executable, perhaps to the operating system. This is particularly true where the attack target is the machine or virtual machine itself. Remember that some cyber criminals make their living by renting "botnets," networks of attacker-controlled machines. For this attack goal, the compromise of a machine has attacker value in and of itself (without promulgating some further attack, like keystroke logging or capturing a user session). In the world of Advanced Persistent Threats (APT), the attacker may wish to control internal servers as a beachhead, an internal

---

* We will examine another exception below: Critical pieces of code, especially code that handles secrets, will be attacked if the secret protects a target sufficiently attractive.

machine from which to launch further attacks. Depending upon the architecture of intrusion detection services (IDS), if attacks come from an internal machine, these internally originating attacks may be ignored. Like botnet compromise, APT attackers are interested in gaining the underlying computer operating environment and subverting the OS to their purposes.

Probing a typical computer operating system's privilege levels can help us delve into the factoring problem. When protecting an operating environment, such as a user's laptop or mobile phone, we must decompose down to executable and/or process boundaries. The presence of a vulnerability, particularly an overflow or boundary condition vulnerability that allows the attacker to execute code of her or his choosing, means that one process may be used against all the others, especially if that process is implicitly trusted.

As an example, imagine the user interface (UI) to an anti-virus engine (AV). Figure 3.4 could represent an architecture that an AV engine might employ. We could add an additional process running in user space, the AV engine. Figure 3.8 depicts this change to the architecture that we examined in Figure 3.4. Many AV engines employ system drivers in order to capture file and network traffic transparently. In Figure 3.8, we have a generalized anti-virus or anti-malware endpoint architecture.

The AV runs in a separate process space; it receives commands from the UI, which also runs in a separate process. Despite what you may believe, quite often, AV engines do not run at high privilege. This is purposive. But, AV engines typically communicate or receive communications from higher privilege components, such as system drivers and the like. The UI will be running at the privilege level of the user (unless the security architect has made a big mistake!).

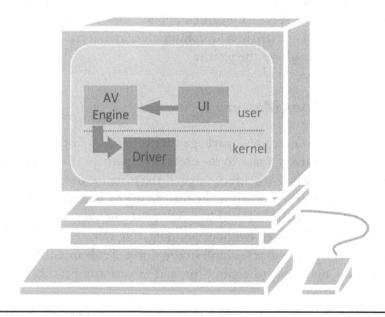

Figure 3.8 Anti-virus endpoint architecture.

In this situation, a takeover of the UI process would allow the attacker to send commands to the AV engine. This could result in a simple denial of service (DOS) through overloading the engine with commands. But perhaps the UI can turn off the engine? Perhaps the UI can tell the engine to ignore malicious code of the attacker's choosing? These scenarios suggest that the communication channel from UI to AV needs some protection. Generally, the AV engine should be reasonably suspicious of all communications, even from the UI.

Still, if the AV engine does not confirm that the UI is, indeed, the one true UI component shipped with the product, the AV engine presents a much bigger and more dangerous attack surface. In this case, with no authentication and validation of the UI process, an attacker no longer needs to compromise the UI! Why go to all the trouble of reverse-engineering the UI, hunting for possible overflow conditions, and then building an exploit for the vulnerability? That's quite a bit of work compared to simply supplying the attacker's very own UI. By studying the calls and communications between the UI and the AV engine, the attacker can craft her or his own UI component that has the same level of control as the product's UI component. This is a lot less work than reverse engineering the product's UI component. This attack is made possible when the AV engine assumes the validity of the UI without verification. If you will, there is a trust relationship between the AV engine and the UI process. The AV process must establish trust of the UI. Failure to do so allows the attacker to send commands to the AV engine, possibly including, "Stop checking for malware."

The foregoing details why most anti-virus and malware programs employ digital signatures rendered over executable binary files. The digital signature can be validated by each process before communications commence. Each process will verify that, indeed, the process attempting to communicate is the intended process. Although not entirely foolproof,[*] binary signature validation can provide a significant barrier to an attack to a more trusted process from a less than trusted source.

Abstracting the decomposition problem from the anti-virus engine example, one must factor an independently running endpoint architecture (or subcomponent) down to the granularity of each process space in order to establish trust boundaries, attack surfaces, and defensible perimeters. As we have seen, such granular depth may be unnecessary in other scenarios. If you recall, we were able to generally treat the user's browser atomically simply because the whole endpoint is untrusted. I'll stress again: It is the context of the architecture that determines whether or not a particular component will need to be factored further.

---

[*] It is beyond the scope of this book to delve into the intricacies of signature validations. These are generally performed by the operating system in favor of a process before load and execution. However, since system software has to remain backward compatible, there are numerous very subtle validation holes that have become difficult to close without compromising the ability of users to run all of the user's software.

For the general case of an operating system *without the presence of significant, additional, exterior protections*, the system under analysis can be broken down into executable processes and dynamically loaded libraries. A useful guideline is to decompose the architecture to the level of executable binary packages. Obviously, a loadable "program," which when executed by the operating system will be placed into whatever runtime space is normally given to an executable binary package, can be considered an atomic unit. Communications with the operating system and with other executable processes can then be examined as likely attack vectors.

3.8 Applying Principles and Patterns to Specific Designs

How does Figure 3.9 differ from Figure 3.8? Do you notice a pattern similarity that exists within both architectures? I have purposely named items in the drawing using typical mobile nomenclature, rather than generalizing, in the hope that you will translate these details into general structures as you study the diagram. Before we explore this typical mobile anti-virus or anti-malware application architecture, take a few moments to look at Figure 3.8, then Figure 3.9. Please ponder the similarities as well as differences. See if you can abstract the basic underlying pattern or patterns between the two architectures.

Obviously, I've included a "communicate" component within the mobile architecture. Actually, there would be a similar function within almost any modern endpoint

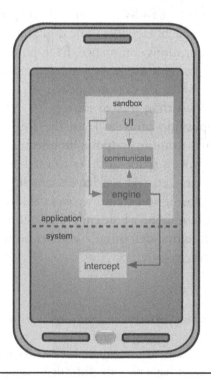

Figure 3.9   Mobile security application endpoint architecture.

security application, whether the software was intended for consumers, any size organization, or enterprise consumption. People expect their malware identifications to get updated almost in real time, let's say, "rapidly." These updates* are often sent from a central threat "intelligence" team, a threat evaluation service via centralized, highly controlled Web services to the endpoint.†

In addition, the communicator will likely send information about the state of the endpoint to a centralized location for analysis: Is the endpoint compromised? Does it store malware? What versions of the software are currently running? How many evil samples have been seen and stopped? All kinds of telemetry about the state of the endpoint are typically collected. This means that communications are usually both ways: downwards to the endpoint and upwards to a centralized server.

In fact, in today's mobile application market, most applications will embed some sort of communications. Only the simplest application, say a "flashlight" that turns on the camera's light, or a localized measuring tool or similar discreet application, will not require its own server component and the necessary communications flows. An embedded mobile communications function is not unique to security software; mobile server communications are ubiquitous.

In order to keep things simple, I kept the communications out of the discussion of Figure 3.8. For completeness and to represent a more typical mobile architecture, I have introduced the communicator into Figure 3.9. As you may now see, the inclusion of the communicator opens up all kinds of new security challenges. Go ahead and consider these as you may. We will take up the security challenges within a mobile application in the analyses in Part II. For the moment, let's restrict the discussion to the mobile endpoint. Our task at this point in the journey is to understand architectures. And, furthermore, we need to understand how to extract security-related information from an architecture diagram so that we have the skills to proceed with an architecture risk assessment and threat model.

The art of architecture involves the skill of recognizing and then applying abstract patterns while, at the same time, understanding any local details that will be ignored through the application of patterns. Any unique local circumstances are also important and will have to be attended to properly.

It is not that locally specific details should be completely ignored. Rather, in the interest of achieving an "architectural" view, these implementation details are overlooked until a broader view can be established. That broader view is the architecture. As the architecture proceeds to specific design, the implementation details, things like specific operating system services that are or are not available, once again come to the fore and must receive attention.

---

* These updates are called "DAT" files or updates. Every endpoint security service of which the author knows operates in this manner.

† For enterprises, the updated DAT will be sent to an administrative console from which administrators can then roll out to large numbers of endpoints at the administrator's discretion

I return to the concept of different architecture views. We will stress again and again how important the different views are during an assessment. We don't eliminate the details; we abstract the patterns in order to apply solutions. Architecture solutions in hand, we then dive into the detail of the specifics.

In Figure 3.8, the trust boundary is between "user" space and "kernel" execution area. Those are typical nomenclature for these execution areas in UNIX and UNIX-like and Windows™ operating systems. In both the Android™ and iOS™ mobile platforms, the names are somewhat different because the functions are not entirely same: the system area and the application environment. Abstracting just what we need from this boundary, I think it is safe to declare that there is an essential similarity between kernel and system, even though, on a mobile platform, there is a kernel beneath the system level (as I understand it). Nevertheless, the system execution space has high privileges. System processes have access to almost everything,* just as a kernel does. These are analogous for security purposes. Kernel and system are "high" privilege execution spaces. User and application are restricted execution environments, purposely so.

A security architect will likely become quite conversant in the details of an operating system with which he or she works on a regular basis. Still, in order to assess any architecture, one needn't be a "guru." As we shall see, the details change, but the basic problems are entirely similar. There are patterns that we may abstract and with which we can work.

Table 3.1 is an approximation to illuminate similarities and, thus, must not be taken as a definitive statement. The makers of each of these operating systems may very well violently disagree. For instance, much discussion has been had, often quite spirited, about whether the Linux system is a UNIX operating system or not. As a security architect, I purposely dodge the argument; a position one way or the other (yes or no) is irrelevant to the architecture pattern. Most UNIX utilities can be compiled to run on Linux, and do. The configuration of the system greatly mirrors other UNIX systems, that is, load order, process spaces, threading, and memory can all be treated as similar to other UNIX variants. For our purposes, Linux may be considered a UNIX variant without reaching a definitive answer to the question, "Is Linux a UNIX operating system?" For our purposes, we don't need to know.

Hence, we can take the same stance on all the variants listed in Table 3.1—that is, we don't care whether it is or is not; we are searching for common patterns. I offer the following table as a "cheat sheet," if you will, of some common operating systems as of this writing. I have grossly oversimplified in order to reveal similarities while obscuring differences and exceptions. The list is not a complete list, by any means. Experts in each of these operating systems will likely take exception to my cavalier treatment of the details.

---

* System processes can access processes and services in the system and user spaces. System processes will have only restricted access to kernel services through a formal API of some sort, usually a driver model and services.

Table 3.1 Common Operating Systems and Their Security Treatment

Name	Family	Highest Privilege	Higher Privilege?	User Space
BSD UNIX	UNIX[1]	Kernel[2]		User[3]
Posix UNIX	UNIX	Kernel		User
System V	UNIX	Kernel		User
Mac OS™	UNIX (BSD)	Kernel	Administrator[4]	User
iOS™	Mac OS	Kernel	System	Application
Linux[5]	UNIX-like	Kernel		User
Android™	Linux	Kernel	System	Application[8]
Windows™[6]	Windows NT	Kernel	System	User
Windows Mobile™ (variants)	Windows[7]	Kernel	System	Application

Notes:

1. There are far more UNIX variants and subvariants than listed here. For our purposes, these variations are essentially the same architecture.
2. The superuser or root, by design, has ultimate privileges to change anything in every UNIX and UNIX-like operating system. Superuser has god-like powers. The superuser should be considered essentially the same as kernel, even though the kernel is an operating environment and the superuser is a highly privileged user of the system. These have the same privileges: everything.
3. In all UNIX and UNIX descendant systems, users can be configured with granular read/write/execute privileges up to and including superuser equivalence. We ignore this for the moment, as there is a definite boundary between user and kernel processes. If the superuser has chosen to equate user with superuser, the boundary has been made irrelevant from the attacker's point of view.
4. Mac OS introduced a preconfigured boundary between the superuser and an administrator. These do not have equivalent powers. The superuser, or "root" as it is designated in Mac OS documentation, has powers reserved to it, thus protecting the environment from mistakes that are typical of inexperienced administrators. Administrator is highly privileged but not god-like in the Mac OS.
5. There are also many variants and subvariants of Linux. For our purposes, these may be treated as essentially the same operating system.
6. I do not include the Windows-branded operating systems before the kernel was ported to the NT kernel base. These had an entirely different internal architecture and are completely obsolete and deprecated. There are many variants of the Windows OS, too numerous for our purposes. There have been many improvements in design over the years. These variations and improvements are all descendants of the Windows NT kernel, so far as I know. I don't believe that the essential driver model has changed since I wrote drivers for the system in the 1990s.
7. I'm not conversant with the details of the various Windows mobile operating systems. I'm making a broad assumption here. Please research as necessary.
8. Android employs OS users as application strategy. It creates a new user for each application so that applications can be effectively isolated, called a "sandbox." It is assumed that there is only a single human user of the operating system since Android is meant for personal computing devices, such as phones and tablets.

It should be readily apparent, glancing through the operating system cheat sheet given in Table 3.1, that one can draw some reasonable comparisons between operating systems as different as Windows Server™ and Android™. The details are certainly radically different, as are implementation environments, compilers, linkers, testing, deployment—that is, the whole panoply of development tooling. However, an essential pattern emerges. There are higher privileged execution spaces and spaces that can have their privileges restricted (but don't necessarily, depending upon configuration by the superuser or system administrator).

On mobile platforms especially, the application area will be restricted on the delivered device. Removing the restrictions is usually called "jail breaking." It is quite possible to give applications the same privileges as the system or, rather, give the running user or application administrative or system privileges. The user (or malware) usually has to take an additional step*: jail breaking. We can assume the usual separation of privileges rather than the exception in our analysis. It might be a function of a mobile security application to ascertain whether or not the device has been jail broken and, based upon a positive result, take some form of protective action against the jail break.

If you now feel comfortable with the widespread practice of dividing privileges for execution on operating systems, we can return to consideration of Figure 3.9, the mobile security application. Note that, like the endpoint application in Figure 3.8, there is a boundary between privileges of execution. System-level code has access to most communications and most services, whereas each application must be granted privileges as necessary. In fact, on most modern mobile platforms, we introduce another boundary, the application "sand box." The sand box is a restriction to the system such that system calls are restricted across the privilege boundary from inside the sandbox to outside. Some system calls are allowed, whereas other calls are not, by default. The sand box restricts each application to its own environment: process space, memory, and data. Each application may not see or process any other application's communications and data. The introduction of an execution sand box is supposed to simplify the application security problem. Applications are by their very nature, restricted to their own area.†

Although the details of mobile security are beyond this book, in the case of a security application that must intercept, view, and perhaps prevent other applications from executing, the sand box is an essential problem that must be overcome. The same might be said for software intended to attack a mobile device. The sand box must be breached in both cases.

For iOS and, most especially, under Android, the application must explicitly request privileges from the user. These privilege exceptions are perhaps familiar to iPhone™ users as the following prompt: "Allow push notifications?" The list of exceptions

---

* There are Linux-based mobile devices on which the user has administrative privileges. On these and similar systems, there is no need for jail breaking, as the system is not restricted as delivered.

† There are many ways to create an isolating operating environment. At a different level, sandboxes are an important security tool in any shared environment.

presented to an Android user has a different form but it's essentially the same request for application privileges.

Whether a user can appropriately grant privileges or not is beyond the scope of this discussion. However, somehow, our security application must be granted privileges to install code within the system area in order to breach the application sand box. Or, alternatively, the security application must be granted privileges to receive events generated by all applications and the system on the device. Mobile operating systems vary in how this problem is handled. For either case, the ultimate general pattern is equivalent in that the security system will be granted higher privileges than is typical for an application. The security application will effectively break out of its sandbox so that it has a view of the entire mobile system on the device. For the purposes of this discussion (and a subsequent analysis), we will assume that, in some manner, the security application manages to install code below the sandbox. That may or may not be the actual mechanism employed for any particular mobile operating system and security application.

Take note that this is essentially a solution across a trust-level boundary that is similar to what we saw in the endpoint software discussion. In Figure 3.8, the AV engine opens (or installs) a system driver within the privileged space. In Figure 3.9, the engine must install or open software that can also intercept application actions from every application. This is the same problem with a similar solution. There is an architecture pattern that can be abstracted: crossing an operating system privilege boundary between execution spaces. The solution is to gain enough privilege such that a privileged piece of code can perform the necessary interceptions. At the same time, in order to reduce security exposure, the actual security engine runs as a normal application in the typical application environment, at reduced privileges. In the case of the endpoint example, the engine runs as a user process. In the case of the mobile example, the engine runs within an application sand box. In both of these cases, the engine runs at reduced privileges, making use of another piece of code with greater privileges but which has reduced exposure.

How does the high-privilege code reduce its exposure? The kernel or system code does as little processing as possible. It will be kept to absolute simplicity, usually delivering questionable events and data to the engine for actual processing. The privileged code is merely a proxy router of events and data. In this way, if the data happens to be an attack, the attack will not get processed in the privileged context but rather by the engine, which has limited privileges on the system. As it happens, one of the architectural requirements for this type of security software is to keep the functions of the privileged code, and thus its exposure to attack, to an absolute minimum.

In fact, on an operating system that can instantiate granular user privilege levels, such as UNIX and UNIX-like systems, a user with almost no privileges except to run the engine might be created during the product installation. These "nobody" users are created with almost complete restriction to the system, perhaps only allowed to execute a single process (the engine) and, perhaps, read the engine configuration file. If the user interface reads the configuration file instead of the engine, then "nobody" doesn't even need a file privilege. Such an installation and runtime choice creates strong protection against a possible compromise of the engine. Doing so will give an attacker no additional privileges. Even so, a successful attack may, at the very least, interrupt malware protection.

As in the endpoint example, the user interface (UI) is a point of attack to the engine. The pattern is exactly analogous between the two example architectures. The solution set is analogously the same, as well.

Figure 3.9, the mobile malware protection software, shows an arrow originating from the engine to the interceptor. This is the initialization vector, starting the interceptor and opening the communication channel. The flow is started at the lower privilege, which opens (begins communications) with the code running at a higher privilege. That's a typical approach to initiate communications. Once the channel is open and flowing, as configured between the interceptor and the engine, all event and data communications come from higher to lower, from interceptor to engine. In this manner, compromise of the engine cannot adversely take advantage of the interceptor. This direction of information flow is not represented on the diagram. Again, it's a matter of simplicity, a stylistic preference on the part of the author to keep arrows to a minimum, to avoid the use of double-headed arrows. When assessing this sort of architecture, this is one of the questions I would ask, one of the details about which I would establish absolute certainty. If this detail is not on the diagram, I make extensive notes so that I'm certain about my architectural understanding.

We've uncovered several patterns associated with endpoints—mobile and otherwise:

- Deploy a proxy router at high privilege to capture traffic of interest.
- Run exposed code at the least privileges possible.
- Initialize and open communications from lower privilege to higher.
- Higher privilege must validate the lower privileged code before proceeding.
- Once running, the higher privilege sends data to the lower privilege; never the reverse.
- Separate the UI from other components.
- Validate the UI before proceeding.
- UI never communicates with highest privilege.
- UI must thoroughly validate user and configuration file input before processing.

As you may see, seemingly quite disparate systems—a mobile device and a laptop—actually exhibit very similar architectures and security solutions? If we abstract the architecture patterns, we can apply standardized solutions to protect these typical patterns. The task of the architecture assessment is to identify both known and unknown architecture patterns. Usual solutions can be applied to the known patterns. At the same time, creativity and innovation can be engaged to build solutions for situations that haven't been seen before, for that which is exceptional.

When considering the "architecturally interesting" problem, we must consider the unit of atomicity that is relevant. When dealing with unitary systems running on an independent, unconnected host, we are dealing with a relatively small unit: the endpoint.* The host (any computing device) can be considered as the outside boundary of the system. For the moment, in this consideration, ignore the fact that protection software might be communicating with a central policy and administrative system. Irrespective of these functions, and when the management systems cannot be reached, the protection software, as in our AV example, must run well and must resist attack or subversion. That is a fundamental premise of this type of protection (no matter whether on a mobile platform, a laptop, a desktop, etc.) The protections are supposed to work whether or not the endpoint is connected to anything else. Hence, the rule here is as stated: The boundary is constrained to the operating environment and hardware on which it runs. That is, it's an enclosed environment requiring architectural factoring down to attackable units, in this case, usually, processes and executables.

Now contrast the foregoing endpoint cases with a cloud application, which may exist in many points of presence around the globe. Figure 3.10 depicts a very high-level, cloud-based, distributed Software as a Service (SaaS) application. The application has several instances (points of presence and fail-over instances) spread out around the globe

---

* An endpoint protection application must be capable of sustaining its protection services when running independently of any assisting infrastructure.

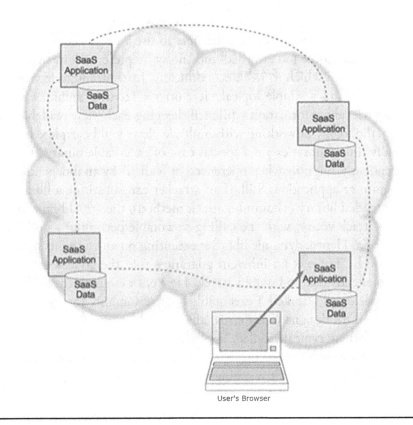

Figure 3.10   A SaaS cloud architecture.

(the "cloud"). For this architecture, to delve into each individual process might be "too hard" a bed, too much information. Assuming the sorts of infrastructure and administrative controls listed earlier, we can step away from process boundaries. Indeed, since there will be many duplicates of precisely the same function, or many duplicates of the same host configuration, we can then consider logical functions at a much higher level of granularity, as we have seen in previous examples.

Obviously, a security assessment would have to dig into the details of the SaaS instance; what is shown in Figure 3.10 is far too high level to build a thorough threat model. Figure 3.10 merely demonstrates how size and distribution change the granularity of an architecture view. In detail, each SaaS instance might look very much like Figure 3.4, the AppMaker web application.

In other words, the size and complexity of the architecture are determiners of decomposition to the level of granularity at which we analyze the system. Size matters.

Still, as has been noted, if one can't make the sorts of assumptions previously listed, if infrastructure, runtime, deployment, and administration are unknown, then a two-fold analysis has to be undertaken. The architecture can be dealt with at its gross logical components, as has been suggested. And, at the same time, a representative server, runtime, infrastructure, and deployment for each component will need to be analyzed in detail, as well. ARA and threat modeling then proceed at a couple of levels of granularity in parallel in order to achieve completeness.

Analysis for security and threat models often must make use of multiple views of a complex architecture simultaneously. Attempts to use a single view tend to produce representations that become too crowded, too "noisy," representations that contain too much information with which to work economically. Instead, multiple views or layers that can be overlaid on a simple logical view offer a security architect a chance to unearth all the relevant information while still keeping each view readable. In a later chapter, the methodology of working with multiple views will be explored more fully.

Dynamically linked libraries are a special case of executable binary. These are not loaded independently, but only when referenced or "called" by an independently loaded binary, a program or application. Still, if an attacker can substitute a library of attack code for the intended library (a common attack method), then the library can easily be turned into an attack vector, with the calling executable becoming a gullible method of attack execution. Hence, dynamic libraries executing on an endpoint should be considered suspiciously. There is no inherent guarantee that the code within the loaded library is the intended code and not an attack. Hence, I designate any and all forms of independently packaged ("linked") executable forms as atomic for the purpose of an endpoint system. This designation, that is, all executables, includes the obvious loadable programs, what are typically called "applications." But the category also extends to any bit of code that may be added in, that may get "called" while executing: libraries, widgets, gadgets, thunks, or any packaging form that can end up executing in the same chain of instructions as the loadable program.

"All executables" must not be confined to process space! Indeed, any executable that can share a program's memory space, its data or, perhaps, its code must be considered.

And any executable whose instructions can be loaded and run by the central processing unit (CPU) during a program's execution must come under assessment, must be included in the review. Obviously, this includes calls out to the operating system and its associated libraries, the "OS."

Operating systems vary in how loosely or tightly coupled executable code must be packaged. Whatever packages are supported, every one of those packages is a potential "component" of the architecture. The caveat to this rule is to consider the amount of protections provided by the package and/or the operating environment to ensure that the package cannot be subverted easily. If the inherent controls provide sufficient protection against subversion (like inherent tampering and validity checks), then we can come up a level and treat the combined units atomically.

In the case of managed server environments, the decomposition may be different. The difference depends entirely upon the sufficiency of protections such that these protections make the simple substitution of binary packages quite difficult. The administrative controls placed upon such an infrastructure of servers may be quite stringent:

- Strong authentication
- Careful protection of authentication credentials
- Authorization for sensitive operations
- Access on a need-to-know basis
- Access granted only upon proof of requirement for access
- Access granted upon proof of trust (highly trustworthy individuals only)
- Separation of duties between different layers and task sets
- Logging and monitoring of sensitive operations
- Restricted addressability of administrative access (network or other restrictions)
- Patch management procedures with service-level agreements (SLAs) covering the timing of patches
- Restricted and verified binary deployment procedures
- Standard hardening of systems against attack

The list given above is an example of the sorts of protections that are typical in well-managed, commercial server environments. This list is not meant to be exhaustive but, rather, representative and/or typical and usual. The point being that when there exist significant *exterior* protections beyond the operating system that would have to be breached before attacks at the executable level can proceed, then it becomes possible to treat an entire server, or even a server farm, as atomic, particularly in the case where all of the servers support the same logical function. That is, if 300 servers are all used as Java application servers, and access to those servers has significant protections, then an "application server" can be treated as a single component within the system architecture. In this case, it is understood that there are protections for the operating systems, and that "application server" means "horizontally scaled," perhaps even "multitenant." The existing protections and the architecture of the infrastructure are the knowledge sets that were referred to earlier in this chapter as "infrastructure" and "local environment."

If assumptions cannot be made about external protections, then servers are just another example of an "endpoint." Decomposition of the architecture must take place down to the executing process level.

What about communications within an executable (or other atomic unit)? With appropriate privileges and tools, an attacker can intercept and transform any executing code. Period. The answer to this question, as explained above, relies upon the attacker's access in order to execute tools at appropriate privileges. And the answer depends upon whether subverting execution or intra-process communications returns some attacker value. In other words, this is essentially a risk decision: An attack to running executables at high privilege must return something that cannot be achieved through another, easier means.

There are special cases where further decomposition is critically important, such as encryption routines or routines that retrieve cryptographic keys and other important credentials and program secrets. Still, a working guideline for most code is that communications within an executing program can be ignored (except for certain special case situations). That is, the executable is the atomic boundary of decomposition. Calls between code modules, calls into linked libraries, and messages between objects can be ignored during architecture factoring into component parts. We want to uncover the boundaries between executable packages, programs, and other runtime loadable units. Further factoring does not produce much security benefit.*

Once the atomic level of functions has been decided, a system architecture of "components"—logical functions—can be diagrammed. This diagram is typically called a "system architecture" or perhaps a "logical architecture." This is the diagram of the system that will be used for an analysis. It must include every component at the appropriate atomic level. Failure to list everything that will interact in any digital flow of communication or transaction leads to unprotected attack vectors. The biggest mistake that I've made and that those whom I've coached and mentored typically make is not including every component. I cannot stress this enough: Keep questioning until the system architecture diagram includes every component at its appropriate level of decomposition. Any component that is unprotected becomes an attack vector to the entire system. A chain is only as strong as its weakest link.

Special cases that require intra-executable architectural decomposition include:

- Encryption code
- Code that handles or retrieves secrets
- Digital Rights Management (DRM) code
- Software licensing code
- System trust boundaries
- Privilege boundaries

---

* Of course, the software design will necessarily be at a much finer detail, down to the compilation unit, object, message, and application programming interface (API) level.

While it is generally true that executables can be treated atomically, there are some notable exceptions to this guideline. Wherever there is significant attack value to isolating particular functions within an executable, then these discreet functions should be considered as atomic functions. Of course, the caveat to this rule must be that an attacker can gain access to a running binary such that she or he has sufficient privileges to work at the code object or gadget level. As was noted above, if the "exceptional" code is running in a highly protected environment, it typically doesn't make sense to break down the code to this level (note the list of protections, above). On the other hand, if code retrieving secrets or performing decryption must exist on an unprotected endpoint, then that code will not, in that scenario, have much protection. Protections must be considered then, at the particular code function or object level. Certain DRM systems protect in precisely this manner; protections surround and obscure the DRM software code within the packaged executable binary.

Factoring down to individual code functions and objects is especially important where an attacker can gain privileges or secrets. Earlier, I described as having no attack value a vulnerability that required high privilege in order to exploit. That is almost always true, except in a couple of isolated cases. That's because once an attacker has high privileges, she or he will prosecute the goals of the attack.

Attackers don't waste time playing around with compromised systems. They have objectives for their attacks. If a compromise has gained complete control of a machine, the attack proceeds from compromise of the machine to whatever further actions have value for the attacker: misuse of the machine to send spam; participation in a botnet; theft of credentials, data, or identity; prosecuting additional attacks on other hosts on the network; and so forth. Further exploit of another vulnerability delivering the same level of privilege holds no additional advantage.* However, in a couple of interesting cases, a high-privilege exploit may deliver attacker value.

For example, rather than attempting to decrypt data through some other means, an attacker might choose to let an existing decryption module execute, the results of which the attacker can capture as the data are output. In this case, executing a running program with debugging tools has an obvious advantage. The attacker doesn't have to figure out which algorithm was used, nor does the attacker have to recover keying material. The running program already performs these actions, assuming that the attacker can syphon the decrypted data off at the output of the decryption routine(s). This avenue may be easier than a cryptographic analysis.

If the attacker is after a secret, like a cryptographic key, the code that retrieves the secret from its hiding place and delivers the key to the decryption/encryption routines may be a worthy target. This recovery code will only be a portion, perhaps a set of

---

*The caveat to this rule of thumb is security research. Although not intentionally malicious, for some organizations security researchers may pose a significant risk. The case of researchers being treated as potential threat agents was examined previously. In this case, the researcher may very well prosecute an exploit at high privilege for research purposes. Since there is no adversarial intent, there is no need to attain a further objective.

distinct routines, within the larger executable. Again, the easiest attack may be to let the working code do its job and simply capture the key as it is output by the code. This may be an easier attack than painstakingly reverse engineering any algorithmic, digital hiding mechanism. If an attacker wants the key badly enough, then she or he may be willing to isolate the recovery code and figure out how it works. In this situation, where a piece of code is crucial to a larger target, that piece of code becomes a target, irrespective of the sort of boundaries that we've been discussing, atomic functions, binary executables, and the like. Instances of this nature comprise the precise situation where we must decompose the architecture deeper into the binary file, factoring the code into modules or other boundaries within the executable package. Depending upon the protections for the executable containing the code, in the case in which a portion of the executable becomes a target, decomposing the architecture down to these critical modules and their interfaces may be worthwhile.

3.8.1 Principles, But Not Solely Principles

[T]he discipline of designing enterprises guided with principles[22]

Some years ago, perhaps in 2002 or 2003, I was the Senior Security Architect responsible for enterprise inter-process messaging, in general, and for Service Oriented Architectures (SOA), in particular. Asked to draft an inter-process communications policy, I had to go out and train, coach, and socialize the requirements laid out in the policy. It was a time of relatively rapid change in the SOA universe. New standards were being drafted by standards organizations on a regular basis. In my research, I came across a statement that Microsoft published articulating something like, "observe mutual distrust between services."

That single principle, "mutual distrust between services," allowed me to articulate the need for services to be very careful about which clients to allow, and for clients to not assume that a service is trustworthy. From this one principle, we created a standard that required bidirectional authentication and rigorous input validation in every service that we deployed. Using this principle (and a number of other tenets that we observed), we were able to drive security awareness and security control throughout the expanding SOA of the organization. Each principle begets a body of practices, a series of solutions that can be applied across multiple architectures.

In my practice, I start with principles, which then get applied to architectures as security solutions. Of course, the principles aren't themselves solutions. Rather, principles suggest approaches to an architecture, ideals for which to strive. Once an architecture has been understood, once it has been factored to appropriate levels to understand the attack surfaces and to find defensible boundaries, how do we apply controls in order to achieve what ends? It is to that question that principles give guidance. In a way, it might be said that security principles are the ideal for which a security posture strives. These are the qualities that, when implemented, deliver a security posture.

Beyond uncovering all the attack surfaces, we have to understand the security architecture that we are trying to build. Below is a distillation of security principles. You may think of these as an idealized description of the security architecture that will be built into and around the systems you're trying to secure.

The Open Web Application Security Project (OWASP) provides a distillation of several of the most well known sets of principles:

> — *Apply defense in depth (complete mediation).*
> — *Use a positive security model (fail-safe defaults, minimize attack surface).*
> — *Fail securely.*
> — *Run with least privilege.*
> — *Avoid security by obscurity (open design).*
> — *Keep security simple (verifiable, economy of mechanism).*
> — *Detect intrusions (compromise recording).*
> — *Don't trust infrastructure.*
> — *Don't trust services.*
> — *Establish secure defaults.*[23]

Given the above list, how does one go about implementing even a single one of these principles? We have spent some time in this chapter examining architectural patterns. Among these are security solution patterns that we've enumerated as we've examined various system architectures. Solution patterns are the implementation of the security principles.

It should be noted that running with least privilege or failing securely are part of a defense-in-depth. The boundaries between the principles aren't discrete. Not trusting an infrastructure is a part of minimizing attack surfaces, which is a part of the defense-in-depth. A single security control can relate to a number of security principles and supply a solution to one or more attack surfaces. Concomitantly, any attack surface may require several orthogonal security controls. Remember, specification of a defense is a matrix problem across many domains and technologies. There are few, "if this, then do that" solutions. Solutions are more often like, "if this, then do this, and that, and maybe a little of this other, too, if you can."

Hence, using security principles is a starting point not an ending. It's a matter of applying solutions to achieve the principles. If you see the principles begin to emerge out of the security requirements that you specify, then you have achieved an understanding of security architecture as well as having achieved a practice of applying information security to systems.

> *Contrary to what most users and even many developers assume, security functionality does not necessarily provide genuine security; security is a systems property emerging from the totality of system behavior.*[24]

Summary

As we have seen in this chapter, in order to assess systems for security, the assessor has to have a grounding in the practice of system architecture. Specifically, he or she must understand logical and component architectures well enough to uncover attack surfaces, trust boundaries, and defensible units of composition. For convenience, we call this process "decomposing in architecture" to a functional granularity such that these units can be factored into security significant components.

Rarely will a single architectural view suffice, especially for complex system architectures. Often, a security analysis will make use of multiple views. Each view typically serves for a particular stakeholder group or community. Enterprise architects have one view, business architects another view, solutions architects yet another view of a system, and infrastructure architects have a different view entirely. Each of these views usually holds some of the security information required. And thus, for a review, each stakeholder view has some validity.

By abstracting general architectural patterns from specific architectures, we can apply known effective security solutions in order to build the security posture. There will be times, however, when we must be creative in response to architecture situations that are as yet unknown or that are exceptional. Still, a body of typical patterns and solutions helps to cut down the complexity when determining an appropriate set of requirements for a system under analysis.

Our security principles will be the ideal towards which we architect security solutions. As solution patterns are applied and requirements specified, the security principles should be the emergent properties of the solution set. There is no one-to-one mapping. Still, the set of solutions will together enable a system architecture to achieve a security posture that exhibits the set of security principles from which the security architect is working. In this way, the art of securing systems is the craft of applying information security such that the system's architecture will exhibit the qualities described by a set of security principles.

References

1. Zachman, J. A. (2007). "Foreword." In *Handbook of Enterprise Systems Architecture in Practice*, p. xv, Saha, P., ed. IGI Global.
2. Ibid.
3. Saha, P. (2007). "A Synergistic Assessment of the Federal Enterprise Architecture Framework against GERAM (ISO15704:2000)" (Ch. 1). In *Handbook of Enterprise Systems Architecture in Practice*, p. 1, Saha, P., ed. IGI Global.
4. *Merriam-Webster's Collegiate Dictionary.* (2004). 11th ed. Merriam-Webster.
5. Sherwood, J., Clark, A., and Lynas, D.. "Enterprise Security Architecture." SABSA White Paper, SABSA Limited, 1995–2009. Retrieved from http://www.sabsa-institute.com/members/sites/default/inline-files/SABSA_White_Paper.pdf.

6. Zachman, J. A. (2007). "Foreword." In *Handbook of Enterprise Systems Architecture in Practice*, pp. xv–xvi, Saha, P., ed. IGI Global.

7. Ibid., p. xvi.

8. Godinez, M., Hechler, E., Koenig, K., Lockwood, S., Oberhofer, M., and Schroeck, M. (2010). "Introducing Enterprise Information Architecture" (Ch. 2). In *The Art of Enterprise Information Architecture: A Systems-Based Approach for Unlocking Business Insight*, p. 33. IBM Press.

9. Ibid.

10. Berners-Lee, T. (1989). "Information Management: A Proposal" CERN. Retrieved from http://www.w3.org/History/1989/proposal.html.

11. Godinez, M., Hechler, E., Koenig, K., Lockwood, S., Oberhofer, M., and Schroeck, M. (2010). "Introducing Enterprise Information Architecture" Ch. 2). In *The Art of Enterprise Information Architecture: A Systems-Based Approach for Unlocking Business Insight*, p. 74. IBM Press.

12. Zachman, J. A. (2007). "Foreword." In *Handbook of Enterprise Systems Architecture in Practice*, Saha, P., ed., pp. xv–xvi. IGI Global.

13. Godinez, M., Hechler, E., Koenig, K., Lockwood, S., Oberhofer, M., and Schroeck, M. (2010). "Introducing Enterprise Information Architecture" (Ch. 2). In *The Art of Enterprise Information Architecture: A Systems-Based Approach for Unlocking Business Insight*, p. 74. IBM Press.

14. Schoenfield, B. (2011). "How to Securely Process and Allow External HTTP Traffic to Terminate on Internal Application Servers." *ISA Smart Guide*. SANS Institute.

15. *Oxford Dictionary of English.* (2010). 3rd ed. UK: Oxford University Press.

16. Ibid.

17. Buschmann, F., Henney, K., and Schmidt, D. C. (2007). *Pattern-Oriented Software Architecture: On Patterns and Pattern Languages*, Vol. 5, p. xxxi. John Wiley & Sons.

18. Open Web Application Security Project (OWASP). (November 2013). OWASP Application Security FAQ, OWASP.org. Retrieved from https://www.owasp.org/index.php/OWASP_Application_SecuriFAQ#Why_can.27t_I_trust_the_information_coming_from_the_browser.3F.

19. Ramachandran, J. (2002). *Designing Security Architecture Solutions*, p. 43. John Wiley & Sons.

20. Godinez, M., Hechler, E., Koenig, K., Lockwood, S., Oberhofer, M., and Schroeck, M. (2010). "Introducing Enterprise Information Architecture" (Ch. 2). In *The Art of Enterprise Information Architecture: A Systems-Based Approach for Unlocking Business Insight*, p. 33. IBM Press.

21. Schoenfield, B. (2014). "Applying the SDL Framework to the Real World" (Ch. 9). In *Core Software Security: Security at the Source*, pp. 255–324. Boca Raton (FL): CRC Press.

22. Saha, P. (2007). "A Synergistic Assessment of the Federal Enterprise Architecture Framework against GERAM (ISO15704:2000)" (Ch. 1). In *Handbook of Enterprise Systems Architecture in Practice*, p. 1, Saha, P., ed. IGI Global.

23. Open Web Application Security Project (OWASP). (2013). *Some Proven Application Security Principles*. Retrieved from https://www.owasp.org/index.php/ Category:Principle.

24. Redwine, S. T., Jr. and Davis, N., eds. (2004). "Processes to Produce Secure Software: Towards more Secure Software." Software Process Subgroup, Task Force on Security across the Software Development Lifecycle, National Cyber Security Summit, March 2004.

Chapter 4

Information Security Risk

It's about contextual risk.
— Anurag Agrawal, in conversation with the author, 2014

The success of the assessment depends greatly upon the assessor's ability to calculate or rate the risk of the system. There is the risk of the system as it's planned at the moment of the assessment. And there's the risk of each attack vector to the security posture of the system. Most importantly, the risk from the system to the organization must be determined in some manner. If computer security risk cannot be calculated in a reasonable fashion and consistently over time, not only does any particular assessment fail, but the entire assessment program fails. An ability to understand, to interpret, and, ultimately, to deliver risk ratings is an essential task of the architecture risk assessment (ARA) and threat modeling.

The word "risk" is overloaded and poorly defined. When discussing it, we usually don't bother to strictly define what we mean; "risk" is thrown around as though everyone has a firm understanding of it. But usage is often indiscriminate. A working definition for the purposes of security assessment must be more stringent. "Risk," for our purposes, will be defined more formally, below. For the moment, let's explain "risk" as Jack Jones does: "the loss exposure associated with the system."[1] This working definition encompasses both the likelihood of a computer event occurring and its negative impact.

4.1 Rating with Incomplete Information

It would be extraordinarily helpful if the standard insurance risk equation could be calculated for information security risks.

$$\textbf{Probability * Annualized Loss = Risk}$$

However, this equation requires data that simply are not available in sufficient quantities for a statistical analysis comparable to actuarial data that are used by insurance companies to calculate risk. In order to calculate probability, one must have enough statistical data on mathematically comparable events. Unfortunately, generally speaking, few security incidents in the computer realm are particularly mathematically similar. Given multivariate, multidimensional events generated by adaptive human agents, perhaps it wouldn't be too far a stretch to claim that no two events are precisely the same?[*]

Given the absence of actuarial data, what can a poor security architect do?

4.2 Gut Feeling and Mental Arithmetic

Security architects generate risk ratings on a regular basis, perhaps every day, depending on job duties. Certainly, most practitioners make risk ratings repeatedly and regularly. There's a kind of mental arithmetic that includes some or all of the elements of risk, factors in organizational preferences and capabilities, the intentions of the system, and so on, and then outputs a sense of high, medium, or low risk. For many situations referencing many different types of systems and attack vectors, a high, medium, or low rating may be quite sufficient. But how does one achieve consistency between practitioners, between systems, and over time?

This is a thorny and nontrivial problem.

I don't mean to suggest that one cannot approach risk calculation with enough data and appropriate mathematics. Jack Jones, the author of Factor Analysis of Information Risk (FAIR), told the author that the branch of mathematics known as casino math may be employed to calculate probability in the absence of sufficient, longitudinal actuarial data. Should you want it, the FAIR "computational engine" is a part of the standard.[†2] For our purposes, it is sufficient to note that the probability term is difficult to calculate without significant mathematical investment. It isn't too hard to calculate likely loss in dollars, in some situations, although it may be tricky to annualize an information security loss.

Annualizing loss may not be an appropriate impact calculation for information security, anyway. Annualizing a loss obviously works quite well for buying insurance. It's also useful for comparing and prioritizing disparate risks. But we're not talking about

---

[*] A significant amount of study has been devoted to data breaches. In particular, please see the breach reports from the Poneman Institute (http://www.ponemon.org). However, by the time a breach has occurred, we are at a very different point in the computer security cycle. ARA is meant to prevent a breach. And a data breach is only one of the many types of possible successful impacts.

[†] A computational engine for FAIR is protected by patent, however.

an ability to directly insure the risk of a computer system attack in this book.* In order to create some risk treatment, some protection, periodic premiums are usually paid to a trusted third party, the insurer.

Generally, the cost of security technology occurs one time (with perhaps maintenance fees). It may be difficult to predict the useful life of technology purchases.† The personnel needed to run the technology are a "sunk cost." Unless services are entirely contracted, people are typically hired permanently, not on a yearly subscription basis (though some security firms are attempting a subscription model). In any event, this book is about applying computer security to systems such that they will be well-enough defended. The insurance, such as it may be, comprises the capabilities and defenses that protect the systems. Although logically analogous to insurance, the outlay structures for preventative system security follow a different cost model than paying for insurance.

The problem with sophisticated math is that it may take too long to calculate for the purpose of assessment. Generally, during an analysis, the security assessor must repeatedly calculate risk over multiple dimensions and over multiple items. If there are numerous attack surfaces, then there are numerous risk calculations. It would be onerous if each of these calculations required considerable effort, and worse if the calculations each took an extended period. Any extended time period beyond minutes may be too long. If there's significant residual risk‡ left over after current protections and future treatments are factored into the calculation, then the assessor must come up with an overall risk statement based upon the collection of risk items associated with the system. Taking a few hours to produce the overall risk is usually acceptable. But taking weeks or even months to perform the calculations is usually far too long.

Experienced security architects do these "back of the napkin" calculations fairly rapidly. They've seen dozens, perhaps hundreds, of systems. Having rated risk for hundreds or perhaps many more attack vectors, they get very comfortable delivering risk pronouncements consistently. With experience comes a gut feeling, perhaps an intuitive grasp, of the organization's risk posture. Intimacy with the infrastructure and security capabilities allows the assessor to understand the relative risk of any particular vulnerability or attack vector. This is especially true if the vulnerability and attack vector are well understood by the assessor. But what if one hasn't seen hundreds of systems? What does one do when just starting out?

---

* It is possible to underwrite liability from computer security incidents. That is one risk treatment. However, the point of architecture analysis for security is to try and reduce the possibility of loss in the first place. Either are treatments for the risk. These are not mutually exclusive.

† Digital technology changes rapidly. On the other hand, the investment in building upon and around core systems may discourage change, thus extending the useful far beyond predictions.

‡ Residual risk" is that risk that remains *after* all treatments and/or mitigations have been applied. It is the risk that cannot or will not be adequately mitigated.

Indeed, the computer security language around risk can be quite muddled. Vulnerabilities are treated as risks in and of themselves. Tool vendors often do this in order to produce some kind of rating based upon vulnerability scans. Typically, the worst possible scenario and impact is taken as the likely scenario and impact. And unfortunately, in real systems, this is far from true.

As an example, take a cross-site scripting (XSS) error that lies within a web page. As was noted previously, depending upon the business model, an organization may or may not care whether its website contains XSS errors.* But how dangerous is a XSS error that lies within an administrative interface that is only exposed to a highly restricted management network? Even further, if that XSS can only be exercised against highly trained and highly trusted, reasonably sophisticated system administrators, how likely are they to fall for an email message from an unknown source with their own administrative interface as the URL? Indeed, the attacker must know that the organization uses the vulnerable web interface. They have to somehow induce technically savvy staff to click a faulty URL and further hope that staff are logged into the interface such that the XSS will fire. Indeed, on many administrative networks, external websites are restricted such that even if the XSS error did get exercised, the user couldn't be redirected to a malicious page because of network and application restrictions. Since no URL payload can be delivered via the XSS, the exploit will most likely fail. In this scenario, there exist a number of hoops through which an attacker must jump before the attacker's goal can be achieved. What's the payoff for the attacker? Is surmounting all the obstacles worth attempting the attack? Is all of this attacker effort worthwhile when literally millions of public websites reaching hundreds of millions of potential targets are riddled with XSS errors that can be exploited easily?

I would argue that a XSS error occurring in a highly restricted and well-protected administrative interface offers considerably less risk due to factors beyond the actual vulnerability: exposure, attack value, and difficulty in deriving an impact. However, I have seen vulnerability scanning tools that rate every occurrence of a particular variation of XSS precisely the same, based upon the worst scenario that the variation can produce. Without all the components of a risk calculation, the authors of the software don't have a complete enough picture to calculate risk; they are working with only the vulnerability and taking the easiest road in the face of incomplete information: assume the worst.

In fact, what I've described above are basic parts of a information security risk calculation: threat agent, motivation, capability, exposure, and vulnerability. These must come together to deliver an impact to the organization in order to have risk.

A threat is not a risk by itself. A vulnerability is not a risk in and of itself. An exploitation method is not a risk when the exploit exists in the absence of a threat agent

---

* An attack against the session depends upon other vulnerabilities being present (it's a combination attack) or it depends upon the compromise of the administrator's browser and/or machine, which are further hurdles not relevant to this example.

that is capable and motivated to exercise the exploit and in the presence of a vulnerability that has been exposed to that particular threat agent's methodology. This linking of dependencies is critical to the ability of a successful attack. And, thus, understanding the dependency of each of the qualities involved becomes key to rating the risk of occurrence. But even the combination so far described is still not a risk. There can be no risk unless exploitation incurs an impact to the owners or users of a computer system. "Credible attack vector" was defined in Chapter 2:

Credible attack vector: A credible threat exercising an exploit on an exposed vulnerability.

4.3 Real-World Calculation

For the purposes of architecture assessment for security, risk may be thought of as:

Credible Attack Vector * Impact = Risk Rating

where

> *Credible Attack Vector (CAV) = 0 < CAV > 1*
> *Impact = An ordinal that lies within a predetermined range such that 0 < Impact >*
> *Predetermined limit (Example: 0 < Impact > 500)*[3]

I do not claim that guessing at or even calculating in some manner the credible attack vector (CAV) will calculate a risk probability. It's merely one of any number of risk rating systems. The following explanation is one approach to risk that rates a collection of dependent conditions that must be taken together as a whole. One cannot simplistically grab a vulnerability and assume the other factors. The following is one way to decompose the elements of probability, an approach to impact that has been used over hundreds, perhaps even more than a thousand risk assessments over a number of years. It is certainly not the only way, nor the "True Way." Credible attack vector is presented as an example for a cyber-risk calculation rather than a recipe to follow precisely.

The point of describing this one approach is for you to understand the complexity of computer risk, especially when the risk ensues from the activities of human attackers.

In order to assess computer systems, one must have a reasonable understanding of the component attributes of risk and one must be facile in applying that risk understanding to real-world attackers and actual vulnerabilities within real computer systems, where a successful attack is likely to cause some harm. Credible attack vector rating is a simple and proven method to account for the many connected and dependent factors that, taken together in some measure, make up the probability calculation for cyber risk. Use

CAV as a starting point for your understanding and your organization's methodology, if it helps to get a handle on this thorny problem.

If we can consistently compute CAV and also rate Impact within a chosen scale, their multiplication will result in a risk rating. This is precisely how the Just Good Enough Risk Rating (JGERR) computes risk. The rating will always be some ratio of 500. JGERR users must choose what portion of 500 will be low, what the medium risk range will cover (presumably, centered on 250?), and the remainder will be high. Or, as we did at Cisco Systems, Inc., the range might be divided up into five buckets: low, medium-low, medium, medium-high, and high. Depending upon the needs of the organization, the buckets need not be symmetrical. Greater emphasis might be placed on higher risk by skewing towards high risk through expansion of the high bucket. Simply start the high classification from a lower number (say, "300"). Or an organization with a more risk-tolerant posture might decide to expand low or medium at the expense of high. Skewing around a particular bucket guarantees that the security needs of the organization are reflected within the rating system's buckets.

We will come back to the terms making up any similar calculation at a later point. First, let's define what risk means in the context of computer security.

As in the entire assessment process, there is significant craft and art involved in risk rating. Because of this, a key tool will be the assessor's mind. Each of us unique human beings is blessed (or cursed) with her or his own risk tolerance. Effectively rating risk can only be done when the assessor understands his or her personal risk tolerance.

Effectively managing information risk and security, without hindering the organization's ability to move quickly, will be key to business survival.[4]

4.4 Personal Security Posture

Personal risk predilection will have to be factored out of any risk calculations performed for an organization's systems. The analyst is not trying to make the system under analysis safe enough for him or herself. She is trying to provide sufficient security to enable the mission of the organization. "Know thyself" is an important maxim with which to begin.

Faced with the need to deliver risk ratings for your organization, you will have to substitute the organization's risk preferences for your own. For, indeed, it is the organization's risk tolerance that the assessment is trying to achieve, not each assessor's personal risk preferences. What is the risk posture for each particular system as it contributes to the overall risk posture of the organization? How does each attack surface—its protections if any, in the presence (or absence) of active threat agents and their capabilities, methods, and goals through each situation—add up to a system's particular risk posture? And how do all the systems' risks sum up to an organization's computer security risk posture?

4.5 Just Because It Might Be Bad, Is It?

What is "risk"?

An event with the ability to impact (inhibit, enhance or cause doubt about) the mission, strategy, projects, routine operations, objectives, core processes, key dependencies and/or the delivery of stakeholder expectations.[5]

At its core, risk may be thought of as "uncertainty about outcome." In the risk definition quoted above, the author focuses on "impact" to an organization's goals, and impact to the processes and systems that support the mission of the organization. In this generalized approach, "impact" can be either enhancing or detracting, although, as Jack Jones says, risk equates more or less with general "uncertainty."[6] The focus in classic risk management is on uncertainty in how events outside the control of an organization may affect the outcomes of the efforts of the organization. The emphasis in this definition is on uncertainty—events beyond the sphere of control—and the probability of those events having an effect.

Given certain types of attacks, there is absolute certainty in the world of computer security: Unprotected Internet addressable systems will be attacked. The uncertainty lies in the frequency of successful attacks versus "noise," uncertainty in whether the attacks will be sophisticated or not, how sophisticated, and which threat agents may get to the unprotected system first. Further, defenders won't necessarily know the objectives of the attackers. Uncertainty lies not within a probability of the event, but rather in the details of the event, the specificity of the event.

Taking any moment within the constant barrage of Internet-based system programming and deployment, we know with some certainty that sophisticated attackers are active in pursuing objectives against a wide range of targets. The question is not whether an attack will occur or not, so much as how soon, using what methods, and for what purposes?

Because we are concerned with the assessment of systems that are likely to be attacked and specifying protections to prevent success of the attacks, we may constrain our definition of risk. For the purposes of this book, we are not concerned with the positive possibilities from risk. We focus here on negative events as they relate to human actors attempting to misuse or abuse systems for goals not intended by the owners of those systems. In other words, we are interested in preventing "credible attack vectors" from success, whatever the goals of the attackers may be. We are constraining our definition of risk to:

- Human threat agents
- Attacks aimed at computer systems
- Attack methods meant to abuse or misuse a system

Just for the purposes of this book, we exclude nonhuman events (though certainly, in many information security practices, nonhuman events would also be considered). We also exclude any event whose impact may unexpectedly enhance the desired objectives of a computer system. Although those factors that we have excluded are, indeed, a part of the risk to an organization, these are generally not under consideration in a "risk" assessment of a computer system. So, just for the purposes of this book, we may safely exclude these.

It is worth noting once again that many[*] human attackers focused on computer systems are:

- Creative
- Innovative
- Adaptive

It is in the adaptive nature of computer-focused threat agents where a great deal of the uncertainty lies in gauging security risk. It has been said that, "whatever can be engineered by humans can be reverse engineered by humans." That is, in this context, whatever protections we build can ultimately, with enough resources, time, and effort, be undone. This is an essential piece of the probability puzzle when calculating or rating computer security risk. The fact that the attackers can learn, grow, and mature, and that they will rapidly shift tactics, indicates a level of heuristics to the defense of systems: Expect the attacks to change, perhaps dramatically. How the attackers will adapt, of course, is uncertain.

Calculating risk may seem a daunting task. But perhaps a little understanding of the components of information security risk can help to ease the task?

4.6 The Components of Risk

[W]ithout a solid understanding of what risk is, what the factors are that drive risk, and without a standard nomenclature, we can't be consistent or truly effective in using any method.[7]

---

[*] There are attackers who only run well-known, automated attacks. These "script kiddies," as they are commonly called, have little skill. Attack methods regularly move from innovative to automated, thus becoming available to the less skilled attacker. Defenses must account for automated, well-known attacks as well as the creative and new ones. Defending against well-established attacks is a slightly easier task, however, since security vendors regularly update their products to account for these well-known attack methods.

There is a collection of conditions* that each must be true in order for there to be any significant computer security risk.† If any one of the conditions is not true, that is, the condition doesn't exist or has been interrupted, then that single missing condition can negate the ability of an attack to succeed.

"Negate" may be a strong term? Since there is no absolute protection in computer security, there can be no surety that any particular exploit against a known vulnerability will not take place. Although Internet attack attempts are certain, there is no 100% surety about which will be tried against a particular vulnerability and when that particular attempt will take place.

However, even in the face of intrinsic uncertainty, we can examine each of the conditions that must be true and thus gain a reasonable understanding of whether any particular attack pattern is likely to succeed. "True" in this context can be thought of as a Boolean true or false. Treating the sub-terms as Boolean expressions gives us a simple way of working with the properties. But please bear in mind that because there is no absolute surety, these conditions are not really binary but, rather, the conditions can be sufficiently protected to an extent that the probability of a particular attack succeeding becomes significantly less likely. When there are enough hoops to jump through, many threat agents will move on to the next target or be sufficiently delayed that they either give up or are discovered before harm can take place.

> To illustrate how network defenders can act on their knowledge of their adversaries' tactics, the paper lays out the multiple steps an attacker must proceed through to plan and execute an attack. These steps are the "kill chain." While the attacker must complete all of these steps to execute a successful attack, the defender only has to stop the attacker from completing any one of these steps to thwart the attack.[8]

In short, for the purposes of ARA, we can treat each term as Boolean, though we rationally understand that no strict Boolean true or false state actually exists. We are simplifying for the purpose of rapid rating. Treating the sub-terms as Boolean terms allows for rapid risk ratings. Treating the sub-terms as Boolean terms allows us to proceed with a more easily practiced methodology. In the words of the "kill chain" analysis quoted above, the defender must interrupt the kill chain. The risk rating system proposed (actually in use by some organizations) provides a taxonomy for a general purpose kill chain risk model.

---

* The work presented here is based upon Just Good Enough Risk Rating (JGERR). JGERR is based upon "Factor Analysis of Information Risk" (FAIR), by Jack Jones. The author had the privilege of attending a number of in-depth sessions with Jack Jones during the later development of FAIR.

† In this context, we are only concerned with risk from attacks originating from humans.

Surety in the computer security risk arena is much like the proverbial story of the bear and two backpackers ("trekkers"). In this archetypical story, one backpacker asks the other why he's carrying a pair of running shoes. He replies, "for the bear." The first backpacker responds, "You can't outrun a bear." "I don't need to outrun the bear. I just need to outrun you," quips the second backpacker.

In the same way, if exercising an attack method becomes too expensive for many attackers, or the exploit exceeds the attacker's work factor, that is, the attack exceeds the amount of effort that the attacker is willing to put in to achieve success, then the attacker will move on to an easier target, to a less well-defended system. The system with the best "running shoes" will remain uncompromised or unbreached.

There are certain types of attackers who possess far more resources and patience than most organizations are willing to muster for their security protection. As we saw earlier in describing various threat agents, certain types of attackers are incredibly determined and persistent. Each organization will have to decide whether it will try to outlast this type of attack, to "outrun" such a determined bear. It may not be worth it to the organization to expend that much energy on its security posture. Or only the organization's most critical systems may get the appropriate resources to withstand such persistent and sophisticated attacks. This will have to be an organizational risk decision. No generalized book can presume to make such an important decision for any person or any organization.

4.6.1 Threat

Whatever the organization's stance towards advanced persistent threats (APT) and their ilk, the first condition that must be met is that there must be active, motivated threat agents who are interested in attacking systems of the sort that are under assessment. The "threat agent" is an individual or group that attacks computers. The term "threat" is scattered about in the literature and in parlance among practitioners. In some methodologies, threat is used to mean some type of attack methodology, such as spoofing or brute force password cracking. Under certain circumstances, it may make sense to conflate all of the components of threat into an attack methodology. This approach presumes two things:

- All attack methodologies can be considered equal.
- There are sufficient resources to guard against every attack methodology.

If one or both of the conditions above are not true, it will make more sense to develop a more sophisticated understanding of the "threat" term. A threat can be thought of as consisting of three qualities that could be considered independently and then combined into the "threat" term.

- Threat agent: an individual or group that attacks computers.
- Threat goal: the usual and typical value that the threat agent hopes to achieve through their attack.
- Threat capability: the typical attack methodologies that the threat agent employs.

You may have encountered one or more of the more sensational threat agents in the news media. Certainly, at the time of this writing, certain types of cyber attacks gain a fair amount of attention. Still, many threat agents labor in relative obscurity. It is no longer newsworthy when a new computer virus is released. In fact, hundreds of new varieties appear daily; most variations are used only a few times. There are literally hundreds of millions of malware variations. Perhaps, by now, there may be billions? Who writes these viruses and for what purpose? When we pose this question, we walk into the components of threat. Who are the threat agents? What are their goals? What are their methods?

I would add two more significant dimensions to threat: How much work are they willing to put into achieving their goals? I will call this the "work factor." And what is the threat agent's risk tolerance? What chances is the attacker willing to take in order to achieve his or her goals? Does the attacker care if the attack is discovered? What are the likely consequences of getting caught for these particular attacks and goals? Are these consequences a deterrent? These are key questions, I believe, in order to understand how relevant any particular threat agent is to a particular attack surface, impact or loss to the organization, and the level of protection required to dissuade that particular type of attacker.

- Threat agent
- Threat goals
- Threat capabilities
- Threat work factor
- Threat risk tolerance

When we put all these terms together, we have a picture of a particular threat agent as well as their relevance vis-à-vis any particular system and any particular organization. Ultimately, if we're not going to treat every attack as equal (the easiest course), then we have to come up with some yardstick (risk!) in order to prioritize some attacks over others. That is the point of the risk calculation. We are trying to build an understanding of which attackers and which attacks are relevant and which are less relevant or even irrelevant. This will vary from system to system. And this will vary significantly depending upon organization. Luckily, there are patterns.

In Chapter 2, we examined three different threat agents. Table 4.1 summarizes the attributes that can be associated with cyber criminals. Focusing for a moment on cyber crime, we can dig a little deeper into the questions posed above.

Table 4.1 Cyber Criminal Threat Attributes

Threat Agent	Goals	Risk Tolerance	Work Factor	Methods
Cyber criminals	Financial	Low	Low to medium	Known proven

Cyber crime is a for-profit business. The goal is monetary gain from attacking systems and system users. Cyber criminals go to jail when prosecuted; the goal is to *take*, that is, steal (in one way or another, scam, swindle, confidence game, black mail, outright theft) assets or money without getting caught and then successfully prosecuted. In other words, theft without punishment. As Kamala Harris wrote, *"cybercrime is largely opportunistic."*[9]

Like any for-profit business, there is more profit given less work to generate revenue. For that reason, cyber criminals tend to use proven methods and techniques.[*]

Hopefully, at this point, you have some sense of how to analyze a particular threat in terms of its components. It will be important for you to construct a reasonably holistic picture of each type of attacker whose goals can be met by attacking your organization's computer systems. Then, in light of the attackers' methodologies, consider which systems are exposed to those attack methodologies. In this way, you will begin to build a threat catalog for your organization and your systems. Again, no two threat catalogs are identical. Threat catalogs tend to be very organization and system dependent.

4.6.2 Exposure

Now let's consider the "exposure" portion of a risk calculation. Exposure in this context may be defined as the ability of an attacker to apply the attacker's methodologies[†] to a vulnerability. The attacker must have access to a vulnerability in order to exercise it, to "exploit" the vulnerability. At its most basic, if a vulnerability is not exposed to an attacker that's interested in that vulnerability, then the likelihood of that vulnerability being exploited goes down. As has been said, there is no zero possibility of exploitation. Still, when exposure can only be achieved through a significant amount of effort, hopefully too much effort, then the probability of exploitation can be considered to be low, or even very low, depending upon the protections. An attack cannot be promulgated unless a vulnerability is exposed to that particular methodology. The attacker needs access. And the attacker's methodology has to be matched to the type of vulnerability that has been exposed. There are many classes of vulnerability. Attacks tend to be quite specific. Many attackers specialize in a limited set of attack methodologies. Only the

---

[*] It's important to remember that cyber criminals may tend towards the well known, but that doesn't mean that they, along with other threat agents, won't also be creative.

[†] Attacker methods are often called "exploits." It is said that a computer attacker exploits a vulnerability. The specific technical steps necessary to successfully exercise a vulnerability are termed an "exploit."

most sophisticated attackers have at their disposal a wide range of methodologies, the complete gamut of attack possibilities. The more difficult a vulnerability is to reach, the harder it is going to be to exploit. Thus, "exposure" is a key component of the likelihood of an attack succeeding.

As an example, highly trusted administrative staff often have very privileged access. Certainly within their trust domain, a database administrator can generally perform a great many tasks on a database. In situations in which the database administrators are not being monitored (their activities and tasks on the databases not independently watched), they may be able to pretty much do anything with the data: change it, steal it, delete it. They may even have sufficient access to wipe away their "tracks," that is, delete any evidence that the database administrators have been tampering with the data.

In organizations that don't employ any separation of duties between roles, administrative staff may have the run of backend servers, databases, and even applications. In situations like this, the system administrators can cause catastrophic damage. As an example, I bring up the case of a network administrator for the City and County of San Francisco, California, USA. For whatever personal reasons, he became disgruntled with his employer. He changed the administrative password to the network routers for the internal network. Only he knew to what he had changed the password. No other administrative staff had access to work on the internal routers. Nothing could be changed. No problem that occurred could be fixed. All network administrative activity ceased. It was an unmitigated disaster. The employee refused to disclose this single, unlocking password for some number of weeks. He even endured a jail stay while refusing to comply. The City and County of San Francisco were held hostage for weeks on end because a single administrator had the power to stop all useful network administrative activity.

Even in mature and well-run shops, administrative staff will have significant power to do damage. The excepted protections against misuse of this power are:

- Strict separation of duties
- Independent monitoring of the administrative activities to identify abuse of administrative access
- Restriction of outbound capabilities at the time when and on the network where administrative duties are being carried out
- Restriction of inbound vectors of attack to administrative staff when they are carrying out their duties

It is beyond the scope of this book to detail how these security controls would be implemented. There are numerous ways to solve each of these problems. Still, despite the deep trust most organizations place in their administrative staff, the possibility of privileged insiders taking advantage of their access is usually met with a series of controls. The larger and more complex the organization, the more formal these controls are likely to be. The important point to take away from this example is that insiders, especially trusted insiders, have a lot of access. Vulnerabilities are exposed to the trusted insiders; if they so choose, they have the capability to exploit many, if not all, vulnerabilities. We can say that the "exposure" term* has a high value for the trusted insider, at least in the domain for which insiders have access.

Now let's contrast insider exposure to an external threat agent. An external attacker must somehow exploit a weakness to attain the intended goals. The weakness might be a computer vulnerability. But it can just as well be a human vulnerability: social engineering. Social engineering, the manipulation of a person or persons to gain access in order to eventually exploit computer vulnerabilities, is part of the one, two (three, four, . . .) punch that many sophisticated attacks employ. Much of the time, exploitation of a single vulnerability is not enough for the attacker to achieve her or his goal. Single vulnerability exploitation only occurs in the instance where the attack value is directly achieved through that single vulnerability: SQL injection or complete system takeover through remote code execution vulnerability, to name a couple of single vulnerability instances. In the case of executing SQL injection vulnerabilities that were thought to be protected by the authentication, if an attacker is not using any data that actually points back to the attacker—the attacker is using a false name, false address, false identity, and stolen credit card—the attacker can proceed to carry out injection attacks as long as the account remains open. There will be no consequences for the attacker if the attack is essentially anonymous.

The data is the goal. If the SQL injection is exposed to the attacker, as in cases in which an injection can be promulgated through a public Web interface that requires no authentication then, of course, a single vulnerability is all that the attacker requires. Occasionally, various runtimes will have vulnerabilities that allow an unauthenticated remote attack to be promulgated. The PHP web programming language has had a number of these that could be exploited through a PHP coded webpage. Certain Java application servers have had such vulnerabilities from time to time.

But, oftentimes, in order to get through a layer of defenses, like requiring an internal user name and password for privileged access, the privileged user becomes the target. This is where social engineering comes into play. The attacker delivers a payload through some media, email, phone call, malicious website, or any combination of two or more of these, such that the privileged user is tricked into giving up their credentials to the attacker.

In the world of highly targeted phishing attacks, where a person's social relations, their interests, even their patterns of usage, can be studied in detail, a highly targeted "spear-phishing" attack can be delivered that is very difficult to recognize. Consequently, these highly targeted spear-phishing techniques are much more difficult to resist. The highly targeted attacks are still relatively rare compared to a "shotgun" approach. If you, the reader, maintain a more or less public Web persona with an email address attached to that persona, you will no doubt see your share of untargeted attacks every day—that is, email spam or phishing attacks.

---

* The controls in the list above are mitigations to the high exposure of vulnerabilities to insider staff.

Certainly, if Nigerian prince scams did not work, we would not see so many in our email inboxes. Unfortunately, there are individuals who are willing to believe that some distant prince or government official has indeed, left them an exorbitant sum of money. In order to become instantly rich, a person has only to be willing to give bank account details to a complete stranger. And the same may be true for buying diet preparations and other "medicines" through unsolicited email. People do buy that stuff. People do respond to emails from "friends" who say they are in trouble and without funds and are, therefore, stuck in some distant city. You may delete every one of those emails. But rest assured, someone does respond.

Trusted insiders who are sophisticated system administrators are not likely to respond. These people are typically not the targets of the general level of spam email that you may see in your inbox day after day. An attacker is going to have to socially engineer, that is, fairly tightly target a sophisticated user in order to succeed. In today's interconnected work environment, most staff expect to receive and send email, both work-related and personal. Every connected person is exposed to generalized social engineering through email and social networks. Depending upon your job role, you may also be exposed to more targeted attacks. This is the human side of exposure in the digital age. We all visit websites on a fairly regular basis. At least occasionally, one or more search engine hits will be to a malicious website rather than a genuine service. We are all exposed to social engineering to some extent or other.

> [I]t was revealed that the Target hackers managed to sneak their way into the company's systems by stealing credentials from a contractor. From there, they planted malicious code targeting the retailer's payment terminals. In the wake of the attack, some Target customers have been hit with fraudulent charges, forcing banks to replace millions of credit and debit cards.[10]

In the computer sense, an attacker must be able to reach the vulnerability. Obviously, taking the foregoing explanation into account, if the attacker can trick someone into giving up credentials, the attacker can bypass access restrictions. But, in contrast, let's examine a common approach to restricting access for publicly available Software as a Service (SaaS) products.

Where the service is being offered for free but requires a valid credit card in order to register, there may be some illusion that the account and resulting access links to a legitimate individual. The last time I had information (some years ago), valid credit card numbers cost $.25 apiece on the black market. Email addresses are readily available for free. It is not too much of a leap to believe that a cyber criminal might tender a credit card that's still valid (briefly) with a free email address and, in this manner, get access to many "freemium"* services. Even if the access exists only until the stolen credit

---

* "Fremium" services offer a basic or limited package for free. Additional features require a subscription (the premium offering). A combination of the words "free" and "premium."

card fails, the attacker has unfettered access during the window before the fraudulent account is closed.

Occasionally, a legitimate user will carry out attacks as well; these may be thought of as a variation of the trusted insider.

"Exposure" is the ability of an attacker to make contact with the vulnerability. It is the availability of vulnerabilities for exploitation. The attacker must be able to make use of whatever media the vulnerability expresses itself through. As a general rule, vulnerabilities have a presentation. The system presents the vulnerability through an input to the system, some avenue through which the system takes in data. Classic inputs are:

- The user interface
- A command-line interface (CLI)
- Any network protocol
- A file read (including configuration files)
- Inter-process communication
- A system driver interface
- And more

Really, any input to a system may offer a channel for an attacker to reach the vulnerability. There are other, more subtle attack channels, to be sure. Among the more sophisticated methods are reverse engineering and tight control of code execution paths within a running binary. Let's constrain ourselves to inputs, as the vast majority of attack surfaces involve programmatic or user inputs to the system.

Even if a vulnerability is presented through an input, it still may not be exposed to a particular threat agent. Some inputs may be purposely exposed to a wide range of attackers. Think of a public, open website like a public blog. In fact, when the author opened his very first website, the web designer used the administrative user ID as the password. On Friday night, a first version of the site was completed. By Sunday morning, the website was defaced. Again, on the public Internet, attack is certain.

Some inputs, however, may be available to only a very restricted audience. Highly restricted management networks—unconnected machines in tightly controlled physical environments (which might be someone's home, depending on circumstances)—come to mind. If the input is not in the presence of an attacker who has the capabilities, knows about, and sees value in attacking that particular input, then the vulnerability is not exposed.

The exposure of a vulnerability, then, needs to be factored into our calculation of "credible attack vector." Without the necessary exposure, the vulnerability cannot be exercised by the threat agent. Thus, our credible attack vector term contains a false condition greatly lowering any risk rating that we might make. A vulnerability that is easily accessed by a threat agent interested in exploiting that particular vulnerability would then greatly raise the risk of exploitation. Exposure is a key contributing factor in our ability to assess the likelihood of a successful attack.

4.6.3 Vulnerability

Considering our constrained definition of risk (above), "vulnerability" should be defined with respect to computer security risk.

Vulnerability is any characteristic of the system that allows an attacker to commit cybercrime.[11]

As may be apparent from the definition above, we are particularly concerned here with software and design errors and flaws that have relevance to human attackers misusing a system in some manner. There are other definitions of vulnerability that are broader. And depending upon the role of the security architect and the context of ARA, a broader definition may be in order. For the purposes of this book, we confine ourselves to the simpler and more direct case: any weakness in the system that allows a human attacker an opportunity to use the system in ways not intended by the designers of the system, not in line with the objectives of the owners of the system, and, perhaps, not in line with the objectives or safety of users of the system. The techniques outlined in this book can be applied to a broader definition of threats or vulnerabilities. The definition is constrained in order to provide a more thorough explanation and examples around the most typical attack vectors and vulnerabilities that will be part of most assessments.

An enumeration of all the different types of vulnerabilities and their many variations is beyond the scope of this book. One only need to roll through the Common Weakness Enumeration database (www.cwe.mitre.org) to understand how many variations there are in the many classes of vulnerabilities. From the author's experience, an encyclopedic understanding of vulnerabilities is typically not required. Although an in-depth understanding of at least one variation in each class of vulnerability comes in handy during assessments, an in-depth understanding of many variations doesn't enhance the assessment a great deal. Treatments to protect against the vulnerability tend to apply to many variations of that vulnerability. Hence, the security architect performing assessments must know the classes of vulnerability that can occur for that kind of system. Understanding each variation of that class of vulnerability isn't necessary. Instead, what is required is the understanding of how those vulnerabilities occur and how they may be protected. And that can usually be done at a higher level of abstraction—a grosser level of granularity working with classes of vulnerability rather than specific vulnerability variations.

For instance, The OWASP "XSS Filter Evasion Cheat Sheet" contains 97 XSS variations, with some variations containing several to many subvariations.[12] The security architect might make a study of one of more of these to understand the mechanisms required of an attacker in order to exploit an XSS. What the architect must know is that the attacker needs access to a vulnerable page. The attacker must also induce the target user to load the page with browser scripting enabled. The language used in the attack must be specifically enabled in the user's browser. The attacker must include in the

URL attack the script that is the initial attack. All of these high-level conditions must be true irrespective of the details of the actual method used to execute the attacker's exploit script. A security architect who is assessing a web front end should understand XSS at this level in order to effectively design controls and in order to understand precisely what the target is and what is at risk from the successful exploitation of the vulnerability. And finally, developers are more likely to respond to a request for code changes if the security architect can speak authoritatively about what the coder must implement.

The treatments that are typically applied to XSS vulnerabilities are input validation and, where possible, some assurance that output does not include any encoding that allows an attacker to express any sort of scripting semantics. Additionally, defenders typically restrict access such that the system can't be probed by the millions of attacks hunting for weakness on the Internet. Although authentication by itself isn't a protection against XSS, it can reduce the attack surface somewhat for many, but not all situations. The amount of attack surface reduction depends upon the amount of restriction to a more trustable population that the authentication achieves. We explored this somewhat above.

Similarly, exploitation of any heap overflow will be unique to the organization of memory in an executable, on a particular operating system. The techniques can be generalized; the exploitation is always particular to a particular vulnerability. There are literally thousands of exploits. Anley et al. (2007)[13] include three examples of heap overflows in their introductory chapter and several chapters of samples under major operating systems, such as Windows, Linux, and Mac OS X. Again, a security architect assessing a system that is written in a language that must handle memory must understand the nature and attackability of heap overflows and should understand the generalized value gained by the attacker through exploitation. But an encyclopedic understanding of every possible heap overflow isn't necessary in order to proceed with a system analysis.

To prevent heap overflows, coders must handle system memory and heap memory with great care by allocating the size that will be needed, releasing memory properly, and never reusing the memory. In addition, restricting access to input channels may reduce the attack surface, as well.

I noted above that it's useful to understand the workings of at least one variation of each class of vulnerability. In order to apply the right treatments or the right security controls, which, ultimately, will be the requirements for the system, one needs to understand just how vulnerabilities are exercised and what exercise "buys" the attacker, that is, what is gained through exploitation.

As has been noted previously, resources are always limited. Therefore, it almost never makes sense to specify security controls that provide little additional security value. Each control should be applied for specific reasons: a credible attack vector that, when exercised, delivers something of attacker value. Since there is no one-to-one mapping between control and attack vector, one control may mitigate a number of vectors, and, concomitantly, it may take several treatments, or defenses, to sufficiently mitigate a single attack vector. It's an M:N problem.

Furthermore, it is typical for smart engineers to question requirements. This is particularly true if a security assessment has been mandated from outside the development team. The assessor, you, will need ammunition to build credibility with the development team. Your influence to make requirements and recommendations will be enhanced, once they have confidence that you actually know what you're talking about, understand the relevant threats and how real they are, and how they will attack the system. In the author's experience, engineers can be quite suspicious of security pronouncements and ivory tower requirements. Sometimes, the security assessors must prove their mettle. There's nothing like describing how a system can be misused, and stating some statistics about how often that happens, to clear the air and create a sense of common purpose. As usual, it's a mistake to ignore the people side of information security. Security architecture is probably as much about relationships as about anything technical.

Vulnerabilities can be introduced during the coding of the system. Issues such as XSS and the various types of overflows are almost always, at least in part, coding errors—that is, they are bugs.

Importantly, there's another type of miss that creates vulnerability in the system. These are the missed security features and design elements (sometimes architectural elements) that don't make it into the architecture and are not then designed into the system. Gary McGraw, Chief Technical Officer of Cigital, Inc., and author of *Software Security: Building Security In*, told me that "flaws" are 50% of the errors found in systems.* In my experience, when working with mature architecture practices, the number of architecture and design misses tends to be much lower. I can only speak anecdotally, because I have not kept any metrics on the distribution.

It may be worth noting that terming architecture and design misses as "flaws" might not serve a security architect integrating with other non-security architects. If comparing a system under analysis to the ideal security architecture, missing key security capabilities is certainly a flaw in that architecture. However, the term "flaws" might be received as a comment upon the maturity of practices, especially with senior management. But I'm pretty sure it certainly won't make any friends among one's sister and brother architects, one's peers. If I begin working with a development team and I then tell the hard-working members of that team that they had created a bunch of flaws in their design, I probably wouldn't be invited back for another session. "Flaw" might not be the most tactful term I could employ? Maybe this is a difference between consultation services and having spent a career working with and integrating into enterprise-level architecture practices?

---

* I don't know where Gary gets this number. However, the number of design misses or "flaws," in Gary's parlance, is not really important for our purposes. A single security requirement that has not been put into the system can open that system to misuse, sometimes catastrophic misuse. ARA is not about cumulative numbers, but rather, thoroughness.

I prefer the term "requirement." Architects proceed from requirements. This is a common term within every architecture practice with which I've worked. During the assessment, one builds the list of security requirements. Then, during the architecture phase, the security architect will likely be engaged in specifying how those requirements will be met. Finally, during the design phase, the architecture is turned into specific designs that can be implemented and coded. Delivering a set of architecture requirements fits neatly into the overall architecture process. Your "mileage," the needs of your organization, may, of course, be different.

The design makes the architecture buildable. Programmers work from the design.[14]

As may be seen, there must be some sort of weakness—whether it's a missing security feature such as authentication or encryption, or a coding error—a bug that exists, before an attacker can misuse the system as per our definition above. Thus, vulnerability is a key component of our credible attack vector term.

Hopefully, it's obvious that vulnerability is not the only term for calculating risk? Vulnerabilities are key. Without them, an attacker may not proceed, but, in and of themselves, vulnerabilities do not equate to risk. The other factors combined into our term, credible attack vector, must each be in place. And therein lays one of the keys to building a defense. We will take this up in a subsequent chapter. In short, interrupting the terms of the credible attack vector is a way to disrupt the ability of the attacker to promulgate a successful compromise. Restricting or removing terms with a credible attack vector delivers defense. Hence, not only is it useful to understand the nature of credible attack vectors in order to rate risk, it's also essential to building a defense-in-depth.

Obviously, if there are no vulnerabilities, we might require less robust and layered cyber defenses. It's important to note that even if a system contains no vulnerabilities, it still might need security features and controls in order to meet system objectives. For example, in an online banking system, each user must only access her or his own account details. Each user must not have access to any other user's details. This banking system requires an authorization model of some sort. Although it may be argued that failure to implement an authorization model actually introduces a vulnerability, failure to implement authorization properly also misses one of the key objectives of the banking system: safety and privacy of each user's financial details. The intertwining of vulnerability and necessary security features points back to our list of assessment prerequisites. Particularly, the assessor must understand the system's intended purpose, objectives, and goals. And it is good practice to understand how the system's purpose contributes to the organization's mission. It's probably a mistake to chase vulnerability in and of itself. Although important, vulnerability is not everything to the assessment, to the objectives of the system, or to risk calculation.

We have explored the subcomponents, the contributing factors, to a credible attack vector. A credible attack vector may substitute nicely in everyday risk assessments for the probability term. (For more in-depth information on the aforementioned, please refer to the following: Brook Schoenfield, "Just Good Enough Risk Rating," SANS Institute Smart Guide, released 2012.) Because risk calculation without sufficient data can be quite difficult and perhaps mathematically lengthy, we build a technique that is sufficient to deliver reasonable and consistent risk ratings—namely, a technique that is lightweight enough and understandable enough to be useful "in the trenches." I make no claim as to the mathematical provability of using the term credible attack vector as a substitute for a risk probability term. However, to its credit, there are literally thousands of system assessments that have used this calculation. There exist longstanding teams that have been recording these values over an extended period of many years in order to manage risk. I believe that credible attack vector is based upon sound concepts gleaned from the FAIR risk methodology.

I encourage you to break down the elements that make up the likelihood of the chain of events for successful compromise in whatever terms or scheme will work for you and your organization. As long as your terms represent, in some manner, the factors involved in connecting attackers to vulnerabilities through the attacker's exploits, any complete set of terms will probably suffice. I offer credible attack vector as only one possible approach, perhaps overly simplistic? My intention is to seed consideration on the nature of the probability problem. And, as has been mentioned, we can use the sub-terms of credible attack vector as a starting point for building defenses.

However your organization and you personally choose to calculate probability, please bear in mind that it's a complex of various elements, each of which should be considered before you can arrive at a probability of an attacker succeeding. Failure to honor this complexity will be a failure of your risk rating approach.

4.6.4 Impact

There is one term remaining in our pseudo-risk calculation. This is the loss value, or "impact" of a successful attack. If a monetary loss can be calculated, I believe that is generally preferable. However, when we consider losses whose monetary value may be more difficult to calculate, I use the term "impact" to reach beyond monetary calculations into the arena of general harm. Impact to a system, a process, a brand, or an organization is meant to be a slightly broader term. I use "impact" to encode all of the CIA elements: confidentiality, integrity, and availability. Impact may include the good will of customers and partners, which is notoriously difficult to estimate. Although it may be possible to associate monetary values to some losses, there are situations where that may be more difficult, or even impossible. However, understanding an impact as high, medium, or low is often sufficient.

As a simple example, consider an organization that maintains thousands of servers for its Internet accessible services. In this scenario, loss of a single server may be fairly insignificant. However, let's say that customer goodwill is exceedingly important to the business model. Given the importance of customers trusting an organization, should the compromised server get used to attack customers, or to display inappropriate messages, such a situation might result in a more significant loss. What if that server has become a base of operations for attackers to get at more sensitive systems? In any of the foregoing scenarios, a single compromised server among thousands that are untouched may be seen as a much greater loss.

Once again, we see that accounting for more than the vulnerability by itself yields different risk results. I cannot stress enough the importance of accounting for all the sub-terms within the credible attack vector. Once accounted for, the impact of exercising CAV depends, as we have seen, upon the risk posture of the system within an organizational context. To divorce these various component items from each other may yield no more than a "finger to the wind" gauge of possible risk values.

I reiterate that many vendors' products, vulnerability scanners, Global Risk and Compliance (GRC) systems, and the like often offer a "risk" value for vulnerability or noncompliance findings. Be suspicious of these numbers or ratings. Find out how these are calculated. I have sometimes found upon asking that these ratings are based upon the worst case scenario or upon the Common Vulnerabilities and Exposures (CVE) rating of similar issues.* Without context and relative completeness, these numbers cannot be taken at face value. This is why the Common Vulnerability Scoring System (CVSS) adds an "environmental" calculation in order to account for the local circumstances. There is no shortcut to gauging all the terms within CAV (or similar) and rating organizational impact in order to derive a reasonable sense of risk to a specific organization at a particular time, and in light of the organization's current capabilities.

4.7 Business Impact

There is obviously a technical impact that occurs from the exercise of most vulnerabilities. In our XSS examples, the technical impact is the execution of a script of the attacker's choosing in the context of the target's browser. The technical impact from a heap overflow might be the execution of code of the attacker's choosing in the context of an application at whatever operating system privileges that application is running. These technical details are certainly important when building defenses against these attacks. Further, the technical impact helps coders understand where the bug is in the code, and technical details help to understand how to fix the issue. But the technical impact isn't typically important to organizational risk decision makers. For them, the impact must be spelled out in terms of the organization's objectives. We might term this "business impact," as opposed to "technical impact."

---

* A simple search of CVE returns XSS vulnerabilities rated in a range from 1.9 (very low) to 9.3 (severe).

Continuing with the two examples that we've been considering, let's examine a couple of business impacts. As was explained earlier, a XSS attack is usually an attack via a web site targeting the user of that web site. The goal of the attacker will be something of value that the user has: his identity information, her account details, the user's machine itself (as a part of a botnet, for instance). The attacker is attempting to cause the user to unwittingly allow the attacker to do something to the user or to the user's machine. There are too many possibilities to list here. For a security architect who is trying to assess the risk of an XSS to an organization, it is probably sufficient to understand that the user of the web site is being attacked (and possibly hurt) through a mechanism contained on the web site. The organization's web site is the vector of attack, linking attacker to target.

From the web site owner's perspective, a web site becomes a tool in service to an attacker. The attacks are directed at the web site's users, that is, the organization's users. For example, consider an organization offering an open source project, providing a set of executable binaries for various operating systems (the "application") and the source code to which developers may contribute. Most open source project sites also foster a sense of community, a web site for interaction between users and coders. So, there's usually some sort of messaging, discussion forums, and search function. All the above functions are offered besides static and dynamic web content about the project.

Open source projects often don't have "leaders" so much as leadership. But imagine, if you will, that those who take responsibility for the project's web site must consider XSS vulnerability, which I'm sure, many must. What is the business impact of letting attackers target the users of the project's web site?

I would guess that such a site might be able to sustain an occasional user being targeted, since success of the attack is not guaranteed, given an up-to-date, security sandboxed browser. Further, if the site does not require the user to turn on site scripting in their browser, users are free to use the site in a more secure manner, less vulnerable to XSS.

But if I were responsible for this site, I would not want to squander my user confidence upon XSS attacks from my web site. Put yourself, just for a moment, in the shoes of the people dedicating their time, usually volunteered, to the project. I can well imagine that it is precisely user confidence that will make my project a success. "Success" in the open source world, I believe, is measured by user base, namely, the number of users who download and use the application. And success is also measured through the number of code contributions and contributors, and by the level of activity of code and design discussion. If users do not feel safe coming to the project's web site, none of the foregoing goals can be met.

Hence, the business impact of a XSS to an open source project is loss of user and contributor confidence and trust. Further, if the web site is buggy, will users have confidence that the application works properly? Will they trust that the application does not open a vulnerability that allows an attack on the user's machine? I'm guessing that user confidence and user trust are paramount and must be safeguarded accordingly.

Now, we can assess the risk of a XSS bug *within the context of the organzation's goals.* And we can express the impact of a successful attack in terms that are applicable to a given open source project: "business impact."

Let us now consider the heap overflow case above. Like XSS, an overflow allows the attacker to run code or direct an application's code to do something unintended (such as allowing the attacker to write to the password store, thus adding the attacker as a legitimate user on the system). Heap overflows occur most often in programs created with languages that require the programmer to directly handle memory.* The word "application" covers a vast array of software scenarios, from server-side, backend systems to individual programs on an endpoint, laptop, desktop, smart phone, what-have-you. Apple's iOS phone operating system, a derivative of the Mac OS X, is really a UNIX descendant, "under the covers"; iOS applications are written in a derivative of the C programming language. Because the universe of applications written in memory handling languages is far too vast to reasonably consider, let us constrain our case down to an endpoint application that executes some functionality for a user, has a broad user base (in the hundreds of millions), and is produced by a company whose mission is to produce broadly accepted and purchased software products. Examples might be Microsoft or Adobe Systems. Each of these companies produces any number of discreet applications for the most popular platforms.

A heap overflow that allows an attacker to misuse a widely distributed application to attack a user's machine, collect the user's data, and ultimately, to perhaps control a user's machine really is not much different, in a technical aspect, from XSS. The attacker misuses an application to target the user's endpoint (and, likely, the user's data). The difference is one of scale. Scripts usually run in the security sandboxed context of the user's browser. Applications run directly on the operating system at the privilege level of the logged-in user. For broadly distributed applications, privilege might be restricted (typically on enterprise-supplied computers). But most users run personally owned computers at "administrator" or some similar high level of privilege. If the attacker can execute her or his code at this level, she or he has the "run of the box," and can do with the computer whatever is desired. Users are thus at great risk if they use their computers for sensitive activities, such as finances and medical information. In addition, at this level of privilege, the computer might be used by the attacker to target other computers, to send spam (perhaps through the email accounts of the user?), or to store illegal digital materials.

I believe that it isn't too much of a leap to imagine the business impact to an Independent Software Vendor (ISV) from a widely distributed heap overflow that

---

*Though it must be remembered that even languages that protect application programmers from memory handling typically program the runtime environment with a memory handling language such as C/C++, at least partially. Therefore, although the application programmer may not have to worry about overflow issues, the runtime must certainly be coded carefully.

allows execution of code of the attacker's choosing. Again, the ISV is staring at a loss of customer confidence, in the software, in the brand, in the company itself.

4.7.1 Data Sensitivity Scales

Chapter 2 introduced data sensitivity as a determinant of system criticality. Uncovering the sensitivity of the data flowing and stored by a system is a key part of an architectural assessment and threat model. Sensitive data is likely to be a target of attack and may offer value, sometimes great value, to potential attackers, the threat agents. But just as importantly, the reason data is classified as sensitive should be due to the potential harm to the organization if the data is disclosed before the organization intends to disclose it.

Obviously, the customer's personal, health, and financial data must be protected, for customer trust and goodwill and by law, at least in the United States.* But there are numerous other reasons for declaring data sensitive. In the United States, insider trading laws prohibit the sale of publicly traded stock with knowledge of financial results for the company before the public has the information. These laws were put into effect in order to provide a fair trading environment in which everyone has the same information. The laws also prevent the manipulation of stocks based upon prior, "inside" knowledge. Because of these laws, anyone who has access to such information before it is disclosed must be considered a financial insider, whether they are aware of their status or not.

That awareness is important because a database administrator who has access to pre-announce financial information, even casually, while doing other unrelated tasks, is still bound by the insider trading rules. If she or he inadvertently and unintentionally sells company stock during a quiet (no trading) period, this administrator might have broken the insider trading law. Due to the broad applicability of the law, pre-announcement financials are typically considered to be among a public company's deepest secrets. The moment the financial results are announced, however, they become part of the public domain.

Patented prescription drug formulas have a similar shape. They are financially key company intellectual property that must remain proprietary and protected so long as they are in development. Once the formula receives approval for marketing, it is patented and thus protected by law. The formula becomes part of the patent's public record and need not be held secret at that point.

For a software maker, the algorithms that make up the unique properties of the code that produces the company's revenue will typically be a closely guarded secret. Even when the algorithm is protected under patent law, the algorithm's implementation may be considered secret, since a competitor, given knowledge of the source code, could

---

* Many other countries have more stringent personal data protection laws than the United States, of course. But privacy protection law is beyond the scope of this work.

potentially build a similar product without incurring the research and development cost for an original design. Security software, especially cryptography implementations, tend to be held quite closely even though the algorithms are public. This is so that if there is an error in the implementation, attackers will not find out before the implementer can fix the error.

These are a few examples of data that may be considered "secret" or "proprietary," or closely held by an organization. Each organization must decide which types of data, if lost, will represent a significant loss or impact to the company. There will also be information that may incur impact if disclosed, but which won't be key or critical. And most organizations have public information that is intended for disclosure.

A mature security architecture practice will understand the data sensitivity rating scale of the organization and how to apply it to different data types. By classifying the sensitivity of data, the assessor has information about the required security posture needed to protect the data to the level that is required. Further to the point of this section, loss or impact can be expressed in business terms by noting which data are targets and by understanding the potential effects on the system and the organization when particular data are disclosed or tampered with. Data sensitivity, then, becomes a shorthand tool for expressing the business impact of a risk.

Understanding the business impact of the exercise of a credible attack vector is the goal of a risk rating. Although severity is one dimension, ultimately, it is the amount of effect that can radiate from a compromise that is important. With that in hand, decisions about how much risk to tolerate, or not, are properly informed.

4.8 Risk Audiences

There are different audiences, different stakeholders, who need to understand risk through unique, individualized perspectives. It's a good practice to craft risk messages that can be understood from the perspectives of each stakeholder group. As has been noted, decision makers, namely, organization leaders, typically prefer that risk be stated in business terms, what I've termed "business impact." Business impact is the effect that the successful exercise of a credible attack vector will have on the organization's operations and goals.

But as we've already seen, there also exists a purely technical impact. Defenders need to understand the sorts of things that can happen to the attacked computer system. Without this understanding, defending the system adequately is not possible. Security defense must be matched to attack method and is always implemented to protect something of value. Further, one can be more precise when one understands the technical targets of particular attack methods.

There are other audiences beyond the purely technical. Each audience may need its own expression of impact. For instance, program and project managers will want to understand how successful compromise will affect their deliverables: implementation phases, schedules, resources, and budgets. Project managers are also likely to want to know whether they have missed some step in the development lifecycle. Architects will require an architectural view of impacts: which components are affected, which data can no longer be considered trustworthy, and what communication flow will need protection. Developers will want to know what features should have been delivered or what the correct behavior should have been.

Of course, not every impact will have relevance to each of these perspectives. And some stakeholders will only want impacts (executives, usually), while others (engineers) may need to understand the attack vector, as well. The wise practitioner couches risk communication in the terms best understood by the different viewpoints. "Impact" may be expressed in multiple ways so that each person can understand a risk and why it's important to address the risk. Impact can be tailored specifically, depending upon which decisions are being made surrounding a risk. Usually, people need to understand why a risk is important to them before they will be willing to make changes in order to mitigate the risk.

4.8.1 The Risk Owner

Which brings us to the "risk owner." Depending upon the organization's structure and mission, there may be people who are held accountable for decisions that accept or mitigate organizational risk. In my years of very unscientific surveys of enterprise information security professionals, my sense is that many enterprise-sized organizations let business leaders (usually, a vice president or above) decide about what risk to take, how much residual risk to accept rather than treat, and which attack vectors can remain unmitigated. But certainly, even in my casual (though lengthy) observation, organizations big, medium, and small differ, sometimes dramatically, with respect to exactly who can make these decisions.

Since one of the purposes of ARA is to uncover risks from digital systems, naturally the process is going to search for and find risk. Not all of that risk can be mitigated. And in some organizations, none of it will be mitigated until a decision maker chooses to apply a treatment.

In some organizations, the risk assessor may be empowered to make decisions, anywhere from making all the computer risk decisions to only those that fall within organization guidance, standards, or policies. A decision split that I have seen numerous times is constrained to where a risk can be entirely treated by following an organization standard or industry standard, or similar. The assessor is empowered to decide upon a design to fulfill the requirement. However, if the risk cannot be treated to at least an industry standard approach, then it must be "raised."

Raising risk means bringing the untreated or residual risk to a decision maker for a risk decision. These decisions typically take one of three mutually exclusive forms:

1. Assumption of the risk: "proceed without treatment," that is, the organization agrees to bear the burden of the consequences, should an impact occur.

2. Craft an exception to treating the risk immediately, that is, "fix the risk later, on an agreed-upon schedule."

3. Treat the risk immediately.

In order to raise a risk for a decision, one must know to whom to raise the risk. The person who can make this decision for an organization is the "risk owner." This is the person or persons who have sufficient responsibility to the organization that matches the scope of the risk.

[R]isk owner: person or entity with the accountability and authority to manage a RISK[15]

In large organizations, there may be an escalation path based upon the impact of the risk, from team, to group, to division, to enterprise. Depending upon how much of the entire organization may be impacted, the risk owner might escalate from the project team (project delayed or over budget), to the director for a group (operations of the group are impacted), to a vice president of a division, or even to the top tier of management for risks involving the reputation of the entire enterprise. In short, it is the impact of the risk that dictates at what level a decision can be made. But of course, there is subjectivity when scoping impact. Although this subjectivity needs to be acknowledged, it is still usually possible to ascertain the scope of impact in terms of organizational levels and boundaries. If in doubt, go up a level. It never hurts to have clear decision-making power. On the other hand, if a decision is made by those without the authority to make it, they put the organization at risk. Risk decisions made at a level insufficient to the scope of the impact will then likely be hidden from those that do have the authority. Impact surprises from risks that had previously been discovered but have not been made known to decision makers are rarely "fun."

Before any assessments are performed, the assessor should have a firm grasp on just which roles have decision-making power over particular impact scopes. At each level (whether a single level or many), the role with the decision-making authority will be the risk owner. Having a clear understanding of just who is capable of making which decisions is critical so that any residual risk that is uncovered will be dealt with appropriately. Whether decisions are made collectively by all participants, or the organization has a strict hierarchy (with all decisions made at the top level), whatever the form, the assessor must understand the form and the roles. Given the difficult and changeable nature of cyber risk, there is sure to be residual risk for which hard decisions will need to be made, and risk assumed or treated.

Along with risk ownership is the escalation path of decision making. This is also an important prerequisite to assessment. Of course, fully collective organizations, where decisions are made by all the participants, have no formal, hierarchical escalation path. But that doesn't mean that there's no formal escalation path at all. The escalation might be from a working group to the governing body. In organizations that make decisions in a fully participatory manner, the escalation will be to a time and place where everyone can participate, where all can be a part of the decision.

In enterprises that make some decisions through some form of informal consensus, there is usually a deciding "vote" in case of a deadlock at each peer level. Typically, that structure will be the escalation path. And in the typical, hierarchical corporate or government organization, the decision making structure is usually laid out clearly. In these more hierarchical organizations, the security architect must understand just how much or how little each level may decide, to what amount of harm, and for what organizational scope of impact. This might be given in dollar amounts: Managers may decide for $15,000 of harm, which is confined to their team. Directors may have $50,000 discretion, with impact bounded strictly to the director's group. And vice presidents might have $250,000 discretion, which is confined to their division. These numbers are merely examples, not a recipe. Each organization decides these things locally. The key is to find out some measure of risk discretion confined to impact to an organization boundary *before* having to escalate a risk. In other words, know who the risk owners are within the organization and for how much and how wide the risk owners may decide.

4.8.2 Desired Security Posture

The ultimate goal of an ARA for the security of any system is to bring that system to a desired security posture. The operative term is "desired" or "intended." Since there is no possibility of "100% secure" (since the world is full of unknowns), and particularly since merely connecting systems together and interacting through automation is fraught with cyber risk and cyber attacks against vulnerable software, a certain level of defense is almost always called for. But what is that "level of defense"?

There is no easy prescription or recipe to determine the desired risk posture. One can turn to the organization's security policy and standards as a starting point. In organizations whose cyber-security function is relatively mature, there may exist standards that point the way to the controls that must be implemented.

Experienced practitioners may have a good "gut feeling" for what level of risk is acceptable and what is not. A mature GRC function may have conducted research into the organization's risk tolerance and concerns. Desired posture may be calculated as a percentage of system cost or expected revenue. Or any combination of the foregoing may provide sufficient clues to derive a security posture.

In the absence of any of the above, it may come down to conducting interviews and listening to what is acceptable or not among the decision makers. In any event, it helps mitigate the influence of one's personal risk tolerance to understand what the organization seeks from risk assessments, how much security needs to be implemented, and what risk can be tolerated.

4.9 Summary

The calculation of risk is fundamental to security assessment and threat modeling. Ultimately, some reliable and repeatable risk methodology will have to be adopted in order for priority decisions to be made about which attack surfaces will receive mitigation, how much mitigation to build, and which risks can be tolerated without unduly impinging on an organization's mission.

In an effort to simplify risk calculation such that it can be performed rapidly during security assessments, we've proposed a rather simple approach: All of the terms in our "credible attack vector" must be true in order for a threat agent to be able to exercise a vulnerability. Even if there is a credible attack vector, the impact of the exploit must be significant or there is no risk.

The terms in a credible attack vector are:

- Threat (exploit)
- Exposure
- Vulnerability

Each of these terms is further broken down so that the aspects of a successful attack can be assessed in separate and distinct terms. In fact, we propose substituting credible attack vector for the probability term in the standard, well-known insurance risk equation that was presented at the beginning of this chapter.

When we build security defenses, we can use a simplified Boolean approach to each of the terms in credible attack vector. To interrupt any single term is to prevent an attack. This simplified approach allows us to more precisely specify security controls as we build our defense-in-depth.

In this chapter, we have narrowed the scope of the term "risk" to precisely fit the purpose of security assessment and threat modeling. We have proposed one methodology as an example of how risk can be understood and rated fairly easily. Whatever methodology is used, it will have to be repeatable by the analysts who'll provide security assessments, build threat models, and provide requirements for a system's security posture.

References

1. Jones, J. A. (2005). "An Introduction to Factor Analysis of Information Risk (FAIR)." Risk Management Insight LLC. Retrieved from http://riskmanagementinsight.com/media/documents/FAIR_Introduction.pdf.
2. Ibid.
3. Schoenfield, B. (2012). "Just Good Enough Risk Rating." *Smart Guide*. SANS Institute.
4. Harkins, M. (2013). *Managing Risk and Information Security: Protect to Enable*, p. xv. Apress Media, LLC.
5. Hopkin, P. (2012). *Fundamentals of Risk Management: Understanding, Evaluating and Implementing Effective Risk Management*, 2nd ed., p. 14. Institute of Risk Management (IRM). Kogan Page.
6. Jones, J. A. (2005). "An Introduction to Factor Analysis of Information Risk (FAIR)." Risk Management Insight LLC. Retrieved from http://riskmanagementinsight.com/media/documents/FAIR_Introduction.pdf.

7. Ibid.

8. U.S. Senate Committee on Commerce, Science, and Transportation. (March 26, 2014). A "Kill Chain" Analysis of the 2013 Target Data Breach. Majority Staff Report For Chairman Rockefeller.

9. Harris, K. D. (February 2014). "Cybersecurity in the Golden State." California Department of Justice.

10. Welch, C. (February 14, 2014). "Target's Cybersecurity Team Raised Concerns Months Before *Hack*." The Verge. Retrieved from http://www.theverge.com/2014/2/14/5412084/target-cybersecurity-team-raised-concerns-before-hack.

11. Mansourov, N. and Campara, D. (2011). *System Assurance: Beyond Detecting Vulnerabilities.* p. xv. Morgan Kaufmann Publishers.

12. Hansen, R. (2013). "XSS Filter Evasion Cheat Sheet." OWASP.org. Retrieved from https://www.owasp.org/index.php/XSS_Filter_Evasion_Cheat_Sheet.

13. Anley, C., Heasman, J., Lindner, F., and Richarte, G. (2007). *The Shellcoder's Handbook: Discovering and Exploiting Security Holes,* 2nd ed. John Wiley & Sons.

14. Schoenfield, B. (2014). "Applying the SDL Framework to the Real World" (Ch. 9). In *Core Software Security: Security at the Source*, pp. 255–324. Boca Raton (FL): CRC Press.

15. ISO Technical Management Board Working Group on risk management, ISO 31000:2009, Risk management – Principles and guidelines, 2009-11-15, ICS, 03.100.01. Available from: https://www.iso.org/obp/ui/#iso:std:iso:31000:ed-1:v1:en.

Chapter 5

Prepare for Assessment

In this chapter, we will review the assessment and threat modeling process that has been introduced in previous chapters. The process has been described at a high level, though presented piece-by-piece, wherever a particular step of the process was relevant to fully understand the background material necessary for assessment. In this chapter, we will go through, in a step-wise fashion, a single example architecture risk assessment (ARA) and threat model. The goal is to become familiar with the process rather than to complete the assessment. In Part II, we will apply these steps more thoroughly to six example architectures in order to fully understand and get some practice in the art and craft of ARA. The example used in this chapter will be completed in Part II.

5.1 Process Review

At the highest level, an assessment follows the mnemonic, ATASM:

Architecture ➤ Threats ➤ Attack Surfaces ➤ Mitigations

Figure 5.1 shows the ATASM flow graphically. There are architecture tasks that will help to determine which threats are relevant to systems of the type under assessment.

Figure 5.1 Architecture, threats, attack surfaces, mitigations.

The architecture must be understood sufficiently in order to enumerate the attack surfaces that the threats are applied to. Applying specific threats to particular attack surfaces is the essential activity in a threat model.

ATASM is meant merely as a very high-level abstraction to facilitate keeping the assessment process in mind. In addition, ATASM may help beginning assessors order and retain the details and specifics of the ARA process. There are many steps and details that must be understood and practiced to deliver a thorough ARA. Having a high-level sequence allows me to retain these numerous details while I proceed through an analysis. My hope is to offer you an abstraction that makes this process easier for you, as well.

5.1.1 Credible Attack Vectors

At some essential level, much of an ARA is focused as an attempt to enumerate the complete set of credible attack vectors (CAVs). If you recall from Chapter 2, a credible attack vector was defined as follows:

> **Credible attack vector:** *A credible threat exercising an exploit on an exposed vulnerability.*

Recalling the risk term discussion from Chapter 4, a CAV encapsulates the three threat sub-terms into a single expression:

- Threat
- Exposure
- Vulnerability

Each of these terms is likewise composed of details that were explained in Chapter 4. If you don't feel comfortable with CAV, in particular, and computer security risk, in general, you may want to review Chapter 4 before you proceed.

Risk is the critical governing principle that underlies the entire risk assessment and threat modeling process. Ultimately, we must mitigate those computer attacks that are likely to impinge upon the use of the system under assessment and upon efforts to obtain the objectives of the organization. As my friend, Anurag "Archie" Agrawal, says, "[threat modeling is] all about risk. . . ." Still, you will find that "risk" is not mentioned as much as priorities.

As you walk through the process, filtering and prioritizing, you will be calculating risk. Although a formal risk calculation can be, and often is, a marker of a mature security architecture practice, by itself, simply understanding the risks is only one goal for an ARA and threat model. We also need to know which risks can be treated and which cannot, and produce an achievable set of requirements that will get implemented. Risk is the information that drives these decisions, but it is not the sole end result of the ATASM process. For this reason, risk calculation is built into the steps of ATASM and underlies much of the process, rather than being a separate and distinct calculation exercise.

5.1.2 Applying ATASM

Assume that the analyst (you?) has completed the required homework and has studied the background subjects sufficiently to understand the context into which the system will be deployed. The "context" is both technical and organizational and may be broken down into strategy, structures, and specifications. To reiterate, this knowledge set includes at least the following:

Table 5.1 Required Background Information

Strategy	Threat landscape	Risk posture	
Structures	The set of possible controls	Existing security limitations	
Specifications	Data sensitivity	Runtime and execution environments	Deployment models

Table 5.1 summarizes the typical background information an assessor brings to an assessment. These topics have been arranged with the "3 S's" merely for convenience and to provide an ordering principle.

No matter how one may choose to order these topics, it remains that before beginning an ARA and threat model, one will need to have examined the current threat landscape into which the system will be deployed. Further, investigation will have taken place to understand the risk posture of the organization that will use and deploy the system as well as what the overall risk tolerance of the organization is. One must understand the current state of security capabilities and infrastructure in order to understand what controls are easiest to implement and what will be a future state (perhaps only a wish?). Since no security is perfect, there will be limitations that must be taken into account. Certain approaches or security technologies may be impossible, given the current state of affairs. If the assessor wants to provide real-world mitigations, she or he will need to know what can and cannot be accomplished in the present, in the short term, in the medium term, and perhaps longer still. Each execution environment typically presents a unique set of security services and a unique set of vulnerabilities and security challenges. A system may take advantage of the services but, likewise, must take account of the runtime's weaknesses. Finally, as was noted previously, different deployment models require different architectural approaches to security. Customer premise equipment must be capable of implementing the owner's security posture. Systems destined for an infrastructure that is controlled by an organization will inherit that infrastructure's security weaknesses and strengths.

- Runtime Models
- Deployment
- Deployment Processes

The wise security analyst will arm her or himself with sufficient background knowledge to thoroughly assess a system. The enumerated background subjects create a strong basis for ARA.

Recall from Chapter 2 a list of steps that, taken together, constitute a high-level procedure for conducting an ARA. Figure 5.2 orders those steps by the high-level ATASM abstraction. That is, architecture steps are followed by threat-related tasks. The results of these are applied to an enumeration of attack surfaces, which, when prioritized, can then be defended by building a set of risk mitigations, a defense-in-depth of security controls.

Each of the steps outlined in Figure 5.2 is, of course, what developers call a "non-trivial" activity. We will tease these steps apart more fully below. In this book, the steps

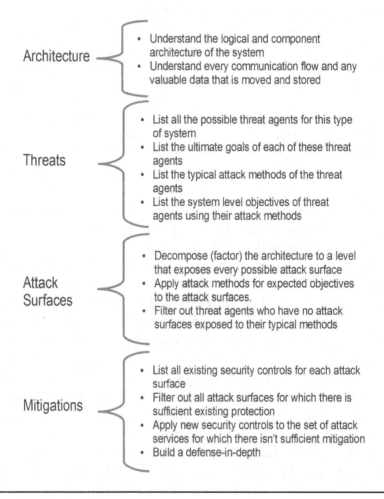

Figure 5.2 ATASM procedure steps.

are presented as a sequenced set of tasks. The first assessments will proceed in this orderly manner. However, in the real world, the process can be more like peeling an onion.[*]

You may factor an architecture into defensible units and then discover that there are other critical systems that were not diagrammed in the architecture, as presented up to that point. Or you may be writing what you think is a complete list of security requirements, only to discover that a security control you thought existed was actually designed out or had been phased out and is no longer available. The implementation team may tell you that they absolutely must deploy a technology about which you know next to nothing. Encountering an unknown technology will normally cause an assessor to research the technology and learn about its security history, its weaknesses and strengths, before proceeding. During many agile development processes, the design (and even the architecture) will change during coding, which can entail shifting security requirements around to accommodate the changing software architecture. There are can be delays obtaining necessary technologies and equipment or changes in scope or schedule.

Any of the above scenarios, in isolation or in various combinations, may cause a threat model to become "stale," to be incomplete or even obsolete. The assessor will have to return to once again achieving an understanding of the architecture and then move through the succeeding steps to account for new information or other significant changes. (In other words, the process begins again at the architecture stage in order to analyze the new material.) The worst case is when there has been no notice of a need for reassessment, the system is near deployment (or already live and in production!), and suddenly, changes made during development surface such that the changes invalidate most or all of the security posture. Such events can and do happen, even in the best run organizations. The short of it is, learn the steps that must be taken. Proceed in as orderly and organized a fashion as possible. But don't expect complex system development to be entirely linear. Change is the only constant.

5.2 Architecture and Artifacts

We spent considerable time in Chapter 3 understanding what system architecture does and why it's important for security assessment. We've looked at a few architectures, both to understand the architecture and from the perspective of what a security architect needs to know in order to perform an ARA. We will examine these architectures in greater depth in Part II. Let us examine what needs to be accomplished with the architecture activities.

---

[*] John Steven, an industry-recognized authority on threat modeling, calls the threat modeling process "fractal." Adding to the organic exploration forays to which John refers, I believe that, in practice, the process tends also to be recursive. John Steven's biography is available from OWASP: https://www.owasp.org/index.php/Threat_Modeling_by_John_Steven.

Part of understanding a system architecture is to understand the system's overall functions and what objectives deploying the system is hoping to achieve. An assessment should start at the beginning by determining the system's intended purpose and how it fits into the overall goals of the deploying organization and its users. This information will "ground" the architecture into the real world and will place the architecture within its intended context. Ascertaining the overall purpose may be enough information to determine the appropriate security posture of the system, especially when the assessor is familiar enough with the risk tolerance and security posture of the organization as a whole.

Try not to start with technologies, if you can avoid it. Instead, steer the conversation back up to purpose and, perhaps, an overall architecture or how this system will fit into an enterprise architecture (if the enterprise architecture is known).

5.2.1 Understand the Logical and Component Architecture of the System

First, of course, one must know what a logical and/or component architecture is. Hopefully, you have some feel for this gained through reading Chapter 3?

The logical architecture represents each logical function that will be in the system. These groupings are irrespective of how many individual units of each function get instantiated and irrespective of the physical architecture. Generally, that there are computers (servers?) and operating systems is assumed and not detailed; the physical network addresses assigned to each network interface are unimportant in the logical view. Instead, functions like business logic versus the presentation versus back office accounting systems versus databases are separated out. It is assumed that all of these are connected by some sort of network architecture. Oftentimes, the system management function will be detailed as a separate logical function, even if the business logic and the management module share the same server. If the functions are different and these functions are separated in some manner (process space, execution environment, what have you), then in a logical architecture, the functions will be shown as separate units.

In a component architecture, it is the various components that are differentiated. For instance, if the business logic has a database and the management function also has separated data, then each of these databases will be detailed. In order to depict the component relationship, the business database can be shown as a part of the business component, while the management database can be depicted as a part of the management component. This makes sense in the component view, even if in actuality, both databases reside in a common data layer, or even if these are different tables in the same database server. The concept is to represent all the units that will make up the architecture, not to represent where and how they will be executing.

As you may see, each of these views, logical and component, has advantages and disadvantages. No one representation can possibly show everything for even modestly complex systems. Hence, there are many possible views. If you remember from Chapter 3, an assessment may take several different views in order to uncover all the relevant information. For more complex systems, you will likely end up stitching together the information from several views because security is the matrix domain that involves and is implemented at many levels, often in many, if not all, of the components of a system.

Until details of implementation are considered, the physical architecture will likely have too many details and may certainly obscure important relationships between functions. For instance, for many years I worked with an eCommerce architecture whose physical network architecture actually consisted of a group of seven or eight huge switches. On the face of it, that might seem a dreadful Internet facing architecture? The networking equipment is one big block? Where are trust boundaries within that single, physical group of switches? What if an attacker gained one of those switches? The whole would be lost, yes? Where are the layers to protect more valuable resources by offering bastion systems that, if lost, would prevent loss of every system connected to the block of switches?

The logical architecture was actually a standard three-tier web architecture, with very strict rules between layers, bidirectional authentications across trust boundaries, valued resource protected by bastion systems that terminated and then validated traffic before passing across trust boundaries, and similar protections. Looking only at the physical architecture would not properly represent the way that traffic flowed and the trust boundaries that existed. It was the logical architecture that appeared to separate out the firewalls (and restrictions) of each layer and that demonstrated how traffic flowed or was stopped. All of this was performed by a group of multifunction switches with different blade inserts for the various functions that implemented the logical architecture. Although ultimately understanding that physical architecture made me a better, more competent system assessor, I didn't need that information for quite some time, as long as I understood the logical architecture of the infrastructure.

When deciding precisely where to place network restrictions or administrative security controls, the physical architecture will be required. Still, for coming to an understanding of a complex system—all of the systems' functions and the components that will implement those functions—the logical architecture is usually the right starting point. As we have seen in Chapter 3, the logical and the component architecture views often get put together into the same view; for the sake of convenience, let's call that view "the logical architecture." Ultimately, in the process of decomposition and factoring, an analysis must get down to components, perhaps even modules, and processes. As has been said, the point of factoring the architecture is to uncover attackable units and defensible boundaries. And as we have seen, the unit down to which we go depends on several factors; there is no single rule to apply; architecture decomposition for security is an art that has to be learned through experience.

As guidance, a logical architecture should start with each function in broad, inclusive categories delineated by functions such that the entire system can be represented. This representation can be along technological groupings, or the delineation can be along business functions, or, often, a combination of technological "stack" and business functions. These two dimensions can be mixed successfully in a "logical" architecture as long as the architecture representation doesn't become too crowded to understand. If the representation, that is the diagram, becomes so busy that it can't be read or lines of integration can't be followed, that's usually the time to come up a level of granularity and group similar units together, at the same time showing the detail in sub views.

The more complex the system, the more likely it is that a security analysis will require multiple views of that system. A guiding principle is to start at a gross level that can be easily understood and then decompose to detail, factoring the architecture in ever more detailed units until all the attack services and all the defensible boundaries are understood. The "units" that will be useful depends on the security assumptions surrounding the system under analysis. As we saw in Chapter 3, a system that is exposed on an endpoint has a different set of boundaries than a system that inherits the security of a well-managed infrastructure. You may remember that one of the important knowledge sets that is brought to an analysis is the deployment model of the system (or all the deployment models that are involved)? And, of course, the execution environment and its boundaries and security capabilities also partially determine just how deep a unit must be, or at what atomicity the architecture will have to be factored.

Essentially, you must begin somewhere and then investigate. Asking implementation team members for a "logical" or a "component" architecture will get the conversation and, thus, the investigation started.

Personally, unless I get a diagram similar to Figures 3.1 and 3.2 (in Chapter 3), which are too gross to have much security meaning, I try to work with what the team produces, moving either up or down in granularity, as necessary. That discovery process is often best done on a whiteboard, captured, and then diagrammed in some more permanent form that can be shared and subsequently become a part of the record of the security assessment. Other experts in threat modeling sometimes provide more direction by providing an architecture template. That's a perfectly reasonable approach, as well. As was explained earlier, I prefer to integrate into any existing processes rather than imposing a different approach from outside. Depending upon your organization's style, either of these approaches can work; the right approach will depend upon the organization and your relationship to implementation teams and any existing architecture practice.

5.2.2 Understand Every Communication Flow and Any Valuable Data Wherever Stored

Starting from a logical architecture, as described above, every communications flow, whether to exchange data or control messages—that is, irrespective of the purpose of the communications flow—should be diagrammed. Recalling the AppMaker architecture introduced in Chapter 3, Figure 5.3 (reprised from Figure 3.4) can be considered a representative "Data Flow Diagram" (DFD). The DFD portrays not only communication

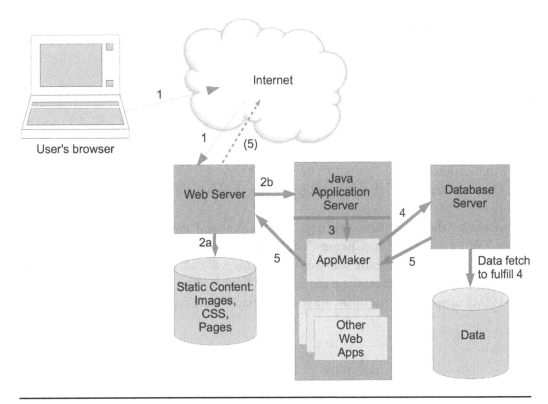

Figure 5.3 Data Flow Diagram of AppMaker.

flows, but their direction, as well. Single-headed (single-pointed) arrows are preferred. Especially in request/response protocols such as HTTP, a response can be assumed.

Since the ordering of authentication and validation is important, and the origination across trust boundaries is critical to understand, the single-headed arrow, from origination pointing to the destination, is by far the preferred representation. This is for security purposes. Other architects may require other views using bidirectionally pointed arrows for their purposes. That's OK. But I caution the security analyst to insist upon understanding origination and destination, especially in client/server applications in which the origination of the communication is going to be critical to getting the security controls correctly placed, and the destination will be the most common attack surface—the attack coming from client to server, from requester to responder. Building a defense will start at the server. (This does not necessarily exclude the client. But the obvious attack surface to be defended is usually the destination side.)

A way to proceed is to start with the logical architecture and add the communications flows. In Figure 5.3, we have an architecture that is separated, both along functional lines:

- Server for static content
- AppMaker application construction function

- Database software
- Data repository
- Content repository

And along technology boundaries:

- User's browser
- Web server
- Application server
- Database server and data repository

Hopefully, the combination of logical function and component can be seen in Figure 5.3? As was noted in Chapter 3, for reasons of clarity, an HTTP response flow was added to this DFD. Again, real-world diagrams will contain exceptions to the usual rules. In this particular case, since the response flow is bifurcated, a response has been added (5) to demonstrate the bifurcation rather than a more typical response assumption.

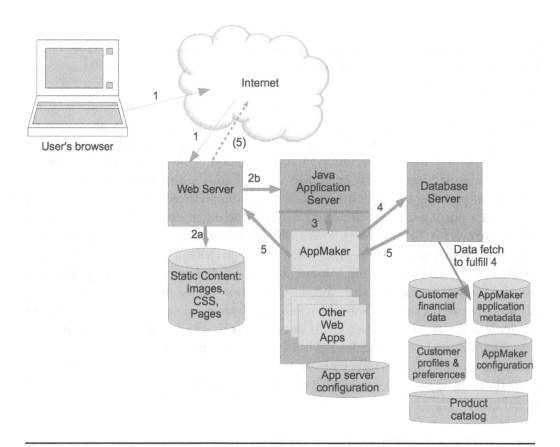

Figure 5.4 AppMaker DFD with data types.

Data types have been added to the AppMaker diagram to create Figure 5.4. There is a co-located repository containing various types of static content to be served to users (customers). Moving further back in the architecture, every application server must contain configuration data and metadata about the applications that the server is running. Usually, but not always, there is local disk storage, or readily available storage for this application server–specific data. Although some application servers use databases for the data associated to the application server's running and to the execution of applications, let's assume, in this case, that this application server makes use of local disk storage or a network disk that appears as a local disk.

Though five different types of data associated with serving customers are shown on the right of the diagram, there is only one arrow, for simplicity. Let's assume that the database server understands how to fetch appropriate data in order to fill in a response made by AppMaker. Thus, the diagram uses a single arrow to represent all data fetches for any type of data, each delineated data set being held in a distinct table.

In this particular use of the AppMaker application, customer financial data, profiles of the customer—that is, the customer's contact information, interests, order history, browsing history among products, etc., as well as the customer's preferences—are kept in a database (or collection of databases that can functionally be considered a single unit). In addition, AppMaker itself has data and metadata associated with the various applications that it builds and instantiates, that is, the applications that are constructed using the AppMaker software. These constructed applications must also draw from a data catalog of products and offerings to be presented to customers for their purchase.

A security assessment must enumerate all the targets of value that will be of interest to the various threat agents who may attack the system. A portion of that enumeration is uncovering the data stored by and processed by the system. Most importantly, data are rated for sensitivity and importance to the organization's goals. For some organizations, the product catalog may be considered entirely public information. However, if that catalog contains prices, and prices depend upon the customer, then the pricing information may be sensitive, even highly sensitive. Data sensitivity rating can be quite unique to each organization.

Even so, we might take some guesses about the importance of some of the data: The obviously sensitive data will be the customer financial data. Under many jurisdictions' laws, financial data is subject to a host of regulations and protections. Any system handling financial data from or that will be stored within one of these jurisdictions will have to meet those regulatory protections. This compliance may dictate the sensitivity of the data. And, in fact, the Payment Card Industry (PCI) standards dictate what can and cannot be done with payment card financial data. PCI also dictates the protections that must be in place for these data. It's probably not too wild a guess to surmise that customer financial data will be considered sensitive by this organization?

For a moment, consider the static content. Much or all of this content may be publicly available to anyone and everyone. Even so, the static content will constitute at least a portion of the public image of the organization. Although the data may be considered "public," a malicious change to the data would normally affect the image of the organization adversely. That is, in classic information security language, the integrity of the data is important to the organization. Even public data may require some form of protection; most organizations don't want their publicly available product catalog to be changed, nor do organizations typically tolerate their public marketing materials being surreptitiously changed.

We will examine all of the data types and their protections in this AppMaker architecture in Chapter 6. For the moment, let's remain focused on the steps of the process that need to be completed in an assessment. One of those steps is discovering the data that is processed and communicated by the system under analysis. Part of that discovery process is rating the data for sensitivity—rating the impact of data loss, malicious change, or unavailability. Data sensitivity is a rating system that codifies the impact on the system and the overall goals of the organization of failure to guard the confidentiality, integrity, or availability (CIA) of the organization's data.

One hint about the data sensitivity step is that in any collection of data there may be multiple levels of sensitivity. It's actually fairly rare that all the data in a particular store or transaction are of the same sensitivity rating. It is the highest sensitivity that will "rule" the collection of data sensitivities. If the high-sensitivity data are scattered among lower-sensitivity data items, the entire collection will have to be protected to the highest sensitivity that is included in the data set. Always ask, "What is the highest sensitivity of data stored in this location?" Or ask, "What is the highest sensitivity of data communicated in this flow?" That will allow you to easily uncover the needs for data protection rather than being taken down rabbit holes of the nature of, "Most of the data are public." The obvious assessor response to a statement about "most of the data" is, "Of what sensitivity is the remaining data?"

It is also important to realize that aggregation of data may raise the sensitivity or lower it, depending on the aggregation. Anonymizing the data, the removal of identifying personal identifying information, will tend to lower the sensitivity of data, at least for privacy purposes.[*]

On the other hand, there are financial data that, when taken separately or in pieces, don't provide enough information to make the overall financial condition of an organization readily understood. However, when those data pieces are collected with other information to create a complete picture, the data become far more sensitive because then the collected data describe a complete, or perhaps even an "insider," financial picture. One aspect of investigating the data sensitivity for any particular system is to examine the data not only in pieces but also explore how sensitivity may change when data are aggregated or presented together.

Experienced security architects may question why I do not make a formal asset list? Lists of every asset within a system are a part of many approaches to threat modeling.

---

[*] Businesses that monetize aggregate consumer behavior, such as Facebook and Google, might consider their anonymized, aggregate consumer data sensitive because of the data's relationship to revenue.

I prefer to focus on assets that are at risk of attack rather than building a list of every object or datum that might possibly be considered an asset. These lists can be quite long. And, I believe such long lists may obscure important prioritization that will have to be made in the face of limited resources.

Instead, I try to understand generally what data are moving through each flow and get stored. After I've uncovered attack surfaces, I can apply prioritized credible attack vectors to assets that will be made available through the vectors. The attackable assets that are not yet sufficiently protected will become a part of the impact calculation that then feeds a risk rating.

By waiting until I have credible attack vectors, I avoid the extra work of listing possibly irrelevant and well-protected assets. I try to focus on those assets that are actually attackable and, thus, whose compromise will most likely affect the system and organization. This is probably just a stylistic preference of mine, rather than a formal methodology? If in your practice, you would prefer or have a need to list all assets, then I would suggest that this is best done during the "architecture" phrase of ATASM.

The AppMaker diagrams, Figures 5.3 and 5.4, do not describe any security component or trust boundary. If security controls exist, these would need to be added to the diagram. As we explore the process for threat enumeration and attack surfaces (ATASM), we will add trust boundaries to the AppMaker logical architecture.

5.3 Threat Enumeration

Once the architecture has been represented in a manner conducive to security analysis, the next step in the ATASM process is the enumeration and examination of threats that will be relevant to systems of the type under analysis. In Chapter 2, we examined a few types of threat agents in order to understand the general background knowledge that security architects bring to the process of system assessment for security. In Chapter 4, we explored how a single threat agent—cyber criminals—contributes to the calculation of information security risk. Each of these threat investigations can be thought of as background to the assessment process. We need to understand the attackers in order to know which of them apply to any particular system. And in order to prioritize attack surfaces and attack targets, we need to be able to calculate the risk of any particular attack occurring. Since it is likely that we won't be able to defend against every attack equally, there has to be a way to prioritize those attacks that will have the most impact and de-prioritize those attacks that are likely to produce an insignificant result.

These higher-priority areas are characterized by the existence of threat agents who have the motivation and capabilities to take advantage of likely methods that will lead them to their objectives – and will in turn cause unacceptable losses . . .[1]

If the assessor has a firm grasp on the threat agents, the capabilities of the threats, and the exposed attack surfaces of the system, then the enumeration of the threats for the system in question is almost complete. However, if threat research and understanding is incomplete, then the threat enumeration must be completed as a part of the system assessment and threat modeling process.

5.3.1 List All the Possible Threat Agents for This Type of System

Using Figure 5.4 as the target architecture, who are the threat agents who will be most interested in attacking Web applications created through AppMaker? Since we know that this particular instance of the AppMaker implements a customer-facing store that processes financial transactions, how does that influence which threat agents may be interested in attacking it?

As explained earlier, any system that is open to public Internet traffic will be attacked continuously. The vast majority of these attacks are undirected or untargeted. Attackers are merely snooping around trying to figure out what might be vulnerable. Information security people call this "doorknob rattling." The vast majority of this traffic comprises unsophisticated, automated scripts attempting well-known attacks against possibly unpatched systems. The motives of these undirected attack sweeps are varied; many of these sweeps are conducted by criminal organizations or independent attackers. But there are many other reasons for running constant vulnerability sweeps, as well. Increasing one's skill as a security tester is certainly among these reasons. Every sweep is not conducted by criminals, though, in many jurisdictions, conducting such a sweep is illegal.

Obviously, there are threat agents interested in stealing the financial information of the customers. Not so obvious, perhaps, are the threat agents interested in various forms of cyber fraud: denial of service attacks (DoS) coupled to blackmail extortion requests. If the website has not been careful in the handling of financial transactions, another fraud scam might be the purchase of products for little or no price, or the theft of products through warranty replacement scams, and the like. If a warrantee replacement product can be delivered to the thief, the thief may resell the product at nearly 100% profit. Identity thieves are going to be interested in the personal details of customers.

Attackers who run botnets (large collections of compromised hosts) for rental will be interested in the servers underlying this web application. Those who sell illegal digital products, such as pirated movies, pirated software programs, or other illegal digital products, will be interested in the web application's storage as a place to keep such illegal digital content. And of course, we must not forget those who would use the web applications as a way to attack customers who will believe they're going to a trustworthy website and instead are being attacked through the website [for example, cross-site scripting (XSS)].

Interestingly, though each of these threat agents has slightly different targets, I believe they can all be lumped together under the class "cyber criminal." As a class, they more or less collectively exhibit the same gross attributes, which were listed in Chapter 2 and revisited in Chapter 4. Ultimately, each of these goals is financial reward. However, the system-level targets differ widely, from raw machines and storage, to information that is financial and/or personal.

Will an activist group be interested in attacking our cyber store? Probably not unless the company fielding the web application is perceived as taking a political stand on a controversial subject. As long as the company that owns and operates our AppMaker web application is seen as relatively neutral, the likelihood of an activist attack is fairly small. Let's assume that our example company stays out of political controversy as best as they can.

How about nation-state or industrial espionage? We don't know what the products are that are being sold through this website. I imagine that if the products are military hardware, the site most definitely would be a nation-state cyber target. In the same vein, if the products are particularly proprietary, industrial espionage is a distinct possibility. However, for a company selling fashionable socks, these two threat agent types are likely to be much less interested in the site or the organization. Let's assume, just for simplicity's sake, that this web site sells socks and nothing else—"Web-Sock-A-Rama"—which leaves us with the various flavors of cyber criminal and the ever-present vulnerability sweeps of the Internet.

There is one additional threat agent with which most public sites and products must contend. Calling security researchers "threats" is somewhat of a misnomer and might be perceived by researchers as an insult? No insult is intended. Still, if an organization is on the receiving end of vulnerability research, the impact to reputation and brand may be approximately the same as what can occur following a successful compromise of systems or data.

Let me explain. It's important to understand that the vast majority of vulnerability researchers have no interest in hurting the systems they probe. These are honest people, in general (just like any other affinity group). A single tricky or difficult to discover vulnerability found within a high-profile product or service can significantly enhance the career and remuneration prospects of the finder. That is a fact.

In addition, once one becomes known for discovering vulnerabilities, there is a bit of a treadmill; the researcher must continue to produce significant results at a level commensurate with expectations or the researcher's career opportunities begin to diminish. It's a bit like being an actor or musician. After a celebrity enjoys a bit of success, a failure to consistently follow up with more successes kills one's opportunities, and ultimately, one's career. In order to maintain a position as a leader, the researcher must find ever more difficult vulnerabilities that must get published, hopefully, through presentations at one or more of the leading conferences. Or the researcher's "hack" must achieve plenty of media attention. In short, there is pressure to continue to uncover vulnerabilities.

Any product or service (or site) that achieves some amount of notoriety (such that vulnerabilities will be seen as significant) is going to receive researcher attention. And these people are smart, savvy, and dogged.*

---

* For clarity, vulnerability researchers number among my personal friends.

My friend, Chris Valecek, calls many of the more difficult to promulgate research attacks ("hacks") "stunt hacks." That is, these attacks aren't really practical for most attack scenarios. The attacks require highly privileged access; many sophisticated attacks even require physical control of the machine; and special tools may be involved, not to mention lots of time and effort in order for the attack to be carried out.

Stunt hacks make great presentations, and even, sometimes terrific theatre (in a computer-oriented, geeky sort of way). And these difficult and tricky exploitations are most certainly highly career enhancing. But the resources and dedication, the one-off, one-time-only nature of the attacks are not suitable for most threat agents (even nation-states). The attack might be too detectable and might require too much physical presence to be carried off without discovery. Consequently, stunt hacks are not really about the security of products so much as they are about the technical skills of the researcher. Irrespective of the usefulness as an attack—a stunt hack against a well-known product, especially a computer security product—has profound effects on the career of the researcher.

Essentially, researchers need to find vulnerabilities. They need to find tricky vulnerabilities and then must publish the research. It doesn't really matter if the vulnerability can result in significant loss for the organization owning the problem. The actuality of an impact does not play a big part of the research equation. Any organization that has had to deal with a well-publicized stunt hack against one of the organization's systems will know full well that the media attention of the research did not benefit the public image of the organization, especially if that organization's customers expect a certain level of security from the organization. That is, security vulnerability research can and does cause significant detrimental impact to an organization's public image, in some cases. If you follow this logic, hopefully you will see that, from the organization's perspective, security researchers can be considered a threat agent, despite the fact that researchers do not steal or otherwise intend to compromise production systems and services. And this consideration is in spite of the fact that the researcher is helping to find and remove vulnerabilities from the organization's systems.

Most researchers that the author knows personally maintain a very high caliber of professional integrity. Despite this personal integrity, a fair amount of the time, there is some negative impact to an organization from receiving a researcher's report,[*] especially if a significant vulnerability has leaked past whatever software (or hardware) security practices are in use by the organization. Security research remains a double-edged sword. Vulnerabilities are found and removed. At the same time, an organization's operational eco-system may be impacted through discovery and publication of the issue in an unplanned manner. Here, we deal with security researchers as a threat agent, despite the obvious fact that, in general, the researcher means to cause no harm and typically sees him or herself as enhancing security, not detracting from it.

---

[*] The extent of the vulnerability research impact varies. Impact might only be an interjection of unplanned work into already committed schedules. Or, impact might be as severe as a loss of customer confidence.

If Web-Sock-A-Rama achieves enough success to garner a significant customer base, researchers are likely to take notice by probing any publicly available system or software for vulnerabilities. Assuming that Web-Sock-A-Rama is one of the most often visited sock purveyors on the Internet and has an international clientele, let's set out the threat attributes for security research (see Table 5.2):

Table 5.2 Threat Attributes of Security Researchers

Threat Agent	Goals	Risk Tolerance	Work Factor	Methods
Security researchers	Technically challenging vulnerabilities	Very low	Very high	Unusual, one-time, unique, complex, specialized

Determining which types of attacks are possible is only the first step. The true value derives from knowing which attacks are most likely to occur.[2]

Web-Sock-A-Rama, as defined, above, appears to have two probable threat agents: cyber criminals and security researchers. In order to more fully understand the attacks that are likely to come from each of these threats, we can base our prognostications upon what we assume the threat agents are ultimately trying to accomplish. If we don't understand what the threats are seeking, what their objectives and goals are, it is more difficult to prioritize some attacks as important while deprioritizing attacks that, even if they were to succeed, would not further the threat agent's goals. Assuming that we do not have the resources to handle every possible attack vector equally, we want to spend our limited resources defending against that which is probable and that which is likely to do the most harm to our organization. We do not want to spin our wheels chasing attack vectors that are not credible because these vectors will not advance the threats towards their goals.

Hopefully, it is clear that cyber criminals are financially motivated. In the end, attacks are not promulgated for fun. Whatever the strategy, cyber criminals are earning a living through some form of theft, be it a confidence game, stealing services and selling these at a profit, outright theft, fraud, or what have you. Although the intermediate steps, including system objectives (which we will examine shortly), may be many, the ultimate reward is intended to be monetary.

Although it might be said that security researchers are also interested in financial reward, that conclusion may be a bit overly simplistic. Most people want to be well compensated in their careers. Narrowing "reward" to simple financial gain also might be perceived as insulting by the many hard-working researchers who see themselves as a positive force for better and increased security in the digital world? Remember please, we are only considering security researchers as a threat from the organization's perspective. There is a world of difference between a cyber criminal and security researcher, even if some of the attack methods are similar.

Hopefully, it is safe to say that career enhancement, technical mastery, and improving security are three typical driving motivations for security researchers as a class of cyber entity that may attack a system. Obviously, individual cyber criminals or security researchers may not fit our stereotype.

Cyber criminals will be satisfied if they can extract financial award from the organization, its customers, or its systems. Security researchers are seeking recognition for their technical mastery and the betterment of systems' security postures. Although financial reward is one likely outcome from industry recognition, there are other, softer rewards that are just as valid. Assuming these two characterizations are more or less working stereotypes, each of these classes of threat agents is motivated by a radically different objective.

5.3.2 List the Typical Attack Methods of the Threat Agents

Like many legitimate business owners, cyber criminals seek to maximize profit for effort expended. In other words, an ultimate goal of financial reward, as much money as possible, leads directly to a corollary of limiting effort expended towards the goal: This is basic capitalism. As a result, cyber criminals try to capitalize as much as possible on the tools and techniques that are available.

Spending months or years creating a new method to execute a series of randomly placed instructions in a program to create an attack simply isn't worth the effort: The research and development costs are too high. At the time of the writing of this book, so-called "gadget" programs take too much time. Running gadgets culled by finding bits of code within widely distributed applications is much more likely to fall into the category of "stunt hack." Cyber criminals are probably not going to waste their time unless there was a readily available tool (even if on the black market) that would make this attack trivial.

Instead, the cyber criminal who is going to attack an organization's system will attempt to use as much pre-existing and proven technology, whether attack methods or attacking tools, as possible. There is a burgeoning black market for cyber attack tools, tools similar to the attack and penetration tool, Metasploit. Generally, the people who make the attack tools aren't usually the people doing the attacking. The toolmakers get paid for the tools, whether legitimately or on the black market.

Indeed, even more telling, the person actually performing the attack may be at a lower rung of the organization, even a technical novice recruited such that if the novice is caught, those higher up are hidden from the authorities. The actual attackers often have quite limited technical skills. Therefore, the attacks have to be well-known, effective, and well packaged so that they can be run like other user-friendly applications. There is very little incentive for cyber criminals, in general, to invent a lot of technology. Such research would entail an unpaid period of development. The need to accommodate a lower technical sophistication of the actual attackers, and the fact that there is so much vulnerable software available to attack leads to the conclusion: Why waste time on unprofitable activities?

The list of cyber criminals' attack methods might be found within the suite of known attack variations in any of the available security-testing tools. If the tool can test the type of system under analysis, its suite of tests makes a good starting point for answering the question, "What are the cyber criminal's attack methods?"

Almost directly opposite the needs of the cyber criminal is a security researcher whose reward can be directly tied to the technical difficulty and complexity of the attack. The reward comes from industry recognition for the technical capabilities and acumen of the researcher. If there are any financial rewards, these will be less directly tied to the attack method, but rather a product of a stronger *curriculum vitae* and the approbation of colleagues. The more difficult it is to execute the attack, the larger the reward.

Since many (if not most?) security researchers are employed, a typical security researcher has the luxury of an income. Although some security researchers' jobs entail finding vulnerabilities, others perform their research "on the side," outside of work hours, as an extracurricular activity. Hence, there isn't much imperative for speed. The investigation will take as long as is necessary. This means that the researcher can take the time needed to achieve success. This spaciousness with time directly influences the technical complexity of the methodology. Unlike the cyber criminal, looking for the fastest payoff, vulnerability research might be seen as an investment in the skills of the researcher, like time spent studying for an additional, higher education degree. The "final exam" in this case will be the researcher's proof that a vulnerability is exploitable. The proof is often delivered as a short example program demonstrating the successful exploitation of the vulnerability on the system under investigation.

Security researchers can and do run readily available, open source and commercial vulnerability scanners. The analyst cannot discount the well-known attack methods. Discovery of known classes of vulnerabilities may not have the prestige of a complex stunt hack; nevertheless, finding these proves the security testing capabilities of the researcher and also helps to get vulnerabilities removed from deployed software. And it is generally better for an organization to have a relatively friendly and probably honest researcher find a vulnerability rather than a cyber criminal who will exploit it for gain for as long as the vulnerability continues to be exposed to the criminal's use of it.

The set of Web-Sock-A-Rama attack methods includes that suite of standard attacks and variations that are understood sufficiently to have been programmed into vulnerability scanning software. But there is also the possibility of extended research probing for more complex issues of a one-of-a-kind nature within the web store software.

5.3.3 List the System-Level Objectives of Threat Agents Using Their Attack Methods

In order to properly defend the attack surfaces, one must understand the intermediate, cyber, digital, or system objectives of the attack methods. For instance, looking once more at XSS attacks, we know that the ultimate objective of a cyber criminal is to extract money from the victim. Of course, there are a multitude of ways that an XSS can be used to do that, from fake product sales (illegal or pirated pharmaceuticals) to theft of personal information like payment card numbers, account information, or an entire identity. But how does the attacker get from the XSS vulnerability to the objective?

For many exploits there is a system-level objective that must be attained in order to prosecute the attack to its goal. For security researchers, the system-level objective—that is, getting a piece of scripting code (javascript) to execute in the user's browser, or gaining system-level privileges—will be sufficient to prove vulnerability. No more need be accomplished.

But for other attackers, the system objective is the steppingstone to an ultimate goal, whatever that goal may be. System-level privileges allow the attacker to "own," that is, completely control the attacked machine. From there, all information on the machine can be stolen. With superuser privileges, the attacker can install software that listens to and records every entry on the machine. If a spy, the attacker could turn on the machine's video camera and microphone, thus eaves dropping on conversations had within the vicinity of the machine. And, of course, an owned machine can be used to stage further attacks against other machines or send spam email. Essentially, a completely compromised machine can be used for the malicious and abusive purposes of the attacker. Hence, the term "owned."

System-level objectives are tied closely to attack methods. Table 5.3 is not intended to be exhaustive. There are plenty of more extensive lists elsewhere, the most complete probably being CAPEC™* at Mitre.org or the lists of attack methods at OWASP.org. Nevertheless, we are studying the ARA/threat modeling process in this chapter. The following is offered as an example of a technique for understanding how the prioritized threats are most likely to misuse attack surfaces.

The first three entries in Table 5.3 are purposely difficult enough to execute that these would not be a consideration for most well-managed websites. Unless there is a serious, unauthenticated, remotely executable vulnerability available via an HTTP request or message into a vulnerable application server or Web server, all the other interfaces should be protected in such a way that getting sufficient privileges to perform one of these first three attacks should be extremely difficult. In order to highlight security researcher "stunt hacks," the first three entries specifically require high privileges or wide access, or both.

The subsequent entries in Table 5.3 are drawn from OWASP.org Top 10.† In order to gain a place in the list, an attack method has to be one of the most popularly executed as

---

* Common Attack Pattern Enumeration and Classification. CAPEC is a registered trademark of the Mitre Corporation.

† Not all of the top 10 attacks are listed. Table 5.3 is just an example to demonstrate the process of understanding the system-level objectives of the likely threat agents. Some of the Top 10 List are vulnerabilities, thus not detailing an attack method. Table 5.3 is limited to technical attack methods only. CAPEC, maintained by the Mitre Corporation, details most known attack methods.

Table 5.3 System-Level Attack Objectives

Specific Attack	System Objective(s)	Threat Agent
String code "gadgets" together into a meaningful sequence that escalates privileges	• User installed (and accepted) application code running attacker's program without having to install an executable on the attacked machine • Call vulnerable system code from within an installed application and exploit to escalate privilege to system or superuser	Security researchers
Bypass the no-execute page protection policy to execute code	Execute code of the attacker's choosing within the context of the currently logged user and a running application	Security researchers
Use a system debugger to exploit a buried overflow condition	Prove that an overflow condition not reachable through inputs can execute code of the attacker's choosing	Security researchers
SQL and LDAP injection	• *execute unintended commands* • *access data without proper authorization*	Cyber criminals
Cross-Site Scripting (XSS)	• *execute scripts in the victim's browser* • *hijack user sessions* • *deface web sites* • *redirect the user to malicious sites.*	Cyber criminals
(exposed) Direct Object References	*manipulate . . . references to access unauthorized data*	Cyber criminals
Cross-Site Request Forgery CSRF)	• *force a logged-on victim's browser to send a forged HTTP request* • *generate requests . . . [that appear to be] . . . legitimate requests from the victim*	Cyber criminals
Unvalidated Redirects and Forwards	• *redirect and forward users to other pages and websites* • *use untrusted data to determine the destination pages* • *redirect victims to phishing or malware sites* • *use forwards to access unauthorized pages*	Cyber criminals

SQL = Structured Query Language; LDAP = Lightweight Directory Access Protocol.
Source: Data set in italics is from the Open Web Application Security Project (OWASP) (2013). *OWASP Top 10 List.*[3]

well as used on a regular and continuing basis. When we analyzed cyber criminals, we noted their predilection for well-known and proven attack methods. The OWASP Top 10 list is representative of the most often used attacks on the Internet. Since the Web-Sock-A-Rama site is a typical web store, it will be subjected to attacks drawn from the OWASP Top 10 list, at the very least. Security researchers will also attempt well-known attack methods in order to find and report vulnerabilities.

5.4 Attack Surfaces

The attack methods and their system-level objectives listed above are targeted against "something." That set of "somethings" are the attack surfaces of the architecture. In most systems—that is, examining most architectures—some attack surfaces will be more exposed than others. Ultimately, the ARA and threat modeling process should prioritize the exposed attack surfaces.

In the ATASM process, we try to enumerate all the attack surfaces before we categorize the importance of each surface. It's useful to avoid the prioritization process during enumeration. Think of it as an attack surface brainstorm: Any discussion about the legitimacy or fitness of an attack surface tends to bog down the enumeration into too many details. In this way, the natural flow resulting from nonjudgmental observation is broken. It's easy to miss an attack surface, especially when it seems inconsequential, or perhaps that function just seems to be "part of the running program." For that very reason, getting a good flow of nonjudgmental inspection can help to uncover all the attack surfaces. Prioritization can come later, once everything has been uncovered. In the process being described in this chapter, we simply enumerate all the attack surfaces and try to avoid discussion of their importance and exposure until a later step.

In order to find the attack surfaces, we first must break down the architecture sufficiently to expose them. If you're not comfortable with the architecture decomposition and factoring process, review Chapter 3, in which these processes are explained in detail.

5.4.1 Decompose (factor) the Architecture to a Level That Exposes Every Possible Attack Surface

When hunting for attack surfaces, it's important to understand the trust boundaries that exist between components in the architecture. Figure 5.5 adds three dashed-line divisions to the AppMaker-based, Web-Sock-A-Rama online store. The three lines represent one possible set of boundaries, based upon industry-standard, three-tier web architecture.

However, many web sites do not employ all of these divisions. Some might only be concerned with the boundary between the Internet and the web server. In this case, the web server, application server, and database server would all exist in the same trust segment. Another often-used web architecture separates Internet and then database into separate spaces, leaving web server and application server at the same trust level. Indeed, many of the leading application servers include a web server that may be used instead of a separate and distinct web server instance. An integrated web server collapses the web tier and application server tier into a two-tiered architecture. Following the security principles, defense-in-depth and fail securely, the three-tier architecture is usually considered a more defensible approach. Web-Sock-A-Rama, as depicted in Figure 5.5, demonstrates the more standard three-tier web architecture.

However the fictitious designers of our web site might have considered trust within this AppMaker implementation for Web-Sock-A-Rama, a strong case may be made that the Internet is inherently dangerous, supporting the boundary between the web server and the Internet. Further, since the web server is a "terminus" and is open to all traffic (in order to sell as many socks as possible to the widest possible Internet populace),

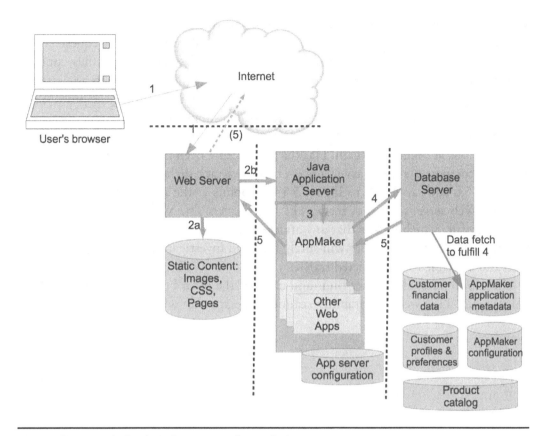

Figure 5.5   Web-Sock-A-Rama trust boundaries.

the web server should be considered a "bastion" or resource that can be lost without losing the entire site. It is on a demilitarized zone (DMZ) to which known bad traffic will have access. Placing a boundary between the web server and the application logic (application server) will offer an opportunity to protect the application code from at least some types of attack that will be stopped at the bastion web server, and not passed onto subsequent tiers.

If the data in the databases were lost or compromised, Web-Sock-A-Rama would not be able to function, revenue could not be generated (or lost through fraud), and the loss of customer financial data might engender legal consequences. In short, the loss of data obtained through the database server would impact the functioning of this business, and might even cause the organization to fail. Further, this data and the infrastructure that serves it must be trustworthy. The operation of the web site assumes that the data are correct. If you follow this logic, you may see that the data layer will be the highest trust area in the architecture.

Some web architectures might consider both the application code and the data to be high trust. If compromised, the application code could have profound consequences for the web store. The reason for putting the application server in a different trust segment is based upon the fact that it must handle messages from untrustworthy sources. Even though web traffic (HTTP) is terminated at the web server, the dynamic requests must be processed by code running in the application server. Messages that possibly contain attacks will get passed through the web server and get processed by web application code running in the application server. For this reason, I would consider the probability that the application server is under attack, thus placing another trust boundary between code and data.

Take a look at Figure 5.5 again. Has the architecture been factored into all the functions and components necessary to uncover all the attack surfaces?

Figure 5.6 adds an arrow to Figure 5.5 that points at the most obvious attack surface: the Web server's Internet facing HTTP receiver. The Web server is open to all Internet traffic, which means that any attacker can probe it. The constant "doorknob rattling" sweeps of the Internet will surely find and investigate whatever interfaces are open and available to unrestricted traffic.

Once an interested attacker finds and catalogs the open HTTP port, then the fun really begins. Like web vulnerability scanners, the attacker will probe every reachable

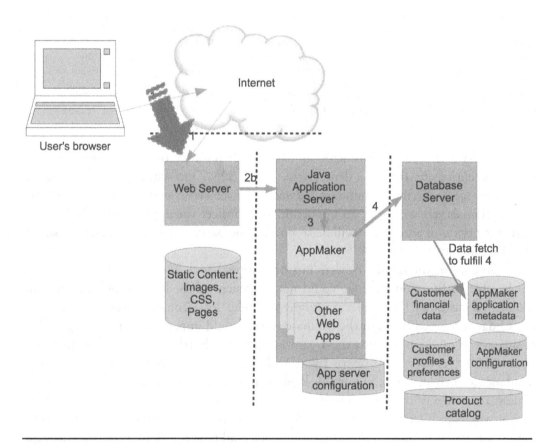

Figure 5.6   An obvious attack surface.

page with every attack variation possible. These probes (and possibly downloads of portions of the site) will be unrelenting. To prevent restriction of the attacker's address, she or he may use multiple addresses or even shift attacking addresses on-the-fly (e.g., fast flux DNS).

But the attacker won't just try attacks at the network or HTTP protocol level. Probes will attempt to catalog every vulnerability of any interest to the attacker. Since cyber criminals sometimes specialize in particular attack methods, one attacker will search for XSS errors, to chase Web-Sock-A-Rama's customers, whereas another attacker might target customer data and payment cards. A third attacker might probe for hosts that can be compromised to add to a botnet or from which to stage attacks either inbound into Web-Sock-A-Rama's internal networks or outbound at other organizations. The possibilities are many.

For every one of the above cases, and for security researchers as well, the web server that is reachable from the Internet will be the first attack surface to examine.

Please study Figure 5.4. What other attack surfaces can you find? We will complete this investigation in the next chapter.

Table 5.4 adds another column to Table 5.3. To which attack surface can each attack that we've uncovered be applied? Assuming that there is only one HTTP/S interface presented to the public Internet, there are only a very limited number of vectors through which the first three, security researcher–promulgated attack methods might possibly succeed. A failure would have to connect a number of fairly unlikely concurrent vulnerabilities: a hole in the HTTP request processing of the Java application server allowing the exercise of a vulnerability in the Java runtime environment (JRE) followed up by exercisable vulnerability in system services or the operating system itself. This combination of events is not impossible; it has been seen a number of times even within the last year or two of this writing. This is what a properly managed website administrative crew must attend to. Streams of announcements of new vulnerabilities for the technology that's been deployed have to be watched on a continual basis. A mature operations practice includes regular patch cycles to plug new vulnerabilities and an emergency process for serious vulnerabilities that need immediate attention.

Just for the sake of this investigation, let's assume that our fictitious Web sock company has a mature web master administration practice. The Java application server is patched for the most serious Java and application server vulnerabilities; its security posture is up-to-date. If this is true, and all other interfaces to the Web server and application server are sufficiently protected (we'll get to this in the next chapter), then I think we can discount the security researcher stunt hacks because they do not have access. There is no exposure, and perhaps no vulnerability?

This leaves the remaining five attack methods from the list in Table 5.4 to apply against our single exposed interface, the attack surface. If you scan through Table 5.4, column 3, you will see that the entries are not the same. Not every attack can be applied in the same way against the same targets, even in this limited set of threat agents and attacks.

Table 5.4 Attack Methods Applied to Attack Surfaces

Specific Attack	System Objective(s)	Attack Surface	Threat Agent
String code "gadgets" together into a meaningful sequence that escalates privileges	• User installed (and accepted) application code running attacker's program without having to install an executable on the attacked machine • Call vulnerable system code from within an installed application and exploit to escalate privilege to system or superuser	None available	Security researchers
Bypass the CPU's no-execute page protection policy to execute code	Execute code of the attacker's choosing within the context of the currently logged user and a running application	None available	Security researchers
Use a system debugger to exploit a buried overflow condition	Prove that an overflow condition not reachable through inputs can execute code of the attacker's choosing	None available	Security researchers
SQL and LDAP injection	• *execute unintended commands* • *access data without proper authorization*	Applications via HTTP	Cyber criminals
Cross-Site Scripting (XSS)	• *execute scripts in the victim's browser* • *hijack user sessions* • *deface web sites* • *redirect the user to malicious sites*	Web Server and applications via HTTP	Cyber criminals
(exposed) Direct Object References	*manipulate . . . references to access unauthorized data*	HTTP responses from applications and application server	Cyber criminals
Cross-Site Request Forgery (CSRF)	• *force a logged-on victim's browser to send a forged HTTP request* • *generate requests . . . [that appear to be] . . . legitimate requests from the victim*	Application server via HTTP (in this case, AppMaker)	Cyber criminals
Unvalidated Redirects and Forwards	• *redirect and forward users to other pages and websites* • *use untrusted data to determine the destination pages* • *redirect victims to phishing or malware sites* • *use forwards to access unauthorized pages*	Web server and applications via HTTP. Possibly also the application server	Cyber criminals

SQL = Structured Query Language; LDAP = Lightweight Directory Access Protocol.

Source: Data set in italics is from the Open Web Application Security Project (OWASP) (2013). *OWASP Top 10 List.*[4]

The injections for downstream destinations, such as LDAP and databases, are aimed at the application server code because that's where the capability to pass on these attacks is typically found. These are then attacks against the application code.

Contrast these injections with a Cross-Site Request Forgery (CSRF) attack. These attacks can be mitigated at several different layers, depending upon how session management is implemented in the website. Although many would consider this a vulnerability of the custom application code, depending upon how the infrastructure is set up, it may be that the application server handles user and transaction states. If so, then a CSRF vulnerability would lie in front of the application code. Another possibility might be the Web server handling session management, or even a specialized piece of hardware running in front of the Web server? Without these additional details, and without knowing the specifics of authentication, authorization, and user state management (against which CSRF attacks), it's hard to put a finger on the precise attack surface in the technology stack. For the moment, let's place this attack against the application server via the HTTP requests that are passed from the Web server. A common CSRF treatment is to add a nonce to every request so as to tie the user and the user's current expected state. One way to generate the nonce is to implement an outbound filter at the application server that lies in front of all applications, rather than having every application developer code a nonce into each individual responder. Alternatively, a common library might be distributed to every developer such that including a nonce is a trivial set of calls to the library. Since this application was built with the AppMaker software, let's assume that the creation of a nonce is the responsibility of AppMaker. In this instance, the CSRF attack will then will be aimed at AppMaker's code.

The exposure of inappropriate data and objects will generally be the fault of the application code. That's assuming a well-debugged Java application server. However, the application server might expose its objects and references, as well. All the code that is involved in building a response—from special, local logic that is programmed in the application, to the code in AppMaker (which builds the application for the developer), through the application server—can cause this mistake. The attacker almost gets this compromise for free, since not much of an attack, beyond taking a look at the HTTP responses, is required. Have you ever gone to a website, caused a website error, and received as a response a page full of what appears to be code? That's what this attack is; if the website makes this error, the attack is trivial. The attacker need do nothing but reap the information gained. It should be noted that static content and a web server can also have this fault, delivering coding information to an attacker unintentionally. This attack applies to every part of the front end and middle tier of the website we are examining.

To complete this step of the process, we find that every type of attack, at least at this gross level, should be applied to every attack surface that is relevant. As attacks are applied it should be obvious which are irrelevant for any particular attack surface. In addition, some attacks will start to fall off, whereas others will gain in importance.

5.4.2 Filter Out Threat Agents Who Have No Attack Surfaces Exposed to Their Typical Methods

Through the process of filling out Table 5.4, we have already filtered out a series of attacks that do not have an appropriate attack surface exposed to them. In fact, by attempting to apply attack methods to attack surfaces, we have even eliminated, or significantly reduced, a threat agent: security researchers. Security researchers' stunt level hacks are unlikely since the attack surfaces required to execute these attacks are not exposed. To simplify the process in order to understand it, we didn't list security researchers in any of the subsequent attack methods in Table 5.4. Nonetheless, security researchers can and will attempt all the other attack methods we have listed. Unless we do something very insecure on this website, stunt hacks on the website are not very likely to occur.

We will continue the filtering process in the next step.

5.4.3 List All Existing Security Controls for Each Attack Surface

The reason that the ATASM process encourages delaying the assessment of existing controls is to ferret out all of the attack surfaces. Discussions start to get bogged down in rating the sufficiency of existing controls. Because of this tendency, this particular approach to the threat modeling process urges us to wait until we have all the attack surfaces and all the attack methods catalogued before applying existing controls in order to prioritize. The essential problem is that we can never be 100% sure that we are sufficiently defended. Furthermore, we have to assume that some of our defenses may fail under sophisticated attack. It comes down to risk: There are no sureties. Risk decisions have to be made in order to account for limited resources to apply to the defense. Those discussions are best had at a later stage of analysis, once discovery has been completed.

In Table 5.4, the existing security controls are not shown. We have made a couple of assumptions for the sake of understanding the process. Namely, we've assumed that Web-Sock-A-Rama has a mature website management and administrative function. In previous chapters, we've listed what those functions typically are. This assumption provides the usual set of controls to the backend of our website. In the real world, I would never make that assumption without investigating first. An ARA has a due diligence responsibility to tie every loose end down, to dot every "i" and cross every "t." The upside is that one usually only has to investigate an infrastructure once to understand its strengths and weaknesses. After that investigation, the infrastructure knowledge can be applied to each system that will be deployed to the infrastructure, instance after instance. The foregoing, of course, echoes and underlines the importance of pre-assessment knowledge, such as understanding the intended deployment infrastructure.

We do not know if some AppMaker applications or some Web-Sock-A-Rama pages require authentication. We don't know if some transactions require authorization. We don't know where the firewalls are, if any. We don't know what actions are monitored, or even if there's a security team who can monitor them (although a mature administrative function would imply security monitoring for attacks).

Because we don't know what security controls exist, we could assume that there are none. If that were so, then we'd be ready to start writing security requirements. We would skip the next step in our process.

However, this chapter is devoted to learning the process. So, just for the sake of completing the process fully in every one of its steps, let's assume that there is a single firewall between the public Internet and HTTP termination. Let's also assume that there's an authentication mechanism for certain operations, like changing a customer's profile. Assume that each individual customer is authorized to change only her or his record and none others. Let us assume, as well, that there are no other controls existing.

5.4.4 Filter Out All Attack Surfaces for Which There Is Sufficient Existing Protection

The difficulty in this step is the word "sufficient." That will be a risk decision, as described in Chapter 4. There aren't easy answers to the question of "sufficiency," because the security needs of organizations and security postures vary. For one system at a high-security-needs organization, "sufficient" may mean layers of protections: network firewall, web application firewall, vetted input validation library, object-level authorization model, inter-tier encryption of communications, inter-tier bidirectional authentication at the function level, DB rights management, and so forth. All the defenses taken together sum to "sufficiency." The foregoing list would be an "industry standard" web security list. However, this list would probably be too expensive for a small shop to implement. In addition, if that small shop's crown jewels are all public, the industry standard list is overkill. Probably good patching and hardening practices, network restriction, and strict input validation are sufficient in this case? The required security posture tends to be somewhat unique, at least to classes of systems and organizations, if not to individual organizations.

Still, let's use industry standards as our basic guide in the absence of organizational policy and standards.

We know that our infrastructure practices are mature. We also have restrictions in place to prevent any but intended HTTP/S traffic into Web-Sock-A-Rama. And we have specified that there is an up-to-date firewall in place in front of our exposed interface. Which of the attacks indicated in Table 5.4 are eliminated, given these controls?

If you said "none that we haven't already eliminated in previous steps" you would be correct. No control we have named will stop any of the five listed attack methods. In fact, authentication (and possibly authorization) increases the value of CSRF attacks. The attacker may masquerade as an authenticated user via a successful CSRF.

Authentication is an interesting security control because, although it does reduce exposure to only those who've been authenticated, there are plenty of techniques an attacker can use to get an account, depending upon the site: steal or crack weak credentials, or perhaps simply sign up for the free version. In addition, once a site or system implements authentication, it now has another system that will need protection! Authentication systems are often considered critical, thus requiring tight security control: a high security posture. Implementing authentication adds significant complexity to the security requirements of the system.

Table 5.5 A Sample Set of Credible Attack Vectors

Threat Agent	Specific Attack	Attack Surface	System Objective(s)
Cyber criminals and security researchers	SQL and LDAP injection	Applications via HTTP	• *execute unintended commands* • *access data without proper authorization*
Cyber criminals and security researchers	Cross-Site Scripting (XSS)	Web Server and Applications via HTTP	• *execute scripts in the victim's browser* • *hijack user sessions* • *deface web sites* • *redirect the user to malicious sites*
Cyber criminals and security researchers	(exposed) Direct Object References	HTTP responses from applications and application server	*manipulate . . . references to access unauthorized data*
Cyber criminals and security researchers	Cross-Site Request Forgery (CSRF)	Application Server via HTTP (in this case, AppMaker)	• *force a logged-on victim's browser to send a forged HTTP request* • *generate requests . . . [that appear to be] . . . legitimate requests from the victim*
Cyber criminals and security researchers	Unvalidated Redirects and Forwards	Web Server and Applications via HTTP Possibly also the application server	• *redirect and forward users to other pages and websites* • *use untrusted data to determine the destination pages* • *redirect victims to phishing or malware sites* • *use forwards to access unauthorized pages*

SQL = Structured Query Language; LDAP = Lightweight Directory Access Protocol.

Source: Data set in italics is from Open Web Application Security Project (OWASP) (2013). *OWASP Top 10 List.*[5]

No attack surface that we have listed has been reduced significantly or defended "sufficiently" from the known existing controls. Therefore, our list of attacks and attack surfaces remains the same after this step.

We now have our set of credible attack vectors (CAV). Table 5.5 removes the attacks and attack surfaces that have been deprioritized. Remaining is a CAV list for the website.

5.5 Data Sensitivity

Please consider Table 5.3 once again. Do any of the general data types named in the diagram indicate the data's sensitivity rating?

- Customer financial data
- Customer records and profile
- Product catalog
- AppMaker application metadata
- AppMaker configuration
- Application server configuration
- Web server configuration

Which of the foregoing seems the most sensitive to Web-Sock-A-Rama's continuing success?

I would pick "customer financial data." Keeping financial data is particularly difficult if the site retains payment card information.* Loss of payment cards typically involves impact to the public image, loss of customer confidence, expensive customer relationship remediations, breach notifications, and, perhaps, lawsuits.

But I wouldn't stop with financial data. What if an attacker can change the configuration of the underlying web components? How about fiddling with AppMaker's metadata to create new, attacker-controlled applications?

The product catalog is public. But the company probably doesn't want anyone to change the sock prices to the attacker's advantage, nor mess with the catalog information, thereby hurting the ability to sell socks, or possibly embarrassing the company.

Using a three-step rating system—high sensitivity, medium sensitivity, or public—where would you place each of the above data types?

It should be noted that a real web store would likely have a number of other data types not shown. We'll ignore these for our process example.

To reiterate why data classification is important, higher-sensitivity data poses a higher attack value target. In order to assess the risk of each attack, we have to understand the

---

* I would try to design the site in such a way as to remove the need to store payment card information. Payment cards are very hard to secure correctly. Note the huge breaches that continue to take place on a regular basis.

impact. And in order to prioritize the credible attack vectors, we have to know where the important data lies.

Data classification is a key component of risk, both for assessing impact and for understanding likely targets in a system. As has been explained earlier, attackers often string more than one attack method together in order to achieve their objectives. An attacker might execute an SQL injection against the payment card database, thereby gaining financial information, if applications accepting user input were poorly written such that SQL injection to databases were allowed. But accepting user SQL statements (or partial statements) to the financial database would be an exceedingly poor design choice. Assuming that there is no direct SQL path from customer to the Web-Sock-A-Rama databases, a potential attacker would have to first gain access to the database server or the inner network before being able to attack the data. That poses at least a two-step set of successful compromises. Even so, we know that payment card data is highly sought after by Internet attackers. Knowing this gives the defender a better understanding of the CAVs that might get employed and, thus, the defenses that will prevent such a combination of attack scenarios. Data classification assists in gauging the impact term and CAVs. That is, it is useful to both risk terms—probability (CAV) and loss (impact).

Data sensitivity musn't become the sole measure of CAV or impact. Each of these risk terms are multidimensional; terms shouldn't be reduced in a simplistic way or assessments will suffer by possibly excluding other key factors. As we've seen, there are system-level objectives, such as executing a script or code, escalating privileges, or causing data to dump, which must be factored into risk, as well. Calculation of information security risk doesn't reduce to a single variable and shouldn't be reduced to one. The approach explained in the chapter on risk reduces calculation to a few terms, some of which can be considered in a more or less binary fashion. That amount of reduction is as much as I think practical. My approximating approach already incorporates considerable condensation. I do not recommend attempting to simplify even further, say, down to data sensitivity alone.

5.6 A Few Additional Thoughts on Risk

Throughout the foregoing process tour and explanation, I've used the work "prioritize" instead of risk. But risk is the principle underlying prioritization as this term has been used in the explanations given above. The goal of risk calculation during ATASM is to identify those CAVs whose lack of mitigation will prevent reaching the intended security posture. Concomitantly, there is an imperative to limit the number of risk treatments to that which is affordable, that which is doable. Few organizations can "do it all." Hence, there has to be a process to eliminate unlikely attacks while prioritizing the most dangerous ones for mitigation.

Risk calculation is taking place throughout ATASM. Assessing risk is built into the steps of the process. An assessor doesn't have to stop and perform an extra calculation, so long as the filtering that is built into the steps takes place. Once the list of CAVs has been enumerated, it may be a good time to then prioritize these, if necessary. Depending upon the organization and the system, it may make sense to treat every CAV in order to build a strong defense. Or it may make business or resource sense to further rate each CAV to produce implementation priorities. The answer to this question is dependent upon the situation.

5.7 Possible Controls

The final steps in the ATASM process build the set of security requirements to achieve the desired security posture. This is the "requirements" phase spoken of earlier. We applied high-level attack methods to each attack surface. It is precisely these attack methods that will suggest the security controls. As has been mentioned several times above, we cannot expect a 1-to-1 mapping of control, of mitigation to attack, though of course, some mitigations will be 1-to-1.

For instance, we've already applied the existing authentication to reduce the attack surface at the application layer. As we explored, adding authentication does provide some control, but it also adds a raft of additional attack surfaces. It's not a panacea; authentication is a piece of a puzzle. Further and importantly, there is the context of this particular authentication; what does it actually add to the defense for Web-Sock-A-Rama? If the store expects to have a large customer base, as big as possible, similar to services such as Facebook™ or Myspace™, identity has to be very inclusive. In these cases, identity is based solely upon possession of a viable email address, and free email addresses are as readily available to attackers as to you, the reader, (not to mention stolen and hacked email accounts). That is, possessing an email address that can send and receive email proves nothing. Think of all the pets who have Facebook accounts. I personally do not know a single dog or cat who actually reads or posts to a Facebook account. Facebook accounts, despite what I believe to be some "best efforts" on the part of the Facebook security team, are easily opened by attackers, just as well as pets, that is, fictitious identities.

In the case of a web store such as we're using for our example, at purchase time, a credit card or other payment option is required. However, several years ago, in a United States Federal Bureau of Investigation (FBI) presentation, it was mentioned that stolen credit card numbers were 25 cents each on the black market. Apparently, one buys the numbers in lots of hundreds or thousands.

Due to the realities of email impersonation and payment card theft, an authentication based upon these factors isn't really worth much, which leaves our Web-Sock-A-Rama website without much attack mitigation based upon authentication. Obviously, the organization's security team will have their hands full with fraud attempts, operationally removing fraudulent and fake accounts as soon as malicious behavior is observed. Still, at account initialization, there isn't much that can be done. One email address looks an awful lot like another; as long as the email server opens a connection, the address is going to verify as active. The foregoing should bring the security person to the conclusion that attackers will have accounts and will bypass authentication.

For a web store, the authentication is as much about business as it is about security. This is true because a store wants to give each customer as personalized an experience as possible. Please consider the following data in Figure 5.4: "customer profiles and preferences." The store retains product browsing history, purchases, interests, and perhaps even reviews and other ancillary data. With this data, the store can offer each customer items of possible interest, thus increasing sales and customer retention. In addition, publishing customer reviews gives customers a sense of participation, not only with the store but also with other customers. Allowing one customer to change another's preferences or profile would be a breach of customer trust. Once authenticated, customers must be only authorized to access their own data, not the data of any other customer.

To be clear, the authentication in front of the store provides little security control. Additional controls are going to be required.

5.7.1 Apply New Security Controls to the Set of Attack Services for Which There Isn't Sufficient Mitigation

We've already examined cross-site request forgery protection: An unpredictable nonce will have to be sent with each authenticated and authorized page. That is the recommended treatment; in this case, attack to mitigation is 1-to-1.

Table 5.6 adds defenses to each of the attack methods that we enumerated in previous ATASM steps. These are the five attacks and their associated attack surfaces (the CAVs) that we believe are applicable to this system, in this organizational context. Table 5.5 summarized attack surfaces with applied attack methods.

Table 5.6 Attacks and Controls

Specific Attack	Attack Surface	System Objective(s)	Control
SQL and LDAP injection	Applications via HTTP	• *execute unintended commands* • *access data without proper authorization*	• Design application code such that dynamic requests to LDAP and to databases are built within the application and not received from users • Dynamic input from users, such as user name or item numbers, must be validated to contain only expected characters • Input not matching precisely constrained values must return an error to the user

(Continued on following page)

Table 5.6 Attacks and Controls (*Continued*)

Specific Attack	Attack Surface	System Objective(s)	Control
Cross-Site Scripting (XSS)	Web server and applications via HTTP	• *execute scripts in the victim's browser* • *hijack user sessions* • *deface web sites* • *redirect the user to malicious sites*	• Dynamic input from users, such as user name or item numbers, must be validated to contain only expected characters • Input not matching precisely constrained values must return an error to the user • Response generation must clear all scripting tags found within stored content
(exposed) Direct Object References	HTTP responses from applications and application server	*manipulate . . . references to access unauthorized data*	• Do not use object revealing protocols similar to Java Remote Method Invocation (RMI) in communications with the user's browser • Remove all debugging and coding information from errors and other user content. Errors shown to user must be user-centric, in plain (nontechnical) language • Do not expose any debugging, configuration, or administrative interfaces over customer/public interfaces • *Use per user or session indirect object references* • Authorize all direct object accesses
Cross-Site Request Forgery (CSRF)	Application server via HTTP (in this case, AppMaker)	• *force a logged-on victim's browser to send a forged HTTP request* • *generate requests . . . [that appear to be] . . . legitimate requests from the victim*	Include a nonpredictable nonce in the response to a successful user authentication. Return the nonce for the session with every authenticated response in a hidden field. Before processing an authenticated request, validate the nonce from the user's session
Unvalidated Redirects and Forwards	Web server and applications via HTTP Possibly also the application server	• *redirect and forward users to other pages and websites* • *use untrusted data to determine the destination pages* • *redirect victims to phishing or malware sites* • *use forwards to access unauthorized pages*	• *Simply avoid using redirects and forwards* • *If used, don't involve user parameters in calculating the destination. This can usually be done* • *If destination parameters can't be avoided, ensure that the supplied value is valid, and authorized for the user* • *Employ an indirect reference to URLs between client and server rather than sending the actual value to the user*

SQL = Structured Query Language; LDAP = Lightweight Directory Access Protocol.

Source: Data set in italics is from the Open Web Application Security Project (OWASP) (2013). *OWASP Top 10 List.*[6]

Some of the defenses are programming requirements. For instance, rewriting errors that will be returned to users in plain language easily understood by users and not containing any programming information is something that will have to be programmed into the applications. Likewise, input validation, which is required to prevent the two injection errors, must be done within code.

Contrast the coding defenses with not using an object referencing or serialization protocol (RMI) to prevent direct code references from escaping to the user. This, like building nonces into responses or using no redirects or forwards, is a design issue. The applications making up the Web-Sock-A-Rama store will have to be designed such that redirects are unnecessary, such that appropriate protocols are used for any code that runs in the user's browser.

Importantly, if you scan through the defenses listed in Table 5.6, you may notice that the usual panoply of security controls don't appear as treatments. Firewalls aren't listed. Intrusion prevention systems are not listed. The treatments given are specific to the attacks. That doesn't mean that firewalls shouldn't be deployed. They should be! In this step, we are hunting for those security controls or defenses that will interrupt each CAV such that we can significantly lower the probability of success for attackers (or eliminate it, if possible). For this reason, defenses tend to be specific and to the point. In the next step, we will build the entire security posture as a defense-in-depth.

5.7.2 Build a Defense-in-Depth

In reality, there are many more attacks that will be received from the public Internet. Because we are exploring the ATASM process, the list of attacks has been truncated to keep the discussion manageable. Network-based attacks, such as distributed denial of service (DDoS), have not been discussed. However, for a real site, these and many other attacks must be defended, as well.

For example, the networking equipment that routes traffic into the site and between its various layers would all be subject to attack. We have not examined the physical, network architecture. But in a real analysis, we would examine everything from top to bottom. Such an examination would, of course, include the networking equipment, the operating systems of the servers running AppMaker, the database servers, the Java application server, and so on.

Instead, we've assumed, for the sake of instruction, that the site is already supported by a trusted and capable administrative and networking staff. That's a big assumption. As was noted above, due diligence requires that we make no assumptions and always actually confirm or deny practices and technologies.

In order to build a defense-in-depth, an assessment would take into account all of the defenses, including firewalls, intrusion prevention systems, anti-malware software on the servers, network black hole route capabilities (for network and DDoS attacks), and so forth.

As mentioned above, I would divide the architecture into three tiers. I would require network restrictions between each layer, allowing only intended traffic from known hosts/subnets over specific protocols to the intended recipients, and no other traffic, especially inbound from the Internet. I would probably also specify an authentication of the web server(s) to the application server to be validated at communication initialization, so that if the bastion network were lost, an attacker would also have to gain access to the web server in order to send traffic to the application server.

Because the system handles sensitive data from users originating from the untrusted Internet, the Transport Layer Security (TLS), most often implemented as HTTPS, must be used between the user's browser and the web server, at least for sensitive data transmission. Some architectures would also require TLS (or more properly, communication encryption of some sort) between the web server and the application server, and perhaps even between the application server and the database server? We assumed that the networks in this system are tightly controlled through a mature administrative practice. Therefore, the networks can be considered a trusted infrastructure. Since we've separated out three tiers, and there is only a single piece of trusted networking equipment separating each tier (a new assumption and requirement), the store doesn't feel the need to encrypt the data as it moves between tiers. There are existing protections, and the data are not moving between multiple network segments while passing between tiers.* Without this assumption of trust, communications-level encryption would, very likely, be a requirement between tiers, as well.

Furthermore, because secure coding is an art as much as engineering, I would try to get a web application firewall (WAF) placed between the Internet facing network equipment and the web server (or it could go between the web server and the application server, as well). A WAF will detect known and typical attack patterns and prevent these from being passed to the application server and the application server code. Programmers make mistakes; vulnerabilities do escape even the most rigorous secure development lifecycles. It's a defense-in-depth to anticipate this by removing known attacks, thus protecting those mistakes from being exercised. In addition, most WAF products allow custom rules, so that if a vulnerability is discovered, attacks directed at that specific vulnerability can be removed at the WAF before they can exploit the error during the period of remediation, which can often take some time.

I would assume that at least those controls that have been placed at the Internet-facing edge can and might get compromised. I assume that programming errors will escape into production. Then I design requirements to supplant and enhance the expected controls such that the failure of any single control does not mean the compromise of the entire system, and certainly protect crown jewel data and systems such as identity and financial data with additional, overlapping defenses.

---

* The PCI standard insists on the encryption of payment information in transit. So, while I believe the architecture as described sufficiently protects the data, compliance with PCI may require encryption between layers. Compliance and security are sometimes not the same thing.

5.8 Summary

In this chapter we walked through a process of architecture risk assessment (ARA) and threat modeling that begins with architecture, uses the concept of a credible attack vector (CAV) to identify attack types and attack surfaces, and then applies security controls, or "mitigations," to build a defense-in-depth. As a mnemonic, we call this ATASM: "architecture, threat, attack surface, mitigation." Each of these steps contains a series of sub-steps that when executed produce:

- A thorough understanding of the architecture from a security perspective
- A list of credible threats
- The set of likely attack methods
- The list of attack surfaces
- A set of security requirements that is specific to this system and its organization's objectives

The attack surfaces and CAV can be considered the "threat model" of the system. However, as we found going through the process, we must start with the architecture and the results of a set of investigations that we bring to the analysis.

If possible, an ARA benefits from understanding the "3 S's": the strategy for the system, the structures that will support it, and the specifications of the underlying environments:

- Threat landscape
- Intended risk posture
- Existing and possible security controls
- Any existing security and infrastructure limitations
- Data-sensitivity classification
- Runtime and execution environments
- Deployment models

With this knowledge set in mind, the architecture is decomposed into attackable components and factored to reveal the defensible boundaries. Architecture decomposition and factoring have been discussed at some length in this chapter and in Chapter 3. The unit to use for atomicity, the granularity at which to decompose, is highly context dependent.

Moving from ultimate attack objectives to the system-level goals of specific attack methods, threats are analyzed and then the relevant ones are enumerated into a list. Those threats' attack methods, now qualified for the system under consideration, are applied to the attack surfaces of the architecture to generate a set of CAVs.

Defenses are applied such that these specifically interrupt each CAV, as was discussed in the chapter on risk. Then, the entire set of defenses is considered as a set of overlapping, interlocking, and supporting defenses to build enough redundancy to create a defense-in-depth. The security requirements should be achievable, relevant, and "real world."

ATASM has been presented as a series of linear steps. However, in practice, an assessment might proceed to requirements and uncover a previously unknown part of the system, thus returning to the architecture stage of the process. Ultimately, the goal of the ARA and threat model is to achieve a unity between security posture and intended risk tolerance, to achieve balance between defenses and resource limitations.

References

1. Rosenquist, M. (Dec. 2009). Prioritizing Information Security Risks with Threat Agent Risk Assessment. IT@Intel White Paper. Intel Information Technology. Retrieved from http://media10.connectedsocialmedia.com/intel/10/5725/Intel_IT_Business_Value_ Prioritizing_Info_Security_Risks_with_TARA.pdf
2. Ibid.
3. Open Web Application Security Project (OWASP). (2013). *OWASP Top 10 List*. Retrieved from https://www.owasp.org/index.php/Top_10_2013-Top_10.
4. Ibid.
5. Ibid.
6. Ibid.

Part I

Summary

The first five chapters of this book are meant to set a context and a basis for the security assessment and threat modeling of any type of system. By "system" I mean not only the implementation of software ("code"), but any sort of digital system integration and deployment. This broader definition will, of course, include the writing of software, as indeed, all digital systems reduce to software. However, there is a higher-order integration that can treat the implementation of blocks of functionality in an atomic way.

Not only has architecture risk assessment (ARA) been a mandate within standards and by organizations for a very long time, but the continuing increase in sophistication and complexity on the part of attackers means that flaws in architecture, missed security features, and weak designs continue to put digital systems at risk of compromise. There is no doubt that we should be analyzing our systems for the security that they require to meet organizational and system security goals. Numerous examples have been provided throughout Chapters 1 to 5 to demonstrate the context in which the practices covered by this book exist.

The first chapter sets the stage on which ARA and threat modeling play out. For many years, security architecture has had the task to ensure that architectures and designs include the security and support the security that will be necessary for systems as they are deployed. However, what that process is and how it is performed has not been well understood outside a coterie of subject matter experts. Indeed, learning to apply computer security to systems has so far been learned almost universally through apprenticeship with a master.

In Chapter 1, ARA and threat modeling have been defined as applied security architecture. Furthermore, there lies a body of knowledge and a practice for applying security architecture to systems of all types and sizes.

In this chapter, I've tried to help the reader understand that it is not just security architects who will benefit from understanding this heretofore obscure practice. Everyone who must interact both with a threat model and its results, from developers and implementers through organizational decision makers, will hopefully benefit through a clearer understanding. I intend to lift at least some of the obscurity to reveal a science and an art that has become a necessary and integral function for system delivery. Chapter 1, then, is the gateway into the remainder of the book.

Chapter 2 defined what a system assessment for security is, and, hopefully, what it is not. We have defined this sort of analysis as "applied information security." Indeed, the subtitle of this book is "Applied Security Architecture and Threat Models," security architecture being the method through which to apply the principles of information security.

An analyst may simply "jump right in at the deep end," which, in this book, might mean jumping to the six example analyses in Part II. Instead, through Chapter 2, we explored the "3 S's" of prerequisite knowledge domains that are typically gathered before system assessment:

- Strategy
- Structures
- Specification

This is a mnemonic abstraction intended to help the practitioner gather and then retain the body of prerequisite knowledge that will be applied to each assessment.

Among the strategies that are required is a working knowledge of relevant threat agents, their capabilities, and their risk tolerance. Each organization has a particular, unique, and individual risk tolerance. The experienced assessor will understand this organizational context as a part of the organization's strategy to meet its goals. The organizational risk tolerance then seeds an understanding of the risk tolerance expected for each system under analysis.

"Structures" is meant to encompass and represent the existing infrastructure, security and otherwise. Any infrastructure will have strengths that can be employed to fulfill security requirements. But every infrastructure also has limitations that will have to be overcome, often through additional system-level security requirements.

Finally, "Specification" is meant to encompass the technical details that will influence not only the threat model but also, perhaps, how the architecture is handled.

A few examples of threat agents were explored in Chapter 2 to highlight how these are to be understood in the context of the ARA and threat model. We introduced attributes such as technical methods, risk tolerance, and the amount of effort typically expended by the agents, which we termed the "work factor." Of course, each of these examinations was highly stereotypical; there are always exceptions and exceptional circumstances. The threat agent profile becomes a key ingredient for prioritization during the threat modeling process.

Chapter 3 was an exploration of the art of security architecture as a practice. We narrowly defined "security architecture" to the confines of the task at hand: ARA and threat modeling. We underscored that this is a subset of what is generally considered security architecture practice.

We were introduced to some of the concepts of enterprise architecture as these are relevant to security architecture. In fact, it is my belief that without a grounding in system architecture and at least a glancing understanding of enterprise architecture, a security architect will be severely hampered when trying to assess systems. This is because the architect will not understand the abstractions and the various types of "views," that is, orderings that architects typically employ to understand and manipulate systems.

With a grounding in what architecture is and what it provides to the organization and to the understanding of digital systems, we explored the different types of perspectives that can be represented in a system architecture. Security assessment generally focuses on the logical and component views; these two views can even be combined within the same diagram. We noted that, at some point, a component view must be expressed as specified technologies in a physical view. A security architect may or may not have to work with the physical view, depending upon the skills of any other teams with whom the architect must interact.

A key security architecture skill is the decomposition of architecture views into units that express the qualities required for threat models: attack surfaces and defensible boundaries. Decomposition is the process by which an architecture is deconstructed into its constituent parts such that it can express these attack surfaces and/or defensible boundaries. These two attributes may or may not be represented at the same level of decomposition. Factoring is the process by which individual units are split into their understandable security boundaries and components. We defined atomicity for these purposes as the need to no longer particularize, as an ability to treat some part of the architecture as unitary. This is a peculiar and local definition of "atomic."

Chapter 4 was devoted to risk as it relates to the attack, breach, or compromise of digital systems. I avoided a larger and more encompassing discussion of risk as beyond the scope of this work. Instead, Chapter 4 is an attempt to provide concepts and constructs with direct applicability to system assessment and threat models solely. Security assessment requires a lightweight, rapid risk rating methodology due to the number of individual risks that will need to be formulated and then combined into an overall risk rating. Typically, the assessor will be pressed for time. Any risk rating system must account for that dynamic and allow the rapid rating of risk.

We were introduced to the "credible attack vector" (CAV), which is a construct for quickly understanding whether an attack surface is relevant or not. Indeed, the individual terms of CAV can be treated as Boolean terms, thus simplifying risk rating. Furthermore, interrupting a single term within a CAV describes a method for applying security controls and mitigations. Consequently, a CAV becomes a useful tool, not only for risk rating but also for threat modeling in general.

Chapter 5 was entirely devoted to the lightweight ARA/threat modeling methodology: ATASM. This acronym stands for Architecture, Threats, Attack Surfaces, and Mitigations. ATASM is, of course, a radical reduction of a complex, multidimensional approach. ATASM can hardly be described as a formal methodology. This abstraction is intended merely to help practitioners organize their thinking as they analyze the systems; it is a pedagogy, not a system.

The remainder of Chapter 5 demonstrated how to apply ATASM to a fictional e-commerce website, Web-Sock-A-Rama. An in-depth ARA and threat model of this example was reserved for Part II of this book, as one of the example analyses. In Chapter 5, we explored it as an approach to assessment and analysis.

Hopefully, most, if not all, of the body of knowledge that experienced security architects bring to ARA and threat modeling has at least been introduced and outlined in these five chapters. Reading and, perhaps, playing with the various concepts will hopefully enable the reader to grasp what is taking place within the analyses presented in the next section of this book.

Part II

Part II

Introduction

Practicing with Sample Assessments

We have gathered the required tools in preparation for an assessment. I'm going to assume that we understand our organization's risk tolerance as it applies to systems of the type under assessment. Of all the possible threat agents, we have selected those that may have the most important impact on our organization's mission and whose methodologies can be applied to systems of the type that we are considering. In other words, in preparation for the assessment, we've taken the time to screen out irrelevant threats and attacks. We understand the infrastructure, the execution runtime, and the deployment model for this type of system. Local variations from industry standards are understood.*

Hopefully, by this point in the book, you have a reasonably clear understanding of the information and considerations that you will need to bring to bear in order to assess a system? Presumably, you have a risk methodology with which you are comfortable? Presumably, you are becoming conversant in architecture representations, diagrams, communications flows? Hopefully, at this point, you've gained a feel for the art of decomposing an architecture?

Now, it's time to apply the knowledge that you've gleaned from the preceding chapters to example† architecture risk assessments and threat models.

The best way to build skill in assessing architectures for security is to assess architectures with security in mind. Perhaps this is the only way to accumulate the skill and

---

* If necessary, each sample assessment will provide sufficient context for that assessment, if this information has not been given elsewhere in the book.

† Every architecture presented in this book is fictitious; the examples have been created for this work and are for teaching purposes only. Although these architectures are based upon real-world systems, any resemblance to an actual product or running system is unintentional.

experience required to do this efficiently and do it well? Six architectures will be examined in some depth. Hopefully, each architecture will build upon the patterns that have been examined in the previous examples. That is the intention, at any rate.

In order to keep the text flowing, I've refrained from repeating the analysis of those architecture patterns, attack scenarios, mitigations, and requirements that we will encounter successively after these have been discussed in the text. Instead, I have tried to note in which previous analysis the information can be found. I hope, in this way, to keep the text moving along without sounding overly pedantic. Each architecture will introduce at least one new pattern for security analysis. Importantly, none of the analyses is meant to be unequivocally thorough; technologies that would normally have to be analyzed in each example have been intentionally excluded so as to keep the assessments focused. Real-world systems contain even more than what is presented here, in almost every case.

Those readers who skip to a particular analysis of interest may find that they will also have to read one or more of the previous analyses in order to understand the entire assessment, as later text sometimes refers to earlier examples. Unfortunately, I've sacrificed six cohesive and independent analyses in favor of what I hope to be a series that build upon each other and that highlight similarities between architectures, common patterns, and common solution sets. At the same time, each analysis should present one or more unique security problems not in common with the previous examples, or the analysis will dig deeper into an area glossed over earlier.

As you gain experience with architectures and their analysis for security, I hope that you see the common patterns that emerge. These tend towards similar treatments. The recurring patterns and their treatments become your standards "book," if you will. At the same time, when analyzing real systems (as opposed to these fictitious examples created explicitly for this book), you will also encounter unique problems and idiosyncratic solutions, whose applicability cannot be generalized. One needs skill with both of these situations—the common patterns and the unique ones. Furthermore, a great security architect can differentiate fairly quickly between the local variations and those problems that are well known. It is the locally unique and exceptional that will most likely require the most attention.

If you, the reader, can tolerate my tired and inelegant prose by reading the entire section, you may find that you've seen a sufficient diversity of architectures such that by the end, you can understand varied architectures, and you can better see the attack surfaces and better prescribe security solutions. That is my sincere hope in having rendered these analyses.

Start with Architecture

The first step is to understand the architecture. Most likely, those presenting the architecture to you will be thinking about how the system works, what it's intended for, and how it will be used correctly. This is very different from the way a security architect must approach architecture. Architects interested in implementing a system focus on "use cases." In a security assessment, the security architect focuses on "misuse cases." This distinction is quite important.

Because we're examining the system for security vulnerabilities and weaknesses, there is a conflict of interest built into the assessment. The people on the other side of the table are concerned with correctness, with implementing the requirements and specifications that have been gathered and are supposed to define the system—that is, its boundaries, goals, and intentions. The implementing team may have been living with this system for some time. They may even have developed their own language of acronyms and aliases that help them speak in shorthand. Implicit within the acronyms are the assumptions that they've already made and the cohesive team's trust boundary. If the security assessor, the security architect, has been a part of the team, this will not be a problem: Everyone will be speaking the same language. Unfortunately, that is not the usual situation.

A Few Comments about Playing Well with Others

On the other hand, quite often the security architect is working with a number of projects, maybe more than just a few.* She or he will not have been a part of the forming of the team and will not be party to the assumptions embedded in the acronym-speak to which the team have become accustomed. It may seem to the team that the security architect has been injected into a smooth and running process. The team's collective understanding and the jargon that represents that understanding—the acronyms, system names, aliases, and such—represent a cognitive, shared team reality. Meanwhile, the security architect assigned to a running project might feel like she or he is stumbling about in an unknown country, trying to make sense of a partially understood dialect.

Architecture reviews are not about enforcement of guidelines handed down from some overarching authority. They should not be conducted in a confrontational manner, nor should they focus on problems outside real technical issues… The quality of technical discussion can be harmed by sidebars into organizational politics, funding problems, unnecessary expansions and contractions of scope during the review, and the absence of key stakeholders. Reviews cannot be rubber-stamp procedures used more as a means to gain a checkmark on some management milestone list. The review team and the project team must forge a partnership with the common goals of validating technical architecture decisions, fostering the cross-pollination of architecture experience across the organization, learning from past real-world experiences, and forming a forum where feedback to upper management can be formulated to state risks and opportunities based solely on technical and business merits.[1]

---

* At one time, I was assigned to review 130 projects simultaneously.

You, the security architect, must work within the parameters of the shared reality of which you may not be a part and into which you've been thrown. You might wish to step carefully across this boundary. At the very first meeting, there may be considerable tension in the room. Obviously, a warm and friendly demeanor won't hurt. But beyond that, it may be useful to ask folks to slow down and explain the jargon terms to which they've grown accustom.

By understanding the team assumptions and by unpacking the team's unique brand of jargon and acronyms, you can begin to enter into their mindset; they may even start to see you as a part of their team (if you're lucky). And being a part of the implementing team is the powerful position, though this may seem counterintuitive. Workgroups tend to defend their boundaries. They spent a lot of time building relationships and trust. Those carefully crafted relationships and the trust that has been earned will often be defended against all newcomers, no matter how friendly the intentions of the outsider. Nobody likes to have their "good thing" perturbed.

You may be entering a team "space" where you have not been given the relationship and trust that the team members have already collectively developed? And, in fact, depending upon what experiences team members may have had with security folk in the past, you could well be at a disadvantage? You may feel that you have the expertise, that you've been nominated by your organization to represent security, that you're empowered to drive security into systems, and that you uphold the policy and standards to which systems and development teams must conform. Although that may be true, a human working group develops boundaries. There is already a process in place with which team members are more or less comfortable. Basically, they have something ongoing into which you are being interposed. The sooner that the team perceives you as a fellow member and not an interruption, the sooner you will have constructive conversations about the security needs of the system. Outsiders may very well be resisted by those who feel that they must defend team boundaries. Insiders, members of the team, are the people who are most likely to receive the benefit of active listening and constructive dialogue. Try to make the assessment not about winning and losing but rather about a collaboration for the good of all.

Nevertheless, even as you try to become an "insider," I caution assessors, especially beginning assessors, from allowing the development team to dictate the entirety of the conversation. It's quite likely that system designers have given some thought to security, especially in today's environment, when cyber security concerns are heightened. Still, they may not have looked at the system holistically. They may have been given requirements that are quite specific about authorization models, authentication, protection of messages in transit, and other parameters at this level of specificity. Or it may also be true that they have looked at the system security quite thoroughly. You won't know until you become familiar enough with the system, its requirements, and the thinking that has gone into the current architecture.

To get the holistic picture, oftentimes, one must pull away from discussions about a single security issue (the "presenting problem"). The conversation will need to be redirected to the architecture, the entire architecture of the system in which the problem manifests. I simply ask the team to explain, in the simplest terms, for what the system is intended. This will usually open a discussion about the gross architecture, which then can facilitate a holistic security discussion, rather than being caught in the weeds of some particular aspect of security.

Always, as has been noted earlier in this work, do not limit yourself to the presenting problem. Whatever the concerns are that the team has raised regarding security, you must learn the entirety of the architecture before you can threat model it. A threat model that does not account for any single, undefended credible attack vector (CAV) builds in a weak link from the start. Irrespective of any particular issue with which the development team is concerned, back up and get an understanding of the entire system, and most importantly, get an understanding about what it is to be used for.

Many of the mistakes that I personally have made have been engendered by my failure to understand the basic assumptions behind a system under analysis. I cannot stress strongly enough that even when feeling pressured to get the assessment completed, taking the time to carefully understand what the system is intended to accomplish for the organization and how the implementing team members are thinking about it will pay big dividends as you begin to actually look for attack surfaces against which to apply your prioritized threats.

Understand the Big Picture and the Context

The first step always is to understand why the organization initiated the implementation of the system and to understand the assumptions that are built into the system's architecture and design.

Start at the very highest level: What is the intention for this system in its entirety? What organizational goals is the system attempting to achieve? Who will use the system and for what purposes? Who will administer the system? Who will consume the various reports and logs of the system and for what purposes? Get a feel at a very high level for what the system is intended to accomplish in the context of the organization into which it is being placed and for whom: these people's relationship to the organization and its goals. Catalog all the potential stakeholders who may have a vested interest in any aspect of the system.

Is the system under assessment to be an application that will be deployed within an ongoing eCommerce site? Or is this system an entirely new eCommerce site? Is this to be a desktop application? Or is this a plug-in to a well-known desktop application? Is this a mobile application that connects and edits documents that have been typically created and changed with some well-known application? Or is this mobile application intended to protect a user's device in some way? Is it a payment processing system? A learning management system? A content production system? An identity system? What is the general purpose of the system, and what is the form of how the system will run? Cloud? SaaS? PaaS? Endpoint? Server farm? Appliance? Hosted? Hybrid?

Understand the basic form and purpose of the system well enough to understand the context in which it will execute and will be used. Understand the system's various user types and why these will use the system, what the system will output to each of its users. Understand what benefit users expect from the system, and what benefit the organization expects to gain. Why is this system important enough to implement and for whose benefit?

Once we have a very high-level "big picture" of the system, we're ready to begin the assessment. As I noted earlier, experienced security architects have a grid of all the steps that will need to be followed in mind as they proceed. This grid or plan will be well inculcated such that the actual assessment may seem more like a conversation than a step-by-step process. Don't be fooled by this apparent looseness, should you observe it. Although an assessor may not be following my steps, she or he will be following a plan, nonetheless. To make it easier as you begin, I will restate the overall process once again. The first example will follow the ATASM outline, as we unfold the security assessment in practice. Later analyses will collapse the process somewhat, to appear more "real," as it were.

You may notice a recursive quality in the later analyses? A component will be examined, which will uncover the need for further investigation, perhaps further decomposition or factoring of the architecture. That is a typical assessment flow rather than a rigid series of steps.

Part II assumes that before actually trying to analyze an architecture, the assessor will have researched threat agents active against the type of system under consideration. This research must then uncover the typical attack methods that the relevant threat agents stereotypically employ and the usual effort that the threats will expend towards success. Finally, some understanding of threat agent risk tolerance will be a factor in determining just how deep and extensive the defense-in-depth will need to be to foil attack success.

With threat information well in hand (as much as one can know about intelligent adversaries), the assessment then proceeds along the following steps (as presented in Chapter 2):

1. Diagram the logical architecture of the system.
2. Decompose (factor) the architecture to a level that exposes every possible attack surface (or defensible components). Pay particular attention to changes in trust levels.
3. Apply attack methods for expected goals to the attack surfaces.
4. Filter out threat agents who have no attack surfaces exposed to their typical methods.
5. List all existing security controls for each attack surface.
6. Filter out all attack surfaces for which there is sufficient existing protection. Remember that interrupting a CAV at any single term invalidates that CAV altogether.[*]

---

[*] Though interrupting a CAV term will not usually constitute a defense-in-depth.

7. Apply new security controls to the set of attack services for which there isn't sufficient mitigation. Remember to build a defense-in-depth. Security controls can fail.

8. The security controls that are not yet implemented become the set of security requirements for the system.

Steps 3 through 7 will comprise a formal threat model of the system. It is possible to draw a diagram strictly for the threat model that highlights attack surfaces and controls (both existing and yet to be implemented). You will notice that the threat model exists in the context of the architecture of the system (as described earlier). Failure to keep the architectural context (and the prioritized threat information) may cause the assessment to chase irrelevant or deprioritized attacks.

Getting Back to Basics

Understand the architecture in its entirety. Understand at the architecture's most gross level, including any and all interactive components and each end-to-end in which the system participates.

Diagram the grossest lines of communication, noting origination and destination (usually a single-pointed arrow pointing from origination to destination). Decide which flows and which subdivisions of the architecture will need to be decomposed further. Depending on system complexity, these may be on the same diagram or sub-diagrams. When working with complex systems, you will likely need to decompose the architecture into its component parts. Factor down to a granularity that presents defensible boundaries.

For each defensible component, gather runtime, deployment model, and the proposed infrastructure. Mark the specific lines of communication between each factored component: origination to destination. Note the highest sensitivity of data going across each communication flow. Note all locations where data is at rest, even temporarily.

Understand the complexity of data within each communication flow. Where there is permanent or temporary storage of data, note what data is being stored and the highest sensitivity of the data in that storage. Catalog every system input—that is, every user type and role; every use pattern at a gross level; every line of communication, especially every point where digital data comes into the system (whether from a human or an automated source). Catalog every transit of data (lines of communication) and every data storage point throughout the system. If data transits more than one network, you will need to understand the trust level and restriction of each network in relation to its adjoining networks. A network boundary is obviously any point at which the network addressing changes. But take note of boundaries where there are any type of network restrictions, as well, and note sensitive data transits and storage. Note levels of trust from inputs.

If the system is simple enough, everything may fit onto a single diagram. If the system is highly complex and interactive, don't hesitate to build layers of representation and sub-diagrams, to break out detailed representations.

The point of this investigation is to thoroughly understand the architecture as it fulfills the intentions of the owners and designers. Enumerating all of the attack surfaces of the architecture cannot be done without a complete understanding. We have discussed at length the task of decomposition and the factoring of the architecture. If you feel uncomfortable with what this means as a practice, please reread Chapter 3. One way to understand the level of detail required is to decompose the architecture down to the level of a defensible component. As we said in Chapter 3, a defensible component is the level at which the security controls and their implementation in and around that particular component can be understood easily. Since different security controls operate at different levels of granularity, you will likely need different views, from gross to granular, of the architecture.

For instance, authentication typically happens at some sort of entry point: the entire Web infrastructure, the application server containing components or applications, the operating system, and so on. One might choose to place an additional authentication at a particular function or application. But it's useful to start at the usual and typical place for each control. Perhaps the expected placement of the control will be sufficient to achieve the intended protection? Do it this way if for no other reason than it's generally cheapest and easiest to implement in an expected manner. (Or the control may already have been implemented, as in the login in order to get access to the operating system. This login is typically built into the operating system from the ground up.)

Authorization is typically applied at a more granular level—the object; a database field, row, or table; a set of Web URLs or pages; a part of a user interface (UI); a particular functionality within an application; permissions for a directory tree (read, write, execute); and so forth. Authorization is often placed in the flow just before the resource is accessed.

Network restrictions and firewalls tend to be applied at gross entry and exit points within a network architecture (which may or may not have been designed with security in mind). People who manage networks want to make these sorts of restrictions as gross and easy to manage as possible. Long, complex lists of network access rules (ACLs) are very difficult to get right; a single additional rule inserted in the wrong place can break the entire rule set.

Network designers and maintainers don't tend to be enthusiastic about placing an individual application within its own highly restricted sub-network or virtual private network (VPN). For ease of maintenance, the people tasked with maintaining network boundaries are going to want to treat every subunit in a unified way. They may argue strongly for "least common denominator." Unfortunately, in security we tend to be concerned with the exceptional case, the critical case, the high-profile or most sensitive and restricted case. In many organizations, there is a built-in tension between the economies of scale achieved through designing for the typical case and the requirement to account for the exceptional. Infrastructure design benefits greatly from consideration of both of these needs: large, easily understood, and gross gradations, while also being able to account for corner cases and exceptions.

Consider these three different cases: authentication, authorization, and network access controls. Each may require a different level of granularity during examination. Authentication may take place at an entry point (web front end, application server, operating system, jump server, or inter-module communications input). Authorization will take place close to the resource that needs to be authorized (file, data object, webpage, etc.) Network access control will take place at a network boundary, segment, or subnet. Each of these is a different view, at a different granularity of the system under analysis.

You will likely have to factor a complex system to granularities that are familiar and understood for each stakeholder within the implementation teams. Still, the assessment will need to be decomposed such that every attack surface that is relevant to the prioritized threat list is uncovered. This implies that for any modestly complex system, you will have multiple views. It may turn out that a view will have to be generated specifically for each type of stakeholder. Each of these views will be unique, highlighting one portion of the holistic information that the security assessment requires at the expense of representing other information.

For instance, the network view might hide information about application logical functions, treating the application runtime (operating system, application server, etc.) as atomic so that the gross network placement of types of systems can be understood: database "zones," Internet "zones," application "zones," and similar distinctions. The networking team won't be concerned about host security controls or application security measures. They will be focused upon what architecture can best support whatever network accesses and restrictions are being enforced by the network, and with what types of networking equipment: routers, switches, and firewalls. They will need to know how many network addresses will be consumed when the system goes into production and what the expected growth will be over the life of the system.

On the other hand, the application architects will want to hide routers and switches in favor of gross groupings of application functions. There may be no physical architecture exposed at all within a strictly application view. The application view will highlight business functions (or some other application-level grouping, such as common layer function—i.e., databases, application servers, user presentation, backend transaction processing, etc.). The network view would then be largely lost in order to construct a logical view of functionality or logical view of components or both.

Due to the necessity for each stakeholder group, from organizational decision makers through the various architects and on to physical implementers, the security architect may have to piece together a puzzle of information from each individual view. Complex systems, whose implementation spans many teams, each with its own perspective, will typically never represent the entire security picture in a single diagram. Attempting to do so may be an energy sink not worth pursuing. The assessing security architect will have to ask his or herself whether this energy is well spent or not.

If I cannot "get," that is, understand, a system, I may attempt to diagram that which I'm failing to comprehend. That is a more focused activity that I find always bears fruit. If I haven't understood, the other architects can then correct the diagram. Working iteratively (usually on a white board), we collectively share what we know until that which was poorly understood comes into clear focus.

At this point, I take generous notes rather than attempting to get everything into a single representation. This has worked for me, over literally hundreds* of security assessments. I offer my approach as one way to tame complex systems. Certainly, your

---

* After I had exceeded 500 cumulative system reviews, I stopped counting.

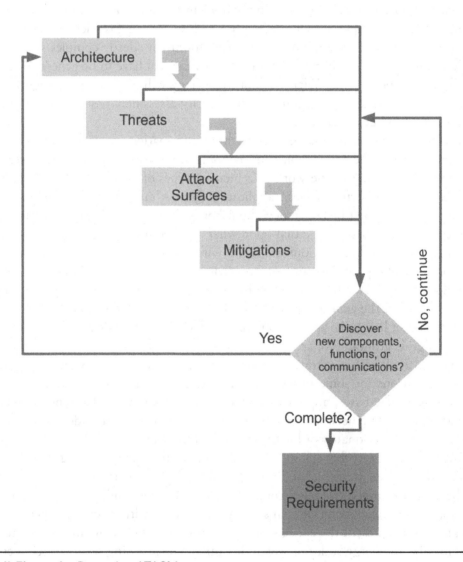

Part II-Figure 1   Recursive ATASM process.

solution will depend greatly on your learning and memory style and the documentation that your organization expects to be produced from your security reviews.

I caution the reader to develop some way of documenting architectures, especially if you will assess many systems, and perhaps even having to undertake multiple assessments running concurrently. Taking good notes alongside reasonable (if incomplete) architecture diagrams has allowed me to assess any number of systems, one after the other and concurrently, and still be able return quickly to where I was in an assessment and what the issues were when I had last looked.

Let's return to a couple of the architectures that we examined previously and start decomposing them into useful parts. Remember, though, as we explore this process, that it is not an exact science as much as an investigative process. We seek to enumerate all the attack surfaces and to understand at which level of granularity controls will have to be applied in order to protect the attack surfaces. Almost by definition then, security assessment tends towards recursion.

Part II-Figure 1 attempts to graphically describe the recursive, investigative nature of ATASM. At any point in the process, as one moves from architecture to threats, then to attack surfaces, and then mitigations, a new element may need to be investigated. The current thread can either complete and then move on to the new items, or the process may be interrupted in favor of the discovery. Each new investigative thread returns to the architecture to begin the process anew. There is both an organic quality to the investigation paths as well as the recursion back to the beginning for each new element that has been discovered.

In Part II, we examine several architectures sequentially, from enterprise level to endpoint, hopefully giving you an opportunity to apply an ARA/threat modeling process to a collection of disparate architectures in order to gain the experience necessary for analyzing real-world systems.

References

1. Ramachandran, J. (2002). *Designing Security Architecture Solutions*, p. 12. John Wiley & Sons.

Chapter 6

eCommerce Website

In this chapter, we will pick up where we left off with the AppMaker Web-Sock-A-Rama web store architecture in Chapter 5. This architecture is reprised in Figure 6.1. We will factor the architecture further into its constituent parts. And we will examine the architecture from different views. We will also complete the ATASM process (Architecture, Threats, Attack Surfaces, Mitigations).

6.1 Decompose the System

Ultimately, the point of the architecture factoring exercise isn't to document a perfect architecture view, but rather, to find those points in the system that are susceptible to likely attack. An appropriate set of defenses can be built from the attack surfaces. In addition, residual risk can be raised for appropriate decision making. As noted above, I will often have multiple views of the same architecture that I consult in order to threat model particular aspects of the system. Security is built at many levels, top-to-bottom, side-to-side, and front-to-back. Security is the architecture domain that interacts with every other domain; it is the "matrix" domain* and must permeate a system in order to build a defense-in-depth.

Looking at Figure 6.1, do you see anything missing? In the chapter about the ATASM process, there were several views of Web-Sock-A-Rama, adding data types, trust boundaries, and an attack surface. Still, in that series of discussions, it was intimated that there must be more; the discussion was purposely kept simple in order to concentrate on the process, in order not to get bogged down in attack details.

---

*I believe that I first heard the phrase, "security is a matrix domain," stated by my former workmate, Richard Puckett (Executive CTO, Enterprise & Security Architecture, at GE).

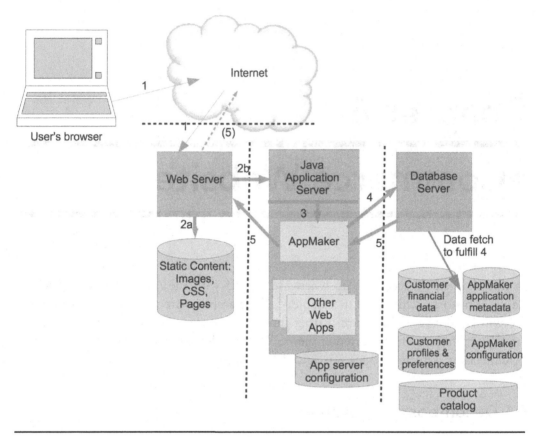

Figure 6.1   AppMaker web architecture.

Over the next series of figures, we will not proceed through the process stepwise, as we did in Chapter 5. Instead, we will proceed in a manner suggestive of an actual assessment. We will analyze what we see and then move on to greater detail. Always, we are looking for ATASM: architecture understanding, followed by credible attack vectors: those qualified threats whose methods have vulnerabilities exposed to them.

When an assessment proceeds stepwise, as in Chapter 5, we try to map a sufficient level of detail during the architecture phase. However, for complex systems found in the real world, a stepwise, strictly linear approach causes diagrams to be overly busy and difficult to understand. As you may see through the following discussions, it often makes more sense to perform a series of mini ATASM assessments, each focused on the level of detail in a particular architecture view showing some workable portion of the system. The mini assessments will often be recursive, as consideration of an attack surface then exposes more components through flows originating at the component under analysis. The summation of risks and requirements then pulls the results from the series of ATASM assessments together into a whole and complete analysis.

6.1.1 The Right Level of Decomposition

I remind the reader, reprising Chapter 5, that the analyst brings the "3 S's"—Strategy, Structures, and Specifications—to each architecture analysis. "Strategy" encompasses the desired risk posture and the threat landscape. "Structures" is about the set of security controls that can be implemented and any existing security limitations that must be taken into account. To understand "Specifications," we have to figure out the data sensitivity, what the runtime and execution environments are, and which deployment model we must analyze for.

As we began to look at the system depicted in Figure 6.1, we discovered that even the obvious attack surface at the web server actually allowed attacks buried in messages and transactions to be passed through to other interfaces in the system. In fact, cross-site scripting (XSS) errors were likely to crop up in the code running in the application server. Structured Query Language (SQL) injections would, if not protected, exploit the database server and data stores. Figure 6.2 adds these two attack surfaces for a more complete picture of the message flow from the Internet and on through to the data tier.

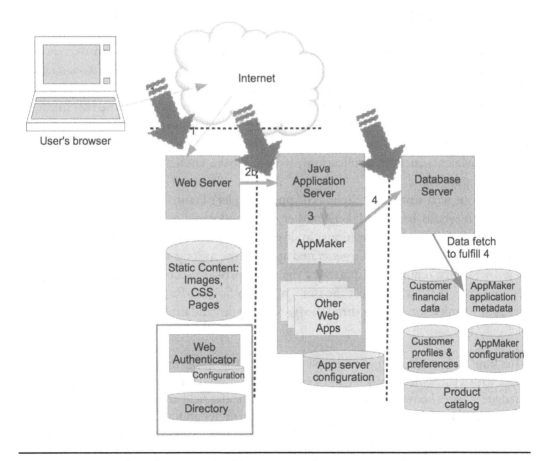

Figure 6.2 Attack surfaces touched by requests from the user's browser.

That is, at arrow 2b, the dynamically handled messages are passed from the web server to the Java application server. The application server calls AppMaker, which in turn passes the message to one of the appropriate applications that were generated by AppMaker. In order to find the appropriate application, AppMaker will have to call the database server (arrow 4) to query the application metadata: data about which application handles which type of message. Then, while handling the request, "other web app" must also query various databases, perhaps customer profiles and the product catalog, in order to build the response for the user. The database server must continue to fetch data ("data fetch to fulfill 4") as requests come in and responses are built. These systems handle multiple requests in parallel.

So, obviously, as called out previously, attacks within messages can be targeted at the web server, at the application server itself (or its configuration), at AppMaker, at one of the generated custom applications that make up the store, or at the database server. In this view, we have uncovered three attack surfaces. That was the conclusion of the analysis in Chapter 5.

6.2 Finding Attack Surfaces to Build the Threat Model

In this architecture view, have we uncovered all the attack surfaces? Can we treat the application server, AppMaker, and the generated applications as a single attack surface? The answer to that question will depend upon how AppMaker works. For the attacks that we've listed previously that target dynamic application code, like the two injection attacks, the bug allowing the injection might lie in the application generation code. Or, it might be fixed within the generated application. Without more information about how AppMaker generates applications, we don't have enough information. There are too many possibilities.

Since our web store has purchased AppMaker, let's assume that wherever the injection lies, it would be AppMaker's maker (the vendor) who would be responsible for the fix. So, in light of this relationship, it probably doesn't matter whether an XSS lies within AppMaker itself or in a generated application, as long as the vendor is responsive to vulnerability reports and practices rigorous software security. Ultimately, it is the vendor's code that must protect the store, not Web-Sock-A-Rama. AppMaker must protect against injection attacks through rigorous input-validation techniques,* as outlined

---

* The kind of generalized application platform that AppMaker represents presents the developer with a particularly difficult and specialized input validation problem. Since *a priori*, the designers won't know what the inputs for any particular field are going to be, they have to design for data-driven validation. That is, AppMaker's design must allow its users to specify the type and allowable sets and ranges for fields at run time. This data will then become a part of AppMaker's application metadata. Input validation routines will need to fetch the relevant metadata that defines a valid input for each field and then validate based upon this metadata. Hard coding data types and ranges isn't possible in this case.

in the tables in Chapter 5. With these types of complex, combinatorial systems, this case often arises, where an organization's security is dependent upon one or more vendors' security practices. In this system, the application server presents an attack surface, as do AppMaker and the AppMaker-generated applications. But responsibility for prevention of application-level code attacks rests firmly with the AppMaker vendor.

We assumed that this web store has an authentication system. Figure 6.2 has added web authentication. We will investigate that component and its flows in a later figure. Still, because authentication systems are often prized targets, the authentication system has been placed within its own separate subnet. Traffic from various components is allowed into the subnet to perform authentications, but traffic from the Internet is not allowed; the authentication system is "invisible" from the Internet; it is not reachable by Web-Sock-A-Rama's customers directly.

The architecture with which we've been working has not been factored into all of its constituent parts. How can an assessor know this with certainty?

Data fetches are not generalized. You will notice in Figure 6.3 that the database server must fetch data from every data store. In previous illustrations, we generalized this for simplicity, showing only a single arrow to represent all data fetches collectively.

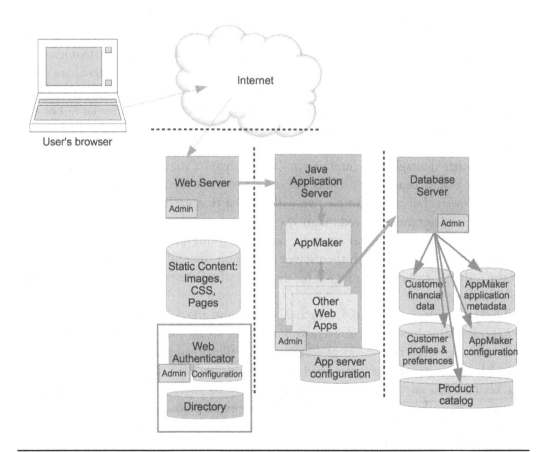

Figure 6.3 Data fetch and management interfaces.

The flow in Figure 6.3 is more coherent with the description given. AppMaker loads one of the generated applications, which in turn must generate a query for various types of data. In this web store, every data store will be used. For each dynamically generated HTTP response, AppMaker must first find (and perhaps in part, build) the appropriate application through its metadata. Then, the application must itself consult the web store and customer data. Hence, the database server is an intermediary between the various data stores and applications (AppMaker and the generated web applications). These flows are shown in Figure 6.3.

Figure 6.3 also shows that each type of functionality must be configured and administered. All web servers, authentication systems, application servers, and database servers have an administrative interface ("admin") that uses a separate network interface and typically have a special user interface (UI) that is presented only to administrators.

Administrators have exceptional powers, that is, "superuser"; they are allowed to start, stop, change, and control the equipment. Therefore, these interfaces are always among the most protected areas of any system. At most of the companies at which I've worked, only "web masters"—highly trusted, proven individuals—are given access to production administration. New hires must demonstrate both skill and trustworthiness over an extended period of time before they are allowed to work on the systems that generate revenue or interact with the public, which are exposed to the dangers of the public Internet. Wise organizations understand that the administrative function has the power to do great harm. In addition, the administrator is likely to be a valuable attack target through which attackers will try to gain access to juicy administrative functions.

What has not been shown is that every separate host among the servers on which this system runs also contains an administrative or management interface. For the operating system, this will be a highly privileged user (that is, the Administrator, super-user, or root account of the operating system). For storage devices and similar, it will be yet another management interface or even a separate management console. A real assessment would factor the architecture down to each of these systems (perhaps in detailed views?). For this example, we will assume that each of the logical functions shown in the diagrams runs redundantly on two or more hosts, and that the hosts are horizontally scaled (additional hosts are added for more processing power). Data are kept on storage devices, which themselves present an integral administrative function. Let the "admin" rectangles in Figure 6.3 represent all of the management interfaces for Web-Sock-A-Rama.

This brings us to Figure 6.4, which diagrams the attack surfaces presented by the management functions. Large arrows are used to indicate the management attack surfaces.

It must be noted that all local configuration files would also be targets and thus should be protected at the same level as the administrative interfaces. That is, if an attacker can add an administrator with the attacker's password to the configuration, or remove all authentication on the interface, or even, perhaps, cause the administrative interface to appear on the Internet, this would significantly impact the system as a whole and the organization fielding the system.

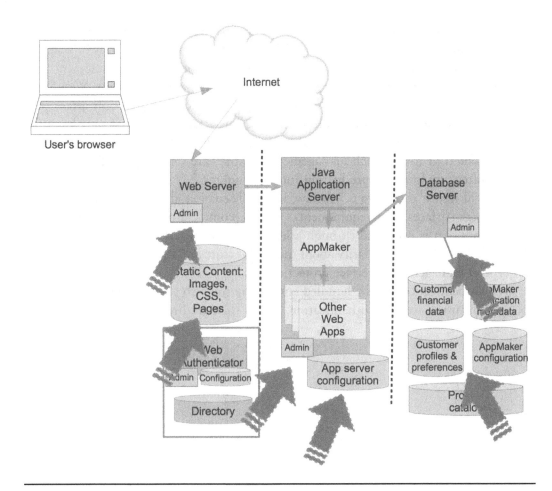

Figure 6.4 Management interface attack surfaces.

Because each system has a set of configuration files and, also, must store some running metadata, attack surface pointers (the large, darker arrows) have not been added to the diagram for these; Figure 6.4 has already become visually busy enough. Still, in the real world, every configuration file and any local, running data set is and must be considered an attack surface. In this case, we have already stipulated that, through the infrastructure practices "investigation" (really, an assumption in this fictitious example system), there are a series of existing controls protecting the servers and their local hard disks. Thus, we concentrate on just a portion of the attack surfaces in order to keep the example focused. In the real world, I would absolutely find out what management practices and protections are implemented to defend the configuration files and metadata sets. Figure 6.7 adds a management access control layer that requires an authentication before administrators can access the management interfaces and configuration data.

Usually, these "jump" servers require dual-factor authentication, often in the form of a one-time token along with the user's password. Once authenticated into the jump server, the administrator then is given access to the management interfaces and consoles only from the jump server protected sub-network. The production system management interfaces only appear on the highly restricted sub-network, which can only be accessed through the jump server. All other access is denied at the network level.

In this manner, an attacker who gains any one of the segments within Web-Sock-A-Rama's web store still cannot access any management interface. The only attack possible is to compromise one of the administrators: The attacker must not only learn the administrator's password, but must also somehow trick or force the administrator to enter the one-time token. Such management networks are very difficult to breach and thus are often employed for production Internet systems.

(We will return to Figure 6.7, below, in the discussion about payment processing flows, attack surfaces, and requirements. A more complete picture of a management sub-network that is restricted through a jump server is pictured in Figure 6.5. Please refer to this figure for more clarity about the architecture and components used to build this type of management interface protection.)

Web authentication can be handled entirely by the web server. The HTTP protocol contains primitives for authentication, which then are implemented in most open

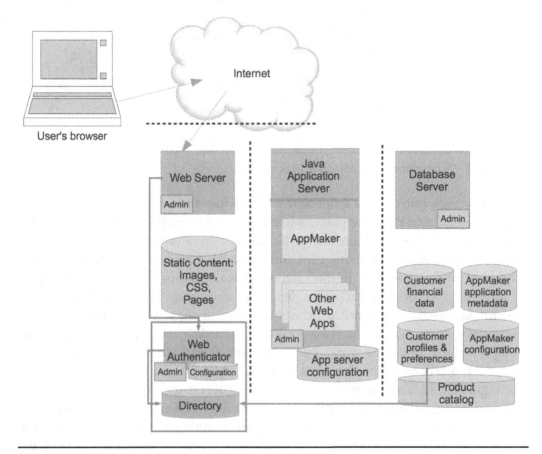

Figure 6.5   Authentication and identity flows.

source and commercial web servers. Many implementations on the web make use of the web server's local or integral authentication services, using the native HTTP authentication messages.

The upside of performing authentication entirely at the web server is simplicity, perhaps even technical elegance (if the integral authentication service is elegantly conceived and carried off). No other components need be put into place beyond the web server. The sensitive authentication doesn't have to traverse a network, most especially the demilitarized zone (DMZ)/bastion network, which is the most exposed zone. Separate protections don't have to be created to protect sensitive authentication systems and data, particularly, credentials. Further, the communications to perform the authentication are likely to be faster when there isn't a network between services. An integral service that has been built with a particular web server in mind is likely to run well as a part of the web server system. Using an included service avoids integration and compatibility problems. Making use of the authentication service included with a web server (whichever web server) has its advantages.

But using the included authentication service contained with or as a component of the web server has some serious disadvantages, as well. First, performing the authentication on the same processor (host) as the web server may slow the web server down. That's not a security concern. But if the web presence must scale to thousands or millions, this factor should definitely be considered. Sometimes, the services included with web servers are not as robust or scaleable as dedicated systems (this is a terrible overgeneralization that may not apply in all cases). Hard evidence should always be sought before making such a decision.

From a security standpoint, if the authentication service is on the web server, where do the credentials reside? Either retrieval calls must be made from the untrusted web server to some other, more trusted layer, or, more typically, the credentials are kept on the server itself, or in storage mounted by the web server. Do you see the security problem in that? With that approach, the credentials are sitting on the least-trusted, most-exposed component in the architecture. That, of course, makes them harder to protect.

If the credentials are kept on the web server or mounted thereon, then all the security controls to protect the web server had better be very nearly bullet proof. Placing that much pressure on the defense of the web server breaks the entire purpose of a bastion system: If the authentication credentials are kept on the web server, it can no longer function as a unit that can be lost in order to protect other systems. The authentication service must not fail—authentication services are security services, namely, security control, which any defense is hoping will not fail or will at least slow attackers down considerably. In other words, the authentication service requires enough defense to provide significant assurance, even in the face of other systems' failures. One does not want to lose customers' credentials! Having lived through one of these scenarios, I can assure you that it is something that any responsible organization will want to avoid.

If you look at Figure 6.5, you will see an alternate architecture. The authentication service lives in a highly restricted network. The only component that can make an authentication request is the web server. Authentication services are not reachable from the Internet, or from any other component in any layer.

In Figure 6.5, you will see an arrow from Customer Profiles to the Directory in the authentication sub-network. That's because user profiles must be attached to user IDs. There should be only one source of truth for user IDs. In this case, it's the Customer Profile. The Directory synchronizes user IDs from the Customer Profiles. As a customer profile is created or deleted, the user ID is populated into the Directory. Passwords are not handled by any of the customer data-handling applications. Instead, control is passed to the authentication service, which then gathers a password from the user (or resets the password, whatever operations must be performed). Only user IDs move from Customer Profile to Directory. The customer onboarding application only has write and delete privileges to the user ID (and any other attributes that authentication requires). In order to protect credentials, no other application may handle or touch credentials in Directory.*

The Web-Sock-A-Rama authentication server and Directory will naturally be valuable targets containing useful functions and data for many attackers. Control of authentication means that an attacker has access to all services protected by authentication. Figure 6.6 has arrows added to some attack surfaces presented by Web Authenticator. Certainly, gaining the authentication host provides complete control of all services running thereon. Less obvious may be the configuration files. If an attacker can reconfigure the authenticator, she or he can control access, as well.

The middle arrow of the three on the left in Figure 6.6 points to the communication flow that goes from Web Authenticator to Directory. If an attacker can view the communications from the service to the directory, then the user's credentials will be exposed. A further level of network attack success might allow an attacker to control authentications: refusing service to some, granting to others (the attacker him or herself?).

Finally, there is an arrow pointing towards Directory, itself, in Figure 6.6. Gaining the directory gives the attacker all the credentials, which are tied to all the user IDs. That very thing happened to a company for which I worked. The attackers compromised every account's password. In other words, attackers had access to every customer account and the services and equipment for which the highest privileged accounts were entitled. Ouch!

But losing customer passwords is worse than that. Many people reuse the same password for multiple web sites. And they reuse their easily remembered user IDs, as well. Consequently, obtaining access to a couple of million passwords probably also gives the attacker access to other web sites. For the successful attacker, acquiring a large password set constitutes considerable success!

---

* These synchronization operations can be implemented in any number of ways: application code, database links, synchronization routines, etc. These implementation details do have security implications. Still we will assume, for the sake of brevity and simplicity, that synchronization is an application function.

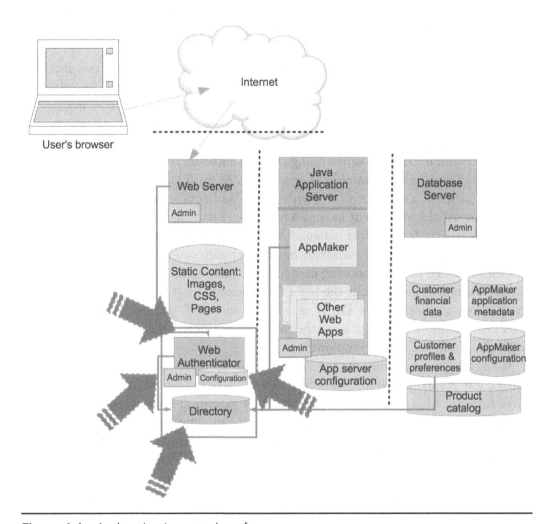

Figure 6.6 Authentication attack surfaces.

If the user ID is the user's email address, the attack also acquires another valuable asset. Active customers' email addresses are a commodity on the black market. The addresses constitute "qualified" spam email targets. A large proportion of the addresses are likely to be in active use, as well as tied to an actual person who can be targeted for phishing attacks, phony drug sales, con games, the gamut of attacks that are promulgated through email. A customer base must include people who buy things with real currency. From the attacker's perspective, "Eureka!" Web-Sock-A-Rama could provide qualified spamming leads in the event of successful compromise of the directory used by the authentication system.

For the foregoing reasons, Directory is a very tempting target. For Web-Sock-A-Rama, the loss impact would include costs of stopping the attack, working with customers over lost information and breached accounts, perhaps socks ordered in a customer's name but sent to an attacker? Then there is the loss of customer confidence in Web-Sock-A-Rama's ability to protect the customer's interests. Future sales may be significantly and negatively impacted?

The Poneman Institute continues to study the direct and indirect costs incurred through the loss of user information. The results of their studies can be sobering. Breaches typically cost companies hundreds of dollars per user. Loss of Directory by itself might well endanger Web-Sock-A-Rama's business, which, of course, means that Directory should be well defended.

The network restrictions surrounding the web authentication service is one layer of defense. Is that sufficient? I would not presume so. As was noted, this component is too valuable to trust to a single defense. Furthermore, authentication requests are tendered by the least-trusted component in the architecture. That component, HTTP termination, resides on the least-trusted network. What additional steps can be taken?

I would reduce the attack surface by having communications from HTTP termination authenticated before processing user authentication requests. That is, the authentication system must authenticate the HTTP component, itself. This will protect against attacks from a compromised DMZ network. And it will protect attempts to spoof HTTP termination. Authenticating the front-end web server does not prevent attacks originating from the web server, however.

We once again encounter the need for rigorous input validation of each authentication request. Although this may seem like overkill to some, I would insist that the maker of the authentication service prove a robust ability to resist ill-formed requests. After all, we must build in an ability to resist the failure of components, particularly those that are highly exposed. It's important to remember that the construction of authentication requests depends upon user (attacker)-supplied data: user ID and password (at least).

Because some data must originate from hostile networks (user IDs and passwords), the authentication services are considered to be "exposed" components. As such, every component that runs as a part of the authentication service must meet the hardening standards for Internet exposed systems. This is the same requirement for every exposed host and application that is a part of Web-Sock-A-Rama's online store. The authentication service, despite its network protections, is no exception. Everything that's exposed must be configured to resist and thwart common web attacks, in case the network protections fail or are compromised.

Naturally, as a high-sensitivity system that is key to maintaining the security posture of the site, administration of the authentication service must only be from the restricted access "jump" server (as described above). The configuration file controls how the authentication service works, so it would be a prime attack target. Therefore, the configuration file must only be accessed by the administration application from the authentication host. In this manner, attackers must first compromise the authentication service or its supporting host before gaining control over the configuration files. And in that situation, the attacker has no further need for exploitation of the configuration file. Configuration file protection is thus dependent upon the defenses of the authentication services and hosts, as previously described.

Any online store will need to handle payments in order to complete sales. Often, the payments are accomplished through payment cards.* Accepting payment cards online immediately subjects the web store to Payment Card Industry (PCI) requirements. These are quite stringent. Some of the requirements specify details about network restrictions and administraative functions. There are encryption requirements, and so on. We will not explore PCI in depth. However, we must briefly touch upon PCI in order to understand how online entities integrate with third-party services.

A merchant does not process the payments for payment card transactions. In most if not all architectures, the supplier of the payment card does not process the payment for the merchant, either. Although there may be situations where a bank or other issuing financial institution will also process payments, these have become rare. Instead, third-party payment processors are employed to actually get funds transfered based upon the credit card or other type of card. From the merchants's perspective, it doesn't really matter who the processor is, as much as the security requirements for the integration.

Whoever the payment processor is, there will be security requirements that the merchant must meet. Usually, the payment requirements are based upon PCI. In addition, there may be contractual obligations to fully meet PCI requirements. In the event of a breach involving payment cards, failure to meet PCI typically involves a penalty against the merchant. I have seen these penalties be quite severe. For our purposes, it is enough to know that significant revenue-impacting penalties are typical when a merchant fails to protect payment cards and/or the payment processor. Adherence to the PCI standard is a critical legal protection, regardless of any actual security value in the standard.

Because our online sock company takes online payments using payment cards, the company will be subject to the PCI standard as well as any additional intricate integration requirements that the third-party payment processor imposes.

PCI requires that every system involved in the chain of handling a payment card must be in a restricted network. The standard also requires that every system on the PCI network meet PCI requirements. Without delving into PCI requirements in any detail, because Web-Sock-A-Rama has isolated its exposed networks and limited the applications and functions allowed on those networks, the company has assumed that the entire online store must meet PCI standards. For our purposes, everything depicted in Figure 6.7 that lies below the Internet, except the isolated authentication service, would be subject to PCI requirements.

Since the authentication service lies within its own restricted network, from a PCI standpoint the authentication service has been separated. The authentication service never handles payment cards and is not involved in financial transactions. Therefore, it lies outside the PCI boundary. Customer's user ID are populated from the customer

---

* There are other types of online payment services. "Wallet" and other, similar services proxy banking and payment card payments for retailers. These services require approximately the same type of integration that we will explore in this example.

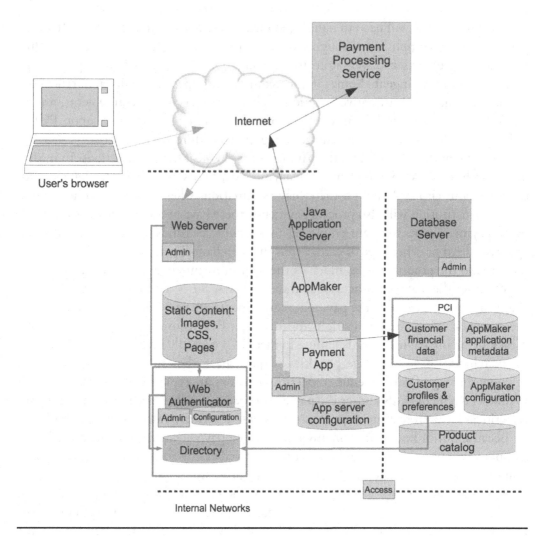

Figure 6.7   Web-Sock-A-Rama payment processing.

database. That is a "push" function; the directory that lies within the authentication service does not call out to the customer data. Therefore, to reiterate, the authentication service is not subject to the PCI requirements.

Even though many of the systems and applications integrated into the online store are not involved in financial transactions, PCI is clear that if systems share a network, then they are subject to PCI requirements. PCI considers the host and the network. It does not discrimiate between applications sharing a host. If a host has not been restricted at the network level from communicating with payment card handling hosts, then it is to be considered within the PCI scope.

You might want to give the PCI proximity requirement some consideration on your own. Does that requirement provide additional security for financial transactions? Is the PCI standard too focused on network proximity versus actual participation in handling the payment card? I'll leave you to consider these questions on your own. The answers tend to be rather controversial.

Regardless of whether the PCI provides an appropriate boundary for security, Web-Sock-A-Rama is subject to the requirements as delineated in the standard. What this means in practice is that the entire application server and all the applications running on it are subject to PCI, since the payment application runs on the application server alongside other applications. Indeed, AppMaker, the online application creation software underlying the web site, is also subject to the PCI requirements. In addition, the database server is subject, as are all the databases, irrespective of whether any particular database contains payment card information. The databases all share the network with the database server. In this way, as stated above, every application lying within the boundaries of the three-tier DMZ architecture is subject to PCI standards. Luckily for the company, the DMZ may be considered carefully restricted (please see the previous analysis).

Because the company is very concerned about protecting its customer financial data and protecting itself against a breach of payment card data, they have chosen to place customer financial data in an additional, isolated, restricted network segment. You will see that Customer Financial Data is isolated within a gray box demarking an isolated network. The isolated network is not required by PCI. It is an additional measure put in place due to the criticality to the business of protecting customer financial data. All of the database network would be considered a PCI segment so long as the database server must move financial transactions. However, as an additional measure, the online retailer has chosen to implement additional protections around the storage of the data.

This extra restriction is implemented through a dedicated network for customer financial data storage.* Only the payment application is allowed to communicate to the financial data store. Naturally, before the payment application may interact with the financial data store, it must authenticate to the financial store (i.e., authentication on behalf of the data store by the database server). The defense of the customer financial data consists of a network isolation, network access control rules (ACL), and authentication of the application before any transactions may proceed through the database server. These security measures are, of course, added on top of management, administrative, and other network and application controls that have already been reviewed. Key will be rigorous input validation by the payment application to protect itself and the data layer from attacks vectored through payment messages.

Although the online retailer handles and then stores customer payment card information, the retailer cannot complete the transaction without the assistance of a third-party payment transaction processor. This is the most common approach to handling

---

* A dedicated customer finance storage network is not mandated by PCI. The entire database zone is subject to PCI due to shared database server(s). The sub-network has been implemented as a part of the defense-in-depth of the online retail website.

payment cards: use of a payment processor vendor. Let's examine the payment processing integration for a moment.

From the perspective of Web-Sock-A-Rama, the payment processor breaches the protective perimeter established around the website architecture. Receipt of messages from the processor add a new attack surface. There have been successful attacks against payment processors. The assumption that the payment processor security is sufficient to protect the company's systems would be foolish. If the payment processor is compromised, the successful attacker has gained an avenue of attack against every retailer making use of the processing service. An attack vectored through the processing service has an entirely different probability than an attack from the Internet. An attack from the payment processor would have far greater access since it would go directly to the payment application. Internet attack is certain; compromise of payment processors is rare, but deadly; the impact of a successful attack coming from a trusted service such as a payment processing service will have critical impact, touching the heart of the relationship between retailer and customer. Therefore, our online retailer must consider what measures should be taken against the rare but serious compromise of the trusted payment service.

Interestingly, the payment service should not trust any retailer. Successful compromise of the retailers' systems would allow attacks to be encapsulated within payment processing requests. Sometimes, a retailer integrates with only a single payment processing service, or perhaps a select few. A successful payment service must integrate with thousands, perhaps hundreds of thousands of retailers. The likelihood that one or more of those retailers will experience a compromise is actually quite high. Again, the payment service would be foolish to assume that every retailer is capable of protecting its systems.

In this example, we have an integration that should be based upon mutual distrust. The two entities must distrust each other at the digital security level, even though there is a fairly high degree of contractual trust. That may seem paradoxical, but remains the better security position for the reasons stated.

Sometimes, the contracts from payment processors can be quite specific and even demanding about the security measures that must be taken to protect the payment processing service. The security architect can easily be pulled away from self-defensive thinking, forgetting about mutual distrust, the fact that payment processors have been breached and might be a vector of attack, and might open an attack surface through the integration. Attacks can go both ways. A holistic approach will not presume adequacy of any entity or system's security. What measures should Web-Sock-A-Rama take to protect itself against a compromise of its payment processor's systems? Are there other defenses that should be taken for the integration?

As is usual for these types of integration, is cheapest to use the Internet for communications between the two parties: Web-Sock-A-Rama and the payment processor. In a later example, we'll explore the use of leased, point-to-point lines to build a private network. That could be a solution in this case, as well. However, the parties have chosen the lower-cost option, the public Internet. But using a known, hostile network obviously presents a security problem. What would be a solution set that would protect all the parties to these transactions? Obviously, customers need to be protected. But, in addition, we have noted that both parties need to be protected from each other as well as from the omnipresent level of attack on the Internet.

Since each party mistrusts the other, each will have to attempt to ensure that attacks are not vectored within the valid and expected messages between them. The actual message stream will be the first attack surface requiring protection. The standard security pattern when one cannot trust the source of input will be to thoroughly validate the input before accepting it: input validation.

The traffic going between the two parties will be the retailer's customers' financial data. When traffic crosses the Internet, one of the features of the TCP/IP protocol is that the routing of any particular packet does not have a guaranteed itinerary. The packet may pass over any router that can handle the path to the next destination router. Although most of the backbone of the Internet passes through major telecom companies' equipment, which implies a probable level of security practice for those routers, such routing is not, as noted, guaranteed. Whatever router is currently available for a path at the moment that a packet arrives will be the router that gets used. A malicious worker, organization, or government might have control of one or more of the routers over which any particular packet must traverse, which, of course, means that Internet routing shouldn't entirely be trusted. Protection of the messages, protection of sensitive customer financial information, is essential.

Consequently, in order to protect their sensitive traffic over the Internet, it must be encrypted in transit. There are two common approaches to this problem: TLS or a Virtual Private Network (VPN).* The application of each of these technologies depends upon the probable length of the connection. And since VPN equipment tends to be more expensive to purchase and to maintain, choice may depend upon the expected return on investment over the connection.

Either of the foregoing transmission encryption choices provides authentication capabilities. And either approach can be kept "alive," that is, active for an extended length of time.† Since our online retailer requires a robust solution and expects a strong return on investment, they have chosen to establish a VPN tunnel for protecting customer payment transactions between its payment application and the payment processing service.

In order to prevent an attacker from establishing a VPN over which to promulgate attacks, the VPN between the two entities must be bidirectionally authenticated. VPN software and hardware is readily available to organizations, individuals, and, of course, attackers. Without the authentication, a wily attacker could very well establish a VPN

---

* A VPN can be implemented with TLS. Or a VPN can be implemented with the Internet Protocol Security (IPsec) protocol. For this example, we will assume that VPN makes use of IPsec.

† We won't compare the relative merits of IPsec and TLS tunnels.

with either the payment application at the retailer, or the payment processing service. Indeed, a perhaps more interesting attack would be to establish a VPN with each party in order to manipulate the transactions flowing between them. This would be a classic "man in the middle" attack scenario. That is, the VPN originating and termination equipment adds an attack surface. Although neither party can protect itself from an attack originating from within the other party, each must do its utmost to protect their end and the other side from a malicious third party. Mutual authentication is the obvious choice. VPN implementations almost always provide robust authentication choices. The one caveat to that statement is that the authentication must traverse the tunnel after encryption has been established unless some other form of credential protection is used, such as an X509 certificate that can be validated. To reiterate, the vast majority of VPN products supply appropriate credential protection, usually in several forms. The specific details of protected credential exchange don't change the basic security requirement.

One additional protection at the network layer is often employed in these types of situations. At the network layer, only the IP addresses of the third-party will be allowed to establish the VPN. In this way, attempts to attack the VPN from other addresses will be eliminated. This "noise" will simply be thrown away at the network level, saving log files for any true, anomalous activity. Furthermore, should there be a vulnerability in the VPN implementation or equipment, there will be some protection at the network level against exploit. Network restriction, then, becomes a part of the defense-in-depth.

Customer service is a function that has not been included in the architecture example. But a customer service function would be a necessity for any successful retailer. Although some portions of customer service can be automated, it's also true that some customers prefer to speak with an understanding human who will take charge and solve the customer's problem. And not every problem is amenable to automation; this is particularly true of complex or multidimensional problems. Sometimes, the service person must act for the customer, viewing and perhaps changing sensitive data, such as payment information and other financial details. Customer service automation integration and customer service representative access are two security problems that will have to be thought through sufficiently. Though we do not take these up in any example architecture, I invite you to take some time to consider issues, attack surfaces, and solutions.

How can appropriate access be given to the customer service representative, while at the same time, making it difficult to steal, either from the customer or the company? The systems and processes for the security of customer service functions could easily fill an entire chapter. Perhaps the material could become a book? We won't take up this subject here, though it surely would become part of the architecture risk assessment (ARA) and threat model of a real web store.

Take a moment to consider the types of access to data that customer service would require to support Web-Sock-A-Rama. Where is the best place to put Support's automated systems? If the Web-Sock-A-Rama company hosts the systems, should these be internal or on one of the external segments? How would the architecture change if customer service were provided by a third party? What other security requirements might support a business decision to outsource this function? Are any of the solutions already presented applicable to these problems?

As an exercise for you to build additional skill, you might consider the customer service security issues listed above as security architecture problems.

6.3 Requirements

Table 6.1 outlines the requirements that we uncovered throughout this chapter's analysis. To provide an organizing principle to the requirements, I've separated them into

Table 6.1 Web-Sock-A-Rama Security Requirements*

Type	Requirement
Administrative	Strong authentication for administrative roles.
	Careful protection of authentication credentials.
	Authorization for sensitive operations.
	Access on a need-to-know basis.
	Access granted only upon proof of requirement for access.
	Access granted upon proof of trust (highly trustworthy individuals only).
	Separation of duties between different layers and duty task sets.
	Logging and monitoring of sensitive operations .
	Monitoring of administrative and management activities must be performed by non-administrative personnel [typically, the Security Operations Center ("SOC")].
	Patch management procedures and service level agreement (SLA) on patch application, depending upon perceived risk of unpatched systems.
	Restricted and verified executable deployment procedures.
	Hardening against attack of externally facing systems.
	Monitor all firewall alerts and other significant events for signs of attack.
	Access control of authentication and authorization systems.
Network	• Implement a three-tier architecture separating HTTP traffic termination (web server) from application server, and application server from the data layer. Allow only required communications between each layer. No other traffic may be allowed to flow between the layers.

(Continued on following page)

---

* A more complete list of typical information security controls and, especially, administrative and management controls may be found in the NIST standard, 800-53.

Table 6.1 Web-Sock-A-Rama Security Requirements (*Continued*)

Type	Requirement
Network (*Continued*)	• Deploy a stateful firewall in front of the HTTP termination.
	• Restricted addressability of administrative access (network or other restrictions). • Administration and management interfaces and configuration files must not be reachable from untrusted networks. Only allow access to administrative assets from the management network.
	• Customer financial data stores must be placed on a restricted, dedicated network.
	• Networks will meet PCI standards • PCI networks must not be visible to untrusted networks. • PCI networks must have restricted access, need-to-access basis.
	• Web authentication systems to be placed upon a restricted network. • Network must not be visible to untrusted networks. Only the HTTP termination may make authentication requests into the web authentication system.
	• The Directory may not be accessed outside the dedicated authentication network, except for Customer profiles and preferences.
	• The authentication service network must not allow any outbound communications to other networks beyond responses to communications that are to be allowed.
	• Use a single piece of trusted networking equipment to separate each tier of the three-tier web processing architecture.
	• Deploy a Web Application Firewall (WAF) between the Internet and the web server. Alternatively, the WAF may be deployed between web layer and application server.
	• Customer financial data between the payment application and the third-party payment processing service will traverse a bidirectionally authenticated VPN.
	• Allow only IP address(es) provided by the payment processing service access to the VPN used to establish an encrypted tunnel between the payment processing service and the payment application. Disallow all other traffic to the VPN.
Application	• Design application code such that dynamic requests to LDAP and to databases are built within the application and not received from users.
	• Dynamic input from users, such as user name or item numbers, must be validated to contain only expected characters. • Input not matching precisely constrained values must return an error to the user. • Response generation must clear all scripting tags found within stored content.

(*Continued on following page*)

Table 6.1 Web-Sock-A-Rama Security Requirements (*Continued*)

Type	Requirement
Application (*Continued*)	• Do not use object revealing protocols similar to Java Remote Method Invocation (RMI) in communications with the user's browser. • Remove all debugging and coding information from errors and other user content. Errors shown to user must be user-centric, in plain (nontechnical) language • Do not expose any debugging, configuration, or administrative interface over customer/public interfaces. • *Use per user or session indirect object references.* • Authorize all direct object accesses.
	• Include a nonpredictable nonce in the response to a successful user authentication. Return the nonce for the session with every authenticated response in a hidden field. Before processing an authenticated request, validate the nonce from the user's session.
	• *Simply avoid using redirects and forwards.* • *If used, don't involve user parameters in calculating the destination. This can usually be done.* • *If destination parameters can't be avoided, ensure that the supplied value is valid, and authorized for the user.* • Employ an indirect reference to URLs between client and server rather than sending the actual value to the user.
	• Customer profiles and preferences must have privileges to insert new user records and to delete records in Directory. No other privileges may be granted to Customer Profiles. No other application not a part of the web authentication service is to be granted privileges in Directory.
	• The authentication service vendor must offer substantive proof of robust fuzz or similar testing on the authentication request processing chain.
	• The authentication service and its hosts must be hardened against attack, as per corporate or industry standards.
	• The authentication service configuration file access must be restricted solely to administrative applications or modules of the authentication service. The configuration file and directories must not be accessible from outside the authentication service network.
	• Applications must pass authentication by the database server before gaining access to databases. • Each application must have a unique database authentication credential.
	• The payment application must validate and verify the correctness of every message received from the payment processing service.

VPN = Virtual Private Network; LDAP = LDAP = Lightweight Directory Access Protocol.
Source: Data set in italics is from the Open Web Application Security Project (OWASP) (2013). *OWASP Top 10 List.* Retrieved from https://www.owasp.org/index.php/Top_10_2013-Top_10.

three areas: administrative, network, and application. These are necessarily somewhat arbitrary; the boundaries between these abstractions are relatively "soft," and perhaps indistinct. Still, I hope this ordering provides at least some organization to the security requirements that we've uncovered from the analysis so that these are more easily digestible.

As we've assumed that there is a mature administrative function for this business, the administrative requirements section is relatively brief. I hope that you, the reader, can make use of any number of available exhaustive explanations or standards describing the secure management and administration of computer systems. Repeating those here, I believe, won't provide much benefit. Most information security professionals are already familiar with this body of knowledge.

For exposed Internet sites, networking restrictions and boundaries can become critically important. Though there are other ways to create trust boundaries, a common way is to use network segments and then control flows between the segments and between the systems in the segments. That's the essential gist of the networking requirements given in Table 6.1.

Each of the requirements listed in the application section should be familiar from the analysis. Although there's always the possibility that I've introduced a requirement into the list that wasn't discussed or that I've missed one that was given in the analysis, I have tried to be thorough and consistent. Hence, if you've read the analysis, you should already be familiar with each of these requirements. As you work through the list, should you find one or more of the requirements as stated to be ambiguous, simply go back into the text and refer to the more complete explanation.

As this is the first analysis in our series of six, I caution the reader to understand these requirements fairly well. In order not to be repetitive, the subsequent analyses will refer back to these wherever they arise. Remember, architectural patterns repeat, and I've attempted to use the same solutions consistently throughout the examples. This is not to imply that any of these is the only solution. Hopefully, I've made that clear? Still, one of the points of this book is that there are patterns and their solution sets that repeat. So I've taken some pains to reuse the same solution set rather than introducing new security defense approaches for the same recurring problem.

Chapter 7

Enterprise Architecture

When a security architect interacts with an enterprise architecture, the work is at a very strategic level. The ATASM process only loosely applies. There isn't sufficient specificity in an enterprise architecture to develop a threat model. Once the architecture begins to be factored into components, it becomes an alternate, logical, and/or component view. Furthermore, even given a component view of the enterprise, we cannot deal with components at a sufficiently granular level to be able to discover actual, technical attack surfaces, or to specify implementable security controls.

Instead, the object of analysis at such a gross level is to uncover the general security requirements that will enable the enterprise architecture to succeed. Instead of representing security as a magic box along the side or underneath as some sort of transformative function that lies within the infrastructure, our task is rather to help our fellow enterprise architects understand the sort of imperatives that security functions will need to fulfill. Indeed, the security requirements that are delivered at the enterprise level will help shape the security strategy for the enterprise. And these enterprise security requirements will then seed the security analyses for each solution (set of systems providing a functionality) that takes its place within the enterprise architecture. Consequently, architecture analysis of the enterprise architecture is formative and informative rather than detailed and specific.

For the security architect concerned with building security systems, there is typically a need for an enterprise security architecture view. Or perhaps like the Open Group's Reference Security Architecture, the strategic vision may be expressed as an enterprise reference security architecture. In this work, we are consuming security systems, not building them.* Therefore, we will skip over this form of "enterprise security architecture"

---

* Though, of course, a security system should be analyzed and threat modeled just like any other system. Accordingly, every security system can be analyzed for its security requirements using ATASM.

in favor of continuing the exploration of securing systems through architecture analysis of the enterprise architecture, while understanding the constraints by which analysis at this level abides.

Instead, at the enterprise level one can concentrate on the security features for major groups of users. Is there a need to keep identities? Identity must be kept for each of the different groups of users. For instance,

- Customers
- Internal analysts
- Customer service and support
- Administrative staff
- Executives

An enumeration such as the above role list suggests an enterprise-grade identity system with sub-systems for external and internal authentication. Or perhaps a single authentication system should be used that can support multiple trust zones securely? Authorization might also be accomplished through the same system, perhaps through group membership (a common, simple approach for implementing authorization).

Naturally, there will need to be perimeter controls, such as firewall systems. These systems suggest a need to gather and analyze the events from low-trust zones, perimeter controls, and perhaps other activities that should be monitored. This implies a Security Information and Event Management (SIEM) system. Using a similar reasoning process, the search would be continued for all the major types and placements of the security systems that will be needed.

Above is an example of the sort of strategic, system-oriented thinking that can be accomplished when analyzing the enterprise architecture. This strategic thinking breaks down that large "Security Services" box in Figure 7.1 into the appropriate functions and components that will be needed to support the enterprise. The enterprise architecture is a panorama that provides an opportunity to think big about security services as features of the organization. Attack surfaces are viewed as the business inputs to the enterprise, rather than trying to provide strategy based upon the surfaces presented at a technology level.

Figure 7.1 reprises the enterprise architecture that was introduced in Chapter 3. Study it for a moment and consider the implications of each of the functions represented. Do presentation layers add an attack surface to the enterprise? How about an eCommerce presence? The supply chain will interact with an entire business ecosystem of many other organizations. Interactions will probably include both people and automated flows. Are these third parties to be trusted at the same level as the internal systems, such as content management or data analysis? Going a step further, are there threat agents whose goals include the business data of the organization? If so, does that make the business analysis function or the content management systems targets of possible interest? Why?

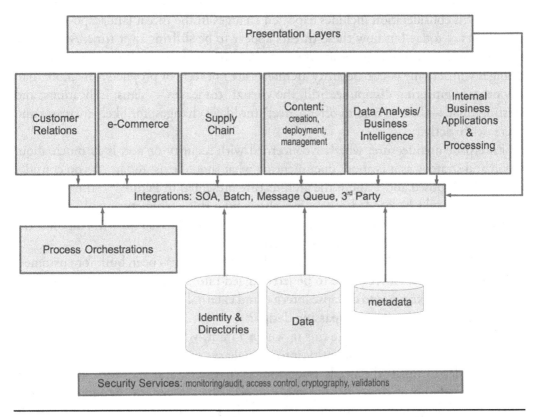

Figure 7.1   Enterprise conceptual architecture.

Considering the "why attack" question for the very gross attack surfaces represented in Figure 7.1 helps to focus the cyber security strategy for the enterprise. Remember, we're trying to see what components will be needed.

Or, more likely, the enterprise architecture practice will follow a period of sustained growth, perhaps years of growth, with little or no enterprise-level architectural order. Certainly, discreet systems will have been architected. But few organizations begin with an enterprise view. We work towards such a view once the number of interacting systems becomes too complex to hold in one person's mind. Due to this natural maturation of architecture practice, the enterprise view must accommodate pre-existing and legacy sub-systems. Naturally, some of those systems will be security systems and infrastructure that have been built to protect what already exists.

Once an organization grows to a complexity that requires an enterprise view, this view usually includes existing systems while at the same time expressing a vision for the future architecture. There will be a mix of existing systems and functions, based upon an existing infrastructure while, at the same time, articulating how the goals of the organization can be accomplished in a hopefully cleaner and more elegant manner.

Thus, the enterprise security model must also account for existing controls while, at the same time, it must consider how the architecture can be protected on into the future. This consideration includes expected changes in the threat landscape—not just the threats of today but how these threats appear to be shifting over time. A three- to five-year horizon is typical, despite the fact that none of us has a line on exactly what changes will actually occur. Security architects are not seers or prophets, any more than any other engineering discipline. Still, the virtual "tea leaves"—signs, indications, and existing trends—can be read to offer a "feel" for likely changes, for likely increases and decreases in activity.

Enterprise architecture, whether concerned with security or not, is as much about vision and strategy as it is about documenting what should exist today. As you consider the questions posed above about the architecture presented in Figure 7.1, think not just about what might be needed today, but about how this architecture will need to be protected on into the future, as it grows and matures. What systems will empower the present while also sustaining anticipated growth?

For instance, what if the existing external identity store has been built for customers only, and internal resources have to be jerry-rigged into a design not meant to include them? Does it make sense to collapse internal and external identities into a single system of truth, into a single all-encompassing design?

I had a situation precisely like this in which a multi-year effort did, in fact, collapse the three distinct systems of identity into a single system. Much design needed to be done in order to fulfill the needs of customers, partners, and the work force (which itself was made up of three distinct sub-groups). Then, a system that could support all the different legacy environments, while at the same time empowering an entirely new infrastructure, had to be architected and then built. Ultimately, the collapse to a single source of truth saved much effort that had been expended to keep all the different systems synchronized. Money was eventually recouped and then saved. The design was much simpler to maintain. As an enterprise-level example, a decision was made to replace functioning systems, including a number of synchronizing applications, all at cost to the enterprise in order to support an emerging enterprise architecture on into the future. These are the types of strategic decisions that are made with enterprise views.

Thinking about the ATASM process, we do not know anything about the purpose of this enterprise architecture, or the organization that fields it. Although we can certainly make some guesses that help, the first step, as previously laid out, is to research the purpose of an architecture in the context of the organization's objectives. Obviously, this architecture is intended to sell something, perhaps something tangible?

Let's find out what kind of enterprise we have diagrammed. As ATASM suggests, "start at the beginning." Even though we will be working at quite a high level, we still must know what it is with which we're working. Of course, if this were an enterprise architecture representing an existing enterprise, a security architect would probably not be encountering the diagram in isolation. Even if brand new to the organization, presumably during the hiring process the architect would've found out what the major goals of the organization are. In other words, encountering an enterprise architecture completely in isolation from the organization itself is a fairly artificial situation. I daresay that a security architect is rarely presented with a conceptual enterprise architecture diagram in the absence of knowledge about the organization supposedly represented by the diagram.

Even though analyzing an enterprise architecture in isolation from the organization is a relatively artificial situation, as a methodology for learning and practicing, let's pretend that we, the security architects, have just encountered an enterprise architecture about which we know nothing. Given our lack of understanding, the starting questions must be, "What does the organization do?" And, "What does the organization expect to get from its digital systems?"

7.1 Enterprise Architecture Pre-work: Digital Diskus

This enterprise is called Digital Diskus. They design, manufacture, and sell networking routing equipment. Digital Diskus' customers are medium and large organizations that must maintain extensive networking infrastructure. The company has a sales force, as well as channel partners—companies that provide networking equipment and networking expertise to their customers. These partners install, configure, and, perhaps, also run large and complex networks. Digital Diskus' vision statement is, "Design and build the most dependable and the easiest to configure networking equipment."

The company offers a wide range of sizes and feature sets to accommodate all portions of the modern, interconnected enterprise. Digital Diskus' products can be used in core networks, throughout the corporate campus, and beyond to satellite offices. Hence, they offer switches, routers, and a whole variety of network-related equipment that would be needed to set up a modern, enterprise-grade network that spans many localities. Although the company does offer security features built into routers and switches, they do not consider themselves a "security" company.

Digital Diskus' sales are placed through the company's Internet facing eCommerce site. Sales can be made directly by a customer via an online store front, through one of the partners, or through the direct sales force. The company tries to automate their supply chain as much as possible, so there is a need for automated interchange between the parties within the supply chain and throughout the purchasing ecosystem, just as there is within the sales process.

Digital Diskus' goal is to provide highly dependable solutions in which customers can have great confidence. Quality is much more important than price. A prolonged mean time before failure (MTBF) is considered a competitive advantage of the company's networking products. The company brand depends on customers who will pay more for the higher confidence and expectation of the company's vaunted dependability. In addition the company's highly trained customer support staff is an aspect of the company's sales pitch.

Nevertheless, the company seeks to maximize profits through careful management of components and inventory when manufacturing its products. Since the company does not compete on price, it cannot afford flaky, poor quality components. Components of the products don't have to be boutique or specially created; components don't have to be of the absolute highest quality. Networking equipment manufactured by the company must perform as described and continue to perform with as few failures as possible. However, high performance is not one of the company's competitive advantages.

The company has not expanded far afield from its core business. Acquisitions and mergers have been strategic to bolster the core networking line of products. Senior management have been reluctant to stray far from a business model and set of technologies with which they are familiar and with which they feel comfortable. Their motto is, "Networks you can depend upon."

Digital Diskus' executive staff are very protective of the brand and the goodwill of the company's customers. The company's customers have been willing to pay a premium for an assurance that they are also purchasing access to significant expertise in networking. A major security incident involving one or more products is viewed as an unmitigated disaster. Consequently, the organization is rather risk averse, especially with respect to cyber security.

Furthermore, the company's designs and manufacturing secrets are considered highly proprietary. Indeed, code that implements encryption algorithms is held very closely; encryption implementations are seen not only as trade secrets but also as a trust that protects the company's customers.

At this point, considering the foregoing, do you have a feel for the company, Digital Diskus? Do you know enough about its mission, its organizational objectives, and its risk appetite to place Figure 7.1 in an organizational context? If not, what more do you need to understand? If something is unclear, take a look at the conceptual architecture diagrammed in Figure 7.1 while considering the introductory paragraphs describing Digital Diskus.

7.2 Digital Diskus' Threat Landscape

Since Digital Diskus' products include encryption implementations, might one or more entities be interested in the cryptography implementations? What if the company's products are deployed by governments, some of whom are hostile to each other? Might one or more of these nation-states be interested in manipulating or compromising cryptography in use within the networks of one of its enemies?

The questions posed in the last paragraph should be asked by those responsible for threat analysis for the company. Whether or not the executive team of our fictitious enterprise have actually considered these questions, we are going to assume that the company believes that it may be the target of industrial espionage. The security team has uncovered a number of incidents that may indicate at least some interest by industrial espionage threat agents. As far as anyone in the company knows, as yet, no major breaches have occurred.

Obviously, as we have previously analyzed, any company that has an Internet presence must be concerned with cyber crime. Beyond the public facing portions of the company's websites, an extensive ecosystem of partners and suppliers is primarily maintained over the public Internet.*

The company is very careful with the brand, allowing only limited use of the logo and name beyond Digital Diskus' marketing materials. Financial data are made available to qualified individuals only. Nevertheless, salesman, sales partners, suppliers, consultants, contractors, and others will access company systems, some of which handle sensitive data. Each organizational member of the ecosystem must guarantee that only qualified and trustworthy individuals have access to the company's systems. In reality, the company have no guarantee of trust, given the extent of the ecosystem and the number of individuals who must have access. Furthermore, given the thousands of people who must interact with the company's systems, it would be foolish to believe that every individual who has access is honest and reliable. It is perhaps also foolish to believe that every connected organization can meet rigorous security practices. Consider the following quote:

> *The attackers reportedly first gained access to Target's system by stealing credentials from an HVAC and refrigeration company, Fazio Mechanical Services, based in Sharpsburg, Pennsylvania. This company specializes as a refrigeration contractor for supermarkets in the mid-Atlantic region and had remote access to Target's network for electronic billing, contract submission, and project management purposes.*[1]

When I worked at a company that had 70,000 employees and also had another 50,000 contractors with access to the network, I often heard people say to me, "but this application is internal only." This statement meant, of course, that the system wasn't exposed since only "trustworthy" people had access. People's faith in the ability of the company to hire and contract only high-integrity individuals was certainly laudable but, perhaps, not entirely well founded? I often responded to these comments by saying, "In any city of 120,000 people, will there be at least a few criminals?" In fact, in any city of 10,000 people, there are likely to be at least a few individuals who are seeking a special advantage, sometimes even a criminal advantage.

Now it is true that enterprises tend to be somewhat picky about who they hire. Indeed, it's common to check criminal records and other similar barometers of integrity before hiring. At least it's common in the United States, where it's legal to do this kind of research. Other countries forbid background checks because they see it as an invasion

---

* At the risk of a complicated fictitious example, several of Digital Diskus' business partners maintain point-to-point connections. These are implemented either with leased lines over common carriers or point-to-point Virtual Private Network (VPN) tunnels that cross the Internet. All of these connections are managed through the company's extranet.

of personal privacy. And in still other countries, the records simply are not good enough to be trusted.

One could be led to believe that through performing some form of pre-employment due diligence, the choice of employees and contractors who've passed muster would eliminate at least some criminal activity. Still, I have personally been party to a number of investigations involving fraud and theft by insiders. Although the percentage of those who might be more criminally inclined is probably less within any global enterprise's employees then the per capita general average, insider attack cannot be eliminated. Certainly, insider attack will not be eliminated when considering populations in the tens of thousands or even hundreds of thousands of individuals, no matter how much prescreening and selectivity has been performed.

The foregoing suggests some possibility for dishonest behavior. In addition, the propensity for humans to make honest mistakes must be added to the integrity angle. The larger the range of experience and sophistication, the more the likelihood of error based upon misunderstanding or just plain inattention. With populations running into the thousands, the probability of error by commission or omission amplifies significantly. People make mistakes; sometimes even careful people make dumb mistakes.*

Taking the above demographics into account, any architecture that includes automation, stretching from post sales back through the sales cycle and on into the manufacturing and supply chain networks and business relationships, will have to account for possible insider threats. In short, those who have been granted access for legitimate business reasons cannot be considered entirely trustworthy.

Because the company provides networking equipment to many companies and organizations, including diverse governments, the company's name has appeared occasionally among the lists of companies related to one controversial issue or another, even being listed as a party to competing controversies. Although the company attempts to maintain a neutral stance politically, its customers do not. Due to this exposure, digital activists have occasionally indicated some interest in the company. Indeed, "hacktivists" have instigated direct cyber actions against lists of companies that have included Digital Diskus. To date, there've been no incidences from digital activism. Still, company threat analysts believe that, in the future, the company may become an unwilling activist target despite its best efforts to take no stance on political or divisive issues.

Beyond the possibility of someone with malicious intent gaining access to the company's systems, the company is also concerned about a disgruntled or rogue insider who must be given privileged access in order to carry out duties. The company employs a fairly extensive technical administrative staff in order to run the various systems that make up the company's digital ecosystem. Should one of these highly privileged individuals, for whatever reason, decide to use her or his access to hurt the company, a great deal of damage might ensue. Thus, technical staff are considered to be among the company's significant threat agents.

---

* Despite my best efforts, I've been known to make very dumb mistakes.

Digital Diskus staff are concerned with four major classes of threat agents:

- Industrial spies
- Cyber criminals
- Cyber activists
- Privileged insiders

7.3 Conceptual Security Architecture

Every single application that interacts with users must have a user interface (UI). This is, of course, obvious. From the diagram shown in Figure 7.1, it might be construed that some economy of scale is sought through building a single enterprise presentation layer through which every application, no matter its purpose or trust, interacts. That would be a great question to ask the enterprise architect who drew the diagram.

Typically, a conceptual architecture is trying to diagram gross functions and processes in relationship to each other in as simple a manner as possible. Simplicity and abstraction help to create a representation that can be quickly and easily grasped—the essence of the enterprise is more important than detail. An enterprise architecture tends toward gross oversimplification.

Although it is possible to build one single presentation layer through which all interactions flow, if legacy applications exist, attaining a single presentation layer is highly unlikely. Instead, the diagram seeks to represent the enterprise as a series of interrelated processes, functions, and systems. A great deal of abstraction is employed; much detail is purposely obscured.

It is rather unlikely that a single presentation layer is actually in use at Digital Diskus, much less planned. Instead, the diagram suggests that software designers think strategically about the sorts of architectures that will enable presentations to be logically separated from business processing. And that is actually the point: This architecture is intended to underline that business processing must not make its way into the presentation layers of the architecture. Presentations of digital systems should be distinct from the processing; systems should be designed such that they adhere to this architectural requirement.

In the same way that this canonical presentation layer is conceived as a part of an enterprise architecture, security is represented by a unitary function that can be abstracted and set to one side. As we have seen several times previously, this notion is patently erroneous. Instead, for modern information security practices at an enterprise level, computer security might be summarized through the architecture security principles that have been adopted by the organization. The organization's architects expect the security principles to emerge from the systems that make up the enterprise architecture.

The following set of security principles from the Open Web Application Security Project (OWASP) are reprised from Chapter 3:

> – *Apply defense in depth (complete mediation).*
> – *Use a positive security model (fail-safe defaults, minimize attack surface).*
> – *Fail securely.*
> – *Run with least privilege.*
> – *Avoid security by obscurity (open design).*
> – *Keep security simple (verifiable, economy of mechanism).*
> – *Detect intrusions (compromise recording).*
> – *Don't trust infrastructure.*
> – *Don't trust services.*
> – *Establish secure defaults[2]*

Of course, parroting typical security principles as a "security architecture" isn't going to be all that useful when building out the security for the enterprise. Very quickly, astute architects and implementers are going to ask, "What do we build in order not to trust the infrastructure? And why shouldn't we, anyway?" Those seem to be perfectly reasonable questions based upon a need to "make the conceptual architecture real."

The trick is to translate principles into high-level imperatives that conceptually outline the security requirements that the enterprise will need. Once we have a handle on the threat agents that are relevant for Digital Diskus, we will attempt to outline the imperatives that will guide the enterprise architecture implementation. It is perhaps useful to reiterate that we must work at a very high, nonspecific level. The "how" part of implementation remains unknown.

7.4 Enterprise Security Architecture Imperatives and Requirements

At a strategic, enterprise level, what other architectural elements, that is, security requirements for the enterprise, might the company consider employing?

As we explored earlier, industrial espionage actors may employ sophisticated attack methods, some of which may have never been seen before.* And, espionage threat agents' attacks can span multiple years. They will take the time necessary to know their quarry and to find weak points in the systems and people who constitute the target. Therefore, at the enterprise level, decision makers will have to be prepared to expend enough resources to identify "low and slow" intrusions.

Furthermore, the company's executive staff should be prepared to respond to a partial breach. An attack may be partially successful before it is identified and can be stopped. With such determined and sophisticated attackers, part of the security strategy must be to frustrate and to slow ongoing, sophisticated attacks. This strategy lies in contrast to belief that defenses are so well constructed that no attack can be at all

---

* So-called "zero day" attacks.

successful. Hence, security alert and event monitoring will be a critical part of the defense in order to catch and respond to events before they become disastrous.

Because of the probability of partially successful attacks, compromise containment can be built into the architecture such that successful attacks cannot be used as a beachhead to move from a higher zone of exposure to less exposed areas. Architectures must emphasize strong boundaries. Crossing a boundary must require higher privileges and hopefully an entirely different attack methodology. These defensive tactics will subvert and contain a successful exploit sufficiently so that the security operations team has time to respond and eradicate. This suggests an architecture in which discrete units of functionality, let's say, applications, have highly limited access to resources beyond their own area.

In Figure 7.1 you will see that almost every function is connected to the integration systems. Whereas all applications, or least most of them, are integrated through technologies such as a message bus, one of the architectural imperatives will be application-to-application and application-to-message bus access control. That is, each contained set of functionalities is allowed only to integrate through the controlled integration system (the message bus) on an as-needed and as-granted basis. No application should have unfettered access to everything that's connected to the integration system (here, the message bus and other integration mechanisms).

Another architectural imperative might be to insist that messages passed to the message bus are generated within the application code. No message destined to cross the message bus is allowed to come from outside the application that sends the message. What this means in practice is that whenever onward-bound data arrive in applications, each application's code must extract the bits that will be passed through the message bus and re-form these into a different message package, a different message construction, before passing along the data. Although such an approach might seem burdensome, it is an effective protocol-level barrier to getting attack payloads through an application to some following target. The attacker must understand the new message form and anticipate the subsequent message processing while still getting the attack through the initial packaging and format. Somehow, an attack destined to be passed through the application has to get through any message validation while also anticipating an alternate encapsulation. While not perfect, this method of protection can slow the attacker down as an attack attempts to go beyond the initial, processing application. Again, containment is not about a perfect defense, but rather about frustration and befuddlement.

Anything engineered by humans can be reverse engineered and understood by humans. This is one of the fundamental laws of computer security. Nevertheless, it takes time and effort to understand something, especially if the "something" is complex. Part of containment can be the art of confusing by introducing unexpected shifts in protocol, message form, transaction state, and encapsulation. It's not that the defender expects the attacker never to figure these shifts out. They will. Rather, the art is to give the defenders' reactive security capability sufficient time to discover and then respond.

One additional imperative for the message bus should be protection of all traffic in transit, perhaps provided by encryption. The encryption would have to be kept appropriately performant. One of the downsides of encryption is that it adds time to overall message delivery. That's a non-security topic that we won't take up here. However, in the real world, experienced architects are going to ask the hard performance questions. A security architect will need to answer these such that encryption gets built that does not degrade overall performance and related service level agreements (SLAs) around message delivery that must be met. Otherwise, the encryption will never get used, perhaps never built.

Ignoring the performance question, we have already stated that the message bus appears to connect to almost every system. That is not a reason to encrypt or otherwise provide message protection. Encryption does not protect the connecting systems from each other; that is not the purpose of encryption. The key determiner for transmission protection is the fact that Digital Diskus networks are highly cross-connected with other entities. Even with strong due diligence activities about the security of the third parties, their security is out of the control of Digital Diskus. Because so many entities are involved, the sheer complexity is a breeding ground for mistakes. Additionally, there are many people who have access to the networks who must have access to various systems, all of which connect to the bus. This level of exposure strongly suggests message protection, if for no other reason than inadvertent disclosure. Add on that Digital Diskus staff are concerned about industrial espionage, and a strong case is made for message protection. The obvious solution to that is to encrypt every message that transits the bus. Alternate protection would be to highly restrict the network equipment, restrict visibility to message bus transmissions, a segmented network, switching rather than hubs, and so forth. As a networking company, these capabilities shouldn't be too difficult. However protection is implemented (encryption or network controls), protecting message bus communications must be an imperative.

Obviously, if our enterprise's risk posture is incident adverse, and the company also intends to be fairly mature in its computer security practices, the company's administrative functions will follow typical, industry-standard practices when maintaining the company's systems. Previously, we surveyed some of the activities that might constitute such a practice. There are numerous works devoted to precisely this subject. Standards such as NIST 800–53 delineate the practices and tasks that are required. Hopefully, there's no need to reiterate these here? Please assume that our digital enterprise is doing its best to meet or exceed access control, configuration and change control, patching, and the panoply of tasks that make up a mature administrative practice.

Even so, as an enterprise security architect, I would underscore the importance of a mature practice. It might be useful to review and assess the current body of practice to identify weak links. This review will be performed on a periodic basis. Such assessment could probably be considered a part of the strategic enterprise security architecture. Given the importance of a mature and solidified practice in this arena when the threat agents and their methods are considered, no matter how comfortable the organization is with what it has done, everyone should remember that sophisticated adversaries will be studying current practices for weaknesses, continually poking at these on a regular basis. In other words, attackers are intelligent and adaptive.

Speaking of the administrative staff, our enterprise is also concerned about a rogue insider who might launch malicious action out of emotional distress. Part of the enterprise security strategy would be maintaining the good graces of those individuals who must have privileged access. It would behoove Digital Diskus' executive staff to try to ensure that technical staff aren't given obvious and compelling reasons to hurt the company. It may seem odd to speak about human resources policies as a part of a security strategy. But indeed, people do get angry. And angry people can do malicious and destructive things.

Beyond the need to try and keep employees happy so that they will perform their functions with integrity, part of the security architecture for the enterprise must be an attempt to limit the damage that any single individual can do. This leads to standard controls (again, NIST 800-53 describes these), such as strict access control. No single individual can be allowed to have control over an entire subsystem and all its functioning parts or infrastructure. For instance, database administrators should only have access to the database administrative functions, not to the administrative functions of the systems upon which databases are run. Strict separation of duties needs to be employed so that only system administrators have access to the system but don't have the credentials to databases. For severe functions, such as changing a critical system credential or bringing a critical system down, several individuals with distinct and separate roles and scope must agree. No single or even pair of individuals, especially those who have the same precise function, should be able to perform any action that could have severe impact on the operation of the enterprise.

Alongside these typical controls, significant activities such as changing the configuration of a production system or database should be performed by independent teams who have no interest in or take any part in the applications and other functions running on the systems. This is standard separation of duties. The concept is used to parcel out privileges such that two or three individuals must agree (i.e., "collude") in order to actually apply critical changes. This control is not perfect, of course.* This control should not be solely relied upon in isolation. Rather, separation of duties compliments access controls and privilege-granting processes. The intention is that any single person cannot have a wide impact when acting alone.

By analyzing the conceptual enterprise architecture, taking into account Digital Diskus' mission and risk appetite, and in light of the relevant threat landscape, we have uncovered the following conceptual requirements:

---

* Prevention of collusion between several people if these have the right mix of privileges is a rather difficult problem to prevent. No doubt, spy agencies have methods of prevention, but typically, information security controls begin to fail when more than two individuals act in concert. Three well-placed people can probably get around most technical control systems.

- Strict administrative access control
- Strict administrative privilege grant
- Mature administrative practices (cite NIST 800-53 or similar)
- Robust and rigorous monitoring and response capabilities (external and internal)
- Strict user access controls (authentication and authorization)
- Access control of automated connection to integration technology, especially the enterprise message bus
- Policy and standards preventing unfettered send or receive on the message bus, coupled to strict, need-to-communicate, routing on the bus
- Application message recomposition when a message is sent from external to internal systems
- Encryption of message bus communications

Obviously, based upon the previous architecture analysis of a web application, the web presences of Digital Diskus would have the same security needs. Since we've already completed that analysis, I won't add those requirements here. Still, you may want to take some time to review the requirements for Web-Sock-A-Rama, turning these into high-level, conceptual architectural imperatives. What are the web and extranet imperatives that should be applied to Digital Diskus' conceptual architecture?

At the enterprise level, the security architect needs to be thinking about the strategy that will ensure the security posture intended by the organization. The activities and methods listed in the foregoing paragraphs are not intended as a complete recipe. Rather, the activities listed above are offered as samples of strategic architectures (which can include processes) that will become an enterprise security architecture which supports the enterprise architecture at its conceptual level. Indeed, the foregoing discussions indicate particular strategies in response to anticipated threats. These imperatives describe the security architecture as suggested by the conceptual architecture given in Figure 7.1. At this conceptual level, the security architecture remains highly conceptual, as well. Specific technologies are not important. Certainly, specific products are not needed in order to form a conceptual enterprise security architecture. The architecture is "conceptual," that is, expressed as security concepts.

Identity is already represented in Figure 7.1. In order to conduct business within an ecosystem that includes customers through the supply chain, identity management will be essential. Integration is also represented in this conceptual view that every business function will integrate with others: Sales via eCommerce must pull from the supply chain. In order to deliver a presence that can drive commerce via the web, content will have to be created, revised, and managed. Business intelligence depends upon the data generated from the other business functions: commerce, customer relations, and the supply chain, as well as from the internal applications and processing necessary to support these activities. Because this enterprise seeks to automate as much of its processing as possible, the enterprise architecture includes an orchestration conceptual function.

7.5 Digital Diskus' Component Architecture

Figure 7.2 begins the process of separating the conceptual architecture given in Figure 7.1 into its constituent components. We continue to operate at the enterprise

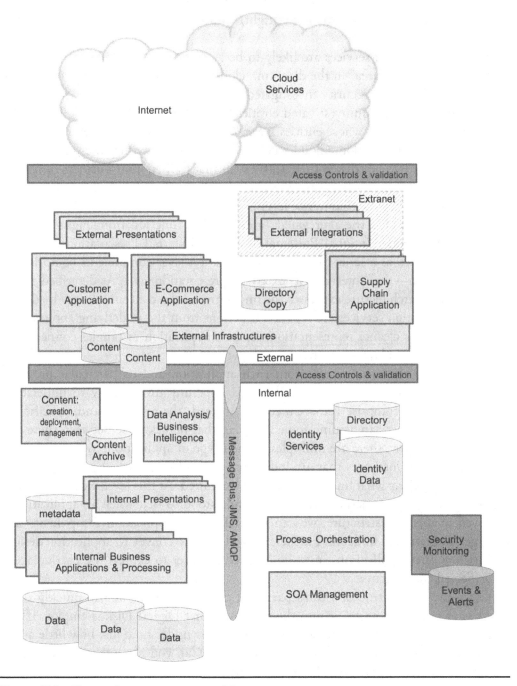

Figure 7.2 Enterprise component architecture.

level of granularity, that is, view the architecture at a very abstract level. Individual technologies and implementations are ignored. This view seeks to factor the concepts presented previously into parts that suggests systems and processes. We have taken the liberty to also introduce a distinction in trust levels and exposure by separating the internal from the external, web presences from business ecosystem connections (the "extra-net" cross hatching in the upper right), and to even distinguish between cloud services and the Internet.

Although the cloud services are likely to be accessed via the Internet (hence, they form a distinguished "area" in the diagram), cloud services will usually be run by entities that have had their security investigated and approved. This is opposed to traffic originating from other, uninvestigated entities on the Internet. The Public Internet is, as we know, a commons whose entities generally must be treated as essentially hostile, given no further information. Cloud services may be viewed with some suspicion, but these services have to be trusted sufficiently such that they support business functions. The Internet deserves no such trust. For this reason, the two abstract areas are viewed as separate clouds, separate assurance levels.

You will notice that the aggregated "presentation" function from Figure 7.1 now has two components: "Internal Presentations" and "External Presentations." Each of these is represented as a series of separate presentation-layer components comprising a larger abstraction—the "internal" or "external" presentation layer. As described above, this component architecture expresses the imperative of the conceptual view by declaring that presentation services are separate functions from the underlying applications. In order to keep a cleaner representation, separate application rectangles connected to separate presentation layers have not been drawn.

At this level, trying to separate out each application and its particular presentation would introduce too much detail and is hopefully unnecessary to understand what components comprise the architecture. Instead, the architect and, specifically, the security architect can assume some mapping that makes sense between these two components. Clearly, there are multiples of each type of application. When reviewing actual application instances that are individual parts of this component architecture, the detail of precisely what links to what will be required. At this level, we are interested in gross groupings of functions that can be understood so that when an application is deployed to this infrastructure, we can understand the application components that must get diagrammed in detail. Further, we will want to convey to application designers just how their applications must be factored in order to express the particulars of the expected components.

Given the architecture of a third-party, off-the-shelf system, we can quickly assess whether or not it's going to fit into the structures that Digital Diskus employ. If you remember Figure 3.2 (from Chapter 3), you may now understand just how little architecturally useful information the diagram conveys? Can you place that "architecture" within the structures given by Figure 7.2? When I was presented with an architecture diagram quite similar to the marketing architecture for a business intelligence product that was previously shown, I was at a loss to place any part of the diagrammed system within the logical architecture with which I was working at the time (which looked somewhat similar to the AppMaker zones).

The component enterprise architecture provides a guide for how to separate the functions that comprise any particular system that becomes a part or expresses the enterprise architecture. Consider the following patterns: Business intelligence applications are internal and will likely be called out as distinct from the internal business applications, processing, and data upon which the intelligence analysis depends. The content management system will also be separately diagrammed, perhaps due as much to maintaining legacy systems as to the introduction of web content as a separate and distinct discipline. Content must be transported and stored in the externally available zone so that it can be presented through those systems. This architecture protects the content creation and management functions from exposure by exporting published content to the external stores. If a new content management system is to be introduced, the patterns listed above (and more, of course) can be applied to create an architecture that will fit into and support the component architecture given in Figure 7.3.

Likewise, integrations and their mechanisms will be distinct systems. In the same way, any system that provides identity services or storage must be internal, while also supporting an external copy that can be hardened against exposure. At the same time, the customer-supporting and business-enacting applications must be available externally. An external infrastructure supports the external applications; these external applications have to be written to that discrete, external infrastructure.

As was previously discussed, a message bus spanning trust boundaries presents a particular security problem. Such a bus may provide a path for attacks to get passed within messages from less trusted, exposed systems, such as the customer or eCommerce applications, to any of the more sensitive or higher-trust systems located in the internal zone. As we noted through the conceptual architecture discussion, great care should be taken to authenticate every bus access, as well as to review the message and transaction paths through the bus such that a compromised application can neither get control of the message bus nor attack systems to which it has not been granted access. In the component architecture given by Figure 7.2, the external versus the internal has been delineated. You will note that the message bus crosses that boundary. Further, the externally accessible portal to the bus is a part of the external infrastructure (the bus crosses the infrastructure box, with an open end on the external side).

There will probably be access-granting policies and procedures that protect the bus from rogue applications. Hence, the bus must pass through the Access Controls & Validation security systems (which, at this granularity, remain largely undefined).

You will note that some of the security imperatives listed for the conceptual architecture appear in Figure 7.2. The monitoring system has been separated as a component. Access controls and validations are diagrammed at the entrance to externally exposed systems and between external and internal zones. The control layer between external and internal must function in both directions. Obviously, harmful and disallowed

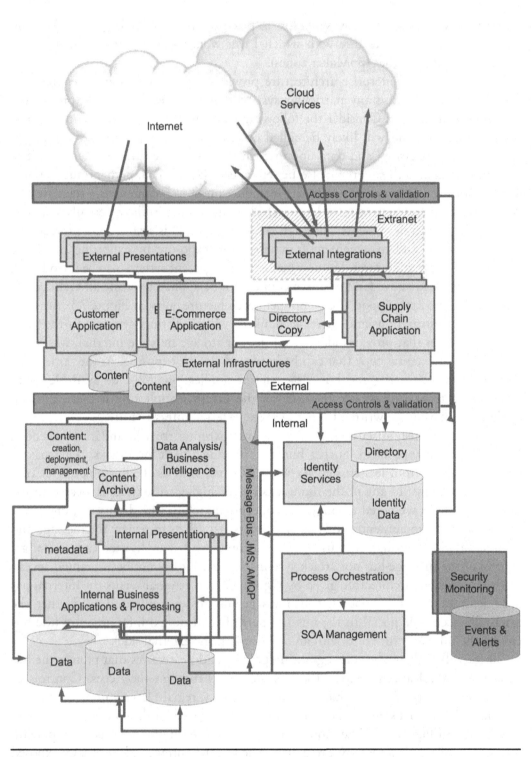

Figure 7.3   Enterprise component flows.

traffic must be kept out of the internal network. In the other direction, those who have no need-to-access external systems, most especially the administrative accesses, are prevented from doing so. Figure 6.7 of the AppMaker web system represented at its bottom an administrative access control layer preventing inappropriate internal to external access. Trying to separate these two layers in Digital Diskus' enterprise view will be too "noisy," or too busy, adding too much detail to grasp easily. Therefore, at this component enterprise level, the two similar functions have been abstracted into a single control layer lying between the two trust and exposure zones.

Figure 7.3 adds data flows between the components depicted on the enterprise components view. Not every component communicates with every other. However, functions such as process orchestration will interact with many applications and many of the databases and data repositories. Each instance of a particular orchestration will, of course, only interact with a select few of the components. However, at this gross level, we represent orchestration as a functional entity, representing all orchestrators as a single component. Hence, you will see in Figure 7.3 that Process Orchestration interacts with a wide variety of the internal systems. In addition, Orchestration has access to the Message Bus, which pierces the trust boundary between internal and external systems, as described above.

Orchestration, for example, is one of the components with a high degree of interconnectivity. Both Data Analysis and Content—creation, deployment, and management—similarly touch many internal systems. Likewise, the Supply Chain applications must interact externally through the External Integrations, as well as send messages through the Message Bus to many business applications and databases. When a complex process must be modeled through automation along the supply chain, orchestrations will likely be created to order transactions properly. The same would be true for eCommerce or customer interactions. In other words, many of the systems, external and internal, must interact through various communications means. The number of attack surfaces multiplies exponentially as these complex systems integrate.

Take a moment to consider which threat agents are likely to attack the various systems in this architecture. Then consider their attack methods: Which are the juicy, valuable targets shown here? Where might particularly proprietary trade secrets lie? Company financial information? Customer information (subject to privacy issues, as well)?

You may observe that security monitoring takes events from both access control layers. But there are a few other systems that also deliver events to be monitored and perhaps acted upon. The external infrastructures and Service Oriented Architecture (SOA) management have flows to Security Monitoring. The Message Bus would normally, as well. Any system that breaches trust boundaries has the potential to vector attacks and, therefore, must be watched for attack-like and anomalous behavior. In a real enterprise, the Security Operations Center function (SOC) would take events and alerts from almost all the disparate systems with any potential for misbehavior. SIEM could be a topic for an entire book, itself.

After adding these gross level flows to the enterprise component architecture, as seen in Figure 7.3, hopefully you will see that the diagram becomes unwieldy. There are too many arrows connecting to multiple systems to easily delineate the relationships between any particular subset. This is intentional on my part in order to highlight the need for breakout views of subsystems. An overly crowded diagram becomes as meaningless as an overly simple one.

Take as an example, the directory copy (often, an LDAP[*] instance) in the external area at the upper end of Figure 7.3. Many of the external applications within each application type, as well as presentation layers, authentications, and so forth, must interact with the directory. In addition, the directory copy must be updated from the master directory that exists within the internal network. Even at this gross level, where particular applications are not specified, there have to exist arrows pointing to Directory Copy from almost every external component. Given that these components also must communicate outwardly, receive communications inbound, and send messages through the message bus to internal components, just the representation of Directory Copy's interactions, by themselves, multiplies communication flows beyond the eye's ability to easily follow and beyond easy comprehension.

Figure 7.3 then becomes too "busy," or "noisy," to be useful, even if this figure does represent in some manner, flows between components. At this point in an assessment, the architecture should be broken down into subsystems for analysis. Hence, we will not continue the assessment of this enterprise architecture any further. Even using a gross component view at the enterprise level, an assessment focuses upon the general security strategy for the enterprise:

- Threat landscape analysis
- Organizational risk tolerance and posture
- Security architecture principles and imperatives
- Major components of the security infrastructure (e.g., identity and security operations)
- Hardening, system management, and administrative policies and standards

Our next architecture assessment will be of the data analysis and business intelligence component of this enterprise architecture. This subsequent Digital Diskus analysis will afford us an opportunity to dig into subsystem particulars in more detail.

7.6 Enterprise Architecture Requirements

At the enterprise level, security requirements are generally going to devolve to the security infrastructure that will support the enterprise architecture. That is, the conceptual

---

[*] Lightweight Directory Access Protocol.

"security services" box in the enterprise conceptual diagram will have to be broken out into all the various services that will comprise those security services that will form an enterprise security infrastructure.

Because we have moved infrastructure security architecture outside the boundaries of our scope and focus, there are no specific requirements given beyond the examples outlined in this chapter. Certainly, each of the following architectures that has some relationship to a larger organization will necessarily consume portions of a security infrastructure. Therefore, we assume for the relevant subsequent assessment examples that a security infrastructure is in place and that it includes at least the following:

- Firewalls that restrict network access between network segments, ingress, and perhaps, egress form the enterprise architecture
- An ability to divide and segment sub-networks to trusted and untrusted areas that define levels of access restriction
- An administrative network that is separated and protected from all other networks and access to which is granted through an approval process
- A security operations Center (SOC) which monitors and reacts to security incidents
- An intrusion detection system (IDS) whose feeds and alerts are directed to the SOC to be analyzed and, if necessary, reacted to
- The ability to gather and monitor logs and system events from most if not all systems within the enterprise architecture
- An audit trail of most if not all administrative activities that is protected from compromise by administrators
- An enterprise authentication system
- Some form of enterprise authorization

The foregoing list, while not exhaustive, will provide touch points into the enterprise security architecture for the example analyses in Part II.

References

1. U.S. Senate Committee on Commerce, Science, and Transportation. (March 26, 2014). A "Kill Chain" Analysis of the 2013 Target Data Breach. Majority Staff Report for Chairman Rockefeller.
2. Open Web Application Security Project (OWASP). (2013). *Some Proven Application Security Principles*. Retrieved from https://www.owasp.org/index.php/ Category:Principle.

Chapter 8

Business Analytics

An enterprise architecture can be thought of as a map of the interactions of the individual systems that comprise it. One of the systems expressed in Figure 7.2 is the business intelligence and analytics system. Typically, these systems handle business proprietary and sensitive data about the performance, strengths, and weaknesses of business execution. Therefore, business intelligence systems are usually not exposed to untrusted networks and to untrusted parties. The Digital Diskus data analysis and business intelligence system exists only on the company's internal network. No portion of the system is exposed on either of the external zones (Internet and Extranet).

8.1 Architecture

We begin with the first "A" in ATASM: "architecture." First, we must understand what a business analytics/intelligence system does and a bit about how the analysis function works. The diagram given in Figure 8.1 has had enterprise components not directly connected with the business analytics and intelligence system removed. Figure 8.1 may be thought of as the gross enterprise components that are involved in business data mining for Digital Diskus.

> [D]ata science is a set of fundamental principles that guide the extraction of knowledge from data. Data mining is the extraction of knowledge from data via technologies that incorporate these principles.[1]

Like many enterprises, Digital Diskus has many applications for the various processes that must be executed to run its business, from finance and accounting to sales, marketing, procurement, inventory, supply chain, and so forth. A great deal of data is

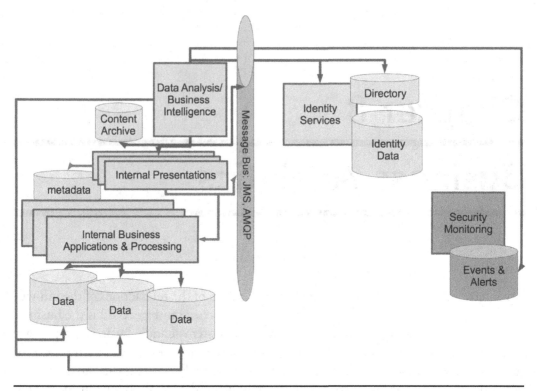

Figure 8.1   Business analytics logical data flow diagram (DFD).

generated across these systems. But, unfortunately, as a business grows into an enterprise, most of its business systems will be discreet. Getting a holistic view of the health of the business can be stymied by the organic growth of applications and data stores. A great deal of the business indicators will either be localized to a particular function or difficult to retrieve from specialized solutions, such as spreadsheet calculations. A business analytics system will then be implemented in order to gain that holistic view of the data that has been lost due to growth. Data mining is a general term for the function that a business analytics system provides. The data mining must reach across the silos of data in order to correlate and then apply analysis tools.

In order to analyze the activity and performance of the enterprise functions, a business intelligence system will pull data from many sources. Thus, there are obvious connections to the backend databases. What may be less obvious is that the analytics will make use of the message bus, both as a listener to capture critical data as well as a sender to request data. Analysis has to tie transactions to entities such as customer, partner, or employee, and messages to things like item catalogs and pricing structures. Each of these data types may reside in a distinct and separate data store. The internal content archive will also be used for analysis, which is, again, another completely disparate storage area.

As is typical for business intelligence and analytics systems, the system will want to make use of existing business processing functions such as the internal business applications that produce statistics, for example, sales bookings and fulfillments. Sometimes, needed processing results can be obtained from databases and other repositories. In these cases, the analysis engine will have to fetch results that may only be available in the user interface of a particular application. As a result, the data analysis and business intelligence system also has a "screen scraping"[*] capability that accesses the presentations of the business applications. Another important analytics source will be the metadata associated with individual business applications. Metadata may describe what data is to be pulled and how it may be processed.

It's fairly usual for a business intelligence and analytics system to touch pretty much all of the backend systems and data stores. These analysis systems contain code that understands how to crawl flat file directories, parse spreadsheets, read databases, HTML and other content representations, and includes code that can parse various data interchange formats. You may think of a business analysis system as being a data octopus. It has many arms that must touch a great deal in order to collate what would ordinarily be discontiguous, siloed data and systems. That is the point of business intelligence: to uncover what is hidden in the complexity of the data being processed by the many systems of a complex business. It is the purpose of business intelligence to connect the disconnected and then provide a vehicle for analysis of the resulting correlation and synthesis.

The system shown in Figure 8.1 comprises not only the business analytics and intelligence but also the many enterprise systems with which analytics must interact. In order to consider the entire system, we must understand not only the architecture of the business analysis system itself, but also its communications with other systems. The security of each system touched can affect the security of business analytics. And conversely, the security of business analytics can impact the security posture of each system it touches. Consequently, we must view the interactions as a whole in order to assess the security of each of its parts. Figure 8.1 diagrams all the components within the enterprise architecture with which business analytics must interact. Not all of these interactions involve the analysis of data. Other interactions are also critically important.

Consider the data flow "octopus," as shown in Figure 8.1. How can the analysis system gather data from all these sources that, presumably, are protected themselves?

If you arrived at the conclusion that the business analysis system will have to maintain credentials for almost everything, much of which is highly proprietary or trade secret, you would be correct. One of the most difficult things about a business analysis system is that it has to have rights—powerful rights—to almost everything at the backend of the enterprise architecture. The security posture of the business analytics system, therefore, can significantly affect (perhaps lower) the posture of the system to which it connects. Since it has rights to a great deal, the system can be considered a repository, not only of the sensitive data and results that it produces but also of access rights. If

---

[*] "Screen scraping" is an automated process that grabs data from a user interface as though it were a human interacting with the system.

these rights are not protected sufficiently, business analytics puts every system from which it must gather data at greater risk of successful attack.

In the illustrated use case, business analytics also listens to the message bus to gather information about transactions coming from the external zones. As you think about this, does that also expose the business analytics system to any potential attacks?

We haven't yet considered everything shown in Figure 8.1. Identity systems and security systems are shown on the right of the diagram. We will return to these after we consider the data analysis system itself. I purposely left all the components as they were represented in the component enterprise architecture so that you can see how business analytics fits into and interacts as a part of the enterprise architecture. Each component diagrammed in Figure 8.1 is in precisely the same place and at the same size as these components were represented in Figure 7.2.

Since the flows have become rather crowded and hard to visualize, I've broken them out in Figure 8.1. I have removed those flows that represent connections between

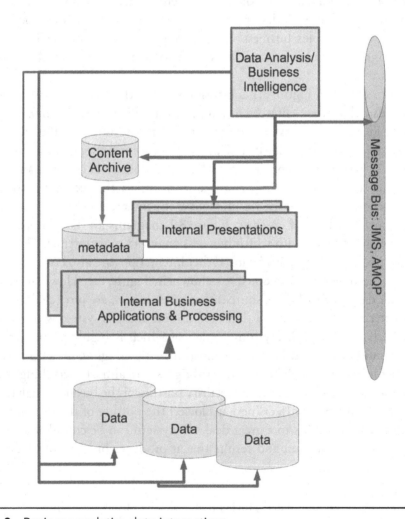

Figure 8.2   Business analytics data interactions.

non-business analytics components in order to highlight only the flows to and from the business analytics system. Please refer back to Figure 7.3 if you don't understand how the various components interact.

Figure 8.2 is a drill down view of the data gathering interactions of the business analytics system within the enterprise architecture. Is the visualization in Figure 8.2 perhaps a bit easier to understand? To reiterate, we are looking at the business analysis and intelligence system, which must touch almost every data gathering and transaction-processing system that exists in the internal network. And, as was noted, business analytics listens to the message bus, which includes messages that are sent from less trusted zones.

8.2 Threats

Take a moment to consider Figure 8.2 as a series of targets for an attacker. Think about the threat agents that we outlined for Digital Diskus and what each might stand to gain by compromising one or more of the components in Figure 8.2. This consideration is based upon "T"—threats—as we've already outlined as active against Digital Diskus.

As we move to system specificity, if we have predefined the relevant threats, we can apply the threats' goals to the system under analysis. This application of goals leads directly on to the "AS" of ATASM: attack surfaces. Understanding your adversaries' targets and objectives provides insight into possible attack surfaces and perhaps which attack surfaces are most important and should be prioritized.

Industrial spies will be interested in which products are most important to the market, what sells best and to whom, and for what reasons? Competitors want to understand on what particular characteristics Digital Diskus' success rests. They will be looking to steal Digital Diskus' technical advantages. The technical advantages are likely to rest within the intellectual property and trade secrets of the company. Spies also might be interested in current sales bookings, future sales, revenues, and the like. Are there other espionage targets?

Cyber criminals might be interested in personal data and financial details, including any account data. This would be the most direct financial attack. They might also be interested in areas in which inventory items, recalls of products, and information about customer returns are stored, in case there's an opening for equipment theft and resale. They may also be interested in employee information, since it's likely that at least some of Digital Diskus may make healthy salaries.

Are there any internal targets that digital activists might attack? How about a rogue insider seeking to disrupt or take vengeance?

In light of the "octopus" nature of this business analytics system, its connections to other systems and communications flows will be prime targets for many attackers. Knowing this, we can move on from threats to cataloging targets, which leads to attack surfaces.

Much key business data will be presented to analysts and decision makers in the reports and analysis screens of the business intelligence system. Obtaining access to this critical business information will most certainly be a target. The business analytics system presentation of the analysis, its reporting and viewing capability, will most certainly be a prime target for several classes of threat agents. (Please see Figure 8.3, to which we will return shortly.)

Because the business analytics system must be given enormous rights, the system itself should be considered a gateway to the many other juicy targets with which it interacts and from which it pulls data. At what level of sensitivity would you place the business analytics system? In order to provide its functionality, business analytics must be connected to much, if not all, of the existing business relevant data, irrespective of where that data gets generated or is stored. And this access is irrespective of whatever security protections have been placed around the data.

Will business analytics have to handle and store credentials? Credentials to what? The data sources and applications from which the analytics system gathers its information. This is a fundamental property of business intelligence systems. That is, if each source is protected through authentication, the analytics system will have to maintain

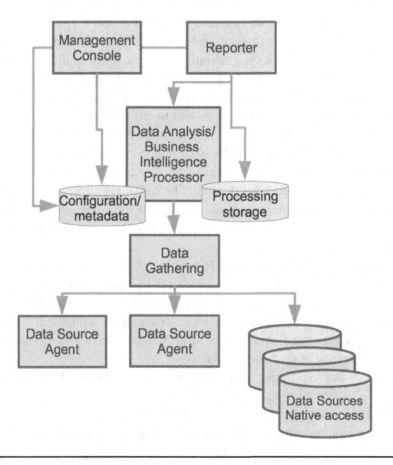

Figure 8.3 Business analytics system architecture.

a user ID (account) and credential for each system that it must touch. Therein lies one of the first security issues that an architecture analysis must deal with.

Not only are the user interfaces of the analytics system obvious attack surfaces, but so will be any storage mechanisms. The security picture is more complex than just protecting the credentials themselves. For instance, if an attacker can change the configuration of the system, she or he might add themselves as an administrator, thus gaining rights to manipulate or steal the source credentials. Consequently, the running configuration and metadata of the system will also present an interesting target opportunity.

It's useful to understand a highly connected system like business analytics *in situ*, that is, as the system fits into its larger enterprise architectural context. However, we don't yet have the architecture of the system itself. Figure 8.3 presents the logical components of this business analytics system.

There are five major components of the system:

1. Data Analysis processing
2. Reporting module
3. Data gathering module
4. Agents which are co-located with target data repositories
5. A management console

There must be disk storage for the processing module to place temporary items and to store the results of an analysis. Of course, there is also storage for configuration of the system. The management function writes out the configuration and metadata to the configuration files. When the processing module starts, it reads its running configuration.

Reporter must also read its configuration. The management console will place configuration data onto permanent storage for each component, which is then available during initiation.

Since Reporter must present results to users, it reads Processing Storage. It also can initiate processing sequences, so Reporter communicates with Processor, as well as reading from the temporary storage set aside for Processor.

Data Gathering gets started by Processor, which then reads its configuration data. All the communications to the data sources are performed by Data Gathering. Processing tenders a request that a particular set of data be collected from across a set of sources and then delegates the task to the gathering module. Gathering supports two distinct access methods: native accesses (such as SQL[*] database queries), SOAP[†] (SOA) calls, and so forth.

---

[*] Structured Query Language.
[†] Simple Object Access protocol.

The data gathering module also supports agent software. So-called "agents" are small pieces of code that include a set of libraries and commands (provided in several languages) that implement a communications stream from Data Gathering to an agent. There is also an Application Programming Interface (API) that must be implemented so that commands from the gathering module will get processed properly. Agents then run on instances of a data source for which Data Gathering does not have a native access method implemented or where such a protocol does not exist. The agent is co-located with the data source. Each agent contains code that understands the unique properties of a data source for which it has been implemented.

Agents for many standard data sources are supplied by business analytics. Additionally, users may program their own agents to a standard API and library set, allowing Data Gathering to call specialized custom code agents written by data analytics' customers. Through this extensibility, this business analytics system can retrieve data from virtually any source.

The system is built such that each module could be run on its own separate server, that is, on separated hosts, using the network for the intra-system communications. However, Digital Diskus has chosen to install the processing module, the data gatherer, and Reporter all on the same host. Their communications consequently are made between the modules locally on the host and do not cross the actual network (i.e., these use "localhost" as the destination). The management console runs on a separated host, as we will explore below.

8.3 Attack Surfaces

In this context, where several components share the same host, how would you treat the communications between them? Should these communications be considered to traverse a trusted or an untrusted network? If Digital Diskus applies the rigor we indicated above to the management of the servers on which business analytics runs, what additional attack surfaces should be added from among those three components and their intercommunications when all of these share a single host?

Given that we already know that Digital Diskus requires and maintains a rigorous set of security standards for its administrative functions, how does this "infrastructure" influence the attack surfaces? This is one of those situations in which the architecture of the system under analysis inherits security capabilities from the infrastructure upon which it's deployed. There are no standard users maintained on the hosts on which business analytics is running. There are only high-privileged users who were charged with keeping the host, as well as the applications running on that host, maintained, patched, and hardened—that is, all the administrative tasks that go into running industrial-strength enterprise systems. This situation is quite unlike a user's endpoint system, which will be exposed to whatever the user chooses to do.

Please remember that Digital Diskus' administrators are supposed to be sophisticated and highly trained individuals. Presumably, they have been issued separate, individual corporate systems on which to perform their usual, digital tasks: email, Web research, calendaring, documents, and spreadsheets. They do not use the servers they administer for these tasks; that would be against policy. Therefore, the only users that business analytics servers should be exposed to are the administrative staff. Although the administrative staff maintaining these hosts does have high privileges on the systems, it is assumed that they know how to protect these appropriately. Working within the strictures of appropriate separation of duties, these individuals would not have any rights to the interfaces of the business analytics system itself. That is, they shouldn't have access to Reporter, Management Console, the processing module, or Data Gathering. They are not entitled to view the results of the business intelligence analysis. Still, despite the separation of duties that prevents administrative staff from being users of the business analytics system, they will have rights to the operating system that runs the applications and thus, they will inherit rights to all the data that is kept locally or mounted onto those servers. So, although the user interfaces of the system might not pose a potential attack surface for an insider attack, the data stores of the system most certainly do.

If I were analyzing this particular business analytics system placed within the context of the enterprise in which it is supposed to be run, I would not worry about the communications flows between the modules that are co-hosted. My reasoning is that the only access to these communications is via the high privileges of the administration accounts. If these accounts have been lost to an attacker, a great deal more than the intra-module communications is at stake. We have already stated that the privileges on these servers are protected by a number of controls. These controls are inherited by the business analytics system and will be taken into account in the threat model. The controls, if executed properly, are likely to prevent or significantly slow an attack to business analytics from its operating environment. However, you may note that we have opened up another attack surface that can come from one of our threats: rogue insider attack to the very sensitive data that business analytics produces.

Communications from the data gatherer to data sources will be of interest to many attackers. Before analysis, some of the raw data will be sensitive and proprietary. Even the internal network, considering the breath of the Digital Diskus business ecosystem, cannot be considered entirely trusted. Therefore, communications of sensitive data must have protection going over the network. The network communications to data sources are an attack surface. Which brings us to the agents.

The data gathering agents are located on various data stores or within the stores' associated data access services. An agent is required in every instance in which a native data protocol cannot be used to pull data from the storage or application. An agent will be written for each proprietary, nonstandard access protocol. It might be written to parse an XML data format, or to read a proprietary file of one kind or another, for example, a Microsoft Word document or Excel spreadsheet. The agent must have rights to read the data source. In this instance, when a data-retrieval operation is instantiated, the data gatherer sends the credentials down to the agent for the operation. Credentials are not stored at agents.

If an attacker can retrieve the API and libraries, then use these to write an agent, and then get the attacker's agent installed, how should Digital Diskus protect itself from such an attack? Should the business analytics system provide a method of authentication of valid agents in order to protect against a malicious one? Is the agent a worthy attack surface?

I would ask the business analytics vendor what protections they had placed in the protocol or interchanges between agent and data gatherer to preclude an attacker writing a malicious agent. The agent's software is a target, in and of itself. With a rogue agent, an attacker can send data of the attacker's choice to the business analytics system, as opposed to real data. Furthermore, a badly written agent, API, or libraries could open a vulnerability that could be misused by the attacker to take over whatever host the agent is running on. Therefore, the data gatherer must protect itself against malicious agents; there's one attack surface. And each agent is potentially an attack surface introduced to the system on which it's running.

The native access interchanges will be protected by whatever native defenses are available for that access method. These, then, would be out of the assessment scope of the business analytics system, by itself.* However, this does not place out of scope the credentials used for those native access methods. These, like all of the other credentials, must be considered a prime attack surface of the business analytics system.

The management console has direct control over the configuration of all the other components. Indeed, credentials for each access method and data source will be input to Management Console. That makes Management Console, in its entirety, an attack surface: every input and every output.

Why should the output of Management Console be considered an attack surface?

Previously, the point was made that all inputs should be considered attack surfaces. However, when the outputs of the system need protection, such as the credentials going into the business analytics configuration files and metadata, then the outputs should be considered an attack surface. If the wily attacker has access to the outputs of Management Console, then the attacker may gain the credentials to many systems. Further, the attacker will know which data sources exist and, quite possibly, the access methods for those data sources (because the protocol and/or agent for each access must be configured). Because of the foregoing, this particular set of outputs contains critical and sensitive information that affects the security posture not only of the business analytics but of many other systems, as well, and should be considered an attack surface.

Naturally, the configuration files are also a prime target themselves, as stated above. What may be less obvious is that when Management Console reads the configuration files, this also creates an attack surface at Management Console. If the attacker can insert attack code to exercise a vulnerability in the configuration file processing

---

* Though, most certainly, each native protocol should be considered within the larger scope of the organization's security posture.

routines, the attacker might gain Management Console, or even privileges on the host that runs it. Remember, Management Console is running on a separate host in this implementation. That server is, of course, a target that inherits the protections of the administration function at Digital Diskus. But a subversion of Management Console itself might give access to all the functions that Management Console controls, which are, of course, sensitive.

Access controls to Management Console itself, authentication and authorization to perform certain actions, will be key because Management Console is, by its nature, a configurator and controller of the other functions, a target. Which brings us to Figure 8.4.

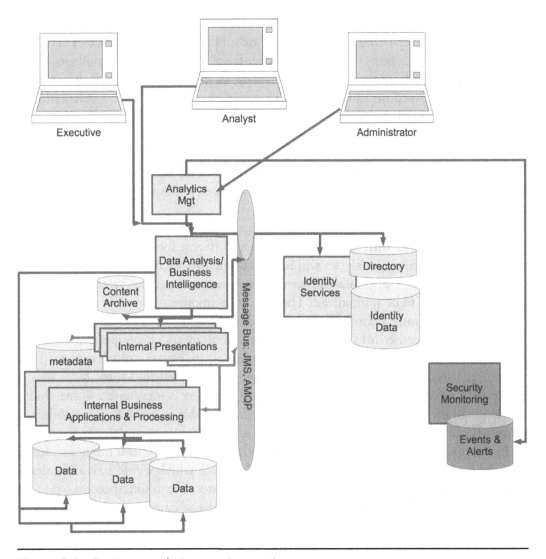

Figure 8.4 Business analytics user interactions.

Figure 8.4 returns to a higher level of abstraction, obscuring the details of the business analytics modules running on the host.* Since we can treat the collection of modules as an atomic unit for our purposes, we move up a level of granularity once again to view the system in its logical context. Management Console has been broken out as a separate component requiring its own defenses. The identity system has been returned to the diagram, as has the security monitoring systems. These present possible attack surfaces that will need examination. In addition, these will become part of the defenses of the system, as we shall see.

Each of the two user interfaces, Analytics Management and Reporter's interface, is implemented as a Web server. User interactions take place over the HTTP protocol. These web interfaces go beyond standard HTML pages. They present dynamic content. And particularly, the reporting module (i.e., "Reporter") must be able to dynamically generate sophisticated data representations, charts, visualizations, tables, and similar views of data. The reporting module needs a rich, HTML-based interface. This interface makes use of scripting and other browser-based presentation technologies. Still, while sophisticated features in the browser, such as JavaScript and XML processing, will need to be turned on in order to make use of the interface, the representation is entirely browser based. No special extra software is downloaded to a user's endpoint.

The foregoing indicates that business analytics web code must resist all the usual and well-known Web attack methods. Further, the reporting module interface must be coded with care to disallow attacks against the data through the interface, such as SQL injection attacks. The interfaces are attack surfaces, and, specifically, they are Web attack surfaces.

Beyond a malicious agent, there is another attack surface in Data Gathering.[†] In order to process many different kinds of data in different formats and presentations, some part of the business analytics will have to normalize the data and put it in a form that can be correlated. The data will have to be parsed and perhaps reformatted. Data will certainly have to be normalized. There is a fair amount of preprocessing that any correlation system must perform before data from different sources in different formats can be brought together into a holistic picture. From an attack perspective, this pre-processing means that the data will have to be read, its context and metadata (field names, etc.) understood, and then the data will be rewritten into some form that is reshaped (normalized) into a standard format. If attackers can exercise a vulnerability that exists in the data processing routines, they may be able to use that vulnerability to subvert the data preprocessing or even go beyond that to the operating system.

Depending upon the vulnerability, Data Gathering at the very least might be caused to simply stop functioning (denial of service—"DOS"), which would halt all business intelligence operations. Without accurate data updates, the results become stale, or perhaps even false. But what if the attacker can cause the data to change? Then false

---

* "Host" in this instance means a "logical" host. There will be several of these servers to scale the processing and for redundancy, in case of failure.

[†] Data Gathering is shown in Figure 8.3.

information will go to Digital Diskus decision makers. Poor or perhaps even disastrous decisions might result. The decision makers are dependent upon the accuracy of the business analytics.

An overflow condition as data are being processed could cause the data gathering module to exit into the operating system and give escalated privileges to an attacker. In order to exercise this sort of vulnerability, the attacker must present the exploit code encapsulated within the data that's being processed.

How might an attacker deliver such a payload? The obvious answer to this question will be to take over a data source in some manner. This, of course, would require an attack of the data source to be successful and becomes a "one-two punch." However, it's not that difficult. If the attacker can deliver a payload through one of the many exposed applications that Digital Diskus maintains, the attack can rest in a data store and wait until the lucky time when it gets delivered to the business analytics system. In other words, the attacker doesn't have to deliver the payload directly to Data Gathering. She or he must somehow deliver the attack into a data store where it can wait patiently to be brought into the data gathering function.

You may remember from the architecture examination that Data Gathering is running concurrently with the business analytics processing system? This means that a data gathering compromise might affect much of the core business analytics system due to the manner in which business analytics has been deployed at Digital Diskus. Each of the three modules running concurrently and in parallel on the processing server becomes an avenue to take over not just the server, but the other two modules. In other words, the security posture of each of the three modules running on that core server profoundly affects the security posture of all three.

The reporting module primarily presents a user interface. To do so, Reporting reads data that's been processed by the business analytics system. As such, it certainly has an attack surface in its user interface. And one could make a case that an attacker might get through all the processing that takes place within Data Gathering and the analysis engine, thus delivering an attack into the results store. However, there's a great deal of processing that happens between Data Gathering and processing. The data will have been read, preprocessed, and continuously manipulated in order to produce results. It is far more likely that an attack will have an effect on either the Data Gathering or processing so long as the reporting module does not take data in any native format. In this system, the reporting module does not handle data from any sources. Its input is strictly limited to the processed results. In Figure 8.3, you can see that Reporting's arrow points towards the processing store—this indicates a read operation initiated from Reporting.

The architecture, as described, leaves the system dependent on the defenses that are built into Data Gathering. If it doesn't do its job to protect the entire system from malicious or bad data, an attack could slip through into the processing module. An attack might even make it all the way through into the results, at least hypothetically.

If I were designing the business analytics system, I would place my defenses within the data gathering module ("Data Gathering"). However, Digital Diskus has purchased the business analytics system and thus has little or no control over the innate protections that have been built into the system. With no further information, an assessment would have to mark as a significant risk malicious payloads within data. We can, at the very least, count Data Gathering as one of our attack surfaces for further investigation into what mitigations may exist to protect the business analytics system. I would have important questions for the programming team of the business analytics vendor.

A further investigation over which Digital Diskus does have direct control will be into the protections that the source data systems provide against a malicious payload aimed at business analytics. If an assessment cannot, with some certainty, mitigate an attack surface, the assessment can move outwards to other protections that lie beyond the system under assessment, that is, what protections exist within the connected systems (in this case, the data sources). Or, failing there, move continuously outward through the chain of interactions and perimeters to build a set of defenses. Perhaps it is actually rather difficult for an attacker to get a payload into any data source due to the layers of defense surrounding the data sources?

If there is high confidence that the protections are in place around and within data sources, then the likelihood of a successful attack through Data Gathering will lower significantly. Since business analytics is a third-party system, the best defense will be to find the attack surfaces leading to primary attack surfaces of the business analytics and to secure these. These other systems are under direct control, as compared to this third-party system, business analytics.

There still remains a possible attack surface in the processing store. If an attacker can introduce a payload to the reporter, they may be able to compromise that module, or even compromise the core system. Although we have noted that passing an attack through all the processing that takes place from data source to the processed results should be fairly difficult if business analytics is written defensively, if the permissions to the data store are not set correctly, this would allow an attacker to drop an attack to the Reporter "from the side," that is, by compromising the results store directly. The results most certainly present an attack opportunity if the permissions on the results store are not set defensively, which, in this case means:

- Processing store is only mounted on the host that runs Processing and Reporter
- Write permission is only granted to Processing
- Read permission is only granted to Reporter
- Only a select few administers may perform maintenance functions on the processing data store
- Every administrative action on processing store is logged and audited for abnormal activity

In Figure 8.3, you can see an arrow from Reporter to Processing. This is a command and control channel allowing users to initiate processing and analytics while they are viewing results. This is, of course, an additional attack surface to Processing. If an attacker can either gain control of processing or slip a payload through the reporting module's inputs specifying processing actions, then a payload might be delivered to the processing module. As we noted above, the communications between the two modules are taking place entirely through the machine, that is, the localhost network that is entirely contained within the kernel of the operating system on the host. In order to subvert these communications, an attacker would already "own," that is, would have completely compromised the superuser privileges, the underlying host's operating system. At that point, the attacker has complete control and, thus, has no reason to prosecute another exploit. There is no additional attacker value to subverting the localhost communications, as these and the process execution space of all three modules are under attacker control.

There are two other systems whose connections with business analytics we have not yet examined. The identity system provides authentication to the various interfaces of the business analytics system. And you will see that there is a security event monitoring system that collects events of interest from business analytics, as it does from many systems within the enterprise architecture.

Because business analytics was written as an enterprise-grade system, not only does it have an integral authorization mechanism, but it can also make use of either of two typical enterprise group membership functions: Microsoft Active Directory or an LDAP directory. Since Active Directory can also function as an LDAP, systems requiring authentication and group membership (pseudo authorization) services can leverage either or both of Active Directory's supported protocols. It is rare that an enterprise-grade system does not, at the very least, support the LDAP protocol. Organizations that manage their identities through Active Directory can make use of that identity system for the whole enterprise rather than programming authentication and authorization information into each application. This is precisely the case with this business analytics system at Digital Diskus. Digital Diskus maintains Active Directory as a foundational enterprise infrastructure system.

Consolidating various identity systems that had become unmanageable through organic accretion some years ago, Digital Diskus collapsed customer, partner, and employee identities into its Active Directory. Therefore, at the company, there is a single identity system that the other applications may make use of. Indeed, the company makes broad use of Active Directory groups such that membership in a group may be used to give rights to the various applications that make use of Active Directory. Although not a true role-based access (RBAC) system, this approach is quite common. Before permission for access is granted, membership in the appropriate group is consulted, providing a fairly simple approach to enterprise authorization. Digital Diskus has provided a self-service interface for group creation and maintenance. In addition, some of the most coarse-grained groups, such as employee, partner, or customer, are automatically populated; membership in one of these enterprise-wide groups depends upon which relationship the identity has with Digital Diskus.

The details of identity management are beyond the scope of this book. However, security architects typically have to have a fair sense of how identities are managed, what systems are employed for identities, how identities get populated if groups are being used, and which groups get populated through automation and which groups are populated manually. Furthermore, the system for granting permissions and group membership should also be understood, as, obviously, if an attacker can gain membership to a restricted group, they then gain those privileges inappropriately.

The business analytics management console and the business analytics reporting console restrict users based on authentication to the active directory. In addition, rights to the coarse-grained roles within the system, such as user, executive, and administrator, are granted through group membership. Membership in the appropriate group is granted through an approval process. Not every employee or any other class of identity type is summarily granted access to the sensitive system. There is an approval process; for the purposes of this example assessment, we don't need to go into the details of that approval process. Nevertheless, in this type of assessment in a real organization, the assessor should understand the group membership process since it must be considered as a part of the system's defenses.

An interesting question poses itself when considering these two systems, both of which are considered very sensitive by the company. Which system provides an attack vector to the other? When the business analytics system requests an authentication, is it possible that an attack could be promulgated from the Active Directory backwards in the response? When the business analytics system requests a determination on group membership, likewise might a response contain an attack?

On the other hand, can Active Directory be attacked through authentication and authorization requests?

The answers to each of these questions I believe would be, "Yes." Each system is at risk of attack from the other. There are two mitigating factors that may be considered. Active Directory is a trusted system to every other system that makes use of the authentication and authorization services. If Active Directory fails, many other systems that are dependent upon it will also fail. Identity systems such as Active Directory are typically considered to be among the "crown jewels" of any organization's data and systems. Consequently, an organization that doesn't sufficiently protect its identity system has already degraded its security posture dramatically. The subject of identity system protections, just as identity systems themselves, can and should be an entire book by itself.

Indeed, the identity system, though interacting with our business analytics system, is out of scope. Identity systems are typically regarded as part of the infrastructure. As we know, the strengths and the weaknesses of the infrastructure are inherited by the systems that are deployed upon them. And any system that is foundational to customer interaction, the business ecosystem, and the internal business systems must be regarded as highly sensitive. Nevertheless, the identity system does not depend upon the business analytics but rather the reverse. That will be a key factor in answering the question about which system poses a danger to the other.

Data Gathering most certainly presents an attack surface when it reads the identity stores: to gather data about the various entities, such as employees, partners, and customers, whose identities are maintained by Active Directory. Similar to any data source, the identity data might contain an attack to the data gathering function. Since data from identity are gathered via native Active Directory protocols, business analytics must maintain credentials that have privileges to read this data.

As we have noted above, Active Directory is highly protected by this organization. Therefore, although we have uncovered an attack surface, attack from this data source, as compared to the many other data sources from which Data Gathering must collect, is probably unlikely. However, the astute assessor will note that business analytics now becomes part of the Active Directory security posture because Data Gathering must have privileges to the identity store in order to correlate other business data with identities and identity metrics. Although Active Directory as a system is outside of scope, because Active Directory is at such a deep level of sensitivity, risk for the identity system would have to be noted because of the rights that the business analytics system must maintain in order to access identity formation from Active Directory. In other words, business analytics significantly poses an attack vector to Active Directory, as opposed to the other way around.

As we have underscored repeatedly, security assessment must be done holistically. And further, if the assessment has a due diligence responsibility to uncover risks for the organization, the dependence of Active Directory's security posture upon the posture of business analytics would have to be noted as a part of the threat model for Active Directory at Digital Diskus.

Irrespective of the scope of this particular assessment, systems interconnect. When they do, the security posture of each system can significantly affect or alter the security posture of the other systems to which it connects. In this case, business analytics must become a part of the tight security posture around the identity system. In addition, the security requirements for business analytics must match those of this very sensitive identity system, at least for the credentials.

It should be noted that, most certainly, Microsoft understands the criticality of Active Directory as a foundational part of many organizations' infrastructures. There's no doubt that they take the security posture of the system quite seriously. It's a safe bet that Microsoft attempts as rigorous a set of protections as they can implement, knowing full well that entire enterprise architectures are dependent upon the security posture of Active Directory. With that in mind, let's assume, for the purposes of this assessment, that Active Directory is in fact protectable, in general, and, in this instance, has been configured to be sufficiently protected. With this assumption, we can be satisfied that it will be very difficult to launch an attack through the Active Directory to our business analytics system.

The foregoing analysis hopes to answer the question posed earlier: Which of the two systems affects the security posture of the other? Theoretically, the answer is that influence is bidirectional. However, we concern ourselves with how business analytics affects the security posture of Active Directory and not, for this analysis, the other way around.

There is another system that interacts with business analytics: the security monitoring system. The security monitoring system will monitor the activities and changes on the hosts that support business analytics modules. This would be a normal part of the security of a mature administration function, as we have previously described. Importantly for this assessment, changes to the configuration file are logged; those change logs are audited for suspicious events. In this way, if an attacker does manage to breach the protections around the configuration files, hopefully, such anomalous activities will be noted quickly. The goal of this sort of monitoring is to stop any malicious activity before it can do serious damage. A further goal is to let administrators know that someone is independently paying attention to events. This type of monitoring is typical and would be described in any number of security standards covering the security of administrative activities.

Does security monitoring pose an attack surface for either business analytics or the security monitoring system? Typically, the security monitoring system gathers change logs that are output by a system and by the operating system. Usually, the logs sit on disk until collected, at which point they may be archived or deleted. Similar to the data gathering activities of the business analytics system, the security monitoring system will be at some risk to attacks embedded within the logs. And it would be very difficult to sell a security monitoring and event correlation system if it was easy to compromise the monitoring system. Although such weaknesses have been discovered in security monitoring systems, vendors depend upon the rigorousness of their processing defenses so that they can successfully sell their systems.

The security monitoring and correlation system will also be considered part of the security infrastructure. Furthermore, a security monitoring system will operate as one of the most sensitive systems an organization maintains. Therefore, all due care should be taken in purchasing and implementing as bulletproof a system as humanly possible. One of the differences between a security event managing system and other systems will be that a security system expects to be attacked and should be built with industrial-strength defenses. When implementing such a system, all due diligence should be taken to make sure that purchased components have many integral defenses, that these defenses are in depth, and that the implementation instance takes advantage of all of the defenses possible.

We have yet another situation where a highly sensitive system, security monitoring, might be profoundly affected by the security of business analytics, just as the identity system, Active Directory, was affected by business analytics. Let's assume, for the moment, that the security monitoring system is a rigorous, industrial-strength security system that protects itself very carefully from malicious data in logs and other event sources.

In this situation, the monitored outputs coming from business analytics are not the system's analysis results, but rather, come from the application about its activities. At least some of this output would be the result of the programming logic steps of the application. Items like data accesses, the size of the access, maybe even details about the data retrieved, might get logged by Data Gathering. In this way, a retrieval of data not consistent with the intentions of the programmers of the system might show up as anomalous activity that would then fire a security alert for further investigation.

However, in order to debug systems, application programmers will typically send events about internal processing steps and similar to logs, as well. In more than one system, I have seen user or other credentials that then get exposed in unprotected ways. Thus, the log files themselves might be an attack surface, not to subvert the business analytics system but rather to gain valuable information that probably shouldn't have been logged at all. Application logs tend to be quite uncontrolled compared to other types of system outputs. If the vendor of the business analytics system was foolish enough to have placed data within the logs that contains possible attack value, that would be yet another conversation with the vendor about software security.

Nevertheless, if the log files contain juicy data about the workings of the business analytics system, or even worse, hints about the nature of the analytics results, then these would constitute a significant attack surface. One of the investigations that should be conducted would be to discover exactly what goes into the logs, ascertaining just how sensitive the information, log item by log item, or when aggregated, might be. Thus, the very act of logging data for the security monitoring system uncovers yet another attack surface.

The logs might be an attack surface against the security monitoring system, including all the mitigations that are in place against log file tampering as well as protections against attacks contained within log items. Since the logs originate solely in the business analytics application, and can only be written by business analytics for read only by security monitoring, this is a fairly long shot for the attacker. Presumably, the only people with access to business analytics code are those authorized to change it. How do they even know which security systems one of their customers may use (attacks are usually quite specific to application and execution environment)?

But the logs themselves may constitute a target if the data they contain is useful. In this case, these are simply flat files on disk. Technically, these are not a part of the formal architecture of the system but rather an output that must then be managed properly. Nevertheless, a prudent assessment would ascertain the data contained in the log files. And a prudent assessment would consider the log files as a possible target.

At this point, I urge you to consider the diagrams of business analytics once again. Do you see an attack surface that hasn't been discussed? As far as I know, given the constraints and background information that has already been described, all the relevant attack surfaces have been uncovered.

One of the biggest mistakes that I've made has been overlooking a detail during assessment. That's why I make liberal use of peer review in my assessments, because it's easy to miss something important. I ask you, the reader, to be my peer reviewer. Have I missed anything? This is not a trick question. Pretend that I've performed an assessment and that now I'm asking you to peer review my work.

Another advantage of a peer review is a diversity of opinion. Each of us has a unique sense of risk, and each of us favors a unique security posture. As such, I believe it's important to consider alternate views when prioritizing attack scenarios. I've given my views on several of the attack scenarios presented in this analysis that should be de-prioritized. What's your opinion? Do you agree with me, or would you change the prioritization to raise an attack surface or attack vector or to lower one that I've considered important?

I suggest that you take some time and imagine yourself as the security architect responsible for the enterprise architecture of Digital Diskus. If you were implementing the business analytics system for this enterprise and enterprise architecture, how would you protect the business analytics system and the systems with which it interacts?

The following section comprises a list of the attack surfaces that have been uncovered during this analysis.

8.3.1 Attack Surface Enumeration

- Data gathering credentials store
- Data source credential inputs
- Data gathered from sources
- Business analytics message bus listeners
- Analytics results store
- Analytics results presentation ("Reporter")
- Configuration files and system metadata
- Management console inputs
- Management console configuration outputs
- Management console host
- Processing module input from Data Gathering
- Processing input from Reporter (commands)
- Processing module configuration file
- Data Gathering module
- Data Gathering module configuration file
- Data Gathering inputs, especially from data sources
- Data source agents
- Communications with data sources
- Reporting module user interface
- Reporting module configuration file
- Business analytics activity and event log files

8.4 Mitigations

As you consider the attack surfaces in the list above, what security controls have already been listed?

I have stressed the importance of industry-standard administrative and system management controls as they apply to the business analytics system. Because of the importance and sensitivity of the system's configuration files, the temporary results and analytics results files, these two storage areas require special attention beyond the usual and typical that we have already stressed. As was already explained, each of these storage areas represents an opportunity not only to control the business analytics system, but perhaps to have far-reaching consequences for the entire enterprise architecture. Due to this sensitivity and the comprehensive consequences of a successful attack to either of these areas and data, particular attention must be paid to the execution of access restrictions and the separation of duties.

Essentially, no matter how particular and careful Digital Diskus is about the implementation of access controls, some administrator, at least one, is going to have access rights to each of these areas. That's because there will need to be someone who can execute those tasks that require superuser privileges. Unfortunately, modern operating systems require someone who, at the very least, has privileges to firefight during a crisis.

Let's suppose that a junior engineer makes a grand mistake by corrupting a couple of key operating system shared libraries on several of the business analytics hosts. Let's suppose that it's an honest mistake; the engineer thought that he was executing a script designed to check the validity of packages, mistyping the command line parameters to the script at a time when he had sufficient privileges to damage the systems. And let's suppose, just for the sake of an example, that the mistaken script causes several systems to reboot in a state from which the system cannot recover. Usually, operating systems survive such unexpected crashes without damage. But to give an example in which firefighting capabilities might be required on a critical system, let's suppose that several of the redundant processing module hosts come up with damaged operating system files that can no longer execute. This is not a far-fetched example. Such crashes do occasionally happen; someone has to come in and get the systems up and running. Often, in these situations, there may very well be significant management pressure demanding that the systems are fixed as quickly as possible. This could especially be true at a time when financial records are being closed or at some other business inflection point.

With the kind of pressure described in the example above and the criticality of the business analytics systems, solutions to such situations often take a very senior engineer with much system experience and deep understanding of the application, as well. This individual must "smoke jump" the problem by using superuser privileges to rebuild the operating system.

The questions that then will be asked for this type of critical system that maintains highly sensitive data will be something like, "Who should have these privileges and how many people need them?"

Oftentimes, the easiest and most manageable solution to who and how many people need high privileges is to give everyone who may have to alter the system the ability to work at the highest privilege level. In a situation in which there are only three system administrators, the tactic of giving everyone high privileges may make a good deal of sense? After all, on a small team, if someone makes a significant error or, worse, is dishonest or downright malicious, one or both of the other two people are likely to notice.

However, organizations that field large administrative staff cannot rely upon a system based upon personal checks and balances over the actions of any particular individual. If there are 100 administrators spread out globally in different time zones, who knows who's performing what actions at any particular time? Furthermore, what if most of those administrators are responsible for every machine on the network, so that the administrative duties can be handled around the clock, 365 days per year? Many individuals may be given very similar duties, so that the absence of any single individual will not be missed. This is very typical in organizations that administer hundreds or even thousands of machines across the globe.

Generally, system administrators are among the most trusted staff at any organization. They have to be: They can bring systems up or down, and they certainly have access to at least some of the critical files and data of the organization. Indeed, it's easier on everyone if privileges and access controls are kept simple. Generally, it's prudent to eliminate as many special cases as possible in order to reap the rewards of economies of scale and efficiencies of task.

Competing against simplicity and economies of scale are the differences in data sensitivity and system criticality. In the case of business analytics, there appears to be a clear need to protect the configuration files and the results files as carefully as possible leaving as small an attack surface as can be managed. That is, these two sensitive locations that store critical organizational data should be restricted to a need-to-access basis, which essentially means as few administrators as possible within the organization who can manage the systems effectively and continuously.

A typical requirement for this kind of system would be to limit the number of administrators who have access to it to a small number. What that number is will need to be determined by taking the factors of global, round-the-clock support and appropriate levels of personnel redundancy into account. There is no hard and fast number that will work for every organization. One of the factors influencing the decision will essentially be the number of individuals who have the experience and proven trust to execute the task. If there are seven of these, that may be a better decision than a smaller number simply because the difference between six and seven poses no or little additional risk to the organization. I would avoid attempts to pull a number out of the air since, in my experience, no such perfect number exists. And time may be wasted and relationships hurt if the number question turns into a tug-of-war between four versus seven, a tug-of-war between system administrators and security.

Instead, it may be more fruitful to examine individuals' past history and expertise, management chains, line management capabilities, and other direct factors that will influence the ability of the individuals to carry out the duties and carry this burden of responsibility successfully.

The requirement would read something like, "superuser privileges may only be granted to high trust, master administrator-level personnel on a need-to-know and need-to-support basis." Keep requirements like these at a high enough level that those charged with execution can implement them without being micro-managed or blocked, as conditions and technologies unfold and develop.*

There are tools readily available (but sometimes expensive and nontrivial to implement) that can help to control high-privilege access, especially in situations as confronted by Digital Diskus' implementation of business analytics. These tools grant privilege levels only for the duration of the session or task. When the task is completed or the designated period ends, the privileges are revoked and must be requested from the system once again.

Access can be granted in a granular manner by tools of this type. That is one of the primary functions of a server access and change management system. Implementing a server administrative privilege control tool would allow the extensive administrative function at Digital Diskus to provide one level of access across most of the servers, while reserving critical server access to a limited, higher-trust set of individuals, precisely as required for the business analytics system.

Such an access and change control tool will also log actions taken by administrators on systems (remember that all actions on the systems are being monitored by the security monitoring system). Consequently, every action taken can be audited, both for malfeasance and for inevitable human mistakes. Typically, a tool controlling highly privileged access can also dole out permissions in such a way that for some systems or some operations, only the most highly trusted individuals are granted permission.

If Digital Diskus hasn't deployed an administrative access control tool, the implementation of business analytics might be seen as an opportunity to upgrade the security controls across the administrative functions. In other words, new complexities to an enterprise architecture often present opportunities for building an architecture that better meets those complexities rather than trying to simply accept additional risk due to the way "things have always been done." Another typical response would be to jerry-rig current systems with high-maintainance manual processes in order to meet the challenge. Although either of these responses may be the appropriate organization decision, an architecture inflection point at which new requirements foster new capabilities is usually an opportunity to discuss strategy as well as any available tactical solutions.

I will point out that since the organization already has a robust implementation of Active Directory groups, an interim solution might be to employ a group membership as a way to restrict access to these two particular storage areas. Such a solution would depend upon the operating system on which business analytics runs and the operating environment for storage areas (both of which are currently undefined) and whether these can make use of Active Directory groups for authorization to particular storage areas.

---

* Steve Acheson taught me to keep my requirements at sufficient specificity to be implementable but not so specific such that implementers cannot adjust to changes without rewriting the requirement.

If we were actually implementing the system, we might have to engage with the operational server management teams to construct a workable solution for everyone. For our purposes in this example, we can simply specify the requirement and leave the implementation details unknown.

The actual data that is pulled into the business analytics system might contain attacks. Some of this data originates from applications that are hosted on the exposed network, the DMZ. Those applications, of course, will be under fairly constant probing and attack. Although Digital Diskus makes a concerted effort to build resistant and self-protective applications, no security measure is perfect. It should be assumed that, at least occasionally, hopefully rarely, a sophisticated attack will breach the protections, input validations, and messaging rewrites that we've already noted have been built into the exposed applications. That is, a strong defense must assume that an attack will come through.

If an attack makes it through, it may lay in wait in data storage until the business analytics system pulls the data that contain the attack and then attempts to process it. At that point, any authentication or communication encryption that is used will provide no defense whatsoever to the stored attack; the attack will be gathered up as a part of the data that's being processed. The business analytics system must be as self-protective and securely programmed as external applications are expected to be. It is important to note that one of the inputs into Data Gathering is from messages that originate from external applications as they pass over the message bus. So an attack that makes it through the external applications might be processed by the business analytics processing module before the attack data are stored. Data Gathering must be robust and rigorous in throwing away any data that is invalid or poorly formed, no matter the source or the timing of the collection.

However, in a system that must process many different forms of data, that processing must be very "plastic." Generalized data format processing must be very data driven so that it can accept just about any form of data imaginable, as the processing code is going to have to process data in many forms and presentations. There is a significant conflict between rigorous input validation and normalization and the processing of many varied data presentations and types. This is what they call in computer design "a nontrivial problem." As has been stated previously, but should be noted again, the implementation and coding of the business analytics system is not within the control of Digital Diskus. What is the best way for Digital Diskus to mitigate the risk from overly generalized data processing?

In Chapter 3, where we examined the art of security architecture, holistic analysis was discussed at some length. The risk of an attack coming through one of the data streams is a good example of how a system's security posture shouldn't be confined to the system itself, but rather, enlarged to include all the systems with which it connects. In this case, the cleanliness of the data, the protection of the data processing module, depends upon a strong defense against malformed data in applications that were likely built without any concern for the business analytics system. In this case, which is a typical timeline for adding a business intelligence to an organization, the business analytics system has been implemented after many of the applications that produce the data to be analyzed were built. Nevertheless, business analytics depends upon those applications' defenses against malicious data. Part of the defense of the business analytics system will be how thoroughly the data is cleaned before it is allowed to pass inwards and onwards to the systems that the business analytics will touch.

However, the defense of business analytics shouldn't rest solely with the quality of applications and other data sources. Below, in the discussion of user interface imports, we will add another assurance step for determining the quality of the business analytics systems' defenses themselves.

There are several user interfaces that require restricted access. When we developed our threat model, the reporting module's user interface and that of Management Console were called out as a likely attack surface. Furthermore, within each of these interfaces, certain inputs were called out as particularly sensitive: the interface provided in order to input credentials for data sources and the interface where the analytics results are displayed.

- Management console inputs
  - Data source credential inputs
- Reporting module user interface
  - Presentation of analytics results ("Reporter")

The data source credential values will be input into a subset of Management Console's user interface. Likewise, the presentation of results is a subset of inputs and outputs within the user interface of the reporting module. Depending upon the granularity of authorization permissions, it should be possible to isolate each of these sensitive areas from the general user interface in a granular manner. That granularity of access and restriction must be finer than a role that is given broad access* to a number of functions or even the entire interface. Fine-grained access in this case may mean single pages, collections of pages, or access that has been confined to individual fields. One of the requirements would then be a fine-grained authorization mechanism.

This business analytics system includes coarse-grained roles, such as system administrator, analyst, and executive, as shown in Figure 8.4. (These are examples and do not comprise an exhaustive list of system roles. Such a list isn't needed for this analysis.) But the system also allows the super administrator to assign privileges in a fine-grained manner. For instance, there can be any number of "administrators" who can add analysts or executives to the system in order to perform typical, day-to-day user management. But each of these administrators should not be given permission to edit credentials that will be used by the system.

---

* The authorization mechanism could be a native business analytics role or membership within an Active Directory group, as we explored above.

This, however, cannot be the entire protection for these sensitive interfaces. Even though all due care must be observed in granting access on a strictly need-to-know basis, it has already been stated that Digital Diskus is concerned about insider attack. The system must implement protections against the various attacks that can be exploited through user interfaces (from web weaknesses to memory handling errors, and so forth). But, as was noted, Digital Diskus doesn't have control over the programming of the system. Has the maker implemented the appropriate input validation and sanitization routines in order to protect the code from user input–based attacks?

From Digital Diskus' viewpoint, since they do not have direct control over business analytics' implementation, they have two (industry-standard) activities that they may use as a risk treatment: study the vendor's security practices, with particular emphasis on software security, and test the system itself for vulnerabilities and attack resistance.

Let us assume that Digital Diskus' security department has conducted a thorough analysis of the vendor's software security practices, with particular emphasis on how the system is built and how the vendor finds and fixes vulnerabilities during the vendor's Secure Development Lifecycle (SDL). Further, a thorough attack and penetration test (A&P or "pen test") was performed by Digital Diskus security personnel on the system before it went into production. Although the pen test did find a few minor issues, no major issues were uncovered. Therefore, Digital Diskus has some confidence in the system's ability to resist attack to its inputs. "Inputs" for the pen test included the user interfaces, the configuration file processing functions, and the data gathering inputs.

Because Digital Diskus' internal network cannot entirely be trusted as a sole control to restrict access because of the broad range of people and organizations that participate in the Digital Diskus business ecosystem, communications from users to the business analytics system and between data sources as data is gathered should be protected in transit. In other words, the network cannot be completely trusted. The business analytics system has the ability to present its user interfaces via HTTPS. HTTPS will meet the requirement to protect user interactions with the system across the less than completely trusted network. And any data gathering access that supports Transport Layer Security (TLS) should be configured to do so. This aspect of the communications is somewhat dependent upon the capability of the data source. To facilitate secured communications, the data agent API and libraries support TLS. Generally, native data gathering protocols pull data from the source. When this is the case, if the data source can act as a TLS server, Data Gathering is capable of being a TLS client. Consequently, in all instances that support a TLS capability, TLS is being employed across Digital Diskus' internal network.

8.5 Administrative Controls

It can't be stressed enough that complex, interactive systems such as the business analytics server presented here require significant administrative protections. This is particularly true when the system integrates and exists within a fairly complex digital ecosystem, as has been described about Digital Diskus. There are too many ways for an attacker to get close enough to the business analytics system to assume that simply because it runs within an internal network, the internal network's perimeter protections will be sufficient.

Adding to the general ecosystem access, privileged access must also be considered, which points directly towards a rigorous web of interlocking administrative security controls and practices, as has been previously described and cited. There is no way around the necessity for the management of this system to enact virtually all the controls described in the various standards.[*]

Several times in our exploration of Digital Diskus, we've encountered a mature and rigorous set of administrative controls. Which of the attack surfaces that we've uncovered do administrative controls protect? At the operating system level, every server that is part of the infrastructure hosting the business analytics modules will inherit the body of practices that Digital Diskus administrators observe.

Access will be restricted to a need-to-know basis. As we have noted, changes to the systems are monitored and audited. At the application level, files and directories will be given permissions such that only the applications that need to read particular files or data are given permission to read those files. This is all in accordance with the way that proper administrative and operating system permissions should be set up. The business analytics systems and tools don't require superuser rights for reading and executing everything on the system. Therefore, the processing unit has rights to its configuration files and data gathering module files. The reporting module reads its own configuration files. None of these can write into the configuration data. Only Management Console is given permission to write data into the configuration files. In this way, even if any of the three processing modules is compromised, the compromised component cannot make use of configuration files to compromise any of the other modules in the system. This is how self-defensive software should operate. Business analytics adheres to these basic security principles, thus allowing the system to be deployed in less trusted environments, even less protected than what Digital Diskus provides.

8.5.1 Enterprise Identity Systems (Authentication and Authorization)

The user interfaces of the system use the enterprise identity system for authentication and then authorization (group membership) to its various privilege levels In addition,

---

[*] It should be noted that many of the largest and most famous breaches were a direct result of an organization's failure to adhere to the entire body of administrative and management controls typically found within the relevant standards. A security architect must continuously bear this fact in mind.

other systems used to support business analytics also make use of the enterprise identity and access control system, Active Directory. The relationship between the identity system and business analytics was examined in some detail above. Authentication via the corporate directory and authorization via group membership still remain two of the important mitigations that have been implemented.

Having reviewed the available mitigations, which attack surfaces seem to you to be adequately protected? And, concomitantly, which attack surfaces still require an adequate defense? Once again, please review the list of attack surfaces that were uncovered during the threat modeling exercise. In the next section, we will prescribe additional defenses necessary to build the defense-in-depth for the business analytics system at Digital Diskus.

8.6 Requirements

The final task of the business analytics analysis consists of finding mitigation for every attack surface that does not already contain sufficient protection to meet the security posture laid out in the description of Digital Diskus, above.

When I do these analyses for a real system, I list every requirement, even those that are already built. In this manner, I document the defense-in-depth through the security requirements. However, for the sake of brevity, the mitigations listed above will not be reiterated in this section. If you believe that an attack surface has not been sufficiently protected through this analysis, then by all means, reread the discussions above.

Since the quality of the software security being built into the system is not under the direct control of the organization implementing it (Digital Diskus), a key requirement will be repeated assurance that the vendor maintains rigorous software security practices, including finding and eradicating vulnerabilities before release; implementing input protections; and maintaining proper memory handling, proper multithreading and multitasking, secure web interfaces, and the rest of the panoply of software security design and implementation requirements[*] that secure software must meet. This requirement can be fulfilled by performing an attack and penetration test on all the inputs of the system and its software updates before the software is allowed to go into production. Particular attention will have to be paid to Data Gathering; Data Gathering and subsequent processing functions will require fuzzing tests in order to achieve some assurance that attacks will be rejected properly.

In order to prevent an attacker from obscuring an attack or otherwise spoofing or fooling the security monitoring system, the business analytics activity and event log files should only be readable by the security monitoring systems. And the log files permissions should be set such that only event-producing modules of the business analytics

---

[*] For further information, please see my chapter, "Applying the SDL Framework to the Real World," in *Core Software Security*, by James Ransome and Anmol Misra (CRC Press, © 2014).

system may write to its log file. Although it is true that a superuser on most operating systems can read and write any file, in this way, attackers would have to gain these high privileges before they could alter the log files that will feed into the security monitoring system.

The administrative requirements for well-managed servers and services have been listed previously in several places. Table 6.1, for Web-Sock-A-Rama, contains a number of examples. And NIST 800-53 has been cited several times. For the purposes of brevity, the functions necessary to create a strong administrative defense will not be reiterated for business analytics (or for any succeeding architecture analysis). Please assume that the same requirements hold true for this system as it is analyzed in this assessment.

Table 8.1 summarizes the additional security requirements that Digital Diskus will need to implement in order to achieve the security posture required for this sensitive system, the business intelligence and analytics system. As we noted previously, requirements are broken down into three large categories: administration, network, and application. These categories are for convenience. Any other suitable abstraction can be used. The important point of the categories is to note that defenses are implemented at different layers throughout an operational execution stack. And, indeed, some of the requirements are not technical but rather process and even personnel oriented.

Table 8.1 is not intended as a complete listing of requirements from which the security architecture would be designed and implemented. As I explained above, when I perform a security architecture analysis, I try to document every requirement, whether the requirement has been met or not. In this way, I document the defense-in-depth of the system. If something changes during implementation, or a security feature does not fulfill its promise or cannot be built for some reason, the requirements document provides all the stakeholders with a record of what the security posture of the system should be. I find that risk is easier to assess in the face of change when I've documented the full defense, irrespective of whether it exists or must be built.

However, this is a pedagogical work, not an analysis of a living system. These architectures are merely examples* intended to help you, the reader, become more facile at analyzing the security of a system. As examples, I hope that you feel free to reread or even study any portions of the analysis, as you require. Consequently, Table 8.1 only lists those requirements that would be in addition to the mitigations that have already been documented above, in the mitigations section. In this way, I hope to keep the analysis more focused.

It's always possible that I've missed something. If you will remember, at the end of the attack surface section, I asked you to check my work. Perhaps you came up with something that has not been discussed? If so, how would you protect that attack surface? That analysis lies at the heart of this book. Your risk sense may not coincide with

---

* Every system presented in this book is based upon real-world systems that the author has assessed. Nevertheless, these systems are entirely fictional. Any resemblance to actual systems or products is purely coincidental.

Table 8.1 Business Analytics Security Requirements

Type	Requirement
Administrative	Typical industry standard controls have already been specified earlier. Please refer to these.
	All modules and executables of the system must be hosted by one of the formal, corporate administrative teams.
	All modules and executables of the system must be run on corporate-maintained hosts.
	Administrative access to the storage areas for system configuration files and temporary and final results for the analytics must be restricted to a need-to-know basis and only to a small number of highly trusted and time-of-service proven administrative personnel.
	Access to the permanent storage for the configuration files for the system and to the storage area for processing results will be granted only for the period required to perform an administrative task and then privileges will be revoked. Privileges will be granted only on a need-to-know basis.
	Read and write privileges for system log and event files must be set in order to protect the files from inadvertent or malicious alteration. Only the business analytics module producing the event file may have write permissions, and only the security monitoring system may read the event or log file.
Network	All executables of the system must run within the corporate internal network.
Application	Fine-grained authorization to Reporter and Management Console functions will be employed. In particular, permission to add, delete, and write data source credentials must be restricted to a need-to-know basis. In addition, access to "executive" aggregations of business data must be restricted only to vice president or above personnel.
	Authentication must be enabled before access is granted to the system for every user role and access. Authentication will be against the corporate, standard identity system.
	Every input of the system must be self-protective and prevent malformed and other input injection attacks. Since coding of the system is not under Digital Diskus control, the vendor must demonstrate a successful attack and penetration test to include input fuzzing against all system inputs. All high- and medium-severity findings must be fixed in each software update before it may be installed on a corporate network.
	For every data source that supports authentication, an authentication must take place before data may be accessed by the system.
	For every data source that supports encrypted communications, encryption must be enabled to protect data as it is transmitted to/from the system.
	Data gathering agents will be run only with sufficient system privileges to read the data to be gathered. Write/execute privileges on raw data sources are not required and must not be granted. Care will be taken to run data agents at a lower privilege than root, superuser, or administrator, if possible. If the operating system allows, a data agent should be run under a unique User ID assigned expressly to the data agent. Under no circumstances, should the data agent be run under the User ID of the user of the system or an administrator.

mine. I invite you to add or subtract from my lists as you see fit. For, in that way, you begin to make ATASM your own.

By now, I hope that you are becoming more comfortable with the ATASM process. Assuming that you no longer need to be reminded of the steps and how each contributes to the understanding of the whole and to each other—Architecture, Threats, Attack Surfaces, and Mitigations—I will no longer note the process as we analyze the remaining architectures in the following example assessments. Furthermore, in order to pace the remaining analyses, I will not list out the attack surfaces that are uncovered after the threat model phase of assessment. Instead, we will focus on the two most important products of architecture analysis for security: security requirements and residual risk left over after the requirements are implemented.

The requirements that result from the ARA/threat model process comprise the security posture of the system. It is the architecture requirements (mostly, the controls that will make up the system's defense-in-depth) that become the security inputs into the architecture, as its developed, which then must be expressed by the design, and subsequently implemented in the software, hardware, infrastructure, operating system, execution environment, processes, and practices of those who will use, administer, and maintain the system. Without requirements, "securing" must be removed from the title of this book; only a risk assessment has been accomplished from the analysis. This book is about the process, tools, and craft of bringing systems of any size and type to a desired risk posture. The requirements that specify those mitigations and controls that exist and will be built comprise one of the essential goals of ATASM—that is, the "mitigation" phase of the process.

In a case where the requirements that can be built do not bring the system to the desired security posture, there is residual risk,* as described in Chapter 4. Clearly stating any residual risk is also a key output of the ATASM process: Decisions will need to be made. Should the organization accept the risk? If not, must the organization invest in new capabilities in order to treat the risk? Does the system go live with the risks untreated? Or should the project be stopped until treatment, that is, mitigation is possible?

The task of the assessor is to present the residual risks in a manner that can be understood by each stakeholder community, each stakeholder type. In the organizations in which I've worked, it has not been the task of the security architect to render risk decisions (though in some organizations, it is). Instead, the security architect is the organizational "truth teller" who tries to convey risks in a manner that facilitates decision making. The architect has been charged with uncovering risks and assessing their organizational seriousness, a due diligence task for the organization, for which the security architect has been fully empowered.

It has also been the task of the security architect to understand who the appropriate decision makers are, depending upon the scope and seriousness of the risks that are to

---

* We are concerned only with negative risk. Positive risk is out of scope of the process of architecture risk assessment (ARA) and threat modeling.

be raised for a decision. The architect (or peer reviewing architect team) must decide the scope of the risk's possible impact (consequences). The scope of the impact dictates at what level of the organization risk decisions must be made. The decision maker(s) must have sufficient organizational decision-making authority for the impacts. For instance, if the impact is confined to a particular system, then perhaps the managers involved in building and using that system would have sufficient decision making scope for the risk. If the impact is to an entire collection of teams underneath a particular director, then she or he must make that risk decision. If the risk impacts an enterprise's brand, then the decision might need to be escalated all the way to the Chief Operating Officer or even the Chief Executive, perhaps even to the Board of Directors, if serious enough. The scope of the impact is used as the escalation guide in the organizations for which I've worked. Of course, your organization may use another approach.

Thus, there must be two primary outputs of the ATASM process, at the very least[*]: a set of architecture, design, implementation, and testing requirements and a statement of any system risks that the requirements do not adequately address in the presence of the threats the system will face when it goes live. In the succeeding analyses in this section, we will focus on these results.

In order that the remaining analyses are as brief as possible, we will proceed in a more realistic manner. As the architecture is understood, attack surfaces are uncovered. While fresh in the mind, requirements will be suggested at that point in the text. There will be no more lists of threats, attack surfaces, or mitigations. Rather, we will strive to develop as complete a set of security requirements as we can for each system analyzed.

References

1. Provost, F. and Fawcett, T. (2013). *Data Science for Business*. Sebastopol (CA): O'Reilly Media.

---

[*] This does not preclude other outputs, such as a threat model or a description of what has been analyzed, the list of threats that have been considered, and similar artifacts.

Chapter 9

Endpoint Anti-malware

Let's now leave the world of Digital Diskus and turn to a set of architectural problems that is different from securing enterprise architectures. You may remember the discussion of endpoint antivirus software from Chapter 3. Figure 9.1 diagrams a more complete set of the components that might be used within endpoint antivirus software.

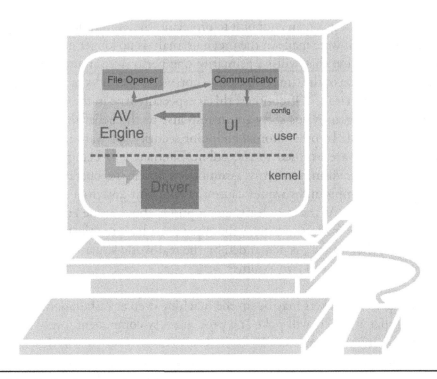

Figure 9.1   Endpoint security software.

As was explained in Chapter 3, the granularity to which level software must be decomposed is radically different compared to the previous analysis—business analytics. If you recall, we didn't have to break down the executable package(s) that comprised the three core modules of the business analytics system. That's because we could make assumptions about the running environment, the underlying host and its security posture. For the business analytics example, we knew something about the protections— both technical and process—that were applied to the host and operating system upon which the core of the business analytics system runs in that environment. Consequently, we discounted the ability of an attacker to listen in on the kernel-level communications, most particularly, the "localhost," intra-kernel network route. Additionally, if an attacker has already gained sufficiently high privileges on the system to control processes and perhaps even to access process memory, "game over." That is, the attacker no longer has any need for exercising most of the typical vulnerabilities since she or he can do whatever is desired. The only users on these types of systems are high-privileged users who perform maintenance tasks. Users of the software's functionality don't have to also be users of the operating system.

9.1 A Deployment Model Lens

For software that must go on an endpoint to protect it, the assumptions about operating system detections that were made in the previous analysis no longer hold true. Software intended for a machine that will be primarily one person's computer and which will likely run at least some of the time on possibly untrusted networks mustn't even assume that the endpoint is "clean." Oftentimes, this is especially true in the consumer market. The user is installing antivirus software in response to the belief that the machine is already compromised. In other words, endpoint security software must assume that, very similar to software exposed to the public Internet, it is being installed into an aggressively hostile environment. Any assumptions about the operating system being free of successful compromises would cause the endpoint antivirus software, itself, to become a juicy target. At the very least, assumptions about a safe environment might lead security software makers to believe that they don't have to take the care with their security posture that, in fact, is demanded by the real-world situation.

The foregoing leads us to two axioms:

- Assume active attackers may be on the machine even at installation time.
- Assume that attackers will poke and prod at every component, every input, every line of communication.

As you may see, this is somewhat analogous, though at a different level of granularity, to the threat landscape for exposed inputs to the Internet. However, in that situation we were able to make assumptions about protections to hosts and networks that were under the control of sophisticated staff (repeating what's been previously stated).

In this situation, the network must be assumed to be hostile. The system "administrator" may have very little understanding of computers, much less security. Even so, that user may be running with significant privileges so they can install software. Consumers typically give themselves greater privileges simply to make life easier as they go about their daily business with the computer. This is a very different situation from having a professional administrative staff providing protections to the system. And, the endpoint situation is radically different from a situation of restricted, need-to-access privileges.

Due to the likelihood of elevated privileges, endpoints (especially consumer endpoints) make juicy targets. Compromise of the user account is equal to compromise of the operating system, since the user is the administrator. Compromise at administrative privileges means that the attacker controls the machine and every user action taken upon it. All data belongs to the attacker. In addition, the attacker may use the machine for her or his own purposes, quite likely without the owner of the machine knowing or understanding what is taking place. This level of control offers attacker value in and of itself.

Every threat agent that has so far been mentioned will be attacking broadly distributed security software. Although consumers probably don't need to worry about state-sponsored industrial espionage, if the antivirus software is aimed at businesses, especially enterprises, and is in use by consumers, the maker of the software should consider these threat agents among those likely to be attacking the software.

Of course, cyber criminals will want to get around any protections of the antivirus software. They may even test the software for vulnerabilities that allow them to masquerade (spoof) as the antivirus software during attacks. Indeed, I think it's not too much to say that every type of attacker and researcher is "gunning" for every type of security software, including antivirus software intended for endpoints.

If the maker of antivirus software wants to be successful, the software has to be as close to bulletproof as the maker can possibly make it. Nothing is perfect; we certainly should understand at this point that no software can be proven bug free and that no security posture is 100% risk-free? As an aspiration, in my experience, security software vendors understand the level of attack that their software must resist. Failure to do so will put the company's future at significant risk.

9.2 Analysis

As we explored in Chapter 3, there is a natural division of privilege and access between user and kernel execution. Even at administrative privileges, this boundary is still important to acknowledge and protect. Gaining the kernel, the attacker has everything, absolutely everything under attacker control.

Since it's so dangerous, why would designers install software into the kernel at all (or make use of kernel software)? In order to capture events and activities across every application, as we noted in Chapter 3, security software will have to "breach" or get out of its assigned process space. The kernel has visibility to everything—all drivers and their associated activity flow through the kernel. In order to gain access to all this activity, and protect against anything abnormal or malicious, security software has to first achieve full visibility. This is typically achieved by running software within the kernel.

The user mode application must initialize and start the kernel software (usually as a driver). But after the kernel software has been started, the flow should be from kernel to user. In this way, attack from user to kernel is prevented once the entire security system has been started. That still leaves the attacker an avenue to the kernel through the initialization sequence of the kernel driver during startup. That call cannot be eliminated; kernel drivers must get started; kernel services need to be initialized and opened. This one opening call remains an attack surface that will need mitigation.

In Figure 9.1, there is only one kernel mode component, the module that "watches," that is, catches events taking place throughout the operating system and from within applications.

The kernel driver should not allow itself to be opened from just any binary. Doing so, allowing any user mode binary to open it, opens up the attack surface to whatever code happens to get an opportunity to run on the operating system. Instead, the attack surface can be reduced if the kernel driver performs some sort of validation that only allows the one true Antivirus (AV) Engine to open it. Depending upon the operating system's capabilities, there are a few methods to provide this authentication: binary signature validation over a binary hash, which can then be re-calculated. What the kernel driver must not do is simply check the name of the binary. Filenames are easily changed.

Cryptographic signatures are best, but not all operating systems can provide this capability to kernel mode processes. The solution to this problem, then, is operating system dependent. Hence, without knowing the operating system specifics, the requirement can be expressed generally. It may also be true that our endpoint security software must run under many different operating systems. We can express the requirement at a higher level, requiring authentication of the AV Engine binary, rather than specifying the authentication method. Whatever executable validation method is offered by the operating system will fulfill the requirement.

Previously, we examined three components that are shown in Figure 9.1. A user interface is shown that allows the user to control and configure the security software to meet the user's needs. There is an AV Engine that performs the security analysis on files, network traffic, and other events. The events are captured through the kernel driver sitting across the kernel/user mode trust boundary. Obviously, the user interface must be accessible by the user; it must run as an application in "user mode," like any other application. However, unlike a word processor or spreadsheet application, the user interface can set security policy, that is, the user can turn off and turn on various security functions, such as whether files are scanned as they're opened ("real-time scanning"), or set policy such that suspicious files are only scanned at scheduled times at a periodicity of the user's choosing. From a security perspective, this means that the user interface has the power to change how security is implemented on the machine—the power to change how well or how poorly the machine is defended by the security software.

In consumer-oriented products, the user will have the ability to turn security functions off and on. In corporate environments, usually only system administrators have this power. The user interface can take control of the security of the system. That, of course, makes the user interface component an excellent target for attack.

Likewise, the AV Engine performs the actual examination to determine whether files and traffic are malicious. If the engine can be fooled, then the attacker can execute an exploit without fear of discovery or prevention. Consequently, a denial of service (DoS) attack on the AV Engine may be a very powerful first step to compromising the endpoint. To contrast this with the user interface, if the attacker is successful in stopping the user interface the security services should continue to protect, regardless. On the other hand, if the attacker can stop the AV Engine, she or he then has access to an unprotected system. Each of these components presents an important target; the targets offer different advantages, however.

As was explained in Chapter 3, any component that runs in the kernel should be considered a target. The kernel acts as the superuser, with rights to everything in the operating environment and visibility to all events. If a kernel component contains an exploit, the consequences of exercising the exploit are catastrophic, at least in the context of the running operating system.

Testing shows the presence, not the absence of bugs.[1]

Despite best efforts, no software can be proved error free. With that fact in mind, the defense should be built such that the impact of a vulnerability, perhaps a vulnerability that can be used to run code of the attacker's choosing, will be minimized. If we can't prevent the leak into production of a dreadful vulnerability, at least we can make the exercise, the access to that vulnerability, as difficult as possible. For security software, we have already stated that rigorous assurance steps must be built into the testing for the software. Still, we shouldn't completely depend upon the success of the testing; rather, we should make it very difficult for an attacker to access a kernel component.

If the kernel driver is written correctly to its requirements (see Requirements below), it should only accept an incoming connection at startup, exactly once, and from the validated engine component only. By meeting these requirements, the attacker must compromise the engine in order to have access to the kernel mode driver. Additionally, since the driver initialization and open happen very early in the startup sequence of the operating system, the attacker must be ready and waiting to take advantage of any vulnerability at that early moment during startup. That places another barrier to the attacker. Although this additional barrier is not insurmountable, it does mean that merely getting the attacker's code to execute in user space does not guarantee access to the kernel driver.

For most operating systems, there's protection to the kernel driver by guaranteeing that only a single open operation may occur. Further, the open call may only be made from a validated binary. An additional restriction can be that the open driver call may only take place during the startup sequence. The attacker has only one avenue through the endpoint security software to get to the kernel. And that avenue is solely through the engine, once, at a point at which there is no logged-in user.

The foregoing implies that an attempt to get from user to the kernel driver will have to be attached to operating system initialization (boot sequence) during normal operation. (Usually, such a system change requires higher privileges.) Then the attacker must either lie in wait or force a restart. A forced restart may get noticed by the user as unusual and unexpected, in response to which the user might perform a security check. This is not an easy or straightforward attack scenario. It has been done. But it's far from ideal and fraught with possible failures.

The AV engine itself will have to be written to be as self-defensive as possible. Even if the AV engine validates the user interface before allowing itself to be configured by the user interface, still, those input values should not be entirely trusted. The user interface may have bugs in it that could allow attacker control. In addition, the user interface might pass an attack through to the engine from external configuration parameters. We'll examine that input in a moment.

The AV engine has another input. In order to determine whether files are malicious, they may have to be opened and examined. Most certainly, in today's malware-ridden world, a percentage of the files that are examined are going to contain attacks. There's nothing to stop the attacker from placing attacks in suspicious files that go after any vulnerabilities that may lie within the file examination path. Thus, the AV Engine must protect itself rigorously while, at the same time, examining all manner of attack code. In fact, the entire path through which evil files and traffic pass must expect the worst and most sophisticated types of attacks. The file open, parse, and examination code must resist every imaginable type of file-based attack.

If the foregoing comes as a surprise to you, I will note that most industrial-grade, commercial antivirus and malware engine examination code must resist attack in precisely this manner; the need for rigorous self-protection has been in place for many years,[*] as of the writing of this book. Rigorous self-protection has become quite normal in the world of security software, and, especially, malware protection software.

That this code is written to be expressively self-protective and resistant doesn't mean that bugs don't get introduced to these sorts of engines from time to time. They do, and will continue to be. But any vendor with some amount of integrity understands this problem and will do their best to avoid getting caught out by a bit of attack code that was in a malicious file. Still, I would count "self-protection" and "attack resistance" as security requirements for the entire examination code path. What that comes down to is careful memory handling, safe library functions, and rigorous input validation.

---

[*] Although the media may trumpet the occasional instances in which malware engines fail, it may place these into context to consider that a typical instance of a malware engine will examine tens of thousands of samples correctly and, most importantly, safely.

Input validation to be implemented in general purpose, data-driven code is actually not a simple problem. This has been mentioned above (the business analytics data gathering and processing modules). For the security person to blithely declare "validate all inputs" begs a very real and somewhat difficult problem. If the coder doesn't know what the inputs are, precisely, how can the input be validated?

Although a complete solution to a data driven, general purpose parsing and examination engine is beyond this book, I do want to note in passing that this remains a nontrivial software design and implementation problem. The solution set is likely to contain data-determined ranges and acceptable input sets based upon each file format. In addition, in order to prove the defenses, a level of assurance may be attained through a formal and thorough set of software fuzzers[*] that become a part of the parser and the examination engine's test plan.

Figure 9.1 introduces a few more components to endpoint security software's architecture. Because the capability to examine many different file types is a specialized function, it's typical to place the file-parsing capability within its own, specialized module. That's how our fictitious antivirus software is written, as well. The makers of the software want to examine as broad a range of file types as possible. This is so that attackers cannot simply package up their attack in some obscure file type, which then allows the attack to slip past the security software. In order to offer the customer as complete a set of protections as possible, the software needs a "can opener" that is a "jack of all trades," readily opening and understanding the formats of just about every file type imaginable that may occur on each operating system that's supported by the software. So, as is typical in this situation, the file-opening software is a separate module.

Suspicious files are passed to the file module to be opened and normalized. The normalized file is then passed back for examination by the engine. The file parsing module only accepts communication from the engine and no other component. If the filing module requires any configuration, it is passed through from the user interface to the engine and then passed when the file parser is started. Would you consider the delivery of configuration information an attack surface of the file-parsing module?

Another special component is the communications module. Figure 9.1 presents a standalone system, so why does it need a communications module? In Figure 9.2, we can see that the system engages in communications with automated entities beyond the endpoint itself. Even if this were not true, a communicator might be employed for inter-module communications within the system. In this case, the simple, independently operating case, it would be a matter of design style as to whether to abstract communications functions into a separate module. The design was chosen in this case, not only

---

[*] Fuzzing is a software testing technique that employs random input values in order to flush out instabilities in software. *Core Software Security: Security at the Source*, by James Ransome and Anmol Misra (CRC Press, © 2014), has a more complete description of fuzzing and its application to security testing.

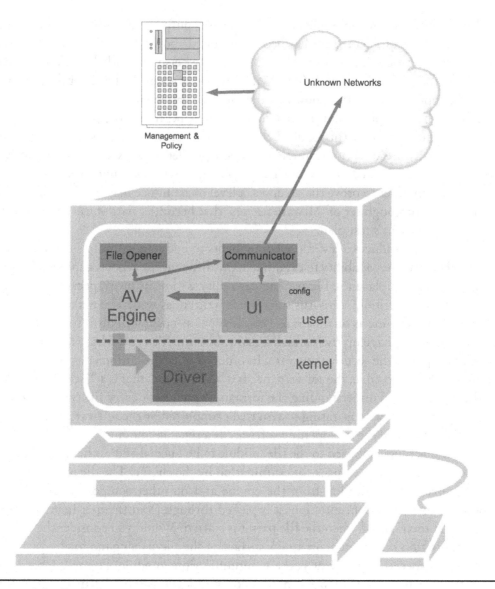

Figure 9.2   Endpoint security software with management.

because the system does in fact support inbound and outbound communications (as depicted in Figure 9.2) but also for reasons of performance.

The engine must react to events in as fast a manner as possible in order to stop an attack or, at the very least, recognize an attack as quickly as possible. Time to identification is a critical factor. The software maker wants to identify attacks in as little processing time as possible. Communications, and especially network communications, can take quite a lot of computer time. Although 250 ms is hardly a blink of an eye (one quarter of a second), a huge amount of processing can take place in 50 ms. Two hundred-fifty microseconds is almost an eon in computer time. By spinning off network communications to a specialized module, the engine code saves processing time for what's important. The engine won't have to block continued processing until a response has been received—the communication module does this instead. In fact, the AV engine won't even waste any precious processing time setting up the asynchronous response handler. All of these time-intensive functions can occur outside the security processing chain. In this system, all communications have been extracted into their own module in order to remove them from performance-hungry examination code.

The engine sends events and alerts to the communications module, which then passes these along to the destination, whether that destination is local, that is, the user, or some other destination. In this system, the communicator is also responsible for any log and event files that exist on the machine.

The user interface passes the communications modules's configuration to it at system startup time. The communications module takes input from the engine in the form of alerts, which then must be passed along to any external management software and to the user, or placed into the log files on local storage. Communications also takes its configuration and any user actions that need to be passed to any destination from the user interface. Where communications are sent is data driven, dictated by the configuration given to the module during its initialization or when the configuration changes.

If the communications module can be stopped by an attacker, malicious actions can thereby be hidden from the user or any management software monitoring events on the machine. If the module can be compromised, the attacker might have the ability to obscure, or even change, events as they're sent onwards. Further, inbound events, such as the management software changing the security policies on the endpoint, could be changed to the attacker's benefit. For this reason, the communications module must validate what it is given and must only allow the other modules in the system to send it messages.

Inward-bound communications, such as software updates, will flow from Communicator to the user interface manager. In this system, the user interface module is also responsible for updating software, such as a new set of malware identity signatures, new policies (and other configuration items), or even updates to the system's modules themselves. We will take up the requirements for inbound communications below, with the introduction of management software in Figure 9.2.

As we have seen with other systems that we've analyzed, configuration files are a prime target. Security policy and the functioning of the system can be changed through the software's configuration file. In a product that must operate whether it has a network connection or not, such as endpoint security software, the product must configure itself based upon files kept on local storage. That's a thorny problem because the configuration files are a target that can change protections. Why?

The software that reads the configuration files, as we have seen, must run in user space and at lower privileges. Typically, this would be the logged-in user of the system. The logged-in user has the right to open any file available for that level of privilege. Since the software is running as the logged-in user and must have the rights to read its own configuration file, under many operating systems, the configuration file can be read by any application running as the logged-in user. That's a problem.

Furthermore, if the user decides to make changes, the user interface software has to be able to write the configuration files back to disk, once again, as the logged-in user. Do you begin to see the problem? If the logged in user's configuration module (the user interface, here) can access and change the files, so can the user. This means that any of the user's applications can change the files. This also implies that all an attacker has to do is get the user to run an application whose malicious task is to change the configuration files. Bingo! Security software would now be under the attacker's control. And that must be prevented. It's a thorny problem.

I'm sure it's obvious to you that the configuration files used by any security software constitute a high-value target. This is no different from other systems that we've examined. And it is a standard pattern, not only for security software but for any software that provides a critical and/or sensitive function, as well. The configuration file is usually (and typically) a valuable target.

Different operating systems provide various mechanisms for addressing this problem. Under the UNIX family of operating systems, an application can be started by the logged-in user, but the application can switch to another user, a specialized user that only has the capability to run that software. This non-human, application-only user will usually only have rights to its own files. The Windows family of operating systems has other mechanisms, such as slipping into a higher privilege for a moment while sensitive files are read or written and then slipping back to the logged-in user for the continuing run. For both of these mechanisms, the superuser can circumvent these protections easily. That is the way the superuser privileges are designed: The superuser can do whatever it wants within the operating system. However, it should be noted that if an attacker has gained superuser privileges, there is usually no need to mess around with configuration files, since the attacker already owns the operating system and all its functions and can do whatever is desired. Further exploits become unnecessary.

Typically, therefore, security software protection mechanisms don't attempt much, if any, restriction of superuser privileges. These "super" privileges are designed into modern operating systems and, as such, are very difficult to protect against. Instead, it is usual to focus on restricting what the logged-in user can do. In this way, the focus is on preventing privilege escalation, rather than preventing what escalated privileges can accomplish.

I will note that some security software in today's market employs sophisticated file restriction mechanisms that go beyond what operating systems provide. For the sake of this analysis, we will not delve into these more extraordinary measures. It's enough to understand that the configuration file, in and of itself, is a target and needs protection. And the inputs in the user interface that read and process the configuration file also comprise an important attack surface that requires protection. For the sake of this analysis, we will confine ourselves to protections that can be provided by the operating system and obvious software protections that can be built into the security software. Protecting files and secrets on local storage could fill an entire chapter, or perhaps even an entire book, devoted solely to this subject. It is enough, for this analysis, to identify the configuration files and the user interface inputs, input fields from the user, and the inputs when the configuration file is read as attack surfaces requiring protection.

There are a few subtle conditions when writing files that may allow an attacker to misuse the output to write files of the attacker's choice. Indeed, there are vulnerabilities in file output routines that can even allow an attacker execution of code. The point is to misuse the user interface file writing routines to play tricks on the application or the operating system to get malicious code onto the machine or to get malicious code executed through the security software's file output routines.

Furthermore, the user interface will have to be written such that items taken from the user through the user interface can't directly be output to the configuration file. That might be a convenient way to get a configuration file attack back through the user interface. The foregoing suggests, of course, that outputs to the configuration file will also require security attention. The output should be considered an attack surface.

It is perhaps obvious, and not worth mentioning except for completeness, that inputs of the user interface are, indeed, an attack surface. We've seen this in previous analyses. The treatment for input attack surfaces is always the same at a high level: input validation. Injections of any sort must be prevented.

Do you see an attack vector surface that hasn't been covered in the preceding text? By all means, once again, check my work. Be my security architect peer review. Has anything significant been missed?

In Figure 9.2, we introduce management of the security software. If for no other reason than updating the antivirus signatures for new strains of viruses, this architecture would not be realistic without this component. Somehow, the AV Engine has to be easily and readily updated on a regular and continuing basis. New strains of computer viruses occur at an alarming rate, sometimes thousands per day. Somehow, that information has to get to our system as there won't be timely protection until it has been updated. This is one of the responsibilities of the communications module. The update has to come from somewhere trustworthy.

If an attacker can control the update of the malware signatures, they may be able to hide an attack. For instance, imagine that the update to the signature set identifies a new strain of virus. If the attacker can prevent the update, through whatever means, then the new virus strain will not be identified and, thus, prevented. Consequently, signature (and code) updates are important targets requiring significant protections.

9.3 More on Deployment Model

As has been hinted during the foregoing discussion, security software does not stand alone, by itself, with no support beyond the endpoint. The days of entirely encapsulated and enclosed endpoint antivirus or anti-malware software have been gone for some time. The most pressing reason that one doesn't simply go to the store, purchase the update, and then come home and install it is that malicious programs mutate and change too much and too often. The rate of change of malicious program types and variations has aggressively increased to the point at which it takes security companies major effort—large analysis systems and teams, as well as hundreds, if not thousands, of samples per day—in order to keep pace.

The upshot of the current situation is that an antivirus program needs updates on a continuing and repeated basis. Sometimes, these updates come more than one per day. The installation of the update has to be seamless such that the user is not inconvenienced. Imagine if every day on your working computer, laptop, tablet, what have you, you had to stop what you were doing two or three times a day to install new security software. That wouldn't be a very good user experience. As of the writing of this work, security software makers have solved this problem by allowing the software to update itself whenever necessary.

The automatic update model, however, poses some significant challenges. How does the endpoint software establish the trustworthiness and veracity of the server that's pushing the update? In fact, when an update event gets posted, how can the software know that this isn't coming from a malicious source?

To make matters more complex, the validity of the update must be established such that it hasn't been tampered with between manufacturer and download at the endpoint (integrity). In fact, most security vendors don't want the threat agents to have the details of what's been prevented nor the details of how protections work. At the least, these proprietary secrets are best kept such that uncovering them requires a significant work factor. Defense is better if the attacker doesn't have the precise details of the strategy and tactics. The foregoing general requirement suggests that communications should be confidential. This is particularly true when the communications must cross untrusted networks. If updates are coming from servers across the public Internet, then the network would not only be untrusted but also hostile.

In Figure 9.2, the management console for the security software is shown as an "unknown" network. That's because the deployers may place the management function wherever is convenient for them. Perhaps management traffic only crosses the local network. But perhaps it crosses the Internet. That decision is up to the owner of the software. In this case, let's assume that the management console is deployed upon an organization's local network. And, for the moment, let's assume that computers are managed on that same network.*

This is only one deployment model. Generally, for consumer-oriented security software, the management console would be a globally available cloud service. We will take up cloud management problems in the next architecture. For this architecture, the management console can be considered to exist on an organization's internal network.

---

* In a real-world situation, laptops leave the organizational network. But they still need to be managed.

With this assumption, we can examine how a customer premise deployment model influences security decisions that are made about a system.

A working concept, when considering the security of customer premise equipment, is to understand that different customers require different security postures. Systems intended for deployment across a range of security postures and approaches will do best by placing security decisions into the hands of the deployers. Indeed, no matter the guidance from the vendor for a particular piece of software, customers will do what is convenient for their situation. For instance, regardless of what guidance is given to customers about keeping the management console for our endpoint system off of untrusted networks, customers will do as they wish. And, having exposed the management console to greater danger, the customer may very well come back and request hardening documentation in order to reduce the exposure. Numerous times, I have seen deployment teams insist that a sensitive management console must be placed so that it's accessible from the Internet. This is generally considered poor security practice. But that statement is meaningless in the face of significant business pressure to do things in some locally unique and idiosyncratic manner.

In a situation in which the software designers also control the infrastructure and have fairly complete knowledge of the management and security practices (as we've seen in earlier examples), a lot of assumptions can be made. For instance, if the system is intended to be deployed to a highly restricted network, then there may be no need to build in extra security controls, such as encrypted tunnels, from the user to the management software. Such features become "nice to have."

Conversely, where one cannot make any assumptions about where the software will be deployed and what the needs of the customer will be, the security features should include a set of protections that can be taken as a whole, or control by control, as required by the deployers. Perhaps at one organization all management consoles are placed on a somewhat open network? In a situation where the network is not providing access control, the software will need to implement authentication and authorization capabilities so that only intended personnel have access. The implementing team ought to be able to configure the system to encrypt communications over their open network. For this example security system, the communications to the endpoint software might include policy and other configuration changes. The sensitive configuration changes proceed across the network from the management console. Hence, deployers may wish to encrypt these sensitive communications. Like the ability to encrypt console to endpoint communications, each security capability needs to be under the control of the administrators managing the system. Each security feature should be individually adjustable for the needs of the deploying organization.

As much as possible, the software should place its security features and configuration in the hands of the deployers. The software maker cannot possibly determine the best settings for every deployment and every organization. Rather, the appropriate approach is to place configuration of the security posture in the hands of the customers, who can then make the best decisions for their instance. In this way, systems intended for a range of independent and locally unique deployments ("customer premise"*) requires an approach that enables the security needs of those who will deploy the system to be met, not those who make it.

Returning to Figure 9.2, the management console in this case is intended to be customer premise equipment. In order to be successful, it will require protection for all communications, both inbound and outbound. Since the management console itself presents an attack surface, as we have seen in previous examples containing management interfaces for various systems, both authentication and authorization must be integral for those organizations that have no standard systems. But for those organizations that do have authentication and authorization infrastructures, the system must also be able to consume these as appropriate. [Lightweight Directory Access Protocol (LDAP) is the most widely supported authentication and group membership protocol.]

Implementing authentication and authorization systems is a nontrivial task. The design must account for the protection of stored credentials, their "password strength," and a host of other details. We will not take these details up here, since there are any number of works that thoroughly cover this subject.

The endpoint security software must be able to validate communications from the management console. There must also be a mechanism to ensure that policy, configuration, and update communications flowing from the management console to the endpoints has not been tampered with or interfered with, en route.

Since the management console and the endpoint software don't run on the same operating system instance (i.e., machine), a vendor binary digital signature that's been generated across the binary at creation doesn't authenticate this particular management instance. There is no way for the signature and hash to be sent in such a manner as to prove that the signature belongs on this one management console. While a vendor's signature can prove the validity of the vendor's binary, it cannot prove the validity of this particular management instance. Without an instance credential, an attacker might set up a rogue management console that pushes the attacker's security policy to all the endpoints under management.

In this case, we need an authenticator that can be transmitted across the network and which has been generated for this instance. There are several ways to accomplish this. The way not to do it is to hardcode a credential in the binary of the endpoint and the binary for the management console as a shared secret. Statically shared secrets, a single shared secret for all instances, is one of the biggest mistakes that is made when designing systems. Such a secret should be considered compromised as soon as there are more than a few instances of the software that are beyond the control of the vendor. Such secrets are fairly easily ferreted out. They get posted to security-related websites and lists, as well as to attacker sites. When thousands of copies of the software are in use

---

* "Customer premise" equipment or software is intended to be used entirely on a customer's premises.

in the field, the secret is not a secret anymore. Furthermore, anyone possessing the secret now has control over every instance of the software that uses that secret. Not very secret.

The important thing is to force whatever credential will be used to be generated at installation and to a particular management context, such as an organization, a group, a department, a network, whatever works for the way that the deployers divide up the management of the software.

The details of particular types of credentials are beyond the scope of this work. X509 certificates could be generated, used, and validated. In this case, the private key used to sign the certificate will need protection. A password generated for only this purpose will work. It then must be protected wherever it is stored. There are a number of ways to achieve the desired result. Numerous and frequent discussions take place among security practitioners about the merits of one approach versus another. I believe that, for this purpose, we can state that the endpoint communicator must authenticate the management console before allowing any communications to proceed. The credential will have to be protected in storage and during transmission (i.e., either encrypted during transmission or some other scheme, such as using a public/private key pair).

The obvious solution to communications integrity is to bring up an encryption tunnel to protect the communications across networks. Typically, this is done with Transport Layer Security (TLS). Again, there's more than one way to do this successfully. The details are beyond the scope of this work. Still, an appropriate security architecture for the management console to endpoint communications must include this requirement.

Before deploying new software, whether the updates are to the running modules or to the malware identification mechanisms used by the engine, the validity of the updates must be established. However updates are obtained for dispersal by the management console, whether by download from the software maker's website, or through some sort of push outwards to the management console, attackers attempting to insert malicious code must be prevented. This validation could be done with a standard binary hash and signature. The hash value can be checked for validity. The signature will be made with the private key that can be checked against the public key for validity. This is the standard approach for this problem.

For most organizations, any system having to do with the organization's security will be considered sensitive and critical. As such, the parts of the security system implementing management of the system are typically considered need-to-know, restricted systems and interfaces. In particular, any system, such as this management console, that can change the security posture of other systems requires significant protection. We explored this topic at some length and depth when examining several of the previous architectures. All of the same reasoning and the same security requirements apply, once again, to this management console. If you have any questions about what those requirements are, please feel free to read those sections once again. Like all critical and sensitive management systems, this management console will also need to be well managed, with careful consideration of access controls to the operating system and storage areas.

9.4 Endpoint AV Software Security Requirements

- Events and data flow from kernel driver to AV Engine only (never from engine to kernel).
- Only the AV engine may open the kernel driver, and only on system startup. "Open" is the only control operation allowed from user mode to kernel driver. No other component may communicate with the kernel driver.
- The kernel driver startup and initialization code must validate, sanitize, and put into canonical form inputs from AV engine.
- Kernel driver initialization and startup must occur during the operating system startup sequence and must complete before users are allowed to log on to the system.
- Kernel driver initialization must complete before user logon to the system.
- Kernel driver initialization must occur as early as is possible during operating system startup.
- Before communications are allowed to proceed between any two or more modules in the system, validation must be performed on the identity and integrity of the calling process/module/binary. The preferred mechanism is validation of a digital signature over the binary. The signature must be signed by the private key of the software manufacturer.
- Every other component except the kernel driver must run in user mode.
- Installation should confine the reading and writing of the configuration files to the User Interface only.
- The system must have the ability to encrypt communications from/to the management console. This must be system administrator configurable.
- The management console must contain a user authentication system.
- The management console must contain a user authorization system.
- The management console must be able to authenticate to an LDAP.
- Management console authorization must be able to be performed by LDAP group membership.
- The administrator must be able to configure the management console to use any combination of:
  - Local authentication
  - LDAP authentication
  - Local authorization
  - LDAP group membership
- The user interface must re-authenticate the user before allowing changes.
- The management console will be able to run in a hardened state. There will be a customer document describing the hardened configuration. Hardening is configurable at customer discretion.
- Input validation coding must be implemented on every system input, with particular care to file parsing and examination path, the reading of the configuration files, and inputs from Communicator.

- The file and event handling paths through the code must be rigorously fuzzed.
- All components of the system must be built using a rigorous Security Development Lifecycle (SDL), with particular emphasis on secure coding techniques, input validation, and rigorous proof of the effectiveness of the SDL (i.e., security assurance testing for vulnerabilities).*
- Vulnerability testing before product release must be thorough and employ multiple, overlapping strategies and tools.

The above list of requirements completes the security analysis upon the endpoint security system. Because the management console is intended to be installed and run by the customer rather than by the vendor, the management console has to have sufficient security features so that the customer's preferred security posture can be implemented: customer "manageable." This is as opposed to hosted systems, which will be managed by the same organization. Manageable (by others) as opposed to managed (by the organization that created the software). This is an important distinction that was called out earlier in this book: "the deployment model."

As was noted, the list of requirements presented here cannot be taken as a complete list, since some of the requirements refer to previous discussions and are not reiterated here. For a real-world system, I would list all requirements, so as to create a complete picture of the security needs of the system. The architectures presented in this book, I'll reiterate, should be taken as examples, not as recipes.

References

1. NATO Science Committee (1969). *Software Engineering Techniques*. Report on a conference sponsored by the NATO Science Committee, p. 16. Quote from Edsger Dijksta, Rome, Italy, 27th to 31st October 1969. Retrieved from http://homepages.cs.ncl.ac.uk/brian.randell/NATO/nato1969.PDF.

---

* Please see *Core Software Security: Security at the Source*, by James Ransome and Anmol Misra (CRC Press, © 2014), for a complete discussion of the SDL and how it can be implemented successfully.

Chapter 10

Mobile Security Software with Cloud Management

We might almost take the discussion for endpoint security software assessed in Chapter 9 and apply it more or less completely to mobile software. Many of the security problems are analogous. The software has to provide protections, whether it's connected to a network or not. On the other hand, configuration and management are delivered over the network when the device is connected. In order to examine yet another architectural pattern, this example mobile security product will make use of cloud-based management software and a Software as a Service (SaaS) "reputation" service. Just for clarity, for many real-world mobility protection product implementations, the customers may deploy their own management servers, which is exactly analogous to the problems we examined for the management console of the endpoint security system. In this example, we will not take up issues related to management from a cloud-based service.

10.1 Basic Mobile Security Architecture

Figure 10.1 presents the architecture for a hypothetical mobile security protection system. Many of the components are the same in the two endpoint security architectures. Incoming and outbound communications have to be established and maintained. An engine must process system events and examine possibly malicious data items. The engine has to respond to these with protective actions while, at the same time, raising alerts to the user of the device and, perhaps, outbound to the management components. These functions will likely be relatively familiar to you, by now?[*]

---

[*] If you have doubts, please re-read Chapter 9's endpoint security analysis.

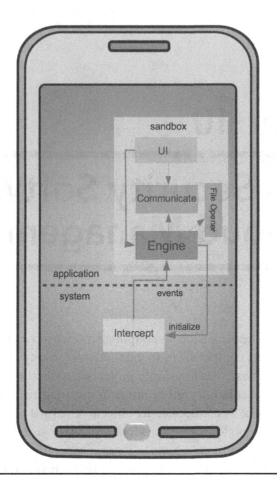

Figure 10.1   Mobile security software.

Once again, as noted previously, the processing engine must be able to examine a gamut of different file types and formats. Everything that was stated earlier about end-point security applies just as well in this situation.

10.2 Mobility Often Implies Client/Cloud

We're going to extend the feature set somewhat for mobility software. As of this writing, most devices are generally not islands unto themselves. For many of these devices, the network is "always on." Except for the devices out of range or off-grid, the network connection is omnipresent as a core piece of the functionality of the device.

The protections from the security software must continue when the device is taken off the network, such as when it's off-grid, or in airplane mode and similar. Still, much of the time, software writers can expect the device to be online and connected, not only to a local network but to the World Wide Web, as well. Web traffic, as we've seen, has its own peculiar set of security challenges. What are the challenges for an always-connected, but highly personalized device?

Most notably, attackers set up malicious websites. These can be returned through search engines, of course. But also, there are the ever-present phishing attacks bombarding users. In addition, people personalize their devices with special purpose applications of all kinds. Malicious website URLs get delivered through many different vectors. This mobility security software includes a URL reputation service running in the cloud. When the user clicks on the URL in order to access a website, an event gets generated from the kernel to the AV Engine, indicating that the URL needs to be checked first before access.

A reputation service is so-called because many behavioral data points are kept about a particular URL, file, or Internet Protocol (IP) Address. Data is collected from various sources about the observed behavior of the object for which reputation is being calculated. A URL (or other object) will fall somewhere in a continuum from absolutely malicious to reputable (good), with various degrees of "gray" in between those two poles. Based upon the reputation rating, software can prevent access, present the problem for user decision, or passively allow the access.

The details of the data used in the calculation are generally proprietary and closely held secrets of the vendors providing the reputation service. For our purposes, it's probably enough to know that reputation services are often implemented in a cloud, generally a global cloud. They are operated as a Software as a Service (SaaS). Reputation is usually checked before proceeding by a piece of local security software (the AV engine, in this case). The check is performed over the Internet via some encapsulation within the HTTP protocol. The backend of the reputation service usually involves "big data," the archive and examination of billions of individual data items that form the basis of reputation calculations.

We will take up the security of the reputation service below, when we analyze Figure 10.2. For the moment, it's important to note that the communicator shown in Figure 10.1 implements all the functions listed previously for endpoint security software. There is one additional communication feature that has been added. The communications module must request reputation from the reputation service before taking action on an individual URL that the user has attempted to access.

Although it may not be apparent when looking at mobile devices, they do have permanent storage. Files are kept on the device's permanent storage. Applications create files. Applications manipulate files. Device users view and edit files. Indeed, on the device's storage, a typical operating system directory structure does, in fact, exist. There is a "tree" of directories ("folders") that is exactly what you would find on your computer or your laptop, regardless of which of the usual operating systems you use. On many mobile operating systems, the file and directory details are hidden from the user. Most of these operating systems assume that there is but a single user who has access to all the files. Since mobile operating systems highlight application functionality, the details of file access are hidden behind application user interfaces.

The details are more or less hidden from the application, as well. Each application has a set of directories assigned within its sandbox. Visibility to other directories is not allowed.

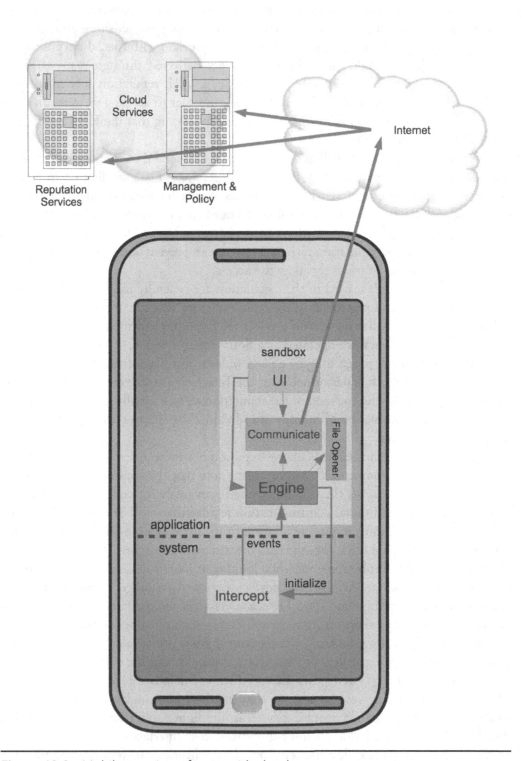

Figure 10.2 Mobile security software with cloud management.

The presence of files implies a security need to examine files to identify those that may be malicious. Included among the user's downloaded applications might be malicious applications. But bear in mind that a "mobile device" is nothing more than an operating system running on a computer. The usual assortment of vulnerabilities that are file based can also exist on a mobile device. As a result, again, just like endpoint security software, this architecture includes a file opener and parser. The same analysis applies as it did in the previous architecture that we examined.

"Intercept" in this architecture replaces the endpoint security software's kernel driver. Analogous to the kernel driver, Intercept vectors events on the device to the engine for analysis. Depending upon the mobile operating system, the intercept module may exist as an operating system service, which is then made available to applications, or the intercept function must be supplied by the software vendor and installed with the security software.

In at least a couple of mobile platforms, no application may install software into the kernel. As was noted in Chapter 3, the "system" area exists between the application mode and the kernel. There are three layers—application, system, and kernel (in Figures 10.1 and 10.2, the kernel is not diagrammed, as it is not relevant to this architecture).

For our purposes, the security issues are approximately the same regardless of whether Intercept exists as a part of the operating system or whether it was written and installed with the application. If the intercept service is "native"—that is, a part of the operating system—obviously its secure coding and assurance is not under the control of the mobile software maker. Still, the design issues are analogous. The secure coding and code assurance activities will be the same in each case. If the interceptor is written for the operating system, the same requirements as given for the kernel driver above apply to the interceptor, as well. If the interceptor is supplied with the operating system, then the security software inherits whatever security strengths and weaknesses have been built by the operating system makers.

Intercept initialization should be performed and communication flows opened early in the operating system "boot" process, before the user is allowed to log on, in order to stymy misuse of the startup calls. We saw this previously in the endpoint example.

As in the previous architecture, events should flow only from system to application, never the other way, just in case an attacker gains control of the application. It is standard design practice to limit communications from lower privilege to higher privilege. The appropriate event flow is, of course, a design requirement.

Even though the file system appears to be closed, more or less, from the normal user of the device, every input we examined in the endpoint security case requires the same security requirements as we uncovered previously. After all, there is the possibility that a malicious program can transcend the sandbox and launch an attack via the device's file system.

Figure 10.2 introduces the cloud aspects for the mobility security software. The diagram shows two different services interacting with the endpoint: management and policy services, and a reputation service.

For mobility architectures that I've encountered, enterprises and larger organizations (or highly security-conscious organizations) tend to prefer to deploy management consoles onto the organization's network. Through local deployment, the organization can control this sensitive function. This situation is analogous to the management console that we examined previously for endpoint security software.

10.3 Introducing Clouds

For the consumer and the small business markets, management is typically provided through a multitenant, shared service run by the software manufacturer. Because the service is shared across many "tenants," the cost of providing the services for each customer is minimized. Economies of scale help to lower the price so that individual consumers and small businesses can purchase protection from their more limited budgets. It is this case that we will examine in this example.

Communications from each endpoint must flow across the untrusted Internet. Any number of networks and Internet providers may be crossed as packets are routed. Hence, in Figure 10.2, the arrow from the communicator reaches into the Internet, whereas disconnected arrows move to the cloud-based services. The disconnect between arrows is to indicate the unknown nature of routing, the unknown networks across which the traffic must pass.

With thousands of devices or perhaps millions to support, communications are instigated from the device to the service. Most mobility operating systems include a service to "push" a "notification" to the device, even to a particular application. In this case, in order to simplify the architecture for study, let's assume that the only push notification issued by the management service is a command to instigate communications in order to receive further commands or updates. Although, in actuality, notifications might be more complex, this one notification would be sufficient to roll out updates, policy changes, and the like. Assuming the architectural limitation of a single, "call home" notification, allows us to state that all communications from the communicator to the cloud services originate from the communicator. Notifications pushed through the operating system service come through the interceptor and appear as an event passed to the engine. Push notifications have a different flow than communications from the application to its services.

Exactly the same problems exist from the management service to the mobile endpoint software that exist from the management console to the endpoint. Communications must be protected over untrusted networks. The device must authenticate to the service, at the very least. The security software must have some method for validating the authenticity and integrity of code and data downloaded from the site to the device. Each of these issues was examined in some length, above. The requirements are the same.

What is different with cloud services are the challenges from multitenancy. In the last, cloud architecture example, we will examine multitenancy at some depth. This is a service problem. It's not really germane to an examination of an endpoint security solution. We will hold off until we investigate the next architecture.

As we saw in the Web-Sock-A-Rama example, simply placing services on the Internet invokes a raft of security necessities: server hardening, layering and trust levels, management interfaces, and so on. If you feel unfamiliar with this coterie of requirements, please return to that earlier analysis for an in-depth discussion of Internet exposure.

Let's turn our attention to the additional feature: the reputation service introduced in Figure 10.2. As we noted above, "reputation" in this context refers to how trustworthy or malicious an object may be. "Object" might be a URL (web destination), a file, an email domain or address, an IP address, and so forth. The calculation of reputation is outside our scope. It is sufficient to acknowledge that security reputation services exist, both free and commercial. The object is presented to the service, which returns a reputation—some sense of how safe or dangerous the object may be to access. Usually, reputation is delivered as a grade along a scale from known to be malicious to known to be safe. Considering the hundreds of millions of websites on the Internet, gathering sufficient information about websites and then calculating a score is a nontrivial, "big data" problem. Significant resources are expended in order to make as good a guess about reputation as possible.*

Usually, the commercial services are "cloud" grade. That is, the services are available across the globe so that user access time is reduced. The services are always available, with failover systems that can pick up upon an instance failure. Cloud services are usually redundant and backed up to various points of presence spread out geographically so that a local catastrophe cannot bring the service down. (We will take a look at the backend architecture of a cloud service in the next analysis.)

One of the big challenges with cloud-based reputation checks is performance. Users don't typically want to wait a few seconds while the reputation of potential URLs is checked. Most of us have come to expect that websites are at the immediate tips of our fingers and that access and loading of the content should take place rapidly and without delay. This presents a tricky security problem.

Since the reputation service exists in the cloud, the challenge can be summed up as, "How can a reputation be securely retrieved without slowing Web access down so much as to create a poor user experience?" The details of cloud performance, points of presence, calculating the shortest distance, data caching, and associated issues are largely beyond the domain of security. We will take a cursory look at some of these issues in a subsequent, cloud-based SaaS service analysis. Still, it's important that the security components of the reputation service don't inordinately affect overall performance. This is one of those cases in which there has to be "just good enough" security, and no more, because security controls often impact performance. For instance, bringing

---

* Business success probably depends upon accuracy. Still, mistakes do get made, and inaccurate ratings get produced.

up a Transport Layer Security (TLS) connection takes a fair amount of computer and transmission time.

One key question when designing a service such as a reputation service is to decide how secret the reputation needs to be kept. Obviously, if attackers know that a malicious site has a poor reputation, they may respond to that situation by changing the domain of the site, or they may take other evasive action. That's an argument for only allowing the mobility software to check reputations and to protect the reputation service from query by any other systems. Further, if the vendor intends the service as a commercial offering for profit, allowing open access to everyone would be a competitive disadvantage.

On the other hand, owners of domains may have their web properties misclassified. Domain owners need a method to check the reputation of a domain and to address a poor reputation rating with the reputation service provider. I personally have had a couple of websites misclassified once or twice over the years and have had to go to a reputation service and complain. Supposedly, all my websites are legitimate. As far as I know, none of my sites allow or foster malicious activities, at least not intentionally. Still, I have been classified as malicious a couple of times. Mistakes get made. Any reputation service that expects to stay viable must offer domain owners a way to check their domains and URLs and to lodge a complaint if misclassified. Obviously, redress can also be abused; no doubt, redress services are abused.

So, what is the right security posture for a cloud-hosted reputation service? The answer to this question is hotly debated regularly. Even within organizations, there will be a diversity of opinions about how much security is "enough." Most security controls, unless it is trivial to implement, are likely to draw significant discussion and generate at least a few strong opinions. Even so, we have a system under analysis. One of the system's components is a cloud-based reputation service that provides proprietary features for commercial mobile security products. Therefore, the reputation service cannot be wide open and without access restriction.

As we have seen, security decisions must be based on the objectives that are to be fulfilled by the security. Earlier examples have explored the issues confronting an Internet-exposed system. Both services in this example require the same protections from constant and unremitting attack from the Internet. This should come as no surprise. These protections must include host and network hardening, as well as all the management security capabilities that have been previously laid out.

10.3.1 Authentication Is Not a Panacea

Generally, Web systems that don't serve public content will require authentication to reduce traffic, and thus exposure, to only the intended population rather than anyone who can send traffic on the Internet. As we saw previously, websites with wide-use demographics may get very little value from authentication. In this case, these services are to be consumed only by paying customers. That, of course, won't stop an attacker from obtaining a paying account from which attacks can be mounted. Authentication can't be the only control in place, for this single reason. Still, and nonetheless, the vast majority of paying customers are looking for security protection, not for a system to attack. Authentication is likely to reduce the attack surface by at least removing exposure to all the automated attack sweeps that are ever present on the Internet.

But in this case, is it the user who should be authenticated? Well, yes and no. The users must be old enough to manage their accounts, manage their devices, configure their security policies, and, of course, pay for the services. For these reasons, there will have to be a user interface and user services. These will presumably employ authentication to tie account and services to users. The architecture presented in Figure 10.2 does not include the web authentication services. We examined these issues previously in the Web architecture example, Web-Sock-A-Rama.

What are shown are the other services that the software uses in an automated fashion. If the user were forced to authenticate every time he or she accessed the URL, I suspect that the security software would not have a very long or useful life on that person's device. Instead, the software will have to authenticate to the services. That's a slightly different architectural problem.

Should the application be the entity that authenticates? Or should it be the device? Again, there are arguments back and forth about this design choice, which we won't go into in this example. There are strong reasons for authenticating the device. And that's the pattern that this system employs. If it's the device that's under management, even if the software breaks down, the management service has some concept of the device itself. If the device is lost, it can contain an identifier, regardless of whether the software on it has been reset by a thief. The mobile carrier interacts with the device; the management service, which is able to identify the device, may interact with the carrier about the device, if necessary. Both the management services and the reputation service authenticate the device, not the user. I reiterate that, in general, mobile operating systems and architectures assume a single user per device.

One way to accomplish the authentication is to issue a certificate to the device. Along with the certificate, which can be validated, when the device is enrolled, its serial number and the carrier's identifier will be tied together. The communicator brings up a TLS tunnel to the server, validating the server certificate, as per the TLS protocol. Then the device certificate is presented. If validated, communications can flow. This means that only enrolled devices are allowed reputation services and are under management.

The foregoing scheme does not protect the system against a rogue or compromised device. It doesn't protect the system against a malicious, paying customer. Other protections will need to be placed around the services in addition to the authentication. Along with the authentication, all the protections together constitute a defense-in-depth. (The SaaS architecture below will delve into other protections.)

10.3.2 The Entire Message Stack Is Important

Once communications have been established, the mobility security software must validate messages, commands, data, and software that come from the cloud services. This is the same problem as was seen between the management console and the endpoint security software. Data and software will have to be hashed and then signed such that the signature over the hash can be validated on the device. This problem is no different from what we explored previously.

Should the communicator authenticate the server? TLS is being used from the device to the server. TLS always validates the server certificate before proceeding. However, that authentication typically only validates that the certificate was issued by a known Certificate Authority and that the certificate is valid for the IP address of the server. In other words, any TLS server that has a valid certificate will successfully pass the server side TLS authentication. What if our mobility security software gets directed through DNS spoofing to a malicious site? And what if that malicious site presents a valid certificate? The TLS will start up with no errors.

Due to the details of server-side TLS certificate validation, in the absence of another authenticator or authentication scheme, a device won't necessarily know that it's talking to the true set of services. TLS server-side authentication usually happens somewhere below the application on mobile devices.

It doesn't make sense for each application to install TLS/SSL services on a device. Mobile devices run on batteries (i.e., must do extreme power management) and tend to be highly storage constrained. This means that the less code an application must install to function, the better. Good mobile applications should use the system services. The foregoing means that a TLS tunnel will be instantiated for an application, then returned as an open connection ("tunnel," "pipe," or "socket"). The details of server-side authentication are opaque to the application. The validation of the server's certificate takes place behind the scenes, from the application's point of view.

Of course, an alternate or extra validation can be performed on the server certificate to ensure that the connection is to the right set of services. That would be an extra validation above the TLS validation provided in the protocol's server-side authentication. In order to effect a validation of the server's certificate (beyond that provided by validating the chain of signing certificates), the server's certificate must be stored for comparison on the device. This validation must be performed after TLS has been successfully instantiated (by the system, as described above).

Is an extra validation necessary in this instance? Will the overhead of an additional certificate validation, and deployment and update of the server's certificate to every device, be worth the additional management issues and, more importantly, the extra time taken to set up the communication channel?

I would argue, "No." Why?

If all significant data and code is validated by hash and signature, what can an evil site do even if connected? This means that validation of signatures over binaries and messages has to be nearly bulletproof. And I've stated many times that a defense should not rely on a single control. If the signature validation fails, then an attack could proceed.

Often, the errors that crop up in cryptography are not issues in the cryptography but, rather, "implementation errors." That is, the implementer made a mistake while coding the algorithm such that the cryptography has been weakened, perhaps significantly. Or, over time, new mathematical understandings or increases in processing power render a particular cryptographic algorithm weaker. These are the dangers of an overreliance on a single cryptographic algorithm, such as a hash algorithm and signature, or relying on a particular implementation. As long as the implementation has no errors and the algorithm stands, the protection remains strong. Over the years, I've noticed that this position of strength can be changed or watered down in almost an instant.*

Since these cryptographic change events are relatively rare, I might, in this case, favor reliance on the signature across the binary. It's a trade-off between performance (customer acceptance) and security. As you encounter similar security situations, you are likely to be faced with such trade-offs on a regular and repeating basis.

10.4 Just Good Enough Security

As was noted above, in this case, we need "just good enough security." Let's dig a little into how I might determine how much "security" will be "good enough."

In order to proceed, an attacker has to successfully line up a number of somewhat difficult exploits: DNS spoofing, a valid server certificate proffered from a malicious site, the signature failure. This is not an impossible scenario. But this set of coordinated and interlinked, dependent attacks is not particularly easy, either. Given sufficient motivation, as we have seen, this attack scenario (and more) can be completed. But I would offer that this attack is probably extraordinary and would likely be highly targeted.

Depending upon the adversaries against whom you are protecting the device, "good enough" might well be a reliance upon the message's digital signature alone. Alternatively, for high-security situations that require more assurance, the addition of a validation of the TLS certificate itself could be added. In addition to validating the certificate authority signing chain, also validate the certificate that is presented by the server. Make it difficult to impersonate the reputation server. There is no "right" answer to this question. It depends upon the security needs of the organization and how much risk can be tolerated.

I invite you to consider this situation. Make up your own mind: What is enough security? What's too little? What might be too much?

---

* Really, the research that achieves these shifts often takes years. Still, once the research has been announced, an algorithm can make a shift, as it were, from "safe" to unprotected very rapidly, that is, in hours, globally.

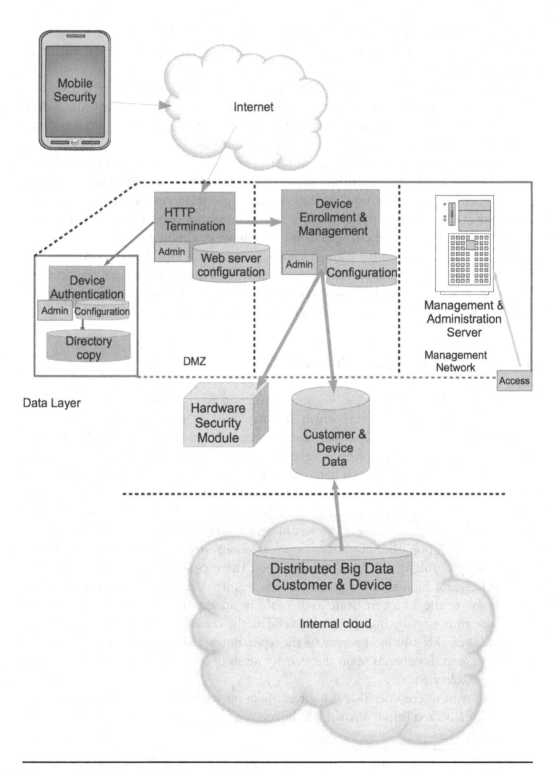

Figure 10.3 Cloud-hosted mobile device management using the Hardware Security Module (HSM).

Since each device will be issued a certificate, device certificates will need to be signed. The signature is generated from a private key so that the signature may be validated with the public key. The private key, then, is an important secret that must be protected from disclosure. If disclosed, anyone possessing the key may create a valid device certificate. Doing so would then invalidate an important authentication, as described previously.

How do you protect a secret like a private key?

The addition of a Hardware Security Module (HSM) can help to protect the private key that will sign each device certificate and all the messages from the management function to the devices (as specified above). But HSM's are not a panacea, just like the use of TLS is not a security cure-all. Deploying an HSM requires some forethought and architecture.

If you glance at Figure 10.3, you'll notice that the HSM has not been placed within any of the outer layers where it would be more exposed. The HSM is placed within the data layer, which only takes communications from the second layer, which lies behind HTTP termination [the demilitarized zone (DMZ)]. The second layer, the "application" layer, has a message flow only from the DMZ or outer, exposed layer. Attackers must first gain the HTTP termination before they may proceed onwards to attack the application layer. The HSM only accepts key signing requests from the application layer. Thus, before an attack can be mounted against the HSM, both HTTP termination and application must be compromised.[*]

Since compromise of the private key will obviate a couple of the security controls in the defense-in-depth, it will need protection, significant protection. A classic situation then emerges: We add a security control, device certificates, which then cause a new target to emerge (the private signing key), engendering attack surfaces that don't exist without the addition of device certificates.[†]

One protection, as described above, is to limit communications flows. Is that sufficient? Probably not.

I would also require that certificate requests be constructed by the communicating layer, in this case, Device Enrollment and Management (the application layer). We've seen this mitigation before (Web-Sock-A-Rama and business analytics) as a method for limiting exposure to inner components. The device certificate will be created and then signed on the HSM. No data need be passed from the outside to the HSM. The

---

[*] Of course, all of these components have to be managed through their administrative interfaces. Administrative communications are restricted as per the AppMaker architecture presented earlier.

[†] In other words, adding device certificates fundamentally changes the architecture of the system. Any architectural change should require a reassessment of the security of the system. I go into some depth on this issue in Chapter 9 of *Core Software Security,* by James Ransome and Anmol Misra (CRC Press, © 2014).

untrusted device cannot originate the message requesting a certificate from the HSM. (We'll examine outbound message signing below.)

Here is the order of processing:

- The user enrolls the security application.
- The user enrolls a particular device.
- A device identifier is generated (must include sufficient entropy to be unpredictable).
- A certificate request is generated for the device identifier on behalf of the device.
- The certificate request is sent to the HSM.
- A signed certificate is returned. The public key of the signing key pair will be included in the certificate.
- A device certificate for that particular device identifier is returned for installation on the device.
- The device can use the public key to verify the certificate signature.
- After enrollment, communications from the device may not proceed before the signature over the device certificate has been verified. This can be done by comparison against a duplicate of the public key, which is kept within the directory copy maintained within the authentication system's restricted subnet. No communication to the HSM is required in order to validate the certificate. The duplicate public key does not require additional, extraordinary protections.

As you may see from the foregoing, as depicted in Figure 10.3, only the enrollment function communicates with the HSM. The certificate request is entirely generated by the enrollment function. No untrusted data is passed to the HSM.

10.5 Additional Security Requirements for a Mobile and Cloud Architecture

In order to derive a more complete list of requirements, please return to the list of requirements from the assessment in Chapter 9. Most, if not all, of those requirements will be relevant to this architecture, as well. The following comprise the additional requirements that must be added to those for an endpoint anti-malware application.

- Use TLS between the mobile device and cloud services. Server-side TLS authentication is required.
- Each enrolled device will be issued a device identifier. Device identifiers must be unpredictable.
- Generate and install a certificate on each mobile device under management. The certificate must be unique to each device. Certificate signature must be validated before cloud services may be accessed. The private key used to sign the device certificate must not be deployed to any device. A single private key may be used

for all devices. A better design generates a private signing key for each customer, although consumers who individually purchase protection may all have their certificates signed by the same private key.*

- The private key used to sign the device certificate must be stored in an HSM or equivalent. The network must be configured such that the HSM will only accept cryptographic operations from the enrollment and management service.
- All data (commands, reputations, policies, configurations, etc.) and all binaries downloaded to devices must be hashed and signed. The device software will validate the signature and the hash before any further processing.

---

* Discussions about Public Key Infrastructure (PKI) in general and certificate revocation in particular have been avoided purposely. Issuing private signing keys would require a robust PKI. When using X509 certificates, certificate revocation must be designed.

Chapter 11

Cloud Software as a Service (SaaS)

In this, our last architecture, we examine the cloud "SaaS" that implements the reputation service that we encountered in the mobility example. "SaaS" is a cloud acronym for "Software as a Service." The meaning of SaaS should become clear through the analysis. If you're unfamiliar with reputation services for security software, it may be helpful to return to the mobility example and refresh your understanding.

11.1 What's So Special about Clouds?

Cloud computing is a model for enabling ubiquitous, convenient, on-demand network access to a shared pool of configurable computing resources (e.g., networks, servers, storage, applications, and services) that can be rapidly provisioned and released with minimal management effort or service provider interaction.[1]

We will not analyze the management portion of the mobility service. Several example architectures in this book have included management components. The cloud aspects of the management service would be roughly equivalent to the other examples, save for the distributed nature of cloud SaaS. The present example will explore distribution in some depth. If this were a real system, security analysis of all the components would be required, not just the reputation service in isolation.

In the mobility example, we represented the management of the mobility clients and the reputation service as servers in the "cloud." Of course, these services require far more architecture than a single or even a horizontally scaled set of servers. Typically, any service offered on the web that must process large data sets, what is commonly known as "big data," will at the very least have an application layer to do the processing, and some sort of data layer. Usually, because of the complexities of processing, presentation, multitenancy, and performance, the application processing can't be done through a single execution environment. There are just too many tasks that need to be accomplished to squeeze all that processing into a single, unitary application.

Even with horizontal scaling to increase the processing, there are distinct phases through which data must flow in order to support an industrial-strength, commercial, data-intensive service. The tasks in the processing chain are relatively distinct and fairly easy to separate out. For this reason, there are more than just "layers." As we shall see, there are groupings of processing that can be assembled to form logical units. This allows for a software architecture to emerge at a gross functional level, which fosters the specialization of programmers in particular types of processing. And it also allows for better security (and architectural) grouping.

11.2 Analysis: Peel the Onion

The data that forms the basis for making reputation decisions will likely come from many sources.* Where data are collected from, and precisely what types of data are involved, are deeply held trade secrets. And this proprietary mix is not germane to the security of the system. From our perspective, we need to know that data are pulled and received from many sources via a data-input function. That function, like the Data Gatherer in the business analytics example, must normalize and parse many different types of data so that the data may be kept in a unitary fashion that can be processed for reputations. One logical function, therefore, is the receipt and initial processing of the various data types. Neither of the figures of the SaaS architecture in this chapter portray reputation data collection. We will not explore this aspect of the service. We concern ourselves with the service as consumed by a mobile security application.

Once the data are in a form that can be processed, a continual process in the backend works through the data, continuously calculating and recalculating reputations. There would be an architectural decision in the development of the reputation service as to whether reputations were calculated upon request for a reputation (i.e., in "real time").

Alternatively, a reputation calculation would perform its processing over every object that had changed based upon incoming data. Each of these possible paths has its pluses and minuses. The decision on which way to architect the system would be made based upon the relative merits and challenges presented by each method. For our purposes, neither of these paths presents a wildly different security problem. Let's assume that there was a decision to make a separate process for calculating the reputation. And that process doesn't receive traffic directly from the Internet.

---

* One of the sources for new objects will be requests about objects that have not been encountered by the service previously. These will be entirely new, having no reputation calculated. We will ignore this typical data input in this example, for simplicity's sake.

The key piece of security information here that I've just laid out is that messages do not come directly from the Internet through to the processing function. If you remember from both the business analytics and Web-Sock-A-Rama examples, one of the key defenses in both cases was a recomposition of requests before the request was passed to an inner, more trusted layer. In this way, an attempt to attack the web layer stays at the web layer and isn't forwarded on further beyond that initial layer. Although such a defense is not always possible, depending upon the nature of the applications in the back-end, it's relatively common that requests that will need to be processed by inner layers are generated at the outer, less trusted layers rather than simply forwarding traffic from even less trusted sources. In this case, the least trusted source would be a mobile device. Although the entire system does attempt to keep mobile devices safe—that's its purpose—there's no guarantee that some clever attacker hasn't breached the device through some means or other. Thus, an attacker could be in possession of a vector of attack in the demilitarized zone (DMZ)–exposed system. Furthermore, as we know, an attacker could very well just buy the software, put it on the attacker's device, and then use that device as a launching pad for attacks against the system. Hence, despite the protections built into our mobile security software, including malware protection and certificate authentication of the device to the service, the reputation service should make no assumptions about the relative safety of communications from the device.

With the foregoing in mind, a more defensive security architecture will be one in which messages are received and processed from devices, that is, requests for reputations via a bastion front end application. The front end "reputation service" to which a device under management connects then regenerates a request for a reputation to the reputation processor based upon the parameters sent from the device.

The URL or other object about which the user is asking must still be passed through to reputation processing. The object data can be inspected, validated for proper form, and sanitized. That processing will take place in the front end. Still, some data that is received from the untrusted source will be moved through the front layer and on to the next. Hold that in mind as we dig deeper through the architecture layers and attack surfaces.

Because of the separation of functions, from a security perspective it doesn't really matter whether the reputation-calculating software performs the reputation calculation when it gets a request or simply retrieves the reputation that's been previously calculated and stored. As long as reputations are kept up to date, that's all that matters to the customer: retrieving the most up-to-date calculation.

It is quite possible that there may be two back-end application functions: reputation calculation and reputation retrieval. For our purposes, this distinction isn't really relevant and doesn't change the security picture of the system. Some piece of software presents an attack surface by receiving requests from a less trusted layer. That's the important security-relevant piece of information. In order to keep our diagrams simple, these two functions have been collapsed into a single component.

Figure 11.1 represents the cloud service as it may look, logically, from the user's, that is, the mobility security software's, perspective. The "cloud" means that the service has

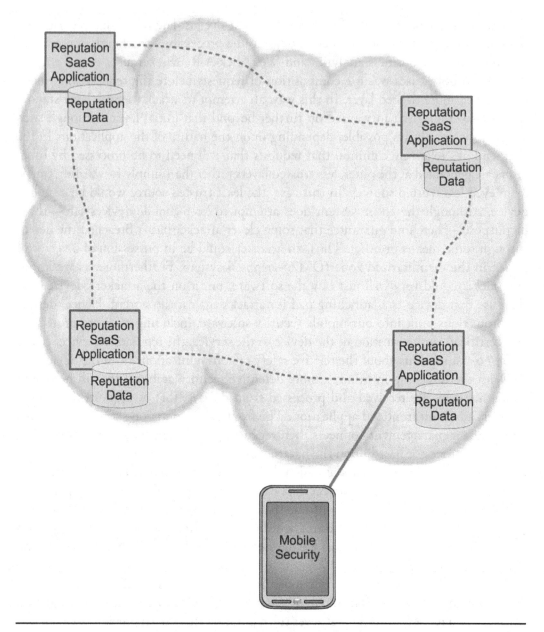

Figure 11.1   SaaS Reputation Service architecture (in the cloud).

multiple points of presence across the globe to be queried. Cloud also implies large scale to support thousands, even millions, of clients. The mobile device software doesn't need to understand any of the details behind that service. In other words, the details of data retrieval, processing, rating, and responding to queries are entirely opaque to the querying software. This is my intention. Even in SaaS architectures, data and structure hiding is a worthy design goal. As long as the messages remain consistent across versions, there's no need for the endpoint software to understand the details of how the query gets answered. This is no different than an API hiding a library or an object hiding its internal processing. This is nothing more than structured programming (a rather dated term) at a very gross, logical architecture level.

Decomposing one of the points of presence, Figure 11.2 shows more detail. If you recall the Web-Sock-A-Rama web store architecture, the application portion of the

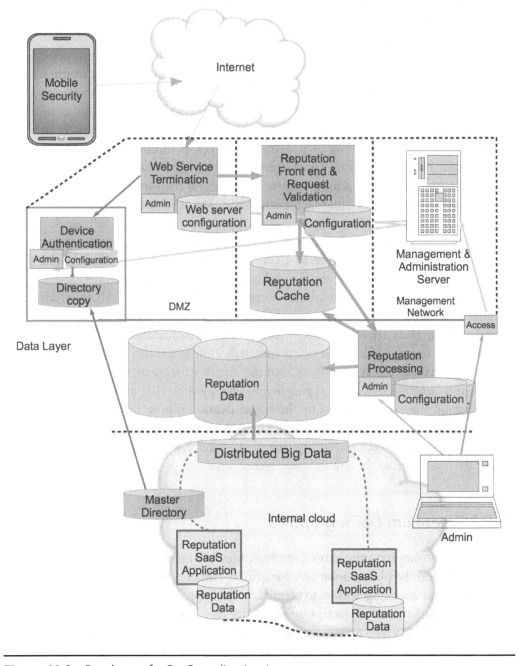

Figure 11.2   Breakout of a SaaS application instance.

reputation service looks surprisingly similar to the previous web example. This is not to suggest that all web applications are the same. They decidedly are not. However, a three-tier architecture, separating the web termination, authentication, and message validation from front end processing logic, which is then separated from further processing, is one very typical architectural arrangement.

In order to represent the many management and configuration functions that support a secure web presence, I have diagrammed a management network, administrative interfaces, and configuration stores. These would all have to be implemented in order to run a cloud SaaS service. Since these were explored in the earlier web example, please refer to that if you have any doubts about the sorts of issues and resultant security architecture that will normally be put into place for the management of Internet-exposed systems. A demilitarized zone (DMZ) management network is employed to ensure that administrative access is highly controlled, just as we saw in the previous web architecture. In this case, access to the management network is through a single constrained point, which then proceeds to a management server. The management server is the only source from which the administrative interfaces on the various DMZ components can be accessed. As before, dual-factor authentication is required before access to the management network is granted.

As we noted in our mobility example, all devices containing the mobility software, which is under management, receive an X.509 certificate issued to that device. Only queries for reputations that present a valid certificate signed by a private key issued by the reputation service for the mobility software will be accepted. All other attempts at communication will be rejected. In this way, all the dross attack attempts that take place on the Internet are consistently rejected. This authentication does not mean that all attacks are rejected. The value of an authentication as a security control is based on its ability to reduce access, that is, reduce the attack surface, by rejecting "untrusted" sources. But "untrusted" is a value judgment. The question that must be asked in order to understand the value delivered by the authentication is how much does the issuance of the authenticator tie to some level of trustworthiness? As we've noted a couple of times, there is the distinct possibility that an attacker can become part of the population of devices running the mobility software.

11.2.1 Freemium Demographics

Taking a slight tangent from our example, it may be interesting to note that different levels of trust can be placed upon any particular "authenticated" population. In a business model that encourages users to create accounts, such as a social media site, there's very little trust that can be placed into the entity that has authenticated access. And, in fact, that's precisely what can be seen empirically. Attackers routinely use their authenticated access for malicious activities on social media sites. The authentication means very little, except that the system has opened an account. I might point out that I personally have seen many accounts purporting to be pets on Facebook despite Facebook's policy of a single account only given to validated humans. This policy is very difficult to enforce, especially where the revenue is based on customers' enjoyment of the site.

Let's compare social media with its relatively wide-open and easy access to a system like a banking or investment site. In the latter case, it's critical that an account be tied to a validated, authentic human. But even more so, that human will have to be trusted to be engaged only in legal activities. The possibilities opened by an attacker with malicious intent who has normal customer access can be quite calamitous. Financial institutions tend to take a very dim view of attempts to circumvent laws and regulations through their services. Hence, a fair amount of due diligence takes place before issuing accounts. And then a fair amount of due diligence and out-of-band authentication takes place before issuing online access.

For a third example, security-conscious organizations, for instance, government intelligence agencies or institutions of any kind requiring a fair amount of trust of the employees, usually go through significant background checks to determine the trustworthiness of potential employees. Even after hire, responsibilities requiring significant trust may be withheld until the new employee proves a level of trustworthiness.

In the last two examples, financial institution account holders and security-conscious institution's employees, an authentication will likely be tied to a much higher level of proven trust; the authenticated entity has been validated through other means. In the case of intelligence agencies, double agents do exist and occasionally get caught. In the case of financial institutions, dishonest employees do sometimes get hired. And account holders are not always as honest as the institution might hope them to be. Therefore, in each case, we can infer that although authentication reduces the attack surface, sometimes a great deal of reduction, it is very rare that authentication eliminates the attack surface. Perhaps, never?

One standard method for dealing with the fact that authentication does not protect against all attacks is to log the actions taken on the system by the authenticated entity. Logging system activity is a typical additional control. Monitoring is often employed so that, at the very least, malicious actions can be tied to a user of the system. In order to monitor, the activity first must get logged. At best, instantiation of malicious action will be noticed and can be stopped before serious damage takes place. For social media sites, logging of action sequences is critical to identifying malicious users and ejecting them from the system before they can harm other users or the system itself.

Since for the reputation service we understand that attackers can gain access, all actions taking place on the service by each device are logged. Anomalous sets of activities trigger an investigation from the 24×7, around-the-clock security monitoring team.

In Figure 11.2, you will see the authentication service. As in the eCommerce example, the architecture has placed the authentication service within its own highly restricted network segment. Only the web front end may issue authentication requests. In this way, the authentication service cannot be attacked from the Internet. First, the front end would need to be compromised.

In addition, the credentials and entities (identity, i.e., device identifiers) are pushed from a centralized master directory that lies within the most protected internal network. In this way, even if an authentication service is lost, it cannot communicate inwards, putting the master directory at risk. Communications are outbound from the master directory only. (The authentication service must also be managed and configured, just as we have seen previously.)

11.2.2 Protecting Cloud Secrets

In the previous mobile security architecture example, we explored the use of Hardware Security Modules (HSM) for protection of cryptography key materials and signing operations. This reputation service has precisely the same problem. There are private keys that are used to sign X.509 certificates that will be used to authenticate devices requesting reputations. In addition, you may remember that all messages and data going to the managed device must be cryptographically signed in order to establish authenticity of the traffic after it has been received by software on the device. This is true for reputation messages, as well as messages from the management service (which we are not exploring in this example).

The use of an HSM is the same pattern, with the same challenges as we examined earlier. Except, each node (point of presence) will either have to communicate with a central HSM, or, alternatively, each node will require its own HSM. The latter architecture will be faster. But it does mean that the same private key will have to be provisioned to each HSM.* If there is a change (e.g., a revocation or renewal) to the key, every HSM will have to be updated. There are interesting timing issues when updating multiple points-of-presence. We will not investigate these.

Of course, each HSM could generate a separate key. But that also has significant issues for a global service. Each node across the globe would have to be able to validate every public key (what is present in the certificate), which requires access to the private key. This is because devices might be accessing from anywhere; devices travel with their owners.

There are certificate chaining validation methods that address this problem. And indeed, if each enterprise customer requires a separate signing key (and most will!), then our cloud reputation service will have to employ a fairly sophisticated certificate signing and validation implementation that accounts for multiple certificate signing keys. Still, messages from the service may be signed with the same private key (so that every device can employ the public certificate/key to validate).

---

* One use case is to generate the private key on the HSM and to perform signing operations with that HSM. This way, the key never leaves the HSM. That isn't the only possible HSM use case.

Introduction of public key cryptography (PKI) into a cloud scenario serving a broad range of customer types requires a robust PKI implementation on the part of the reputation service. Still, ignoring these problems (which are well described elsewhere), an HSM is still the best method for protecting keying materials from both external and internal attacks. This cloud service includes an HSM (for performance reasons) deployed to each node in an architecture analogous to the previous mobility example.

11.2.3 The Application Is a Defense

A further protection at the front end of the reputation service must be the validation of every request for reputation. Those are the only messages accepted by the service. If the message is not in the proper form, in any manner, the system must reject it. Since attackers might possess a device certificate, and thus be authenticated to the service, rejecting any ill-formed request will provide protection of the front end and, thus, any services with which the front end communicates, as well.

Even the best, most security-conscious development teams occasionally allow a serious security vulnerability to leak out into production software. So how can a service like the reputation service ensure that all non-valid input is rejected? Security software testing is beyond the scope of this book. Still, it may be worth mentioning that a typical testing strategy is to "fuzz" inputs that are likely to receive malformed messages (or other input data). When we examined the file processing chain in the endpoint security example, fuzzing was one of our recommended security controls. That software must be made to withstand poor inputs; it will be examining malicious files. In a similar way, the reputation service front end, which must receive requests from possibly malicious sources, will benefit from rigorous fuzz testing. In order to protect services further within the chain of processing, the reputation service vendor will want the front end to be as bulletproof as possible. Fuzzing is an accepted test methodology to assure a robust input defense.

It is worth noting that any web front end requires the same list of management and hardening controls that we've seen in several examples already. The reputation service front end is no different. Despite the fact that the front end will reject requests from all but devices under management, all the usual and typical Internet-exposed controls should be observed thoroughly and completely. I won't reiterate those in this example. If you're unfamiliar with how web-exposed systems are set up and managed, please refer back to any one of the web examples already given (see Chapters 3 and 6).

In order to speed up queries, if a reputation has already been requested for an object, and the reputation hasn't changed since having been previously retrieved from the reputation processing function, it may be placed in the cache where it is accessible only by the reputation query front end. Once the reputation is no longer valid in the cache because it has changed, the reputation will need to be removed so that a query will return the updated reputation for the object as retrieved from the reputation processing back-end. This is an interesting architectural problem, as the cache becomes a bridge between trust levels. Both the bastion front end, and the replication processing back-end (which needs protection) access the cache. Consequently, the cache represents an opportunity to vector attacks from the front end to the next layer.

The sequencing of processing goes something like this:

1. A device requests a reputation for an object.
2. The query response process (front end) requests a reputation from the reputation processor.
3. The reputation is returned to the device.
4. It is also placed in the cache for rapid retrieval, should a subsequent request for the same information be made.
5. New data come in about the object.
6. In the back-end data store, the object reputation changes.
7. The reputation change triggers the reputation processing component to check the cache for the presence of the reputation.
8. If found (i.e., it's still in the cache), the reputation in the cache is deleted, forcing the front end to refresh the reputation when it is next queried.

If the cache is not handled well, and, of course, there are bugs in the chain of processing, a malicious reputation could be stuffed into the cache, which then would be read by the back-end processing software in order to exercise a vulnerability somewhere in the reputation processing component.

How should cache handling be accomplished in order to minimize the ability of the attacker to deliver a payload through the cache? If the back-end processor reads what's been put into the cache, then it receives a payload. However, the back-end could query for the presence of an object and, if present, order the cache to delete all reference to the object's reputation. With this logic, no data have actually been read from the cache. The "if present, then delete" command could be implemented in an atomic way, such that reputation processing simply issues the command to the cache. No communications are returned.

I hope you can see from the last example that the sequence of processing, what is read and what is not accessed, determine whether an attack surface is created or eliminated. If data are never read from the cache, then cache manipulation by the back-end presents a very limited attack surface, if any surface is present at all. It's important to investigate processing sequences and data retrievals and flows thoroughly to uncover attack surfaces. By designing in such a way that data flow is minimized or eliminated when unnecessary, attack surfaces can then be removed.

There is, of course, a flow from the front end backwards. Reputations are requested. We've already examined the controls placed at the front end in order to mitigate this possibility. Still, vulnerabilities do crop up in operating systems, runtime environments, and the like such that an attacker has a potential credible attack vector until that vulnerability is closed. One of our security principles is to plan for the failure of defenses. A good defense will plan for the compromise of the front end. Are the front end defenses, as outlined, sufficient?

I would argue, "No." An attacker might compromise the entire front end processing, despite the steps that have been taken to prevent such a compromise. This reputation service is a key component of mobile security software. It needs to have a strong defense so that customers may rely upon it for their protection. That statement suggests planning for failure or compromise of exposed systems and infrastructure.

A front end compromise might not be due to software created by the vendor. Vulnerabilities may crop up in networking equipment, protocols, operating systems, open source software that's been included, or any number of components over which the security vendor may have little or no control. Therefore, a prudent defense takes into account the loss of even key systems. Although relatively unlikely, the back-end software should make some attempt to reject any request for reputation that does not meet stringent and rigorous validation.

Because reputation requests should have been formed by the front end software, and because the API is well defined, it should be relatively easy to deterministically validate reputation requests. Additionally, the validation should be assured by a rigorous testing program, precisely like that laid out for the front end input validations.

The data that are used to create the reputations are a key commercial resource. Therefore, the defense-in-depth from device to reputation processing is, at least in part, built to protect the reputation data. In the mobile security example, we explored some of the reasons that an attacker might want to influence reputation. For at least these reasons, the reputation data itself is considered a critical, and thus sensitive, resource.

11.2.4 "Globality"

One of challenges that will need to be addressed by a cloud service is updating points of presence of the service across the globe. In Figure 11.2, you will see that the back-end is actually not discrete but connected and replicated to all the points of presence across the globe. This is very typical for a global SaaS service. It's desirable to keep processing as close to the consumer as possible. Consequently, all the reputations must be replicated to each point of presence. This means that across the globe, in each data center that hosts the service, the front end, the processing service, and the reputation data are duplicated. If the reputation service is to be accurate everywhere, this replication of data has to be very fast so that a reputation query in Singapore is as accurate and up-to-date as a query in London or Hawaii. This need for the rapid dissemination of updates and rigorous duplication of data everywhere implies that the back-end can be thought of as one global system rather than discrete points. At the back-end, all the systems are connected, as they must be to achieve the performance and accuracy required from a global cloud service.

Consequently, great pains must be taken to protect the global back-end. Failure to do so could provide an attacker a launch pad for global attack. Of course, such an event would be disastrous for a security software maker. As we have seen, the software maker has built a defense-in-depth to keep attackers from getting through to the back-end data layer.

The same rigor will need to be implemented for reputation data inputs. I reiterate: This is very similar to the robust input protection we examined for both business analytics and the malicious file processor in the endpoint security example. Each of these situations is an example of a higher-order pattern where untrusted data from a wide variety of sources will need to be processed. If you need further detail, don't hesitate to re-read these earlier examples.

An additional challenge for cloud services with many customers is multitenancy. As you consider the reputation service and the needs of customers or individual consumers, as well as, perhaps, large organizations that are security conscious like our fictitious enterprise, Digital Diskus, what will be the expectations and requirements of the customers? Will consumers' needs be different from those of enterprises? Who owns the data that's being served from the reputation service? And what kinds of protections might a customer expect from other customers when accessing reputations?

Interestingly, the reputation service may present a rather unique multitenancy profile. Consider for the moment that it is the software vendor who owns the reputations, not the customers. Customers are purchasing the service that advises them about the trustworthiness of various objects before they're accessed, whether that's the consumer sitting in a café going to a URL on the Internet or an enterprise employee accessing a web property from the corporate network. In each case, the response is unique to the request, as provided by the service. Can you spot what part of this interchange the customer owns?

The request can be tied to the user. And if the user is a member of the customer organization, then the request can be tied to the organization, as well. Requests are likely to have some value. If I know the sorts of web properties in which a consumer is interested, I can direct sales efforts to those interests. And that is precisely how search engines and social media services generate revenue. These services appear to be free, but they are far from it. If the service knows that you're passionate about skiing, it will attempt to sell you skiing equipment, skiing vacations, and so forth based upon your demonstrated interests. This is precisely how social media and search engine revenue is generated; the advertising is highly targeted.

Furthermore, each customer, probably each user, won't necessarily want to disclose their web viewing and interaction habits to any other user. If the string of reputation requests from a user were to be accessed by another user, not only would that be a breach of privacy in many jurisdictions, it might also give the receiver a great deal of information about the habits, interests, and activities of the individual.

In the case of an organization, the interests of its employees might be used competitively to understand future directions, pricing models, customer interactions, sales prospects, and all manner of sensitive business activity. Perhaps any one individual's activities might not be all that useful in isolation from the rest of the organization? But if an attacker could gather information about many of the organization's employee activities, significant information will likely be disclosed. For instance, if several of the researchers or executives access the website of an interesting new startup, a competitor might infer that the company was considering an acquisition. Any particular reputation request in isolation may not be all that significant. But the aggregation of reputation requests that can be tied back to an entity are probably quite valuable.

Hence, a reputation service does indeed have a multitenancy challenge. How can the service make sure that no tenant (or other attacker) can have access to all the other tenants' request history?

One solution would be to toss all reputation requests once the request has been satisfied. If no reputation request history is kept, if all reputation requests are ephemeral, then the best an attacker can get is a picture of the requests at any particular attack moment.* The deletion of all reputation request history is certainly one viable strategy.

However, the software vendor may lose valuable data about the efficacy of the reputation service. Certainly, the reputation service would need to keep metadata about reputation requests in order to compute performance statistics, log failures, spot anomalies from expected usage, and similar telemetry information. Metadata are going to be very useful in order to assess the workings of the service and to spot problems with the service as quickly as possible.

Will metadata be valuable to attackers? Perhaps. But the metadata certainly will not be as valuable as reputation request histories that can be tied to entities of interest. Consequently, another viable security strategy might be to throw away all actual request history and only keep metadata.

Consider the case where only metadata is kept, that is, the case where no data is kept about objects for which a reputation request has been made. Once again, in this strategy, valuable data needed by the software vendor about the running of the service would be lost. For one thing, if there's an error in reputation calculations, it may be impossible to know how many customers were ill-informed. That might be another acceptable business risk? Or not. In order to understand who may be affected, the service would probably have to keep reputation request history for each entity.

If reputation history is kept for each user of the system, then the system has a significant multitenancy challenge. Each customer expects that her or his reputation request history is private to the customer. A number of international jurisdictions have enacted laws, so-called "privacy" laws, which legislate exactly this premise: Browsing or other evidence of personal activity is private and, thus, protected information.

Since our cloud service is global, it will be subject to at least some jurisdictions' privacy laws wherever it serves protected customers. Compliance is, of course, one driver

---

* Attack success beyond a single point of presence for the service implies a global compromise of all the front ends. Not a likely scenario.

of security posture. I would argue that merely to comply is to miss the point of security. There are other business drivers of an appropriate security posture. Large organizations, enterprises, governments, and the like, tend to take a dim view of loss of employee data, whatever that data may be. Meeting a customer's expectation for protection of the customer's data should, in spirit at least, also meet many legal privacy requirements.

Having established the need to keep at least some reputation request history for each user, how can user data protection be implemented? As noted above, this is a significant design problem. We will explore this only in terms of general patterns. An actual design for a specific product is out of scope.

We will not propose what some companies have attempted. Occasionally, a service will build what I call "table stakes" security—firewalls, intrusion prevention, administrative privilege controls, the collection of typical and well-known security infrastructure—and then declare, "Your data are protected." I'm not dismissing these controls. But none of the typical controls deal with multitenancy. Standards such as NIST 800-53 are based upon an implicit assumption that the controls are built for a single organization's security posture.* And that is not the case when infrastructure and processing is to be shared, in this case, highly shared. In the case of multitenant, shared services, customers expect to be segregated from each other and to be protected from the service vendor's access, as well.

There are three architecture patterns that seem to be emerging to provide sufficient tenant data protection.

1. Encrypt data as it enters the service; decrypt data when it exits.
2. Separate processing within the infrastructure. Each customer essentially receives distinct infrastructure and processing.
3. Encapsulate data such that it remains segregated as it is processed.

Which of these patterns should be employed depends greatly upon what services are to be shared and how the services are architected.

1. *Encrypt data as it enters the service; decrypt data when it exits.* Encryption as data enter the service and decryption at exit is the preferred solution from the customer's perspective, as long as the keying materials are held by the customer or the customer's trusted third party. Encryption tends to be the obvious solution. Often, customer security teams will ask for encryption because encrypting the data before it enters the cloud

---

* The assumption that control is for a single organization does not preclude handling others' data. However, NIST 800-53 was originally drafted *before* many of today's privacy standards were enacted. It was certainly drafted before cloud systems become prevalent. In addition, somewhat implicit in the standard is the United States' assumption that once data are given, the data belong to the recipient, not an "owner." Privacy law in the United States is also changing. Perhaps older security standards may one day better reflect current notions of data privacy.

mitigates risk from multitenant compromise as well as vendor compromise. However, as we have seen, proper key handling isn't necessarily easy or obvious. If the vendor has the keys, or worse, if the vendor stores key materials with the data, then encryption doesn't really offer much protection.

When used as a control for cloud data protection, encryption won't work in many situations. In particular, if the data must be manipulated during processing, then the data cannot remain encrypted. For instance, consider a cloud-based business intelligence application that must manipulate data in order to produce "intelligence." Data must be decrypted before processing, which assumes that the service also handles the keys, or no processing can take place.

For cloud services that primarily offer storage of data, encryption from endpoint and back again is ideal. The caveat must be that keys can be properly protected.

An interesting hybrid case is when at least some of the services can be rendered based upon metadata alone. The data can remain encrypted because the processing takes place based upon the metadata associated with and surrounding bits of data. At least one shared meeting service works in precisely this manner. The visual (graphics) and audio are assembled at the endpoint. Hence, if each endpoint possesses a shared secret key, then meeting data can be encrypted between endpoints as the data traverse networks and the service.

There are two downsides to be found within this hybrid model. First, protecting secrets on endpoints isn't trivial if the secret is kept between sessions. The solution to that is to generate a key only for that meeting session. Once the session is over, the key is destroyed. That still begs the question of a compromised endpoint. Still, if the endpoint is compromised enough that a key in memory can be retrieved by the attacker, probably all bets are off, "game over," anyway. The attacker is in control of the endpoint.

The second downside to this hybrid model in which encryption protects data and the cloud service (SaaS) only manipulates metadata is that the customer must forego any additional services that entail the manipulation of data. In the case of the meeting service cited above, if end-to-end encryption is used, then meeting recordings and upload of shared files cannot be used. Either the service can manipulate data or it is protected end-to-end by encryption.

2. *Separate processing within the infrastructure.* Each customer essentially receives distinct infrastructure and processing. Separation at the infrastructure layer is very popular with services that offer a "platform" and infrastructure, that is, Platform as a Service (PaaS) or Infrastructure as a service (IaaS). Usually, these are highly virtualized and automated such that a virtually separated set of services can be easily allocated to each customer. Typically, the allocated services initialize in an entirely "closed" state, closed to all communications except those from the management console. The customer must open whatever communications will be needed, including ordering any storage (which will also be separated at the virtual infrastructure layer). Each customer, consequently, receives a separate and distinct set of services, almost as though a separate network had been purchased.

I have seen SaaS applications that use this model: Each customer gets a separate instance of the service, and nothing is truly shared above the infrastructure. Where shared processing will not deliver economies of scale, this model delivers reasonable multitenant separation. A downside of this approach is that management of many separate instances is not a trivial problem. Furthermore, the service vendor loses whatever economies can be derived from scaling a highly shared application.

3. *Separate data during processing.* If the vendor requires economies acquired from building a highly shared application (many SaaS vendors try to reap these economies), then the simple, obvious solutions will not work. That is, neither #1 nor #2 above apply. I'll reiterate: No matter how strong the vendor's perimeter and operational security controls and practices are, the shared application and perhaps data layers might present a comingling of tenant (customer) data unless the application is built such that data are kept separated even during processing.

To solve the separated data flowing through a shared application, multitenant problem, the shared application must be carefully coded such that it becomes virtually impossible for data from individual tenants to mingle or get mixed up while being processed. The usual way to protect the integrity and confidentiality of each tenant's data during processing is to encapsulate each data message with identifier(s) for each particular tenant.

Encapsulation is used in communications so that each protocol that rides upon a lower (outer) protocol is held within a protocol-level header and footer (beginning and end). This is how the Transmission Control Protocol (TCP) is encapsulated to ride upon the lower IP layer (TCP/IP). HTTP, for instance, places an additional encapsulation (header and footer) around the data that is to be routed over the TCP, which is, of course, riding on top of the IP layer. There are numerous message layers that can be placed within an HTTP message. Protocols are layered like a set of "Russian dolls," one layer (protocol) carried inside the message for a lower layer protocol.

Similar to network encapsulation, each tenant in a multitenant application will be assigned either a header preceding data or a header and footer surrounding data. The encapsulation identifies which tenant the data belong to and ensures that each tenant's flows remain separated during processing. Only a particular tenant's data may flow through a chain of processing intended for that tenant just as a single TCP message will be routed to a single IP address and a unique TCP port number. The encapsulation must be designed such that no tenant's data can be mistaken for another's. Figure 11.3 represents this data encapsulation visually.

Usually, the tag that identifies the tenant is a token tied to the tenant's account, not the actual tenant name or other public or well-known identifier. In this way, the application has no notion of tenant identity. The tag is "just a number." Some other, separate process is used to tie processing to the tenant.

Better than using "just a number," perhaps a predictable number, is to introduce unpredictability, that is, entropy into the calculation of the tag token. In this way, should

Figure 11.3   Multitenant data encapsulation.

the application be breached and one or more flows become compromised, the attacker will have more difficulty associating an unpredictable number to the vendor's clients.

A step above utilizing a high-entropy token would be to add a bit of indirection into the tag. A separate store might associate a client account to the hash. A second temporary storage (perhaps in memory?) would associate the tag token to the hash. At this point, an attacker must breach the hash-to-client store and the token-to-hash store. These should be kept in segregated processing units, perhaps separate network segments? Capture of the flows delivers nothing but a bit of data that is being processed. Wiring that data back to a client would require several more attacks, each successful.

I've seen a data store that used the above scheme to store customer data files. Although the files were all comingled on disk, they were stored under the token name. There were tens of thousands of individual files, each named by some high-entropy number. The number-to-hash store resided outside the data layer. The hash-to-client store was in yet another layer.

At this company there was 24×7 monitoring of data administrator activity. An alert would be generated should any customer file be accessed by an administrator account (administrators had no business reason to look at customer files).

Essentially, administrators who had access to the client/hash store didn't have data access. Data administrators couldn't access the client key. In this way, customers were protected from each other, from the accidental comingling of data, and from accidental or malicious administrator access. A shared application must be designed to keep tenants' data separated sufficiently, both in processing and storage.

The reputation service must employ a scheme similar to that explained in the third protection pattern above (#3) in order to protect reputation histories sufficiently for each customer. Because the reputation histories are saved, they must be protected as customer data when processed and in storage. A high-entropy token will be used as a part of the tag for requests linking these to a particular tenant through a two-level indirection scheme, as described above.

Figure 11.2 doesn't decompose the internal systems that would make up the "Distributed Big Data." Nor have the reputation data collection services been represented. Although these do encompass significant security issues, the issues are akin to those encountered with the business ecosystem of the enterprise architecture that we examined. The internal cloud will require a closed network with highly restricted access. As an architecture pattern, this is not radically different from any restricted network and services. Therefore, these will not be explored again in this example.

Despite the opaque security nature of the internal network, we will consider the global interconnections of all the points of presence for the application into the global data layer. One typical implementation of distributed big data involves the use of products specifically designed to replicate data between instances. The open-source project Hadoop® is one such product. The reputation service under consideration employs a distributed data product. The details may remain opaque, since from a security perspective, we have already discussed internal networks handling sensitive data.

An architecture specific to global cloud products with many points of presence is the network interconnection. One way to achieve this is to establish a series of connections using VPN or IPsec tunnels over the Internet. For a performance sensitive SaaS, the vagaries of Internet routing will influence transmission times. Hence, although essentially secure across the hostile Internet, such an architecture is likely to be unsuitable for this purpose. Instead, where performance and security must both be served, a private network is often the better choice.

Typically, each distinct and separate portion of the logical "internal" network will be joined through the point-to-point link run through a common carrier. If the common carrier network can be trusted, essentially, this architecture builds a distributed, private network. Since common carriers tend to be highly regulated (we're talking about large telecommunication companies), this is how many internal distribution networks are formed. In addition, the connections are point-to-point. Although the traffic does move across the common carriers' equipment, it isn't routed across disparate networks. Essentially, the point-to-point link is to be thought of analogously to a phone call. Only, in this case, the call is connected continuously. And the line should have redundancy and failover. Using point-to-point links, a private network is created over relatively secure channels.

Having created the internal distributed network, the architect is faced with the problem of whether to encrypt the traffic or not. I've seen this question come out both ways. IPsec tunnels can be placed over the point-to-point links. Hardware encryption might even be employed to speed up the traffic.

Alternatively, it may be that the common carrier is sufficiently secure to leave the traffic in the clear. For a large distributed network with numerous point-to-point links, the choice is not all encrypted or all clear. Any particular link traversing a less trusted carrier can be encrypted. Links going over the more trusted link can remain in the clear. Encryption can be implemented on a per link basis, creating a hybrid model.

Once the internal collection of links is established to the security posture desired, the internal network can be taken as a whole to be at a certain level of security protection. In other words, though the network is actually composed of many disparate points, it may be considered the "internal" network.

For the reputation service, private links connect all the points of presence across the globe. These also connect two redundant data centers where the reputation data are stored and processed. It is from these two centers that data is replicated outbound into the data layer we see in Figure 11.2.

11.3 Additional Requirements for the SaaS Reputation Service[*]

The following list of requirements focuses on the different, cloud aspects of this architecture. Earlier chapters covered in some depth other aspects, such as endpoint requirements, web requirements, and administrative needs.

- The calculation processor will not read from the reputation cache. A message will be sent from the calculation processor to the cache to execute a delete of all references to an object in the cache. Failure of the deletion will be logged. No acknowledgment will be returned by the cache in response to the deletion message.
- Reputation request messages must be constructed by the web front end. Only the queried object will be passed to the calculation processor.
- The front end will sanitize and validate messages from the mobile device. Any message that fails validation in form or data must be rejected.
- Before reputation requests will be received, a device certificate, signed by the private key of the reputation service, must be validated by the reputation front end. Certificate validation failure must cease all further communications.
- All customer reputation requests and request histories will be encapsulated with an unpredictable token. The token will be related to a cryptographic hash. The hash is the only value to be associated to service tenants. The hash-to-client relationship must be kept in a separate network segment, under separate administrative control (different team) from the application administrative team and from the storage and data administrators. Hash-to-token correlation will be done by a separate process running in the back-end, unexposed to any processing outside the internal back-end networks. Wherever stored, tenant reputation histories will be tagged with the token only. No mention of customer identity can be placed within that administrative domain or network segment.
- Reputation data will be pushed from the data farm on the internal network to each reputation data instance.
- Reputation data instances will exist on a segregated network that only receives requests from the reputation calculation and processing module.
- There will be four distinct layers, as shown in Figure 11.2:
  a. The DMZ, bastion layer containing the web service termination. Authentication of device certificates will take place before a reputation request may be made.

---

[*] Please see the requirements from the endpoint anti-malware requirements in Chapter 9 and the mobile security example in Chapter 10 for the relevant device requirements.

b. A front end module that validates requests before any processing may occur. Requests will be regenerated before they are passed on to subsequent layers. Objects about which a reputation query is made may only be passed from the front end after careful validation and format check. The reputation cache is placed in this segment. It receives requests only from the front end.

c. The reputation calculator/processor, which only receives reformed requests from the front end.

d. The local reputation instance for a point of presence, which will only receive requests for data from the calculation module.

- The front end request processing input must pass rigorous fuzz testing before release.
- The calculation module's request handling processing chain must pass rigorous fuzz testing before release.
- An HSM will be employed at each node to perform certificate, message, and data-signing operations. Multiple private keys, including customer specific keys, must be supported. Every node must validate every device certificate.[*]

References

1. Mell, P. and Grance, T. (2011). The NIST Definition of Cloud Computing, NIST Special Publication 800-145, Computer Security Division, Information Technology Laboratory, National Institute of Standards and Technology, Gaithersburg. Retrieved from http://csrc.nist.gov/publications/nistpubs/800-145/SP800-145.pdf.

---

[*] The architecture analysis ignores the issues of key synchronization, update, and revocation. A "real-world" analysis would have to grapple with these details.

Part II

Summary

We have now examined the six distinct architectures for security using the ATASM process. In each analysis, the recurring patterns of attack surfaces and security solutions have been highlighted. After reading this chapter, it should be clear that similar situations arise in seemingly disparate architectures. Indeed, whether building an online retail store, an internal business analytics system, the administration interface for enterprise security software, or a cloud reputation service, the security basics around administration and management make up one of the solutions that is required to build a defense-in-depth.

This is not to presume that the precise solutions outlined in this section are the only way to do it. In fact, depending upon the risk tolerance and business objectives in the context, there is no right way to implement management for security. We will explore this a little bit in the chapter on patterns. It is important to note, however, that although we used the same approach in a number of different architecture examples in this section, there are many ways to achieve the same ends, or rather, ends that are appropriate for the context in which the system exists. Despite what some standards seem to imply, security is always best implemented appropriately and not by meeting some formal recipe that offers a binary "right or wrong" way. If you take nothing else away from these analyses, hopefully, you will gather a sense of the craft of security architecture as it is applied to differing systems.

In order to avoid adding even more length to the foregoing analyses, I purposely dodged controversial subjects that are well covered elsewhere. Furthermore, in order to demonstrate that distinct architectures may introduce new aspects and, quite often, repeat the same patterns over and over, as well, I purposely reused the same solution wherever possible in the examples. It may be prudent to remember that the wise security architect often replies, "It depends." That answer is correct so long as the architect can articulate clearly what the dependencies are.

We applied the ATASM process to six example architecture analyses. For the first example, we followed the process closely, in precisely the order given.

The first step is to gather the context in which the architecture will function: business, risk, objectives, and functions. Next, we analyze the overall architecture, attempting to gain an holistic understanding of all the systems and components that function and interact. A further aspect of understanding the architecture is the decomposition and factoring process. The analysis must determine what level of granularity will expose all the attack surfaces. Additionally, the architecture must be factored into its defensible boundaries in order to apply mitigations appropriately. We listed all the mitigations that existed in the architecture before the analysis in order to uncover and prioritize against the enumerated threats those attack surfaces that require additional protection. This last step generates the formal threat model of the architecture from which the appropriate security requirements will be gathered.

The ATASM progression provides an ordering for the complex process of architecture analysis for security. Such an analysis is meant to generate a threat model from which security requirements can be understood. In our first example, we followed the process carefully and in the order given: Architecture, Threats, Attack Surfaces, Mitigations. However, a real-world analysis does not always proceed in a stepwise fashion. Often, an analysis is more like peeling an onion. The analyst must deal with the outer layer. And once that outer layer has been analyzed, successive layers are either discovered or revealed through the analysis. Components and functions are "discovered" that were not expressed in the first layer, the overall architecture diagram. New systems may be uncovered as the assessment proceeds through the architecture's "layers."

To demonstrate in a more realistic fashion the way that analyses proceed, we dispensed with the slavish adherence to the ATASM process. Instead, proceeding as it might unfold on the job, once the context for the architecture was understood, we proceeded through the architecture to understand the structure, uncover the attack surfaces, and discuss the protection needs (risk tolerance), thus generating appropriate security requirements. In other words, we applied a micro-ATASM process to each facet of the analysis rather than to the architecture as a whole.

The danger to an approach that decomposes to generate the threat model can be a loss of the whole picture. In these examples, we had the luxury of adequate, holistic information from the start of the analysis.[*] As you apply the ATASM process to your analyses, you may find that you have to bounce back and forth between analyzing the whole architecture and analyzing particular areas. Once ingrained, architecture risk assessment (ARA)/threat modeling does not require slavish adherence to any particular approach, whether that be ATASM or any other. Essentially, one must make sure that every step is covered for every facet and every component irrespective of ordering or method.

---

[1] The information was adequate because these examples were created for this book. I had the luxury of hindsight to generate precisely the preconditions required to draw the security conclusions presented.

One of the aspects of the craft of security architecture that I attempted to uncover for the reader is the reasoning that goes into choosing one set of security controls over another. Considerable space was devoted to an explanation about why a particular defense was chosen as opposed to some other course. That should not imply that any particular solution presented in these examples was the absolute "right" way. These are typical solutions to often-encountered problems. But the actual solution that gets implemented will most certainly involve local variation.

These lengthy explanations were intended to unpack, at least to some extent, the reasoning that an ARA and threat model must include in order to arrive at appropriate security within the context of an organization and its systems. The intention behind digressions on enterprise authentication systems and PCI compliance (to name two tangents) is to highlight the background behind the choice of one security alternative versus another. Oftentimes, a security architect will have to investigate standards, technologies, and protocols with which she or he is entirely unfamiliar. Part of the "work" of an assessment is to gain enough information to understand the trade-offs such that appropriate decisions can be made. My forays were intended to help you develop skill in identifying a situation in which more background is needed. To seed that, I regularly asked you to consider the situation before the next portion of the analysis. I pray that these questions sparked your interest and creativity.

Hopefully, at this point in this book, you, the reader, have gained enough familiarity with the art of securing systems that you can apply this knowledge to the systems in your organization, and the assessments that you must conduct? For managers and technical leaders, I hope that, at this point, you have a firmer grasp of what your security architects are attempting as they perform your organization's security assessments.

Part III

Part III

Part III

Introduction

There's more to securing systems than analyzing architectures for security requirements. If the process is near perfect in that upper-management support abounds, relationships with all the stakeholders are pristine, perhaps no more would need to be done
than to hand off the security requirements from an analysis and then move on to the
next system?

Unfortunately, in my humble experience, nothing works this well. If for no other
reason than the inevitable business trade-offs between rigorous security and delivering
products to customers, decisions will need to be made. This is why there is an entire
chapter devoted to risk in this volume. Such trade-off decisions will never be easy, and,
for the moment, they generally cannot be automated.

Another dimension is maintaining assessment velocity when scaled to large numbers
of assessments. In today's highly competitive world, software is being produced at an
ever-increasing rate. Some of this can be accounted for by the increase in the number of
organizations producing software and the increase in the number of programmers who
write code. But I doubt these increases entirely account for the explosion in new software.

I don't have hard data on the increase in software production. I do know that many
organizations are implementing methods to increase the velocity of their production of
code. The Agile movement is one such approach. Implemented well, many organizations experience a significant increase in the amount of code, often high quality, that
the same number of people who'd been working using Waterfall can produce within
an Agile environment. Hence, many organizations are chasing the Agile dream of self-
motivated, self-correcting, high-performing, nimble development teams.

Unfortunately, the kind of experience-based security architecture craft that we've
been exploring doesn't scale very well. Though we will touch on some experiments in
Agile security architecture in the chapter about managing programs, it remains that at

the present state of practice, security architecture requires significant human participation and engagement.

In Part III, we explore some of those areas that I've found help to create and maintain a program for architecture risk assessment (ARA) and threat modeling.

We will deepen our exploration of architecture patterns and their associated security solutions. We have touched on this part of the practice from a practitioner's perspective. In Chapter 12, we examine how capturing, standardizing, and applying patterns and standard solutions can help to increase efficiency and maintain delivery teams' velocity.

Once the specter of standards arises, a program will likely have grown to a size that exceeds that at which mere personal influence is an effective tool all by itself. It should be obvious, if you stayed with me this far, that I consider personal skills to be a critical factor and proficiency; make no mistake. However, when a certain size has been reached, there have to exist some formal processes, even a few clear-cut rules, so that everyone participating understands what must be done. If processes and activities are not delineated clearly, delivery teams simply make up whatever is convenient to their situation. Ensuring that the process has been followed is a matter of governance. There are many books covering this area, so we will confine ourselves strictly to those governance aspects that are relevant to security assessments of systems and security architecture in general.

Finally, Chapter 13 will take up, in a somewhat foreshortened manner, those aspects of building a security architecture practice that bear directly upon successful assessments and building functional teams of security architects. Again, there are plenty of fine programmatic works. I feel no need to repeat that which has been well covered elsewhere. Hence, Chapter 13 has been tightly focused on the needs of this work: applied security architecture.

Chapter 12

Patterns and Governance Deliver Economies of Scale

For small organizations, or where there are a sufficient number of experienced security assessors such that each practitioner can hold in his mind all the relevant patterns and solutions that need to be applied, there may not be a need for standardized patterns. When there are enough people to perform due diligence analysis on every proposed system, these practitioners are the governance process for the organization. The need for standards, a standards process, and governance of that process is generally a factor of size, breadth of portfolio, and, sometimes, the necessity for compliance to regulations imposed from the outside.

A well-known result from rigid, standardized processes and heavy governance of those processes is a slowdown in delivery. When due diligence (i.e., security architects) resources are highly constrained, and there exist rigid processes that require those shared resources to assess everything, due diligence will become a severe bottleneck rather quickly. On the face of it and simplistically, it may seem intuitive to enact a "law and order" and/or "command and control" process. Make everyone behave properly. But anyone who's read the legendary book, *The Mythical Man-Month: Essays on Software Engineering*, by Frederick P. Brooks, Jr.,[1] and similar studies and essays, knows that the more administration and bureaucracy an organization installs, the less work actually gets done.

Hence, in this chapter, we take up some approaches to standards and their governance that have proven, at the very least, to put a minimal amount of drag on innovation, creativity, and velocity in software and system delivery organizations. I make no promise that these will absolutely work in your organization and under your regulatory constraints. However, I have seen these things work. Therefore, I offer these for your consideration as you think about security architecture and risk assessment of systems in larger or more complex organizations working on many different kinds of projects in parallel, and delivering multiple, perhaps, many systems in each time period.

A key to Agile velocity is to prevent roadblocks and bottlenecks in the process. In other words, a bottleneck will be introduced if every project must go through a small number of security architects who must pass every single project no matter how small or big. If, like an auditing function, every project must pass a standard checklist of security items, whether any particular security item is relevant to the architecture or not, then a significant bottleneck will have been built into the system. Even after my 15 years of experience working in and building security architecture practices,[*] I continue to be surprised by organizations that insist upon trying to fit every project through the same mesh, the same matrix of checks, no matter how irrelevant some of these may be. They must have more money for resources and time than the organizations for whom I've worked?

It is a truism that it is nearly impossible to capture even 80% of architecture patterns into a checklist. Furthermore, flattening the decision tree into binary yes/no polarities diminishes the ability to synthetically craft situational solutions, thus hampering creativity and innovation.

The ideal model will empower and enable teams to be as self-sufficient as they can be, while, at the same time, maintaining due diligence oversight of results. There is a balance there between these two goals: entirely self-sufficient versus entirely dependent upon expertise. It would be grand if there were enough security architects to participate in every development project that has security needs. I hope this volume, of course, increases the number of people who feel confident and capable of the work. Still, as of this writing, there is a dearth of experienced practitioners; great security architects are a rare breed, indeed.

So what can be done in the face of a scarcity of appropriate capability? When there are standard patterns and solutions that are well understood and well described, many, if not most, teams can simply "follow the bouncing ball" by architecting to standard solutions. As Steve Atcheson[†] says, "make the easy path the secure path."

In most organizations, programmers are typically incentivized to deliver a finished product. If the security solutions provided to applications are vetted, well-documented, and easy-to-use, the "easy" path will be to simply consume the known solution rather than attempting an unknown implementation.[‡] The tendency to build from known

---

[*] As of this writing, I have an additional 15 years in high tech, holding roles from developer to technical leader to chief designer, and once as the Director of Software Development.

[†] Steve Atcheson, besides being one of my first security architecture mentors, my one-time colleague, and my friend, is also the author of "The Secure Shell (SSH) Frequently Asked Questions."

[‡] There does exist at least one case where even a competent developer may stray from the easy path. I have seen developers insist upon including new and exciting technologies, even when

and trusted software "parts" means that supplying standards that include easy or easier to consume solutions motivates developers to take the easy and secure path.

The foregoing suggests that standards and standard solutions can easily unburden overloaded security architecture staff while, at the same time, empowering developers to build correct solutions on their own. Standard approaches, then, become a critical multiplier of velocity. Thus, standard approaches that cover a wide range of cases has been effective at a number of organizations at which I've worked.

For instance, building a web environment that contains most, if not all, of the security services required by a standard web application frees the developer to think about the business logic that he or she is implementing—that is, authentication services, safe storage, key management, TLS services, security layering, and unbreachable sandboxes for each application. Providing these services will eliminate the possibility of error-prone security implementations from the application programmer. When each of these services (and, of course, others) are easily consumable, web programmers can focus on the security aspects for which she or he is responsible, such as secure coding, and any local input validation that must be performed beyond any standard input validation libraries that are available. In addition, the environment will not have to account for and tolerate all the errors that will creep into each local and unique implementation of critical security requirements. That means less critical security vulnerabilities.

As we have seen in performing analyses, architectures differ, thus requiring different implementations of security controls at different granularities. For a low-level BIOS programmer, or for a programmer writing to a hardware interface, the list given for a web environment above is more or less irrelevant. Still, when a team writes BIOS code for any length of time, the relevant security issues and solutions are going to start forming repeatable patterns. The list will be different, but there is a list of patterns and solutions, nonetheless.

Essentially, when a project can match the known solutions, follows the standard patterns, and contains no exceptions, security review can be bypassed; the team then gets a "get out of security jail free" card. In other words, the project or effort can remain entirely self-sufficient, without the need for more intense security analysis. Consequently, security architects who document their recurring patterns, who provide the solutions to those patterns, and who help to get those solutions built into the available services and software from which projects may draw will increase the scale and velocity at which the organization's development teams can operate. In the ideal situation in which there are many easily consumable solutions, security architects mainly handle the exceptional, the new, that which has never been seen before. Contrast this

---

doing so will create more work and perhaps even "torture" an architecture, misusing the new technology in a place where it is not needed or does not really fit. The developer insists upon the use of the inappropriate technology so that it may be included on her or his resume. The use has nothing to do with the fitness of the technology or the "easy" path; the use is intended to enhance the programmer's career.

situation in which standards are documented and services implemented with one in which the security architect is forced to reiterate the same solutions over and over and over again.*

What do architecture patterns look like?

In fact, if you follow along to at least some of the analyses given previously in this book, you've noted that certain attack surfaces were encountered multiple times, perhaps even across seemingly disparate systems.

One classic problem is how to deal with systems that will be exposed to the public Internet. We know, without a doubt, that the public Internet is hostile and that hosts on the public Internet will be attacked. To counter this omnipresent attack level, there are typical solutions:

- Firewall allowing traffic only to the designated public interface that will be exposed
- Bastion, HTTP/S terminating host (or the equivalent, such as a load balancer or virtual IP manager)
- Access restriction to and protection of management and administrative interfaces
- Network and protocol restrictions between traffic terminators and application logic, between application logic and storage or databases. That is, multiple tiers and trust levels
- Security configuration, hardening, patching of known vulnerabilities, and similar
- Authentication between layers of the automated processes and between trust levels
- Restriction to and protection of the networking equipment

The above list is not meant to be exhaustive, but rather representative. The point is, if an organization is going to deploy a system, especially a complex system, to the Internet, the solutions set that the organization will have to implement (whether purchased or built) is fairly well understood. Some organizations will write the "rules" into their policies or perhaps their standards. Others might make it impossible to deploy Internet-facing systems without meeting these requirements. The point being that if the solution for Internet-facing systems is well understood, any system that can follow the well-trodden path probably won't need a security assessment. Again, the "easy path" is the secure path.

In the same manner, a standard solution could be written for critical and sensitive systems management. Several times in the analysis examples we encountered a need to restrict access, both of humans and of automated processes. For instance, using the

---

* I once interviewed for a job where it was clear that the hiring manager was looking for someone who was comfortable treating every project, and, indeed, every developer as a unique, one-off situation. When I objected that a better solution would be to build a program, including services and solutions, he got quite upset. I guess some practitioners prefer treating each problem as unique? I obviously didn't want that job.

"secured" message bus from one level of trust to another was one of the protections that we examined in a couple of architectures. Appropriately governed use of the message bus then might be a standard solution for an organization (e.g., Digital Diskus).

A message bus standard might be: "Allow only well governed applications access to the message bus. Message destinations must be reviewed and approved. All message bus applications must use approved message handling and validation libraries." With such a standard, the need for security "touch" can be minimized. When I was a security architect responsible for an enterprise message bus, that is precisely how we designed the process. The velocity of applications requiring access to and messages from the message bus was larger than the team could handle. Therefore, it became imperative to screen applications that might put the trust of the message bus at risk for security review. At the same time, in order to enable high development velocity, standard applications that met security requirements were allowed to proceed without being delayed by a security review. Much of the access was granted through automated means, with no human touch whatsoever. On the other hand, identifying access requests that might have some information security risk involved was reduced to a couple of questions and requests for access from known to be less-trusted environments.

Management of administrative access to the systems that may be exposed to potentially hostile traffic is a fairly well documented body of practice. For those example architectures in which rigorous management was among the security requirements, in this book I have consistently cited NIST 800–53 as a reference to the body of practices that would fulfill this requirement. The citation is not to suggest that an organization shouldn't create its own standards. Nor do I mean to suggest that the NIST standard is the one and only best standard. It is simply well known and relatively widely accessible. At this point in information security practice, I see no need to regurgitate these "table stakes" requirements. There isn't much mystery or contention about what robust system management entails. In my own work, I simply refer to any one of the reasonably complete standards and use it as a sort of "checklist" against which I can measure the efficacy of the particular management body of practice. "Meet or is equivalent to ⟩" (fill in the blank with any well-known standard) helps me to keep focused on those problems where I can actually add value, as opposed to repeatedly delivering the same security sermons about appropriate management practices.

In any event, however the administrative practices solution is derived, a failure to be complete is liable to leave significant holes and unprotected attack surfaces. This is a standard pattern: robust administrative practices. If a system under assessment requires management, there should be a standard set of administrative practices that can be applied. It is best if developers can simply consume rigorous practices rather than trying to implement these themselves. This general rule falls apart, however, in very small organizations where people play many roles and wear many hats.

Which brings me to the question of scale. At a small or very small scale, what I call "eyeball-to-eyeball security" may be more than sufficient. That is, if everyone in the organization knows each other fairly well, where many have the ability to watch over, that is, govern the actions of any one or two people, eyeball-to-eyeball security may be quite sufficient. If a member of the organization goes rogue, the other members are likely to notice and can take action,* which means that a complex standard requiring many overlapping and interlocking controls such as NIST 800–53 may be quite inappropriate in this situation. A set of management controls such as those found in the NIST standard will likely cost too much and provide very little security versus the participants simply paying attention to each other's actions.

The trick, especially for a commercial organization that may in fact be investigated for its security practices or perhaps must meet detailed standards to gain a required certification, is to write the security policy in such a manner as to describe the controls, that is, people watching each other, that actually exist and which provide sufficient security. In fact, some standards simply say, "The organization must have a security policy." The organization must prove that they follow their security policy. If the organization's policy is, "Do whatever Brook says," and on security matters, everyone does what Brook says, then that organization meets its security policy. An organization could, hypothetically, have a policy that says, "The security policy of this organization is to not have a security policy." If that organization does not actually have a security policy, then by its own policy, it achieves policy compliance. Silly, I know. Nevertheless, hypothetically, such a policy would meet the standard, even though it's obvious that it would be completely ineffective in providing any meaningful security.

The point of the foregoing is not to suggest that you create a toothless security policy, but, rather, that the security policy should change with the needs of the organization. What is appropriate for an organization that gets along fine with eyeball-to-eyeball security is not the same policy that will work for a modern enterprise that must meet many regulations and that is required to be certified to particular security standards. These are, obviously, two very different situations. The trick is to recognize how much of a standard solution any organization at a particular stage of development needs in order to be effective.

I was listening to the presentation of one of the founders of Twitter a couple of years ago. The team was developing a different product and stumbled upon the tweet paradigm. One of their practices, because they were using Agile techniques for development, was to engage in daily meetings about the development, the issues, and the processes. There was a high level of interaction and a high level of trust among everyone who was involved in the project. Systems weren't exposed outside the local network. Everyone, including sales, marketing, and business people, were intimately involved in the details of the organization and its technical systems. In such a situation, what are the security needs? I would argue, very few, if any. As long as there were, at that time,

---

* Malcolm Gladwell devotes a chapter to the subject of group size and personal accountability through the example of W. L. Gore and Associates in *The Tipping Point: How Little Things Can Make a Big Difference* (Little Brown, © 2000).

no outside persons who had access to the systems (think, janitors), security needs would be minimal at that stage.

Once the initial tweeting system was made available outside that local network, security had to raise its head for attention. I believe that the presenter noted that they simply placed some sort of authentication on the system such that only known users could get beyond the login page. For a time, that also was probably sufficient. Once Twitter actually went live as a public offering, everything changed very quickly.

The next revolutionary step into security might have been the moment when Twitter, the product, was made openly available on the hostile, public Internet. Twitter was tested and prodded for security weaknesses and opportunities that were not a part of the original design and intention. In fact, a number of security flaws were encountered by the system in the first months, then within the first year of operation. I'd be willing to bet that as the system grew, administrative staff were hired and increased, and security issues were encountered, the security function and, eventually, the security architecture function grew to meet the changing needs. Quickly, eyeball-to-eyeball security would no longer have been sufficient. With customers now counting on reliable and secure services, the need to implement robust management practices would also increase. I'm willing to bet that the management of Twitter's systems today looks a lot more like NIST 800–53 than it did in the presentation about the founding that I saw. It would not be surprising if, along the way, many standard solutions were uncovered and then documented and then became part of the normal practice both for the management of the systems and to deliver secure development.

Management of systems, then, will have to be appropriate to the security needs of the organization. The example architectures that we analyzed in this book assumed enough scale to require a robust set of practices. In short, at scale, a pattern that we repeatedly encountered was management of systems that could scale to large organizations and complex systems. Such management at scale will normally implement fairly closely those standards that are similar to NIST 800–53.

Another repeatedly encountered pattern is the movement of data from less trusted to more trusted systems. Generally, if the architect follows the data from its entry at the less trusted border through every point of processing and every station of rest, many, if not most, of the systems' attack surfaces will be uncovered. Acknowledging the foregoing truism, we've also seen that program and user inputs don't comprise the totality of all attack surfaces. But for most systems, especially when considering automation input and levels of trust, the data flow will comprise the majority of attack surfaces. The data flow diagram, which by its very nature indicates inputs and, of course, outputs, gives us a methodology for considering each input as an attack surface. Whatever data might have any capability to include an attack, that input must then be considered an attack vector. Every point at which the data is handled or processed in any manner consequently becomes an attack surface.

The repeated solution to attacks vectored through input is a combination of keeping as many attackers out as possible while, at the same time, ensuring that what does come through is as expected. The defense must reduce access, that is, perform an access control, often authentication, but could include a restriction at the system or network level, as well. Even after access has been reduced, there usually is a requirement to validate the data input such that the input does not contain unexpected data. That is what is commonly termed "input validation." Input validation remains a key to input protection.[*] In other words, where data comes from any source that cannot be absolutely trusted to deliver data correctly, and cannot absolutely be trusted to comprise only the data that is expected, the data must be validated before being processed. If the data is incorrect in any manner, evasive action must be taken. Beyond security measures, input validation remains simple, defensive programming.

Input validation is generally performed within the boundaries of the "application." Since "application" is an ill-defined and overloaded term, this boundary is necessarily indistinct and loose. But, there is a way to gain more precision: Since only the coded logic of the application will have full knowledge and understanding of what data it requires and the data's acceptable range and outside bounds, I think it's probably safe to declare that input validation generally must be close enough to that coded logic to be effective. In essence, input validation is almost always coded somewhere either near where the data are input or where they are used (called a "data sink"). In short, "application" in this sense means a part of the coding of the data logic.[†]

Where input validation is an important defense, then, by its definition (above), the application code becomes a part of the defense of the entire system. This is an important facet to take note of. Security models often assume that system defenses entirely surround and are separate from the application code. Remember the "Security Services" box from the conceptual enterprise architecture in Chapter 7? That is a classic mistake in design: assuming that the application will be protected, as opposed to integrating protections into the application. The application code must be a key part of the defense wherever input validation is required.

This is not to suggest that appropriate input validation is easy to implement. A wide range of types of data increases the difficulty of implementing input validation. The more general purpose the data handling routines, the harder it is to filter out and reject bad data. One of the examples we examined was a module whose purpose is to examine possibly malicious files. I can't think of a more tricky input validation problem. An encyclopedic range of file types will have to be supported. Any of these files can contain

---

[*] In the case in which there is high or even extreme trust of persons or systems from which data comes, it might be possible to reduce significantly any reliance on input validation. However, defensive programming still demands that the software protect itself from human error, at least to some extent.

[†] I'm sure that there are generalized cases or data-driven models in which input validation can be placed further from the flow. These are the more difficult cases to implement. And I do not encounter this design often. Input validation within the data processing flow is the far more common case at the time of this writing.

bad data, and it also must be expected that the data will actually be intended to exercise vulnerabilities, possibly in the file processing code.

Since successful exploit within the file examination module will remove the very protections that have been promised, the module has to be rigorously self-protective against malicious data. In such an instance, perhaps "input validation" is too broad and generic a term. As each part of any particular file type is teased apart (parsed), it must be examined against the file specification first, and the entire file marked "bad" if there's any deviation. This processing care must take place before the data within the file can be examined for common malicious data and attack code.

It's necessary to supplement input validation in cases in which the code must be highly robust and self-protective. Vigorous testing techniques intended to prove the self-protective qualities of a module can be added to the security requirements. In other words, input validation alone is not sufficient to build an appropriate defense. The requirement pattern in this case adds an assurance step to prove the effectiveness of the input validation. In low data trust situations, the pattern will include both robust input validation and rigorous proof of the validation through regression, fuzzing, and similar techniques.

We commonly apply the security solution of input validation to the architectural pattern where there is reception and processing of untrusted data, In order to prove the rigor of the validation, I add assurance testing, typically, fuzz testing.

I have recounted a few patterns and their solutions that recur throughout our example architectures. It may be useful to go back to the example architectures to uncover other recurring patterns and solution pairs. As a hint, message and communication protection were consistently encountered. There were problems around the protection of secrets. There were network architecture approaches that cropped up repeatedly. And, of course, data flow restrictions were encountered in a number of places. Where was authentication employed? Why did we make use of digital certificates? And when digital certificates were a part of the architecture, why might we include the use of hardware security modules (HSM)?

Think back to the examples, or open them again, at least to the attack surface enumerations and requirements lists, to see what other architecture patterns emerge across disparate examples as we analyzed systems. At the very least, the patterns we encountered in the examples will become part of your personal, security architecture repertoire from which you may draw as you analyze systems for their security requirements.

12.1 Expressing Security Requirements

Applications rarely have clear security requirements over and above the vague injunction to follow all corporate security policies. The architect is left groping in the dark when confronted with the question, "Does this product support the context in which security appears within my application?"[2]

It may seem that if management mandates that certain processes will be followed by all the stakeholders and they all agree that they will follow them to the letter, that if all agree that each task will be completed, as specified, and that everyone will participate appropriately as needed, then there should be no need for governance.

In my experience, this is not how things play out in the real world. Perhaps, if the organization is sufficiently hierarchical and driven through command and control, and penalties are sufficient for noncompliance and nonperformance, then I can countenance the possibility that simply giving a command will cause all the appropriate tasks to unfold in their proper and respective places. But I haven't ever worked in this organization.

In my real-world experience, governance is as much an art of relationship and influence as it is a mandate or order. Indeed, there is a significant conflict between empowering intelligent, skilled people to be creative and innovative against the necessity to make sure that certain steps are followed and, particularly, that the important, high-priority security requirements get addressed. I believe that it is impossible to simultaneously empower people to think for themselves and also order the same people to do as they are told. When people think for themselves inevitably they are going to form their own opinions. Even more so, highly capable people's divergent opinions might just be correct.

Admittedly, the organizations in which I've worked have largely preferred to form a consensus decision, if at all possible. Not all organizations behave this way. I personally have not worked in a strictly command-and-control situation in my high-tech professional career. Due to this lack of personal experience, it may well be that a strictly hierarchical organization does not exhibit the sort of problems that I regularly encounter? I wouldn't know. My personal philosophy is that it's much better to let thinking people think; complex decisions tend to improve when multiple views and skills are incorporated.

> [A] random group of intelligent problem solvers will outperform a group of the best problem solvers.[3]

12.1.1 Expressing Security Requirements to Enable

In organizations in which stakeholders have influence on a decision (whatever the decision-making style), conflict will inevitably arise between the security requirements and all the many other things that must be accomplished in building and maintaining systems. Issues such as resource constraints quite directly influence whether security requirements will get met, when they will be met, and how long the implementation will take. There are several key approaches to expressing security requirements that can help ease the implementation as well as foster risk-based decision making for prioritizing security requirements among the many competing needs for a system.

Finding the Right Level and Granularity

One of the key skills that can help is writing requirements at the correct level at which the requirements will be consumed. This is often a difficulty for engineers who are used to expressing a technical matter in as much detail as possible. For any but an inexperienced or unskilled implementer, this will be a mistake. There has to be enough specificity that the security requirement can be implemented somehow, that the goal of the requirement can be met. But generally, a requirement shouldn't be written such that it hamstrings the implementers to exactly one particular and narrow implementation.

For example, if we were specifying network restrictions from one web layer to another, how should this be done? One could specify the precise IP address from the web termination to an application server IP address. One would usually specify the port and protocol. One could specify the exact piece of networking equipment that should be used. One could even specify the exact access control list (ACL) that should be placed in the configuration file of the networking equipment. One could even take the entire list of ACL (however those are presented for the particular piece of networking equipment) and show precisely where that line should go in the list for proper ordering. In a situation in which the implementer does not have enough skill to understand how to write and test ACLs, the above list of specifications might actually be necessary.

The IT networking teams with which I've worked have been considerably more skilled than that. The foregoing might have seemed somewhat patronizing, perhaps insulting, to these teams. And patronizing smart people is usually not a very relationship-building approach.

12.1.2 Who Consumes Requirements?

Depending upon the skill of the receivers and implementers, it may be enough to write a requirement that says something on the order of, "Traffic to the application server must only be allowed from the web termination server to the application server. Only allow HTTP traffic. Disallow all other traffic from the web termination network to the application server." In situations in which changes to the exposed networks have to go through significant architecture and design functions within the networking team, a very high-level requirement may be all that's necessary. If the networking function already has significant skill and investment, good pre-existing networking architectures and equipment, the requirement can assume those capabilities. On the other hand, if web layers are an entirely new concept, more specificity may be required, even down to the particular equipment that will manage the layering.

The maxim for getting requirements to the right level of specificity is, "just enough to deliver an implementation that will meet the security goals." In this example, the security architect is not really concerned so much with how the restrictions are implemented but rather that it will be difficult for an attacker to use the terminating network

(DMZ) as a beachhead to attack the application server. The security architect is interested in preventing a loss of control of the bastion network (for whatever reason) to cause a loss of the entire environment, starting with the application server. That means traffic to the application server must be restricted to only those systems that should be communicating with it, with traffic originating from termination to application server, never the other way around. That's the goal. Any networking method employed to achieve the goal is sufficient. Assuming people who understand how to achieve these kinds of security goals, the requirement can be written at a reasonably high level, as I did at the beginning of this paragraph.

There's another reason not to get too specific with security requirements, unless it is absolutely necessary. In situations in which security requirements have a good deal of organizational empowerment, perhaps even force, a highly specific requirement can be a technical straitjacket.

Technical capabilities change. I don't want to write requirements that hamstring the natural and organic evolution and improvement of capabilities. In our example, if a particular piece of equipment had been specified and then, for some reason, was deprecated or even had become obsolete, a hard, specific requirement for a particular piece of equipment, perhaps configured in a very particular manner, might very well prevent an upgrade to a key system at a possible future improvement point.

Besides, the wise security architect may not have the time to assess every shift and technical capability in the many areas in and around complex systems. That is, for large, complex systems, knowing every piece of networking equipment that's involved, and specifying these in great detail, may be way too much effort and may not actually produce security value. I try to stay out of these sorts of details unless there's a good reason to become involved. By writing my security requirements focused on the ultimate security goal, I can avoid dropping myself, or an organization, into a technical dead end.

Sometimes, there is a tendency for security teams to want to specify particular cryptography algorithms and perhaps, key lengths. In the not too far distant past, the MD5 hash algorithm was considered quite sufficient and cryptographically secure. Then, upon the publishing of a single paper, the ability of MD5 to survive rainbow table attacks was called into question. As of the writing of this book, MD5 is considered deprecated and should be replaced.

Consider a requirement that specified MD5 at a time when it was still considered sufficient protection. Not only would every system that had implemented MD5 be subject to change, but all requirements specifying MD5 would suddenly become obsolete. What if MD5 were specifically called out in a corporate standard or, even worse, in a policy? In large organizations, policies are only rarely changed, and only with approval at a fairly high level in the organization, often with several stakeholder organizations (for instance, a Legal Department). In response to the loss of a particular cryptography algorithm that has been specified in a policy, changing the policy and all the requirements to meet that policy becomes quite an expensive proposition.

But what if the standards writers had said something on the order of "an accepted, cryptographically proven hash algorithm implemented by a well vetted, standard library." Although it may be argued that given such a requirement, some systems might choose MD5, other systems might use SHA1, or perhaps SHA128, or any number of algorithms that are currently considered reasonably cryptographically hard to reverse. In this case, only the systems that have used MD5 need to be changed. The standard doesn't need to be rewritten. If the policy merely says something of the order of "follow the standard," then the policy doesn't need to be changed either. And, as new, more resistant, or stronger hash algorithms become available, implementers and maintainers are free to use something better. I want my security requirements to be as future proof as possible.

Part of the art of writing security requirements is understanding, in some depth, existing capabilities. You may remember that when the ATASM process was introduced, one of the prerequisites to analysis was having a firm grasp on current capabilities? Understanding "current security capabilities," that is, existing infrastructure and control systems, allows those security capabilities and mitigations to be factored into a system analysis. This understanding also helps to express security requirements at an appropriate level such that the current capabilities will achieve their security objectives. If well understood, the existing capabilities can be assumed behind requirements, without the need to exhaustively describe them.

In small organizations in which there are only a few people involved, there may not be much separation between architecture and the details of the engineering implementation. In these situations, a security assessor may also be intimately involved in the details of implementation. The assessor and the implementer are often the same person. In this type of small, tightly bounded situation, there might not be a need for formal security requirements; just to do it. The "just do it" attitude obviates, oftentimes, a need for process documentation and process governance. Still, even in this situation, if customers are going to ask what security requirements were built into a system, it may be useful to have documented the security that has been built into a system, even if implementers don't actually need any formal requirements. Perhaps customers will?

Once organizations reach any sort of organizational complexity, with stakeholders responsible for implementing security requirements becoming different from those who write them, then the security requirements become a document of record of the assessment. The security requirements become the formal statement about the future or finished security posture of a system. The requirements, taken in concert with the "mitigations," that is, existing security features and defenses, describe the security posture of the system in a systematic manner. Since each requirement is tied to the set of attack vectors and surfaces, the requirements set out what has been defended and indicate what has not, as well. Consequently, if no other formal documentation is produced from a system assessment, the essential document will be the security requirements. The threat model can be inferred from a well-expressed set of security requirements.

Different stakeholders of the security requirements will need different levels of specificity. The level of specificity that comes out of an assessment, as we noted, depends highly on the capabilities and skill of the functions that will act on the requirements by turning them into implementations. In situations in which the assessor (security architect) will not be involved in the implementation, generating requirements that focus on the goals of the requirement, as opposed to how the requirements will get done, has proven quite effective as requirements are handed off. Even more so, expressing the security value of requirements will avoid technological traps, obsolescence, and dead ends.

When requirements cannot be met, for whatever reason, a risk analysis will help decision makers to prioritize effectively. It's useful to remember that different stakeholders to a risk decision may need to understand the impacts expressed in terms of each stakeholder's risks. We covered this topic somewhat in the chapter on risk (Chapter 4). Although there are many places in the security cycle where risk may need to be calculated and expressed, the prioritization of security requirements against resource constraints, budgets, and delivery schedules remains one of the most common. This is typically a place where the security architect, who has a fundamental understanding of risk and organizational risk tolerance, can offer significant value. When decision makers have built trust that the security function has a method for rating risk in a consistent and fair manner, they may come to depend upon those risk ratings in their decision-making process.

What the security person can't do is continually and repeatedly rate every situation as "high." There always exists the possibility that sophisticated attackers, chaining attack methods and exploits together, with unlimited time and unlimited resources, can turn even minor issues into major impacts. What must be avoided is the tendency to string all the technical "worst-case scenarios" together, thus making nearly every situation a dire one. If the decision maker doesn't simply dismiss the rating out of hand, certainly, over time, she or he will become numb to a repeated barrage of high and critical ratings.

Don't try to get things accomplished by inflating risk ratings. Truly, not every situation has a fair certainty of serious consequences. Some method must be employed to separate the wheat from the chaff, the noise from the signal, the truly dangerous from that which can be tolerated, at least for a while.

Earlier, we proposed some derivative of Just Good Enough Risk Rating (JGERR). I've suggested JGERR not because it's the best or the easiest, but because I've used it, at scale, and I know that it works. Any methodology based on reasonable understandings about what risk is and how it should be calculated will do. Whatever you use, it must produce reasonably consistent results.

One of the keys to helping stakeholders understand how technical computer risks affect their area is to express the risk as it impacts those things that they are charged to defend. For instance, system administrators don't want unauthorized people mucking with their systems. They don't want unauthorized changes, because these changes will make more work for them. Senior management seek to enhance the brand, and they generally don't want bad marks from their peers on their ability to deliver on the organization's goals. Telling senior decision makers that they might have someone inappropriately on a system may not get results. Likewise, telling a system administrator responsible for a few hundred of an organization's thousands of hosts that there might be damage to the company's customers, which might affect the trustability of the brand or lower the stock price, may not get the desired result. Probably neither of these audiences want to know the details of a remote, unauthenticated buffer overflow that allows an attacker to shell out to the operating system command line at high privilege.

Personally, I save the technical details for the background notes at the bottom of the risk assessment. The details are there for anyone to understand how I've arrived at my risk rating. These details can bolster the logic of the risk analysis, if anyone's curious. Instead, I highlight the impact upon the stakeholder's goals and what I believe to be the likelihood of occurrence.

That doesn't mean that I win every risk discussion. I don't. There are many factors that have to be taken into account in these decisions. The likelihood of successful attack is only one consideration. I believe that it's my job to deliver quality information so that security can be considered appropriately. As one vice president told me, "I guess it's my job to stick my neck out." Yeah, it probably is.

It is a truism that in order to build security into a system, security should be considered as early as possible, some security being considered even at the conceptual stage. Certainly, if an architecture is ready for implementation and it does not contain elements to support the security features that the system will require, that architecture must be considered incomplete. Worse yet are designs that make it impossible to build appropriate security functionality.

In fact, assessing an architecture for its security, creating the threat model after the system has been implemented, is usually too late. If the system has many future phases of development, perhaps security requirements can be gathered during one or more of the future phases? On the other hand, if the system is considered essentially complete, then what does one do with unfulfilled security requirements? Probably, one will end up writing security exceptions and risk assumptions. Although these activities do help your organization understand its shifting risk posture, they're essentially nonproductive with respect to the actual system going into production. A risk assumption provides no security value to a real, live computer system.

The various phases of the secure development cycle (SDL) are described in depth in *Core Software Security: Security at the Source*, by James Ransome and Anmol Misra, including the chapter that I contributed (Chapter 9).[4] Some considerable attention was devoted to getting the security of an architecture correct. Security architecture, that is the application of information security to systems, the art of securing systems, is best done as an early part of any development process, as well as being an ongoing conversation as architectures, designs, implementations evolve. Certainly, there is very little that an architectural risk assessment of a system can do if the system cannot be changed.

Consequently, threat modeling is an activity for early in the development cycle. This is not to suggest that threat models are static documents. In fact, in high velocity, or

Agile processes, the breadth and depth of the threat model will emerge throughout the development process. Architectures will change during the development process, which necessitates revisiting the system analysis and threat model as necessary. In Chapter 9 of *Core Software Security: Security at the Source*,[5] I encourage deep engagement between those assessing and creating the security posture of a system and all the other implementers and stakeholders. Agile works best, in my opinion, when security subject matter experts are readily available during the entire process.

The Early Bird Gets to Influence

But there's another, social reason for an early capture of security requirements. People, implementers, and teams need time in order to incorporate the material into their thinking. This is particularly true of complex matters, which security can sometimes be. In a way, it might be said that "the early requirement gets the worm." When designing and building complex systems, the matters that have been in consideration for the longest time will seem like they are an essential part of the system. Surprises, especially surprises about possible technical misses and mistakes, can be difficult to accommodate. This difficulty of accommodation is especially true the later in the development process that issues are discovered.

12.1.3 Getting Security Requirements Implemented

You've performed a thorough analysis of the architecture and built a relevant threat model. The requirements have been written at the correct level for each implementing organization. You're done, right? Sadly, no, the job isn't finished until every requirement has been processed. "Processed" in this context is multifaceted, since for any modestly complex system, there is some possibility that one or more of the requirements cannot be built as specified due to factors outlined above. After we examine strategies for ensuring that requirements are built, we will take a look at some strategies for working through those situations where the requirements must change.

It's A Partnership

Architecture and design represent one important side of delivering a security posture. That's what this book is all about: How does one go about achieving an architecture and an architectural design that represent the security needs for a system? In today's fast-paced, often "agile" software development, how can the secure design be implemented? In my experience, tossing requirements, architectures, and designs "over the wall" and into the creative, dynamic pit of Agile development is a sure road to failure.

Three things, not mutually exclusive by any means, are likely to occur:

1. Artifacts injected into an Agile methodology from the outside will be ignored because the documents appear to be irrelevant.
2. Developments, learnings, and changes during development will cause elements to change, even for assumptions to get invalidated, causing security elements to change drastically or not get accomplished at all.
3. If the Agile team members attempt to adhere strictly to artifacts brought in from the outside and not directly generated by the Agile process, this blind adherance will cause team velocity and creativity to fall, even to stagnate.

The key to Agile is deep engagement based upon trust and personal responsibility. Since Agile processes let designs emerge out of a creative, innovative, self-regulating process, attempts to issue edicts and expect perfect adherence fly directly in the face of how the benefits of Agile are to be reaped. Agile is a direct response to command and control governance processes. Governance based upon strict obedience is bound to fail. Or Agile will fail—these two are diametrically opposed.

Fully Participating

I have seen security and Agile work seamlessly together as a whole, more than once. This process requires that security expertise be seen as a part of the team. That doesn't mean that a security expert needs to be a part of every Sprint, a part of every discussion, although, if possible, a model in which security is another voice on the team will work admirably if the organization can field enough security people to provide this staffing.*

If fielding sufficient staff so that every SCRUM team has an integrated security resource is not possible, the next best thing is for the security expert to be "on call" to several teams who can reach out when there is a security question. This model, in which a single security expert is matrixed across several teams, works best when someone on the Agile team has sufficient security expertise to identify potential security issues. This person doesn't have to be much of a security expert; her or his job is to flag design and implementation problems as they arise, asking for security expert help, as needed. By remaining available to an Agile team, the security person becomes a part of the team's process as designs emerge.

In order to seed an Agile process, there has to be sufficient architecture as well as "armature," if you will—an architecture scaffolding upon which the Agile, creative process can build.† The architecture scaffolding would be created in the usual, water-fall manner before being handed to Sprint teams. Security would, as described in this

---

* Please see Chapter 9 of *Core Software Security: Security at the Source*, by James Ransome and Anmol Misra (CRC Press, © 2014), for a longer discussion of security within Agile processes.
† Noopur Davis told me about the idea of an architecture runway. I believe that she will be publishing about this in the future.

book, participate in this architectural process. This is not different from waterfall system development. The difference is that the architecture team members (who might be working in an Agile manner, as well!) don't attempt to finish the architecture. Enough must be understood so that the Agile teams involved are seeded with sufficient concepts and a set of basic components, those components' likely structure, and some sense of the inter-component relationships. Once Sprints start, the architecture and subsequent design emerges through the Agile process, in partnership between the architects and the implementers. The key is continuing engagement and collaboration.

Remember, whether Agile or not, something (quite likely a few things) will change during development. The longer the development cycle, the more chances for something to change that invalidates or creates problems that challenge the implementation of the security requirements. Rather than taking a binary, win/lose position, I like to remember that there are often multiple ways to achieve a similar security objective. An alternate method may not provide quite the same level of risk mitigation, but it may be sufficient or "just good enough." I'm driving to meet security objectives, not blind adherence to standards. I try to respect the spirit of policy rather than enforcing the letter of it. Problems, as they arise, are creative opportunities. The side effect of flexibility will be the trust of the teams with which you work: This kind of trust, that you will work with rather than against an implementation team, cannot be purchased or empowered by the organization through your formal title and rank. The key is partnership based upon trust and a sense of shared vision and responsibility.

Pain Point Jujitsu

What to do when the implementing group or team simply refuse to fulfill a requirement? I find that outright refusal is fairly rare. This will manifest in different ways, depending upon organization culture and the surrounding culture of the people with whom I'm working.

There's the famous "yes that actually means no." There's the attempt to find some engineering principle that invalidates your position. My favorite stalling tactic is when the engineer who doesn't want to implement a requirement tries to find a hole in my logic or to point out some other vulnerability unrelated to what we're discussing (misdirection). Some cultures are very up front when they disagree with you. But some have a cultural value of appearing to understand without actually agreeing to anything. And some people will more or less revert to however they won arguments as a child in their families of origin. Whatever the strategy—whether passive, assertive, or aggressive—the effect is the same: Security suffers.

It's important that the security assessor has good reasons for each requirement. Data on attack levels, types of attacks, well-known compromises, and the like bolster the reasoning for the requirement. At one job, I learned that our web interfaces received seven million attacks each day. When I had to drive a web security requirement, mentioning that statistic often removed resistance, once people understood that attack was reasonably certain.

Try to couple requirements to specific problems. Encryption across untrusted networks protects against attackers who have access to network routing equipment. Additionally, routing over TCP/IP can change, routes are not guaranteed, and not all the routers on the Internet are run by major telecom companies. Further, can we even trust major telecoms who have invasive government data collection? Once these facts are explained, resistance may dissolve.

If a plain and simple explanation does not work, I use another tactic. I call this "pain point jujitsu."*

> [M]anipulating the opponent's force against himself rather than confronting it with one's own force.[6]

Many times, I have moved through resistance by ferreting out why there's resistance in the first place. Usually, it appears to the implementing group that something they value will be threatened or lost. If I can work their requirements into the security solution, resistance disappears.

I have seen a security need wallow for years, unfulfilled. In one case, a team charged with issuing certificates was keeping private keying materials on servers throughout IT, with every IT administrator having access to the private keys. For years, Infosec complained bitterly about this situation, only to be met with complete refusal to change.

A big mistake is to issue a security requirement that forces another group to interrupt the way it works, the flow that has been carefully crafted over time. In the above example, every solution proposed required the IT team to lose some of their efficiency.

I asked the team how they would solve the problem. I learned that they had a pain point in that they had to handle the certificate requests manually. When we collectively examined the situation, we realized that we could automate the manual process if we moved storage of the keys to a separate, highly restricted server. Bingo! That set of servers was running a month later. Why? Because the implementing team had strong motivation to solve one of their problems while also improving security.

I find out what the refusing team is protecting. Then I either help to achieve the same ends in some way, or improve it while, at the same time, achieving the security objective (around which I try to remain as flexible as possible). Voilà, pain point jujitsu! Figure out what your opponent needs, thus turning them into your ally.

12.1.4 Why Do Good Requirements Go Bad?

One or more requirements may not be implementable as written, possibly not buildable at all. There are many reasons why requirements don't actually get built that have nothing to do with how well the requirements are written. For instance, there may

---

* I beg the forgiveness of readers who are also martial artists. I may be misusing the term, "jujitsu," by misapplying it.

be changes in the business context that cause schedule, budget, or resource shifts. Or assumptions that a design has been built upon may turn out to be incorrect, invalidating requirements based upon those design assumptions.

Let me offer an example: A java application came through that claimed complete adherence to the J2EE* specification that our external, Java runtime was built on. It was a simple blog application, which used a DB for posts (and other data), and the application seemed to consume the infrastructure's authentication. No additional security requirements were added. The application appeared to adhere to the existing security standards.

But when the application was put into the test environment, the assumptions that its security posture was based on were false. The implementing team had not done a thorough enough examination of the actual architecture of the application. It required a local DB, which was disallowed in the infrastructure. In addition, it could not consume infrastructure authentication. Rather, it implemented its own user store, which also stored credentials in clear text. Both of these needs were against the security standards. The situation was a mess; the application could not be deployed as built. People make mistakes. Early mistakes influence what happens downstream.

12.2 Some Thoughts on Governance

Assuming that requirements are written well and at the appropriate level and specificity to enable smart people to deliver them, does that obviate a need for governance? Unfortunately, no. There are a couple of factors that will cause good requirements to go bad.

We've already called out those tough resourcing and priority discussions. When there is more work than can be accomplished within a given timeline, something will have to be dropped. The security advocate may wish to declare, "You can't drop security or the sky may fall in." In other words, there are additional risks incurred when any required security is not delivered. Again, assuming that the requirements are appropriate to the system and its required security posture, leaving a hole in a well-conceived defense-in-depth will, most certainly, add residual risk. The essential governance problem is to make sure that this decision is uncovered and then made at the appropriate level in the organization. Governance is introduced into an SDL or system delivery process not to ensure that everything is perfect, but so that these hard decisions don't slip under the radar and are not made for the convenience of those charged with on-time, under-budget delivery. These people have a built-in conflict of interest and may not have the security and sufficient computer risk background to effectively make these sorts of decisions.

---

* What J2EE represents isn't relevant to this example.

Another way that good requirements go wrong is when the architecture or design has changed during development such that the requirement can no longer be implemented as specified. Sometimes this is a fault of the requirement; remember my story about requiring SSL where SSL couldn't be tied to particular applications? That's a bad requirement (with good intentions, certainly) because it didn't take into account real-world capabilities and architecture of the infrastructure supporting the applications.

But just as often, as the implementation process has unfolded, it will turn out that architecture or design items that security requirements depend on have changed so dramatically that a security requirement can no longer be built, even if expressed in very high-level, goal-oriented language.

Perhaps it turns out that existing equipment between layers is already running very hot (performance or other capabilities close to maximum). In such a situation, separating two components at different trust levels will cause an unacceptable performance degradation. In such a situation, the simple concept of separate network layers may cause serious problems. Hence, the required layering would affect not just the system to be deployed but also impact other critical systems. In any similar scenario, again, governance's task will be to craft an alternate solution that will, at least partially, meet the same security objectives.

Finally, in my experience, smart people sometimes get a bit too clever. If you're being paid to deliver on time, you may think that the shortcut to success is to limit or eliminate as many requirements as possible. Yes, a few people do sometimes try to "game" the system: manipulate the process in order to go around functions that may add items for delivery, as security often does. Governance is there to uncover these instances and to correct them, for the benefit of not just one system delivery but for the organization as a whole.

In each of these cases, governance is there to find the problem. Governance reviews the plan and asks for confirmation that the plan was executed or asks for all divergences. My friend, Eoin Carroll, has even suggested that ATASM be amended with a "G" for governance, "ATASMG".* Without the follow-through that is usually encompassed by governance functions, the security assessment has no assurance that systems are protected by the requirements that were delivered through the assessment.

In my humble but fairly experienced opinion, governance shouldn't attempt to be a policeman, holding projects to the letter of the law, policies, and standards. Rather, the idea is to hunt for solutions that are the best for the organization as a whole. However governance is implemented—reviews, boards, stakeholder sign-off—the people charged with governance concern themselves with the bigger picture. As such, they need to understand how each project fits into and supports a broader vision, perhaps the enterprise architecture, if there is one. Usually a security person governs the security aspects of systems moving through the governance process.

---

* I agree with Eoin that follow-through after the assessment is vital. But I'm not going to add the "G," perhaps as much because I can't pronounce "ATASMG" as for any other reason.

Where priorities must be decided, the "solution" set will have to include risk decisions that include computer security risk, but may also include other risks, as well. We have already discussed decision-making levels. A governance body might be that decision-making authority. Or its task will be to find the right decision makers and present a coherent and digestible picture of the problem to them.

In the case where things have shifted during implementation, the first thing done through governance ought to be some attempt at redesign based upon what is, rather than what was expected. Often, this will "do the trick." As has been noted, there are usually at least a few ways to skin a security cat, to build a reasonable defense-in-depth.

Accounting for those who attempt to bypass security is a tricky issue. If the project is already showing up in the governance review, then, most likely, those driving the project are not attempting a runaround. Mere attendance (unless drastically passive-aggressive) is demonstrable proof of good intentions.

It's those project teams who are not showing up at their security meetings, and not inviting security people to the table, who must be discovered. In large organizations, it's typically fairly easy to fly under the radar, at least for a while, even to the point of deployment. A trick that I've used a few times is to make the ability to deploy have some sign-off or other proof of process participation. At that point, it's usually much too late to remediate anything substantial. But one will catch those attempting to skirt the process, and I have.

We used to assign the DMZ deployment sign-off to a new or very junior architect-in-training. All she or he needed to do was to check our archive of projects that had been engaged—a simple ongoing list. If the project wasn't on the list, it couldn't get deployed. The project manager would then have to back up and engage with a security architect.

At that same environment, if the web application had greater than zero high-severity vulnerabilities from a web scan, or if it had no record of a web scan, it also couldn't be deployed. At that point, a conversation could be started.

Each deploying organization had security architects assigned to it. Thus, there was almost always someone who could be engaged to quickly figure out what had happened and to figure out what, if anything, needed to be done.

We didn't create this safety net to catch projects that had participated in good faith. But I can assure you, the reader, that we'd occasionally catch projects that were attempting to go around the process. For these, the deployment checks were golden.

In order to keep velocity high, the governance check had to be very, very lightweight. Eventually, IT people responsible for deployment were given the project list so that the security engagement check didn't even require a security person (junior or not). It was simply a part of the woodwork. Governance of this nature works best, I think, when it is almost invisible, except for those projects that are out-of-process. And in the certain knowledge that there is a check, both for web vulnerabilities and engagement, only the very brave and/or the foolhardy attempted an end run outside of the process. We let everyone know that these checks were in place.

Summary

The same security architecture patterns turn up time and again, even across seemingly disparate architectures. The high-level solutions to these patterns remain relatively consistent, even when there are local variations in how the solutions are accomplished.

But establishing requirements, even when well expressed and described in ways appropriate for different implementing stakeholders, isn't enough. Security architecture can't end at the point at which the requirements have been delivered. Some things will change. Flexibility and creativity will help ensure that security objectives will be met in the face of change. This is especially true when working in an Agile environment. The key to success is continuing involvement and deep engagement.

Where there is resistance, having concrete examples helps stakeholders understand the reasoning that gives birth to each security requirement. Sometimes, a single, pithy statistic or particular attack example will help others jump on the security bandwagon. For those instances in which there is outright resistance, identifying what is being protected or some other solvable pain point can turn enemies into allies.

No matter what happens, in complex, highly dynamic organizations there must be some governance that security requirements are being fulfilled. This is necessary even when there is a great deal of security buy-in, because there always seems to be at least one clever person who will attempt shortcuts to delivery. There has to be a method that catches these attempts even when they are rare. Otherwise, the defense of other systems may be impacted; there's a due diligence responsibility to ensure that requirements are met or risks raised to decision makers.

References

1. Brooks, F. P., Jr. (1975, 1995). *The Mythical Man-Month: Essays on Software Engineering.* Addison-Wesley.
2. Ramachandran, J. (2002). *Designing Security Architecture Solutions.* p. 48. John Wiley & Sons.
3. Hong, L. and Page, S. E. (Nov. 16, 2004). *Proceedings of the National Academy of Sciences of the United States of America (PNAS),* vol. 101, no. 46, 16385–16389.
4. Ransome, J. and Misra, A. (2014). *Core Software Security: Security at the Source.* Boca Raton (FL): CRC Press.
5. Schoenfield, B. (2014). "Applying the SDL Framework to the Real World" (Ch. 9). In *Core Software Security: Security at the Source.* pp. 255–324. Boca Raton (FL): CRC Press.
6. Takahashi, M. (2005). *Mastering Judo.* Human Kinetics.

Chapter 13

Building an Assessment Program

Security architecture calls for its own unique set of skill requirements in the IT architect.[1]

For security architecture, the main ingredient will be the people and their skills to perform assessments and, ultimately, to craft and then drive security solutions. This comes down to the individuals and how to form your team.

Many books have been written about security policies, managing security programs, and the like. For software security (which does not comprise the whole domain of what's covered by security architecture, as defined in this book), I think that Dr. James Ransome and Anmol Misra's book, *Core Software Security: Security at the Source*, for which I wrote a chapter, will provide a fairly complete program blueprint, including what value security architecture delivers, how its applied, where it fits, and how to manage and govern an architecture program. I set my thoughts down in Chapter 9 of that book, essentially, as follows:

- Pre-architecture engagement fosters discovery and inclusion of required security features.
- For new architectures, security engagement throughout the architecture cycle improves the integration of security requirements (vs. a one-time assessment).
- For existing architectures, only architecture changes need to be assessed and threat modeled.
- Any change in design of security-related portions or components necessitates a security design review.

- Threat models are living documents; they change and, thus, must be kept in sync with changes in architecture and design.
- Agile requires continuous engagement, since architecture and design are iterative and parallel processes (parallel to themselves, to implementation, and to testing).[2]

There is probably no value in my repeating these programmatic thoughts here, beyond the bulleted list, above. Instead, I will focus on the people who will assess and how security architects form into a team.

My goal for my security architecture program is not to be a policing function that enforces a set of laws to which all projects must hew. Although it is important to establish a set of architecture policies and standards, these cannot be immutable laws to which every project must conform or suffer some dire consequences. The world of computer security is far too changeable. And computer security exists as an attribute, an emerging property (or not!) of systems that exist within an extremely rapidly changing context, that is, digital technology. It is simply too difficult to anticipate all circumstances, external and internal, in a policy at this time.

Rather, policy becomes the bedrock to which many systems can mostly conform. The standards that set out how the policy will be enacted create an easy path, a reasonably secure path that can be followed. At the same time, policy and standards help to define areas and situations that will require creativity—those systems, connections, technologies that are necessary but which cannot conform: the exceptions to standards. Sometimes, these exceptions will reduce the security posture. Sometimes, exceptions will offer an opportunity to mature security in new ways or open opportunities to adopt new technologies.

Take, for instance, Agile software development practices. When these were first being widely adopted, like many security practitioners, I was very suspicious and concerned. It seemed that Agile's penchant for changing design during implementation flew in the face of every process we had put into place to ensure that designs would include necessary security. Security assessments and the resulting requirements were heavily front-loaded in our processes; we counted on implementations that followed upfront guidance closely. There seemed to be considerable tension between Agile and security architecture practice, as we had built it (which was as much an industry standard as existed at that time). In any event, the company at which I worked had some teams who were wholeheartedly adopting the SCRUM Agile methodology. A couple of those experiments did, indeed, seem to shift or lose their security requirements through the Agile process. What was I to do?

My first approach was to put governance checks around the Agile process, to circumscribe it with security assurance. Requirements had to be given with a "don't change" caveat. And there was a governance check, with security having a "no go" blocking power once an application was ready for deployment.

I reasoned that if the requirements were clear enough and security had the power to demand change or stop a project before it went live, then due diligence duties to protect the company could be served. I remember presenting about this Agile security approach at a security sharing forum of major companies that I attended regularly. It turned out that my company was the only company with enough Agile to worry over; Agile was not on anyone else's security radar. I was out on the edges, all alone.

Later, I participated in a couple of Agile projects and saw how SCRUM works from the inside. Subsequently, I had SCRUM training (at another organization) and participated in a wholesale convergence of an IT delivery department to SCRUM. Through these experiences, I came to appreciate the Agile approach, the ideals that underlie SCRUM, and the merit to be reaped from Agile adoption. Perhaps you can say that I've been "agilized"; I'm certainly no longer afraid of Agile; I've seen how valuable it can be even for security, when Agile is done well.

The point is that Agile did not fit with the first organization's policies nor its standards. Agile was exceptional. Still, adopting Agile proved to have great value, both to that organization and, ultimately, to our security posture, as well, once I (and we) had allowed ourselves to step into the challenge and reap the opportunity offered. If we had instead taken an enforcement line, the opportunity would have been lost, and, quite possibly, we also would have lost those relationships, the trust, and influence that allowed us to be effective. A law and order attitude would have been disastrous.

If a team is trying to "game" the system, to avoid security assessment and requirements, governance is there to try and avert disaster. But I try not to mistake my due diligence responsibility to the overall security posture and risk tolerance that I hold with a blind adherence to a set of documents that I know will always be incomplete in the face of change.

I'm not suggesting that we throw away policies and standards. If you've come this far in this book, I hope that you understand the importance of these. But I don't want to use these to stunt creativity and innovation. Rather, these are there as a comparator against reality in order to identify the deviant and the exceptional.

My friend and colleague, Ian Savage, says, "It's like community policing. You can sit around waiting for bad things to land in your lap, or you can proactively try to prevent problems." I'd add that not only can we try to "prevent problems," but we can proactively look for opportunities for growth and change for the better.

In this chapter, I will cover four areas:

1. Program relationship building
2. Acquiring and building a team
3. Outputs of an assessment process
4. Measuring effectiveness

I've tried to keep these topics focused on the subjects not usually covered in other works on security programs—that is, policy, organizational structure, and the relationship between security architecture and other aspects of an information security program. These subjects, I believe, have been abundantly explained multiple times and from multiple angles. Due to my focus on that which doesn't usually get described, the following will necessarily be incomplete. I assume that many of you, the readers, either already have running programs or have previously been introduced to the other programmatic aspects that I have not addressed.

13.1 Building a Program

A program cannot be built solely from top down, or completely from the bottom up, or only across a peer network, but rather all of these must come together in parallel, and also such that each vector of program development supports and strengthens the other dimensions. You will want to work on each of these dimensions at the same time. In my experience, there is no proper linear order, though it is true that, without senior management buy-in, very little can successfully take place.

13.1.1 Senior Management's Job

Senior Management must buy into an assessment program, but there must be more than lip service. The program will require senior management's ongoing support in three ways.

First, if there is any hierarchy in your organization at all, there must be a clear directive from the top that security architecture assessments, and, most importantly, the requirements that are output from the threat model must be completed. That is, security requirements must be empowered, which is the same thing as saying that the architects who generate the requirements have been empowered by the organization to design security into the organization's systems.

Senior management communications can be made through their usual channels: newsletters, at organizational all-hands meetings, blog postings, through the organization's hierarchy as "pass downs." The key trick here is that this cannot be messaged just once through one, single media channel. Various formats and vectors combine for a more powerful delivery. No one on the system delivery teams should be surprised when a security architect shows up and asks to see the architecture. This message doesn't have to be constant, but like all similar process-oriented communications, it will need to be repeated regularly.

But there's more that senior management must do; they must stand behind the empowerment. Smart people will push back. Sometimes, the non-security people will have the best course for the company in mind. Remember, we all make mistakes; everyone is fallible.

When there is conflict between the security requirements and other considerations, we have already discussed escalation. If senior management always delegates the decisions back downwards, or worse, typically ignores security concerns, one of two things is going on. Possibly, security's manner of explaining the situation and organizational risk may be faulty. (This work has previously delved into how to express risk and to whom.) But if the risks are clear and senior decision makers simply ignore the situation entirely, then it is likely that the assessment program isn't truly empowered. In that case, the program cannot be successful without full buy-in from the top. It would be time to re-empower the program.

Finally, when push comes to shove around resource priorities, without full support from those who hire, fire, and assign tasks, it doesn't make any difference what has been declared; all those downward communications about the importance of designing security into systems have been lip service, if none of the security requirements will actually be accomplished. Security requirements lead directly to tasks. Those tasks will need people and compute time in order to be accomplished. The best organizational "empowerment" is useless without time, on the ground, to get real tasks completed. Security, like any other organizational goal, has to have sufficient resources for delivery.

13.1.2 Bottom Up?

As soon as the top layers have endorsed a security architecture program, you can begin to find people throughout the organization and, especially, task-oriented people who not only support security, but are interested and motivated to build security into the systems that they create, deploy, and maintain. The "friendlies" comprise the resource base with whom your security architects will work. Your supporters will accelerate your program simply by taking security architect input seriously. The power that a couple of motivated individuals can have on the tone of a group, and that can even ripple out beyond a single team throughout your teams and groups, never ceases to amaze me. It just takes a few individuals, as long as these individuals are supportive in a visible way.

It never hurts to have support, no matter who offers it. However, the classic, introverted engineer who hardly ever speaks to anyone isn't going to have this ripple effect. You need to find people who will actively express their support. For instance, a single security architect sitting with about a dozen other members of a project team is just a voice in the crowd. But if the project manager, an engineer, and another architect actively engage in the security conversation, this has a profound effect on the entire team. Even those who are resistant to security requirements (for whatever reason) won't be able to dismiss the security conversation out of hand.

In other words, when starting the program, plan for time for you and whoever is working with you to get out into the implementation teams and meet people, talk to them about security, find out what they think. More importantly, uncover fears about security, perhaps even poor experiences in the past. The latter is critically important. If you're working with a pre-existing social debt, you need to understand what the history is, how the debt was accumulated, and what pain points originated with this debt.

For instance, at one organization at which I worked, a past administration had declared that every change to a software product had to be threat modeled. This statement alone will garner plenty of resistance: Most engineers will spot the flaw in the logic immediately. That is, not all changes engender a change to the threat model. Cosmetic changes, in particular, typically do not change a threat model at all.

But even worse, in the past program, threat models were considered so secret, so proprietary, that the people running the program thought that the threat modeling and its methodology were too secret to share. One manager told me that when he asked how he was to threat model, he was told that it was a secret. Whatever that administration was thinking, and I wasn't there, so I can't say, it was clear from talking to the group of managers in the meeting where this was said, that they had rejected entirely the concept of threat modeling as a nonproductive activity.

Obviously, my job was to undo that social debt; I had to overturn the organizational resistance to security architecture, in general, and threat modeling, in particular. Since you've presumably worked through at least some of this book, you'll know that I do not believe that every change requires threat modeling. In fact, such across-the-board, simplistic generalizations will immediately be spotted as falsehoods. But further, a lack of transparency—an opaque program—for whatever reason, had moved the probably neutral to a completely resistant position.

By visiting teams and simply listening, one can learn a great deal. That's almost always the first thing that I do when I join a new organization: I go on a "fact-finding mission." Is there any history with security architecture? Have there been failures? And if so, why? What are people currently doing to achieve security objectives? Where do those security objectives originate? Who are the people who are engaged in security and what are their reasons for engagement? If I can, I try to identify those who are resistant, even potential enemies.

Although I prefer to think of everyone I meet as neutral, as a potential supporter, I am not, I hope, so naïve as to dismiss the possibility that some people are opposed to security in general. Furthermore, not everyone likes me; some people with whom I interact will resist me and my program simply because, for some reason, they don't like me or my style or the shape of the program in general. Identifying resistance helps me better formulate a plan to work around it or through it, as much I can.

In essence, during the very early stages of setting up a program, I circulate through as many of the teams that are tasked with delivery as I possibly can. I try to keep an open mind and put my agenda aside so that I can listen and fully understand the situation into which a security architecture program will be inserted. At the same time, I try to identify people who are supportive of the cause, and I also try to identify those who may have had bad experiences in the past or who are resistant.

As assessments take place, I find reasons to interact with my supporters. In other words, I "network" heavily and continuously. This is the outreach part of the work of building a program. I actively seek opportunities to interact that go beyond "your team will need to perform this task." I perform favors as I can. I develop relationships regardless of any particular person's position in the organizational hierarchy; I ignore rank as much as humanly possible. Every potential supporter is golden and worthy of my attention.

After an architecture assessment and threat model, there are likely to be security requirements. And that's where I need every friend I can find. There are many reasons why critical security requirements are going to be difficult to implement. In order to solve problems, I will need at least a faction of supporters, unless I get a majority on a team who are willing to enter into the search for workable solutions. Grassroots support engenders solution-oriented team discussion. I believe that solutions created and supported by implementation teams are much easier to bring to fruition than escalations seeking senior management mandates. Grassroots support will multiply and amplify the efforts of your security architects many times over.

13.1.3 Use Peer Networks

Just as important as the grassroots network is your peer network across line management, senior architects and other technical leaders, and directors (i.e., middle management). When push comes to shove, these are the people who are going to help sort and solve problems. For many decisions that involve risk escalations or risk assumptions, management is going to be empowered in many organizations to make the call and to work through conflicts in their organizations. A hostile director can absolutely kill the security architecture for that organization. I like to say that people don't have to like me, but they have to respect me and my program. This is particularly true for middle management (usually at the director level).

If you are the director tasked with booting a security architecture and assessment program, your peers will be the network through which most of the day-to-day resourcing and priority issues are set. Although it is true that line management often takes care of these task-setting activities, if they run into trouble, it's to your peer network that they will turn. It is through your peer network that you will need to influence priorities.

Just as important as middle management, senior technical leaders strongly influence the success or failure of a security architecture program. First, security architecture fits in as a portion of an overall architecture program and practice. That is, security is a specialty architecture practice that influences, shapes, and changes a system architecture within many organizations. Architects envision systems. Security architects envision the security of those systems. Although it is possible that both roles can be fulfilled by the same person, these are usually different people with separate but highly intersecting bodies of practice. It is a disaster if the architects and, especially, architecture leaders are not supportive of security architecture. In this case, nothing will get done.

Typically, the first security architect is someone who is quite senior. Her or his peer network will be the other technical leaders: senior engineers, senior architects, distinguished engineers and architects, enterprise architects, and the like. Your most senior security architect will need to have the support of some, preferably most (best is all) of the technical leaders who could be involved in understanding and delivering security requirements.

And so it goes, down the seniority hierarchy and through the grade levels. Normally, even beginning security architects are already established architects in their own right. These people will need to have the support of their peer network on the teams for which they are delivering assessments and requirements.

Considering who comprises these peer networks, I try not to forget line management, as they are tasked with delivering real systems. The same is true for project managers who are driving projects. These two roles (and similar, whatever they're called in the organization) will have to invite security in and will have to make sure that requirements are included in the deliverables. If line managers and project/program managers are unaware of the importance of their role, no matter how wonderful your assessments, threat models, and requirements are constructed, again, nothing will likely get done. Furthermore, a project manager who doesn't understand the sophisticated nature of security solution discussions may not allot a sufficient amount of time for creative thinking. Security will only be given five minutes on the agenda when it actually needs forty-five minutes. Again, the result of this will be that security requirements that are difficult are likely to get postponed, perhaps indefinitely.

In order to fully support a security assessment and threat modeling process, line management and project managers will need to have a clear process that is well defined. Each step along the way will need to be executed in some more or less linear time order, or the project can't be project managed. There is resistance built into this problem, as we have seen that there tends to be some retracing of steps during the "peel the onion" assessment (assessment can be an organic and recursive process). For project managers who are more comfortable with strict linearity, these horizontal movements and retracings will produce tension and anxiety.

Much has been written about where in a system delivery process architecture assessment belongs. I set my own thoughts down in Chapter 9 of *Core Software Security: Security at the Source*, by James Ransome and Anmol Misra.[3] However, the entire book contains a lot of material about where these tasks take place: early. This is obviously not the only book on this subject. Early security assessments within a development process should be well-trodden territory. Remember the very first quote of this book calling for early architectural assessment for security?

You'll want to make the timing of activities perfectly clear in your delivery process or project lifecycle. There isn't much that can actually be done when the security assessment takes place a week, or worse, a day before going live. Rarely have I seen decision makers stop deployment, even in the face of the critical security misses discovered during late assessment.

Generally, architecture tasks take place in the early phases of a project or system delivery cycle. The precise timing will depend on the sort of projects you're delivering as well as the rest of your lifecycle—that is, whether you're using waterfall, Agile, or something else. Whatever your process, at least some of the architecture will happen early, as should the beginning of the security assessment. Your project management function will need to understand the lifecycle and where the security assessment fits into it, in detail, in order to support your assessment program and your security architects.

Program effectiveness can be increased while also accelerating the speed of adoption by broadcasting program successes through the peer network. People like to hitch their wagons to anything that is achieving success. It is said that success breeds success. Your partners may view their future success through a lens of your current wins.

Constantly broadcasting one's own or one's team's success may seem like bragging. It isn't just the successes of your own team that you can broadcast but, additionally, those places where your partner teams have successfully implemented security requirements. Indeed, if you can broadcast those sales that have been closed because the security features that customers needed were already built into products, you demonstrate the importance of security as a differentiator in the marketplace. Dr. James Ransome and I successfully used this tactic to drive security deeply into an organization's product management function.

Before James and I arrived on the scene, customer security inquiries were handled out-of-band and out of sight. The product management function for that product didn't receive important information about what customers' security teams were demanding, so few customer security demands were being worked into new and updated offerings, and security was all but invisible. That was the goal of a previous security organization: to make security as invisible as possible.

However, that product was sold (as a SaaS) to many enterprises. Enterprises can be very finicky about giving their data to third parties. The enterprise security teams would be brought into the sale to perform a due diligence review of the prospective vendor and the offering. Of course, the customer security teams would try to make the product fit their internal policies and expectations. In order to meet enterprise policy requirements, the product had to have certain security features. But those requests weren't being captured in an orderly fashion; product management didn't have the correct information about what security their enterprise customers needed.

James and I realized that there was a gold mine lying undiscovered in these security team to security team conversations. We got our security team, mostly James and myself, involved in these sales discussions. But we included the sales team and the product managers, as well. We developed security marketing literature and other artifacts to demonstrate how security was implemented in the product. By articulating more clearly how security was built, we were able to head off customer attempts to redesign security solutions for something they didn't really understand fully.

As enterprise sales started to close without previous security hitches, our partner teams and our peer network, in particular, took notice.

Although these tactics won't eliminate every bit of resistance in a peer network, in this case it was as if we had supplied lubrication to our working with those people who controlled the direction that our product was heading in, that is, the product management team. In addition, these successes went viral through the sales department as sales (and marketing) began to realize how important security was in closing the big enterprise sales. By networking on top of those first few successes, we were able to achieve architecture engagement in the product development lifecycle. We further reaped the rewards of the confidence that salespeople had in the security team's knowledge and business understanding. This confidence rippled throughout the organization, across our peer network, as well as downwards through our peers' organizations. Upper management took notice that the security team was making a difference.

When things go sideways between security architects and another organization or team, it is my practice to take full responsibility for whatever part I may have had or my team has had in the problem. Of course, I don't think it's wise to broadcast these mistakes throughout the various networks—upwards, across, and downwards. Still, for those involved, transparency and a strong sense of accountability goes a long way to building trust. It's not that mistakes happen that is the problem; mistakes are bound to occur. We are, after all, merely human. Rather, your leadership and that of your architects will be judged on how you handle mistakes—yours and any that crop up in the work. Responsibility and accountability for one's actions are a mark of a leader. And make no mistake about it: Security architects must be leaders.

Your security architects may not have people reporting to them, so they may not officially be "people managers." Because part of an architect's job is to influence, and part of the job will be to establish security direction for the systems under assessment, security architects are generally going to be leaders in their organization, at least within the scope of that influence, whatever it may be. Because of this aspect of the role, that is, helping systems achieve an organizational security posture, training in many aspects of leadership is critical.

In my leadership roles, I've consistently been asked to help evaluate the performance of peers, partners, and those for whom I was supposed to be offering leadership. My HR training in these aspects of the management role has come in very handily.

For a practice such as the security architecture as described in this book, support and, ultimately, buy-in in will need to come from the organizational decision makers, the grassroots, and across your network. That is, building a network of support, even when it's relatively few in number—upwards, across, and downwards—will greatly accelerate adoption and follow through for your security assessment program. Even with relatively few numbers of supporters, the organization will achieve that "tipping point" that spells success for the entire program. Communications are important. Repeated communication will likely be a necessity.

In my communication plan, I include obtaining peer and grassroots evaluation and feedback. I don't necessarily take every bit of feedback exactly as it is expressed. But even wild accusations and projections often have a kernel or grain of truth hiding within them. In this way, I can tailor the program to the organization's needs more precisely. Every organization has its local idiosyncrasies. And every organization has its limitations and constraints: Organizations develop a unique and individual culture. General statements such as those in this chapter have to be tuned to the way business is transacted in each organization. I can't know what that tuning is without finding out how people in the organization are used to doing things, what the expectations are, and what the perceptions are about my team, and then finding out about interactions around security.

Just as important as the actual feedback, is a sense of participation, a sense of co-creation. I've been privileged to start security architecture programs several times in my career (as of this writing, four to be precise). This implies that there'll be a sense of new-ness, a sense of innovation, a sense of something to be created. I invite my peer network and the grassroots to help shape the program, though not in its entirety, of course. As you can see from this book, I do have some very definite ideas. Still, there are always plenty of choices, some new problems that crop up in a complex program like security architecture. There's always room for creativity and synthesis.

This sense of participation in something new and interesting is infectious. Rather than trying to be personally charismatic (I'm not!), I make the program, the work, charismatic. People like to have a little fun, enjoy a little creativity at work. Security architecture is so complex, and there are so many variables to getting things done, it's a perfect test bed for innovation. As I've stressed above, mistakes are going to happen anyway. If I can keep disasters from happening, while at the same time, I'm willing to try different ways of achieving ends even if these have some risk of failing, this invitation to play attracts supporters and helps to build towards a tipping point to a success-ful, self-sustaining security architecture program.

Figure 13.1 is a whimsical visual representation of the social networks that need to be cultivated for program success. As shown in the figure, socialize and keep evangelizing and socializing; stay on message. Michele Guel says, "Say it three times, then find a different way to say it." Prepare to perform years of repeated messaging. The effort to move a major public website's authentication from HTTP to HTTPS was the work

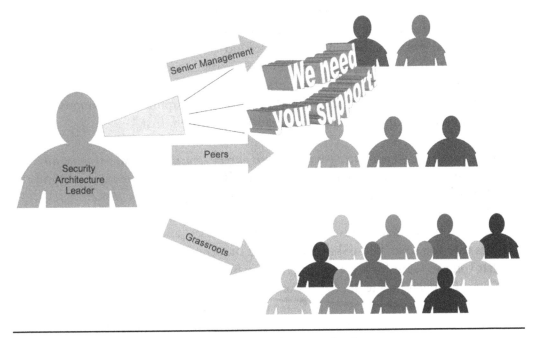

Figure 13.1   Socializing the program across the organization.

of three different security architects and took eight years. It's important not to give up when a security requirement is the "right thing to do," even in the face of significant resistance. Eventually, conditions will ripen such that that the "right thing" can happen.

13.2 Building a Team

Since I have stressed the experience-based quality of the practice of securing systems, it will be obvious that the people who perform this work are a determiner of success. It isn't just the technical skill of the practitioners that is important, but their so-called "people skills" that are an essential factor, as well. Indeed, attitude may be a crucial ingredient. A can-do, optimistic, "we can solve this problem" attitude can even be charismatic, drawing others into solutions, attracting them into the work of securing systems.

How does one go about finding deep technical skills coupled to a love of people and a cheerful, optimistic, solution-oriented attitude? Don't forget that you will have to work closely with each of your team members. (Your personality is important, too!)

I've enumerated what may sound like an impossible combination of skill and temperament. You may notice that I've not added, "has a similar approach"? Diversity among your team members will also be critical. In my experience, motivated people who are dedicated to doing "the right thing" don't need to all be similar. In fact, diversity of approach, style, thought patterns, and work style are not obstacles to overcome but rather gifts to be encouraged.

My teams typically encompass many fairly divergent cultures, most of the world's major religions, every stripe of political viewpoint, and any number of divergent value systems. All of this diversity makes for a rich stew out of which are born innovative approaches and synthetic solutions—if leadership can find value in a wide range of ideas and personality types and then demonstrate that encouragement. I believe that building a truly global, high-functioning team must start with the first person or two, usually those who will be "leaders" of the team. To paraphrase the famous saying, "Physician, heal thyself," we might say, "Leader, lead thyself, first."

> *Authentic leaders demonstrate a passion for their purpose, practice their values consistently, and lead with their hearts as well as their heads. They establish long-term, meaningful relationships and have the self-discipline to get results. They know who they are.*[4]

Again, numerous material is available on how to select and interview people for the qualities that you seek. Those skills are beyond the scope of this book. Instead, assuming that you can select for the above qualities, what do you do, next?

When starting a new team, I focus on relationships first, and not just my relations with other team members. I work to foster trust and empathy between team members. I'm not very goal oriented. In fact, one architect told me, years later, that he initially thought that I "couldn't lead," because I rarely forced decisions on the group. Rather than giving solutions to the group, I often let the group decide, even in opposition to my (rather more experienced) ideas. I let mistakes occur,* followed by their natural consequences. This was all purposive, with the full knowledge and support of my chain of management. Several years later, that same architect told me, "Brook, you made a home for us." That was one of the highest compliments anyone has ever paid to me.

As that team's capabilities and cohesion flowered, so did their ability to climb mountains and conquer seemingly unsolvable problems. The secret was and is in building relationships, first and foremost, while, at the same time, avoiding being overly pressured by goals, at least at first. Measurable objectives come in once the team starts to function and can do so effectively without its "leaders." The team will have become self-sustaining.

If I'm starting from scratch, I have to find that first person. This is harder if the work is already piling up, the architectures are complex, and the velocity is rapid. I've had two situations exactly like this. My first team member will be key to an ability to add lots of different skills sets, experience, and approaches. That first person's temperament and communication skills are as important as the candidate's technical skill.

One of the first additions to the team must foster a spirit of lively interchange directed towards synthetic and creative solutions. This interchange must demonstrate that disagreement does not mean a loss of relationship, but rather a strengthening of trust. If the two of us can set an example of motivation, engagement, and an ability to work through conflict, this will create an environment conducive to diversity. Although it's great to get a first or second addition who is your equal, as long as these people are open to learning, and to being personally empowered, I believe that the right template will be set.

At one job, I had to build a team from absolute zero; I was the only member of the team, though the work was enough for five to eight architects. My first hire did not fit the above profile; that person deferred to my experience far too often to foster an engaged and empowered atmosphere. We then brought in a very junior person to train, which made matters worse.

Understanding this unfolding dynamic, and how it would stunt the growth of the group, I begged my management for a senior person. I then talked a friend of mine, Ove Hansen, who is a very experienced security architect into joining the team. I knew Ove could find the holes in my logic and that Ove wouldn't hesitate to challenge my ideas (though professionally and politely, of course). Within about six weeks of bringing Ove onto the team, the dynamic of the group shifted to lively discussions and synthetic solution sets. The team needed an example; they needed a sign that disagreement with me was not only tolerated but would be encouraged.

---

* Unless, of course, I saw a major train wreck unfolding. Then I would step in and protect the organization from disaster.

13.2.1 Training

How does an organization train people so that they can perform these difficult, architectural tasks? Software security expert Gary McGraw says:

> *For many years I have struggled with how to teach people . . . security design. The only technique that really works is apprenticeship. Short of that, a deep understanding of security design principles can help.*[5]

In *Core Software Security*, I amplified McGraw's wisdom:

> *McGraw's statement implies that, in order to build a qualified team, each organization will either have to invest in sufficiently capable and experienced practitioners who can also mentor and teach what they do, or hire consultants who can provide appropriate mentorship. Neither of these is likely to be cheap. As of this writing, there is a dearth of skilled security architects, much less the subset of those who can and want to impart what they know to others. The architecture and design skills necessary to an SDL program are probably going to require time to build, time to find key leaders, and then time for those leaders to build a skilled practice from among the available and interested people at hand. In one such long-running mentorship, even highly motivated junior people have taken as long as two or three years before they could work entirely independently and start to lead in their own right. This is a significant time investment.*[6]

Up until Michele Guel's Security Knowledge Empowerment program ("SKE," National Cyber Security Award winner, 2011), security training tended to focus on engineering skills, not security architecture skills. Up until about 2010, as far as I know, Gary McGraw hit the nail on the head. That is, security architects learned by following a seasoned security architect through her or his day. That's the way I was trained.

First, the candidate "shadows" the teacher through any number of projects—watching, learning, perhaps trying out ideas under the tutelage and observation of the practitioner. Then there comes a period when the candidate is shadowed by the teacher. In this way, the new security architect has someone to turn to. And, also important for any organization, if the seasoned security architect believes that something dreadful will happen, they can step in and prevent catastrophe. Finally, if all goes as planned, and it often doesn't, the new architect works more independently with regular mentorship and coaching by the teacher for a period of time, often as along as a couple of years.

Almost every architect I know of learned in precisely this manner. The problem is that not everyone learns by following someone around. What if you're assigned to a mentor who you cannot work well with? What happens then? Most likely, the seasoned architect will continue in the role, but the candidate will seem to have failed. I've long thought that this is entirely unfair to talented people who have other learning styles. Not everyone likes to follow me around. Sometimes, even I don't like to follow me around.

Guel's SKE program had an architecture section. Michelle, Vinay Bansal, and I built a curriculum and then attempted to teach it to the class. The class consisted of a group of interested coworkers who had volunteered to attend for the 40 weeks and do the homework. Some of those students went on to a security architect role. More importantly, we proved to ourselves that it is possible to impart at least some of the skills of security architecture in a classroom setting by using lectures, case studies, and class discussion, as opposed to following Michele, Vinay, or Brook around for a couple of years.* We did follow up with formal mentorship for those who were going on to a security architect role.

Today, there are at least a few online videos from conferences describing threat modeling. There have been a couple of books on the subject, as well. And a couple of vendors offer video classes. Still, I believe that there is no substitute for experience, especially when that experience can be held in a container of relative safety.

So what does classroom training look like?

Obviously, you could work through the material in this book. Possible classroom use is one of the purposes that I hope this book will serve. Or use any methodology that works.

Assuming that the students already have some experience in computer security and with system design, I teach in the following manner:

- Introduce security assessment as a part of security architecture
- Introduce security architecture in its entirety, but with a focus on security assessments, in particular
- Delve into understanding architectures
- Practice architectural decomposition and following data flows
- Introduce the ATASM process
- Analyze architectures and present case studies

After students have some feel for what architecture analysis for security and threat modeling is, I've had a lot of success facilitating participatory ATASM sessions. I gather as many of the people who will interact with the threat model on the team as possible. I don't limit the session to just the security architects and those who are directly responsible for implementing the security requirements.

I like to keep these participatory sessions as open as is practical, given constraints of time and proprietary intellectual property protection needs. Even a test engineer who won't be involved in the threat model in any active way will conduct better tests if she or he has some context for attack surfaces when testing. Then, the testing is more likely to, at least in part, prove the mitigations that have been built (i.e., above and beyond the security tests that have been placed into the formal test plan). The entire project benefits from the exposure that active participation in a threat model gains.

I walk through the ATASM process precisely as this book is laid out:

---

* I don't know if SKE marks "the" beginning for formal security architecture pedagogy. But SKE certainly represents "a" beginning.

- Learn the architecture
- Gather all threats (brainstorm)
- Talk about which threats are relevant to this system as it will be deployed for its purposes in the organizational context
- Discover as many attack surfaces as possible
- Consider existing security controls and possible mitigations

The goal of the session isn't to produce a complete threat model. I will often move onto the next step, in consideration of available time, so long as a deep conversation around a particular step in the process has occurred. I don't provide the answers to these questions, though I may fill in towards the end of the discussion to highlight areas that haven't already been covered by the participants. The goal of the class is active participation, nothing else. I want the people present to consider the issues, to delve into the complexities that building a threat model inevitably encounters. I'm after rich discussions, not particular engineering results.

At the end of the class, there may or may not be a complete threat model. That's OK. Even if the threat model is incomplete, the participants now have the skills to finish it.

I know that this format works very well. I've done as many as twenty-four of these in a four-week period, in many locations, spread across distinctly different cultures. Engineers and architects love to consider weighty problems. All that's really required from the facilitator is a willingness to start the ball rolling on each step and, sometimes, a little encouragement to participants.[*]

Once candidates have completed whatever formal training is offered, I then employ a period of "shadowing" an experienced and proven security architect. I described shadowing above.

One of the reasons that organizations perform security assessments is to help ensure that systems don't go live such that the system reduces the security posture of the organization in some fundamental way. This is a "due diligence" responsibility. In other words, the security assessment is, in part, an attempt to keep "bad things" from happening through the implementation and deployment of insecure computer systems. This role imbues the security assessment with a fairly heavy responsibility for the safety of the organization. As such, entrusting this responsibility to someone without the experience to perform the duty might lead to a disaster. The "safety container" is the peer review and coaching (and empowerment) of one or more practitioners with enough experience to carry the load appropriately.

Consequently, except for very small organizations that can get by with just one or two security architects, I favor putting someone in the role first who can carry it off properly. That first practitioner, who has to be good enough at security assessments and

---

[*] If there are managers present, I insist that anything said in the room can't be used against the participants, or for performance review of participants. Or managers have to leave the room. It has to be safe to experiment, or these classes won't work.

threat models to prevent the truly disastrous from unfolding, can then create a container in which others can make some mistakes and gain experience.

But for those readers who feel like they've been placed in the role without having had sufficient experience, I would counsel that your management and their management need to understand the risk the organization has taken.

You will help yourself immeasurably by finding any resources, security or otherwise, who have some architectural experience who can then be your peer reviewers on difficult decisions. Peer review is always a critical part of a good program.

Furthermore, if you find yourself placed in the security architect role and you don't have the background and experience that's been described in this book, I would also suggest that you find seasoned practitioners from whom you can get the mentorship that you will need. Furthermore, you will need an experienced practitioner with whom you can discuss the problems that you encounter and from whom you can receive the necessary peer review that every security architect needs. Again, transparency with your management is critical, since you are likely to make some mistakes along the way. I've certainly made my share; I've made some massive misses and miscalculations. Luckily, my management have always supported me so that I've learned from those experiences.

For others who will have a larger team, for security architects who are working in a team, and, of course, for those who have to build and manage a team of high-functioning security architects, the next section will explain some of the things I think are critical to support your team.

13.3 Documentation and Artifacts

Security assessments must produce some documentation. Personally, I'm a big fan of keeping documentation as lightweight as possible. However, some organizations have more heavy-duty documentation requirements. Any organizations subject to certifications will have to produce sufficient evidence should the certification require proof that systems have been through a security assessment.

There's a joke that goes around the architecture community about 250-page architecture documents that get put into binders, stuck on shelves, and never get read, much less used. This is often called "ivory tower architecture." Unless your organization has a need for these sorts of documents and you can afford to pay architects to deliver binders full of architectural descriptions, such a practice seems like a waste of time.

At the other end of the spectrum, there are teams and organizations (usually small organizations) that produce very little, if any, documentation. I've talked about "eyeball-to-eyeball security." If your organization can make do with informal methods, by all means, only do what's necessary.

In my experience, the minimum documentation necessary to prove that a security assessment has taken place, and to achieve implementation of the security requirements, will be the security requirements document. If nothing else is produced, the requirements document can even imply a threat model. That is, the security requirements document can stand as evidence not only of the assessment, but of the threat model from which the requirements were derived.

If the security requirements artifact is the sole document produced, then I believe it should be as complete as possible. When I set out security requirements, I include those requirements that have already been met or built so that the document makes a complete statement about the security posture of the system.

I try not to make assumptions about what the document reader may or may not know about the system. And furthermore, striving for completeness allows me to hand off an assessment to another security architect with a fairly comprehensive set of documentation about what's already been done and what needs to be done in the future.

As you build your program, the first document that I would focus on is the security requirements document. There are several lists of requirements that have been provided in previous chapters, as well as a discussion of the requirements document itself and the differing requirement expressions that may be necessary for the various stakeholders in the documents. I offer these as possibilities to consider for your organization.

The second document that can be useful outside the security department is the threat model itself. Architects work with various abstract representations of the systems they are building. As we have done in some of the diagrams in this book, attack surfaces and any required security systems can be notated on pre-existing architecture diagrams. That is, integrate security into the evolving architectural artifacts being produced through the architecture process. The threat model isn't (and perhaps shouldn't be?) a separate and distinct diagram that is completely different from those that serve other architectural and design purposes. This will help all the other architects and other engineering functions understand the complete system, including security. In addition, security architects will be using the documents that partner architects already understand; security will be "speaking" the local architecture "language." I try to avoid making security the "special child" or stepchild on the side.

I use whatever representations (as long as they're sufficient representations) are already in use to create the system's threat model. In this way, the threat model that is produced isn't for the security team; it's a living document from which everyone involved can engineer. The goal is not so much about producing a document for security, but rather integrating security into the ongoing architecture process. If there is a requirement for evidence of the threat model and the attacks that have been considered, those could be an adjunct list to the pictorial threat model. In the first example assessment, just such a list was given in this book. Or the attack vectors that have been considered and are to be mitigated could be placed into the requirements document.

There are numerous, creative ways to produce architecture artifacts that are understood and useful to the architects and engineers working on a system. At the same time, the same documents are evidence of the threat model that has been considered, should your organization need such evidence.

Presumably, the organization's architecture practice produces some documentation of the architecture that's being produced? I prefer to use these documents, rather than introducing something different that has to be learned by those who will need to understand the threat model and work from it. My friends at Cigital, Gary McGraw and Jim DelGrosso ("Del"), introduce a threat model template to their consulting engagements. When helping others to "climb in" to the complex process of threat modeling, it may help to offer some structure and linearity to the process? Obviously, going through the ATASM process is intended to offer a "template" of sorts for security assessments. That or any other methodology can be turned into a template that helps guide assessors in some structured manner. I personally haven't felt the need to introduce templates. But I've been asked for them from time to time.

If I was going to introduce a template, I would try to avoid creating checklists of threat agents, attack methodologies, and input types unless, for your organization and your systems, these remain fairly static and discrete. For the organizations in which I've worked, such a checklist approach is bound to cause some attack surface or other to get missed. Many times, I have attended a review of a threat model and have been able to find an obvious attack vector that others had missed because they were following a rigid methodology, working with a limited tool. So I have some fear based upon my experiences that it's too easy to miss something important by doggedly following a predetermined checklist. Instead, I want to empower people's creativity and horizontal thinking. The dictum "think like an attacker" means just that: We, the defenders (the assessors), have to be as creative and inventive as digital attackers are. Attacker creativity is the current situation in which our assessments are taking place. We can't ignore that or we will be well behind attacker methodologies.

Rather than offering checklists and templates, my methodology encourages people to follow every data path, check every flow of interaction, and identify all the inputs in systems. This approach does lead to peel-the-onion scenarios, which inevitably lead to backtracking through the ATASM process as new inputs and flows are discovered. I do find that this process does contain a map for completeness, if followed to conclusion, leaving no stone unturned.

I'll note that I have the greatest respect for McGraw and DelGrosso and their work; I'm sure that the template is an effective tool. If that's a better approach for your organization, by all means then, as your third artifact you might create a template for the ATASM process, or whatever methodology for assessment that you choose to use.

I will note that a requirements document will change its specificity depending upon where in your lifecycle requirements are to be consumed. For instance, at the initial requirements gathering, before an architecture has been created, security requirements will tend to be quite high level: authentication and authorization, protection of the message bus in the internal network, what have you.

As developers begin to code specific parts of the design, they will need to know precisely what to code; they will need the precise algorithms that can be encoded. At this later stage, security requirements are going to be quite specific and detailed. Basically, for implementation, requirements become designs and engineering specifications. But I would argue that these are all expressions of the security requirements of the system in some sense or other. The requirements come out of a security assessment, which starts with an architecture analysis leading through the threat model.

13.4 Peer Review

As I've stated several times in preceding chapters, peer review of assessments and threat models is essential. Responsibility can be overwhelming. By sharing that responsibility, architects can relieve some of the stress that responsibility may cause. Furthermore, the weighty decisions that must be made, the thoroughness that must be applied, the ease with which one can miss an attack surface or vulnerability are all mitigated by having several people look over the results of the assessment. It's just too easy to make a mistake, even for the most experienced architects. For the less experienced or junior practitioners, peer review can help fend off catastrophe.

What does a peer review process look like? When does an assessment require peer review? Who should perform the peer review?

For large, complex, and challenging systems, there's probably no substitute for a formal governance review. A common approach for this is to place senior and leader architects onto an architecture review board. The large or critical systems must pass through the review board and get approved before they can proceed. Sometimes, the review board will also have a checkpoint before deployment into production. This checkpoint helps to ensure that projects that haven't met their deliverables can't move to production to the harm of the organization. A senior security architect will be part of the formal review board and have a "no" vote if there is a significant risk that hasn't been sufficiently mitigated.

On the other hand, forcing every project, no matter how small, through a formal review board can quickly create a bottleneck to the velocity of project delivery. I've seen this happen too many times to count. The desire to have every project get checked by the most trusted and experienced architects is laudable and comes from the very best intentions. But unless an organization has an army of truly experienced architects to deploy, requiring every project to be reviewed by a small group of people who are generally overextended already is going to bring project delivery to a near standstill.

Instead, some other form of review that is more lightweight and nimble needs to be found. I've had success with the following approach.

I may be criticized for being too trusting. Certainly, considering some organization's missions, my approach will be too lightweight. But in the high-tech organizations in which I've worked, we have established a process whereby if the architect is unsure about an assessment for any reason, she or he must find a senior architect (senior to that architect), and an architect who is not involved in the project, to provide the required peer review of the assessment or analysis.

This process does presume that architects will seek peer review. Architects have to perceive peer review as valuable and not a hindrance. If the security architects understand the responsibility that they hold for the organization, my experience is that security architects generally like to receive some additional assurance on their assessments when they feel at all uneasy about what they've found.

I've used this same process four times now, at four different organizations. Those organizations were relatively similar, I admit. Still, in my experience, this works pretty well and catches most mistakes before serious harm takes place. One has to build a culture of support and collaboration or this approach cannot work. It is lightweight and dexterous enough not to interfere overly much with project delivery. And this lightweight peer review process does assume a level of competence of the architect to understand what is in her or his proficiency and what does not. We also encourage architects to seek subject matter expertise as a regular course of their assessments. Nobody knows it all.

13.5 Workload

If a program cannot assign a security architect to each delivery team, security resources will have to be shared across teams or projects in some manner. Therein lies a conundrum: How many projects can a single architect manage and still be effective?

The problem of workload is further clouded by the simple fact that different people have different working styles. Some people can context switch very quickly, and some of these people may be able to retain a great deal of information about many different projects. At the other end, some very brilliant practitioners have trouble switching between contexts at all; even two may be too many.

At one time early in my security architecture career, I had 130 projects assigned to me. Since I was primarily responsible for assigning projects, I wanted to be fair. I didn't notice that I was assigning more projects to myself than any other architect.

To be fair, most of these projects were not active and did not require my attention. Still, this was a rather fragile situation. When three or four projects suddenly "came alive" and needed my immediate attention, every project with which I was engaged would suffer. Clearly, juggling six active projects at a time was too many for me.

I found that I could handle no more than about five and still maintain decent records about what I was doing with each. In fact, for about three months I was the only security architect working on web projects. There were typically about 100+ projects at that time. I could no longer keep reasonable records. In fact, sometimes, I couldn't regain enough context to be useful before I had to switch projects: "thrashing."*

---

* "Thrashing" is a computer term indicating that a multithreaded operating system has exceeded its available work capacity. All that is happening is context switching between processes. No process runs long enough to do useful work.

The point of the foregoing is that there are upper limits that a well-run program dare not exceed. Because each architect is different, it will make sense to pay close attention to the active workload that each architect is carrying. Throttles on the number of active assessments may have to be put into place. Furthermore, you may want to adjust any service level agreements (SLA) that you have with delivery teams so that architects have sufficient time to be thorough.

One last word about workload: In my (very humble) experience, security architects always need time for research. New technologies emerge. New attack methods are discovered. And then there is the personal satisfaction that many security practitioners derive from staying up to date with current security events. The "right" workload also reserves some amount of time for project-focused and basic security research. Besides, up-to-date architects generally deliver better and more efficient assessments.

13.6 Mistakes and Missteps

Although my experience doesn't perfectly match "Murphy's Law," "anything that can go wrong will go wrong," mistakes and missteps do happen, it's true. Perhaps by articulating a few of mine, I can save you from making the same errors?

13.6.1 Not Everyone Should Become an Architect

At one organization that I worked for, as their architecture practice began to mature, management and HR made what I consider to be a fatal mistake. Since architects are generally more senior than engineers (though not always), HR (and Engineering) assumed that the technical growth path was from engineer to architect for everyone. Since in order to be a competent architect its usual for a person to have been an engineer for quite some time, it seemed intuitive that as engineers matured, they would move on to architecture. The new technical growth path at that company, in attempting to account for the emergence of architecture, went from engineer to architect to senior architect to enterprise architect.

But there's a flaw in that logic: Not every person is comfortable with the kind of horizontal thinking that architecture typically requires. In fact, plenty of people become engineers because they like the linearity that engineering typically applies. I'm not saying that architecture doesn't require linear thinking. It does! But architecture also requires patterning, relationships between components, lots of abstractions. Plenty of engineers simply aren't comfortable with the amount of ambiguity that occurs in the practice of systems architecture. For long periods of time, you don't know the details of many of those little boxes in the diagram. You have to be comfortable with that.

Furthermore, as I stated above, architects tend to be leaders, which means, to be blunt, architects have to work with other people. Other people have to like working with an architect. There are a great deal of "people skills" involved in a typical architecture role. There are plenty of engineers who don't particularly enjoy working with lots of people and, even more so, with people who disagree with each other and with that engineer. I like to say, "If you don't like working with people, security architecture is not for you."

At the organization that I described, as soon as the architecture role was opened up as the single technical growth path, one unit immediately promoted fifty engineers to the architect role. Many of these engineers had been in line for promotion for quite a long time. Once the architect role opened up, it seemed natural to management to move these engineers upwards in the new growth path.

You can perhaps see the problem? A number of those people, although perfectly wonderful engineers, weren't very good at thinking about complex relationships and flows between systems. And a number of the same set of individuals didn't like interacting with people all that much. For a few years, it was a mess.

In that situation, there were numerous "architects" who didn't have the capability, perhaps not the aptitude, for what the architect role requires. And remember, these people were senior to a lot of the engineers with whom they were working. That means that even though architecture decisions might not be the best possible solutions, those working underneath these new architects might have to implement something that was not ideal. Indeed, some of the engineers could see the mistakes being promulgated by the new architects, which led to a loss in confidence in the architecture practice.

This one mistake caused a three-year halt in the development of what eventually was an industry-leading enterprise architecture practice. It took several years to filter out those folks who would never gain the right skills or who didn't have the temperament, while at the same time having to wait for the development of those who would take the places of the poorly promoted lot.

Since our security architecture program depended upon the capabilities of the enterprise architecture program, our growth and maturity was somewhat stymied for those same three years. Indeed, we had to deal with a good deal of disruption and outright incompetence during that time. It wasn't fun. Not everyone can be an architect. Not every security person will be successful as a security architect.* The lessons from those three years are burned into the way that I select candidates for the architecture role.

13.6.2 Standards Can't Be Applied Rigidly

Unless you can reduce your security decisions to binary choices, namely, either/or, I would be careful not to place binary thinkers into the security architect role. We were desperate to get some assistance because we were terribly shorthanded and there were

---

* At the risk of being obvious, it's important for organizations to provide an engineering career path for those who prefer to remain in a strictly engineering role rather than halting the growth of great engineers or forcing them to try and be managers or architects in order to advance.

so many assessments, too many projects to review by the staff on hand. We hired a contractor to fill in. The person that we selected seemed darn near perfect. We needed someone who could hit the ground running to be able to review projects immediately. We found someone who had broad security background in several domains. In addition, from the resumé and the interviews, the candidate seemed to have had a hand in the delivery a number of complex systems. How ideal is that?

One thing we didn't interview for was decision-making style. Our contractor had very definite ideas about how security should be implemented. He was well versed in industry standards and the typical policies that a mature organization would normally have. His approach to performing assessments was to make sure that every policy and every standard was adhered to as perfectly as possible; in fact, perfect compliance had to be achieved or nothing.

As I've expounded continuously in this work, I haven't worked at the organization yet where there weren't exceptions, business drivers that trump security, all sorts of reasons for creative and synthetic thinking. At that time, this is precisely how we approached issues encountered in our projects. But our contractor wasn't comfortable with that. That person looked at security as a binary proposition: You either have the right security or you don't. Solutions are simple. Simply follow the standards.

Projects went into his queue but they never came out. Frustrated project teams always had one or more requirements that couldn't be fulfilled as given. Although the requirement was written in such a way that would provide the best security solution possible, as described, many of these requirements were not attainable in that organization with its capabilities and its limitations.

Frustrated teams escalated on a regular basis. Although there was no denying the contractor's security knowledge, the binary, win/lose approach was causing projects to stall, velocity to drop to a standstill, tempers to flare. Though the person was a nice enough person and certainly easy to work with on that team, that architect was not working out at all in any programmatic sense. After all, architects, whether security or otherwise, are there to make projects successful. Part of the definition of "successful" will be to attain an acceptable security posture. "Acceptable" is a qualitative term that cannot be stated for all situations with engineering precision. "Acceptable" has to be uncovered.

13.6.3 One Size Does Not Fit All, Redux

Projects and changes to existing systems come in all variety of sizes, shapes, and amount of change. A successful program is easy to adopt when all who are involved acknowledge this variability upfront and clearly. I can't tell you how many times an IT organization with which I've worked, in the name of efficiency, has built their delivery process around the biggest and most complex systems, only to bury innovation and creativity in a landslide of administration and bureaucracy.

There has to be a fast-track for experiments. And these will need a security sandbox in which to play. At the same time, minor changes don't need to be stultified by documentation requirements. One size definitely does not fit all. In the numerous times that I've seen a one-size approach attempted, the result has universally been a horde of exceptions to the process. Exceptions are generally one of the most expensive ways to handle issues.

13.6.4 Don't Issue Edicts Unless Certain of Compliance

Earlier, I related the story of a security architecture and assessment program from the past that had issued the edict, "all changes will be threat modeled." Much ill will proceeded from that edict, as I noted above.

I avoid mandates, except for the truly essential. Edicts are reserved for what is attainable, such as, "All code will go through static analysis." Or, "Any substantial change to the architecture requires a review of the threat model." "Substantive," of course, is a qualitative term that probably leaves a loophole big enough for an architectural "Mac truck" to be driven through. Still, I'd rather win hearts and minds.

Edicts, unless based on the firm ground of necessity and obtainability, erode trust and support. In addition, if the directive is difficult or impossible to attain, such mandates cause your partners to create strategies of evasion or downright dishonesty, which means that you've made rules that people aren't going to obey and you won't know about it. I don't like to turn delivery teams into liars so that they can get their jobs done. Edicts should be avoided.

13.7 Measuring Success

One of the problems with security architecture is that it is not amenable to absolute measurements. Because of the different sizes and complexities of projects, a measure such as the number of assessments performed is like comparing apples to oranges to bananas to mangoes to tomatoes. And really, how can you count the produce from a single plant and use that quantity to calculate the success of your entire garden? These are not comparable.

A poor measurement is the number of requirements written. A project that adheres to organizational standards will require few to no requirements. The security architect has done his or her job properly in this case. Adherence to standards is to be encouraged. My guess is you don't want your security architects to believe that achieving success is a matter of writing requirements. If you do, you may get a lot of meaningless requirements or even impossible requirements that projects can't fulfill. Bad idea. But I've seen it proposed due to the lack of useful measures of success.

Instead, let me pose a couple of approaches that may help?

13.7.1 Invitations Are Good!

My first measurement for the program itself, and for each security architect, is whether the architect is being included in the relevant architectural discussions? In short, are architects being invited back repeatedly by the teams? Are security architects sought after? Do people call them when there are issues to solve? When they have security questions?

In my experience, project teams are very good at disinviting people and functions from whom they derive no value. Most project teams (development teams, implementation teams, whatever they're called) are typically incentivized through delivery. Delivery within OR under budget. Delivery on time. Delivery, delivery, delivery.

The focus on delivery implies that anything excess that doesn't contribute to delivery is an impediment. If your architects are not being invited to meetings, are not being included in problem-solving discussions, this is actually exquisitely focused feedback. The first measurement for my program always is, are we being invited in and then asked to return?

13.7.2 Establish Baselines

Presumably, you will want to collect data on risk scores of systems (if you're rating or scoring risk), number of projects reviewed, number of escalations, number of exceptions, number of risk assumptions written? None of these alone is a particularly good measure of anything. However, by establishing baselines based upon your most seasoned architects, your most trusted high-performing architects who seem to get things done and are repeatedly sought out, you can get a feel for what performance looks like.

I like to establish baselines of expectations against which I can measure. First, I need to have some architects whose performance I trust. Then, it will take time to establish baselines based upon the throughput of my experienced architects. Doing so will also avoid judgment based upon one or a few outlier projects because outliers always exist in any security architecture practice.

I take the time necessary to establish baselines based upon trusted performance. That means, of course, that I have one or more performances that I trust. I get a sense that security requirements are being met. Certainly not all security requirements will be met, not all requirements will drive to completion. And some requirements will drive to completion with some noise or friction. But when's there's a good flow of projects and requirement completion, then I know I can start measuring.

Risk scores are interesting artifacts. First, these have to be gathered before assessment and sometime around the final governance checkpoint or project go live. Intuitively, one would expect risk scores to decrease. But this is not always what happens.

Take the example of a project that, before analysis, presents as wholly following organizational standards. This adherence to standards will cause the risk score to be low. Then, as the onion is peeled, it is discovered that one or more implementation details of the project present significant organizational risk and are not amenable to the organization standards. Such a situation is not common, but occurs regularly from time to time. I cited an example in a previous chapter. In this situation, the risk score is going to go up during the project delivery lifecycle. But the security architect is doing her or his job correctly; upon thorough evaluation, security issues are brought into visibility. That's exactly the point of architecture analysis: to identify unmitigated attack surfaces.

The point is that risk scores won't always go down, though this is the intuitive expectation. Assessments do sometimes uncover significant or even severe issues; it is not always possible to mitigate all the risk, as required. Each of these is an artifact that the security architect is actually doing the job correctly. Even so, in my experience, the aggregate risk across many projects, from start of project to delivery, should trend downwards. Project teams don't necessarily know what security requirements will be needed. That's why there is a security architect who is a subject matter expert to perform an architectural assessment and threat model.

Over time, if the relationships are strong between the security architects and other team members, you may see a downward trend in the number of security requirements written by the security architect. The teams will take initiative and write the appropriate requirements for themselves. Several IT architects who I worked with for many years began to finish my sentences, quite literally. Over the years of ongoing collaboration, these architects developed assessment skills that they readily applied to their architectures.* When security responsibility starts being taken throughout the architecture practice, this, in and of itself, is a sign of success for the program.

Due to complexity, technical challenges, and dependencies, it can be very difficult to compare the timelines of the projects working their way through a security architect's queue. Hence, the number of projects assessed is not a very meaningful measure. However, over many projects and a significant period of time, say biannually, or over the course of a year, one would expect some of the projects for each architect to move to production. It is a red flag if projects go into the architect's queue, and they don't come out again. It is also a red flag if every project completes successfully. Considering the complexity and difficulty of security architecture, it is almost impossible, working with a broad range of projects, not to encounter some challenges. Both 0% success and 100% success are indicators of some sort of failure. Anything approaching the minimum or maximum should be examined carefully. And, as noted before, by setting an expected baseline, a manager can have some sort of feel for whether an architect is performing successfully. Some projects should complete.

Which brings me to some red flag indicators for the astute manager of the security architecture program.

Smart people working collaboratively will disagree. There should be some amount of friction and some amount of conflict as teams try to juggle security against other

---

* Of course, I've learned a tremendous amount about system architecture through my collaboration with the extraordinary architects with whom I've worked.

priorities. An architect who never has an escalation and never needs help working through to a solution should be a worry. Obviously, an architect who constantly or repeatedly has conflicts is a management problem, as well. There may very well be something amiss in that person's style or communication skills. That would be no different from any other individual who caused more conflict than is normally encountered as people try to work together. Still, people will occasionally push back against a security requirement. This is normal. Pushback should be expected, occasionally. If there is never any friction, something is wrong.

Along with escalations for decisions, occasionally, risk owners or other decision makers will not see eye to eye with security. At such times, the typical practice is to write a risk assumption so that the decision is formally made and can be referred to in the future. Again, like escalations, risk assumptions are a normal part of a well-functioning security practice. At an organization moving around 430 projects a year, with about twelve security architects, we experienced about a single risk assumption each year. Were I managing a program like this and significantly more risk assumptions than one or two in a year were written, such a circumstance might be an indicator that something was amiss in my program.

Of course, not every security requirement will get into the version of the system for which it was written. The usual approach in this situation is to write a time-bound security exception with a plan and schedule for remediation. Like escalations, exceptions are normal. The security architect who writes no exceptions is a worry. On the other hand, if many requirements, or even most requirements, end up as exceptions, this may be an indication that communication is strained or that the architect has not been empowered properly. It could also be an indication of a problem with the amount of influence an architect has within an organization. Presumably, over enough projects and a significant length of time, one could set a baseline of the expected number of exceptions and measure against this. I would expect the trend to be relatively flat in a mature program, neither rising nor falling.

Measuring the success of the security architecture program is not a matter of simply collecting totals for a period of time. As we have seen, however, it is possible not only to measure the relative success of the program but even that of individual architects by maintaining metrics over periods of time and developing baselines. Some measures that intuitively may seem like failures, such as escalations and exceptions, are in fact a normal part of the business of computer security and are to be expected. Even so, extremes are possible indicators of issues. Still, it is possible to quantitatively get a feel for program effectiveness over time.

13.8 Summary

Building a security architecture program is not a simple matter of hiring some smart people and then giving them some training.

A successful security architecture program depends upon the support and collaboration of those who will interact and see the results of the program. Building a strong network of support is one of the key communication activities of the program, even a mature program. Senior management must not only assent to assessments, but they must also support the delivery of the requirements that result from the assessments. Grassroots support is critical to getting things done with the least amount of friction possible. And the inevitable challenges are far more easily solved through a supportive peer network. Building up your network will also be an important contributor to program success.

Finding the right people who have the relevant aptitude is, in and of itself, a nontrivial problem. Care must be taken to select for aptitude in a number of orthogonal areas: technical depth and breadth, communication skills, sociability, and a predilection to think architecturally about systems. I believe that a program will gain more success and proceed more rapidly by finding a seasoned security architect as the first or even first and second hire of the program. Whoever is hired at the beginning must also have the propensity to teach, coach, and mentor those who come afterwards. For most of us, becoming a seasoned security architect takes time, effort, and significant help from those who've gone before.

Training can help to set a firm base upon which to establish experience. Naturally, I hope this book offers at least some basis for training security architects who'll perform assessments. Still, it will be on-the-job experience under the watchful eye of an experienced practitioner through which most of us deepen our craft. A culture of collaboration, coaching, mentoring, and peer review will help accelerate the learning process as well as prevent disaster from ensuing from the inevitable mistakes architects will make as they learn.

The primary output from security assessments must be a set of security requirements. That doesn't mean that there cannot be other outputs; a threat model document can be very useful, not just for the security architects but for everyone who's involved in implementing security requirements. It may also be useful to develop a threat model template in order to seed discovery and discussion that will lead to a thorough threat model. However, I do not favor a checklist approach unless the technology portfolio can be carefully limited to the items in the checklist.

If the program's architects are perceived as adding value, if the architects are repeatedly invited to project team meetings, perhaps even sought out during system conception, this is a very strong indicator of a successful program. There are other quantitative measures. But care must be taken not to take simplistic totals as meaningful by themselves. Baselines built from the performance of successful architects can provide some measure against which performance can be compared. But, generally, even this approach can only indicate the possibility of a problem, not the problem itself.

Typically, security architecture programs don't build themselves. There's a fair amount of care and feeding that necessarily occurs to build a successful security architecture assessment program. Not to be too trivial, but it takes people, process, and technology. I hope that the foregoing tidbits help you on your journey.

References

1. The Open Group (2005, November). *Guide to Security Architecture in TOGAF ADM,* p. 5. Retrieved from http://pubs.opengroup.org/onlinepubs/7699949499/ toc.pdf.
2. Schoenfield, B. (2014). "Applying the SDL Framework to the Real World" (Ch. 9). In *Core Software Security: Security at the Source,* pp. 255–324. Boca Raton (FL): CRC Press.
3. Ibid.
4. George, B., Sims, P., McLean, A. N., and Mayer, D. (February 2007). "Discovering Your Authentic Leadership," Harvard Business Review.
5. McGraw, G. (Jan. 18, 2013). Cigital Justice League Blog: *Securing Software Design Is Hard.* Retrieved from http://www.cigital.com/justice-league-blog/2013/01/18/ securing-software-design-is-hard/.
6. Schoenfield, B. (2014). "Applying the SDL Framework to the Real World" (Ch. 9). In *Core Software Security: Security at the Source,* pp. 255–324. Boca Raton (FL): CRC Press.

Part III

Summary and Afterword

Summary

As we learned in Part I, only the extraordinary person can walk in cold to an assessment and achieve good results. From the organizational through the technical, from system architecture skills to some sort of risk methodology, there is an entire body of knowledge that precedes an actual threat model analysis.

In Part II of this book, a series of six detailed architectural analyses was presented. Each of these was meant to build upon the skills of the previous assessment while, at the same time, introducing one or more new security architecture problems and their possible solutions. There is no doubt in my mind that I've omitted some goals and details: A number of the exclusions were purposive in order to keep the book tightly focused as a course in applied security architecture and threat modeling. And, as was noted previously, these are fictional architectures. Architectures in the real world tend to be even messier than these examples. And throughout the analyses, I have avoided digging down into implementation details, even though these engineering aspects are also critical to the delivery of secure systems.

Instead, the analyses attempt to follow a path as would typically be followed in an analysis. In the first example, we strictly follow the ATASM method. Along the way, we factored an architecture, identified and prioritized threats, applied the threat's methods and capabilities to the attack surfaces, and enumerated existing mitigations. Then after applying a risk methodology to the attack surfaces in the threat model, we prioritized credible attack vectors (CAVs) and developed a series of security requirements to mitigate the enumerated CAV.

After the first example, I tried to follow a more real-world approach such that new discoveries and areas of investigation turned up additional attack surfaces requiring additional defenses. Each of the analyses was meant to demonstrate how a security architect would probably think about these problems and reach decisions about priority and security requirements. None of the analyses was meant to be exhaustive.

In Part III, we took up some facets surrounding the application of security assessment and threat modeling to larger portfolios of projects. Standards become a key tool to allow projects to be self-sufficient and to minimize design and implementation errors. Wherever a vetted standard can be used, the standard solution can be implemented without further need for analysis. This approach saves the human factor for unique and exceptional situations.

Once an organization is delivering multiple systems through writing software, integrating existing systems, or some combination of the two, there will be a need to govern, so that processes and activities actually get executed in a proven and repeatable manner. I explain some of the approaches that have encouraged innovation while at the same time making sure that due diligence processes are, indeed, followed.

When building a security architecture team, appropriate people have to be hired, trained, mentored, coached, and supported so that they can be effective. Since hiring more than a handful of experienced practitioners is difficult at the time of this writing, training and then mentoring through a long process of experience and practice will be a determiner of success. Even though I've tried very hard to clarify and elucidate the kind of thinking that goes into a security assessment, gaining the necessary experience to be able to work independently still requires a significant investment.

Furthermore, in any large organization, there will be many stakeholders with many different perspectives who all have to agree that securing systems is the right thing to do. Organizational support must extend upwards to the highest levels, across through middle management, and downwards through line management and to the grassroots people who are accomplishing the tasks that will ensure the security of an organization's systems. Building communication and relationships through this network is a nontrivial task that will need significant effort and focus.

In Chapter 13, I included some of the larger programmatic mistakes of which I've been a part in the hopes that you, the reader, won't have to make the same mistakes in your program. I hope that these little anecdotes provide at least some insight into the subtleties of running a security architecture program?

If you've made it this far in this book, Bravo! I'm sure that some of my language is not particularly clear. I'm willing to bet that some of the aspects of security that I've tried to cover are fairly dense and perhaps, difficult to understand. There is no doubt that I've made one or more technical mistakes in these analyses. For these, I ask your forgiveness; please don't throw out what is useful because I've made some errors along the way.

Nevertheless, I hope that on this journey of applied security architecture and threat modeling there have been at least some tidbits worthy of the time and effort you've made to slog through this book. As I said at the beginning, if I can add just a little to the emerging practice of security architecture, and perhaps a little controversy, I will be tickled pink.

In any event, always remember that there is more than one way to skin a particular security cat; there are usually at least a couple of different ways to arrive at more or less the same defense.

Afterword

Since I began making notes and an outline for a book on security architecture eight years ago, there have been a number of encouraging security architecture developments.

- The Open Group has created an Enterprise Security Architect certification. One of their first certified architects has subsequently created a few enterprise security reference architectures.
- The SANS Institute hosted three "What Works in Security Architecture" Summits.
- The IEEE initiated a Center for Secure Design. The Center published a "Top 10 Design Flaws" booklet.
- Adam Shostack published Threat Modeling: Designing for Security, and renown threat modeler, John Steven, has told me that he's working on his threat modeling book.
- Anurag Agrawal of MyAppSecurity has been capturing well-known attack surfaces and their technical mitigations within his commercial threat modeling tool, "Threat Modeler."*

In isolation, none of the above developments would be all that significant. Obviously, people think about the practice of security architecture. But the activities described in the abovementioned list have all occurred within the last couple of years, more or less simultaneously. That simultaneity, I think, is significant.

I believe that security architects are coalescing to a consensus on a body of practice. Additionally, influential organizations are recognizing that there is a discipline called "security architecture." And, at least some of the repeating patterns in assessment and threat modeling are amenable to automation.

In my early years as a security architect, some managers and executives were attracted to simple solutions to the problem of software security. Statements like, "Why can't we manually review every line of code?" Or, "Doesn't the static analyzer take care of this problem?" were fairly common misunderstandings and misapplications. I hope that we are all coming to understand the complexity of the problem that we're trying to solve?

The problem of design flaws and missed security requirements will not be solved through a panacea of automation (at least not anytime soon). Although security testing tools are improving, I believe that threat modeling itself will remain, at least in part, a human activity for the foreseeable future.

---

* I have no personal or financial interest in MyAppSecurity.

Penetration testing before or after deployment to production may find design issues, if the penetration tester is sufficiently skilled.* However, the timing of the penetration test is wrong. A penetration test must wait until a system is very nearly complete or until after it's finished. By then, it's usually too late for redesign.

And the complexity of our systems, at least our very large systems in a cross-connected world, far exceeds our ability to reduce the problem to checklists.

I hope that we've moved beyond such simplistic solutions as checklists? The short list of developments, presented above, implies to me that our security architecture sophistication is growing.

This is a hard problem that needs a body of knowledge and some method for learning how to apply that knowledge to real-world systems, that is, a practicum. I believe that we already have a consensus on what needs to be done and the steps to achieve it. When I talk to my peers, we may use slightly different terms; we definitely have different styles. Still, as near as I can tell, we do the same things in an assessment; there's plenty of agreement about what a threat model is and how you create one. What we don't have yet is a pedagogy or even much in the way of coursework; certainly, as far as I know, there is no curriculum that's been established.

I sincerely hope that this book is a doorway to establish a better body of practice, even if you vehemently disagree with the approaches presented here. At the very least, perhaps I've pointed the way towards some sort of methodology and body of practice?

Design flaws, security misses, and mistakes in computer system architecture and design aren't going away by themselves. We must reduce these by dint of hard work in assessments and threat models, as well as by creating and refining our body of knowledge and practice.

B rook

Brook S.E. Schoenfield
Camp Connell, California, USA, October 2014

---

* It is my opinion that at the current state of the art of penetration testing, every test is a unique combination of tester skill and the tool set of that particular tester.

Index

Printed in the United States
by Baker & Taylor Publisher Services